Design and
Construction
of Wood-Framed
Buildings

McGraw-Hill Books of Related Interest

Design and Construction of Wood-Framed Buildings

Morton Newman
Civil Engineer

McGraw-Hill, Inc.

New York San Francisco Washington, D.C. Auckland Bogotá
Caracas Lisbon London Madrid Mexico City Milan
Montreal New Delhi San Juan Singapore
Sydney Tokyo Toronto

Library of Congress Cataloging-in-Publication Data

Newman, Morton.
    Design and construction of wood-framed buildings / Morton Newman.
        p.   cm.
    Includes index.
    ISBN 0-07-046363-8 (acid-free paper)
    1. Wooden-frame buildings—Design and construction.   2. Structural
engineering. I. Title.
TH1101.N423 1995
694—dc20   94-33842
                                                         CIP

    5 6 7 8 9 0 KP/KP 9 0 9 8 7

ISBN 0-07-046363-8

The sponsoring editor for this book was Larry Hager, the editing supervisor was Jane Palmieri, and the production supervisor was Pamela Pelton. It was set in Garamond Light by McGraw-Hill's Professional Book Group composition unit.

Printed and bound by Kingsport Press.

This book is printed on acid-free paper.

To Matilda, my aunt,
who made this book possible

Contents

Preface

Man seems to have always understood the elementary principles of building and to have been blessed with a sense of structure; with similar raw materials—mud, stone and timber—widely scattered groups often built the same type of structure. As time passed, man refined his knowledge through practical experience (and) advances in structural techniques (that) roughly paralleled those in industrialization and mathematics.

ENCYCLOPAEDIA BRITANNICA

I have written this book to present a compiled syllabus of information on engineering methods and materials that can be useful to persons concerned with the structural design and construction of wood-framed structures. Universities can impart a finite amount of essential knowledge within a given period of time. Most of the material presented to the engineering student is rightfully concerned with theory and mathematical development. After graduation an arduous period of learning the practical application of scientific theory begins. I suppose that is why graduation is called commencement. Mark Twain defined *ignorance* as "something that everyone has on different subjects." I hope that this book will help to resolve that condition and to answer questions concerning practical methodology of wood design and construction.

I have tried to compose a book that will act as a source of information for architects, engineers, students, and field construction personnel. There are a number of excellent books concerned with the scientific aspects of wood as a structural material. The purpose of this book is to extend the use of scientific knowledge by presenting a series of practical demonstrations of calculations, methods, and details. It is hoped that the reader can use this book as a working reference in the execution of his or her professional tasks. The narrative and explanations of example design calculations and drawings will cite particular relevant requirements from sections of the *Uniform Building Code* (UBC—1991 ed.); *Timber Construction Manual* (AITC—1985 ed.); *National Design Specification Manual* (NDS—1991 ed.); and the *American Plywood Association* (APA—1993 ed.). The reader should have copies of these publications as source guides in the use of this book. Also, the information presented in Chapter 7 concerning seismic loads was derived and developed from the books by the Federal Emergency Management Agency and the Building Seismic Safety Council of the National Institute of Building Sciences.

Chapter 25 (Wood) of the *Uniform Building Code* specifies the basic structural requirements for wood design and construction. Also, other relevant design criteria are given in Chapter 17 (Loads) and Chapter 29 (Excavations, Foundations, and Retaining Walls). Light-framed wood buildings are classified as Type V structures; that is, they are rated as having a one-hour fire resistance. The matter of building fire rating is not considered in this book except to say that there are circumstances in which the size of lumber can be used to satisfy fire-rating requirements. Sizes of post and beams with nominal dimensions of 6 in or greater are often classified a "heavy timber," which is considered as one-hour fire rated. Additional design calculations are presented to develop the UBC structural load and force requirements for the various parts of a wood-framed structure. There are a number of books which individually address either the methods of design or the standards of construction. However, design and construction are not independent functions; they are an interactive ongoing procedure. The structural details and assembly drawings that are shown in this book translate the structural design calculations into practical field applications. It is important to be aware that building codes specify only the minimum design requirements. Therefore, design examples in several cases are presented to evaluate the result of either an increase in the design criteria or an increase in the strength or size of the materials to be used. This concept confirms a cost-benefit ratio; that is, incremental increases in the structural materials or in the design criteria may not necessarily result in excessive construction costs. Structural designs that satisfy minimum governing code criteria will create an adequate structure with, in some instances, only marginal reserve strength. There are situations in which the addition of hardware or construction materials will significantly increase the strength of a building with only a consequent relatively small increase in construction cost. However, a comparison of cost to strength becomes unrealistic when the increased cost does not buy a commensurate increase in structural capacity, or when the design criteria are beyond a real load expectation. With this in mind, it can be seen that the strength of a design depends not only on the permitted stress values or sizes of members but also on the designer's judgment and the builder's skill and experience.

I arranged the presentation of the material within each chapter in a logical sequence that would tend to increase the comprehension for the reader. In the course of following a narration of a design example, the reader should notice that the calculation sheets have a vertical column of numbers along the left-side margin. These numbers are used as line references or pointers for relevant statements on procedure or source of information. References are made by a notation system which designates the case number or example, the calculation sheet number, and the line number along the left-side margin. For example, S-3, L10 refers to the calculation shown on sheet number S-3 and indicates line number 10. By using this numerical pointer system, the reader can be guided through the design procedure while reading the text for a specific task or condition.

The sheet metal hardware connectors that are shown in the detail drawings are specified as those manufactured by the Simpson Strong Tie Company of California. There are a number of other manufacturers of this type of hardware; however, Simpson products were specified since they are the most prevalent in the industry and are the most comparable to other manufacturers' products. Many of the details presented show manufactured wood products such as glued laminated beams, trussed joists and I-shaped joists such as those manufactured by Trus-Joist Company. It is important to keep in mind that any particular hardware or wood product that is called out on a drawing should have a certified approval of the jurisdiction in which it is being used.

Many of the structural detail drawings used in this book originate from the Praxis Library of Standard Structural Details and the *Standard Handbook of*

Structural Details for Building Construction, published by McGraw-Hill. It is not the intent of this book to offer a "cookbook" methodology for design and construction of wood-framed structures. However, the book endeavors to inform the reader of the various building code constraints and requirements through calculation examples and drawings. It is assumed that the reader has at least a cursory background in the study of strength of materials and engineering static analysis. There is a certain amount of information that is not included in this book. I attempted to deal only with the most significant and the most encountered aspects of wood design and construction of commercial and residential buildings. Many minor design constants or adjustment factors are not specifically considered, but can be referenced from Table 2.3.1 of the 1991 NDS specification.

A great number of people have assisted me in the development of this work. I would like to thank Richard E. Miller and Angelo Caponigro for their advice on field methods of construction; architect Earl Rubenstein advised me on many of the UBC requirements; and Mrs. Brenda Adkins Miller was essential in her encouragement and cross-checking of the work. I have attempted to convey the information and observations gained from over thirty years of structural design of light-framed wood structures. I sincerely hope that you will find this book useful and that it will increase your ability to design and construct safe buildings.

Morton Newman, Engineer

Design and Construction of Wood-Framed Buildings

1

Design and Construction

There is an inclination to think that the current technology used in the construction of buildings is derived from relatively recent scientific development. This commonplace misunderstanding of the evolution of applied technology is perplexing in view of the fact that humanity depends on science to facilitate its basic necessities. It is quite possible for a person who is educated in the humanities to possess only a minimal knowledge of how science serves a civilized population's most ordinary needs. Persons who are trained in science and engineering, however, may not also be reasonably knowledgeable in the social sciences. The two fields of study are not mutually exclusive, but it would not be inaccurate to observe that for some people science and technology will always remain a fiction. The engineering profession can be exciting and is not totally populated by dull or timid persons. The seven wonders of the modern world, listed below, are all civil engineering projects, which serve as clear proof of the magnitude of our creative potential.

1. The Suez Canal—Egypt
2. The Dneproges Dam—Dnieper River, USSR
3. Atomic Research Facility—Harwell, England
4. Alcan Highway—Alaska to Canada
5. Golden Gate Bridge—San Francisco, California
6. The Eiffel Tower—Paris, France
7. The Empire State Building—New York City

The design and construction of buildings is a manifestation of humanity's cumulative knowledge of art and science gained since ancient times. The history of construction shows that humans always had an intuitive understanding of the fundamentals of structure. Many primitive sketches preserved in museums in Europe and in the United States indicate that the earliest builders comprehended the use of some type of structure consisting of columns and beams. Also, it has been observed that with the same materials of mud, stone, and timber, distantly separated cultures built the same types of structures. Depending on the geographic area, early construction was quite advanced; records of an Egyptian mining expedition in the Sinai Desert dated around 2800 B.C. are remarkably similar to present-day construction management procedures. Early Greek and Roman builders and mathematicians such as Euclid, Pythagoras, Pliny, Euler, and Vitruvius, to name only a few, have left a body of scientific knowledge that is still used in modern structural design. Although a great number of their buildings still stand, only a relatively few of these early engineers left any written record of their work; consequently we know very little about them as individuals. The *Ten Books of Vitruvius,* which may be regarded as a predecessor to the modern building code, were written at the time of the Roman Emperor Augustus (A.D. 40–103). The scope of information contained within these books includes subjects regarding architecture; structural design; requirements for residences, temples, theaters, and public works; and strength of materials. It is recorded that Vitruvius stated, "I have not studied with the view of making money by my profession." There are many engineers who believe that in this respect he was much ahead of his time.

The introduction of the science of strength of materials and mathematics of structural statics established a situation in which a building design was created by persons trained in two different but related disciplines. Until this time there was no formal distinction made between the functions of the architect and the engineer. In his first book, Vitruvius writes, "The mere practical Architect is not able to assign sufficient reasons for the form he adopts; and the theoretic Architect also fails, grasping the shadow instead of the substance. He who is theoretic as well as practical, is therefore doubly armed, able not only to prove the propriety of his design but equally so to carry it into execution."

It is indisputable that no building can endure without a sufficiently strong structural frame. This reality may confound those architects who create their designs with little or no regard as to how a building will sustain the predicted natural loads and forces that it may experience. Although the prime prerequisite of every construction is to create a safe human environment, the architect's primary design consideration tends toward creating a building to meet a prescribed function, form, and esthetic. Regardless of architectural considerations, the resultant of the structural design calculations must specify the erection of a structure with the capacity to withstand all expected combinations of loads and forces that it would probably encounter. The strength of any structure should not be diminished below the requirements of the governing design criteria, because without the structure, there can be no architecture.

The design and construction of a building is by necessity a team effort. Each contributing group of individuals on a project provides some aspect of technological expertise or manual skill to assemble the final product. There are times, however, when it is not unusual to get the impression that each of the various trades at the job site are working at cross purposes, and that a hostile attitude of mutually assured destruction exists. The conspicuous damage to the structure resulting from this state of warfare can be caused by such exploits as a plumber running amok with a hatchet throughout the project and chopping 4-in notches in joists and studs to accommodate a 1-in-diameter water line. This type of "tradesperson" can do a lot of mischief before he or she is finally captured and subdued. Frequently it seems that the steel reinforcing workers will find that the foundation excavations offer an excellent location in which to store their empty beer cans. Some electricians can be quite devious, often they will meander about the project looking for points of maximum stress in the beams in which to locate holes for their conduit. The most destructive group may be the plasterers, because their work covers the damage created by other trades. As a result of good wall plastering there exists in many buildings a countless number of invisible electrical junction and switch boxes that may never be seen again until the building is demolished. It is difficult for the engineer to accept the fact that the structural design may not be much better than the least concerned or skilled person on the job, and that all of this is happening under the presumption of applied technology. In the midst of this confusion it is also hard to keep in mind that the engineer and the contractor are trying to achieve the same goal; that is, to construct a safe building. The root causes of design and construction problems usually can be traced to either ambiguous or inadequate design drawings or to the lack of competent supervision at the job site. Quality of design, workmanship, and materials directly relate to the structural capacity of the building. This was verified on many instances by the inspection of wood-framed buildings that were damaged by the Los Angeles/Northridge earthquake.

In order to find solutions to situations that cause delays or damage, it is first necessary to ascertain the source of their origin. A first step in this procedure would be to explore the concerns and duties of the structural engineer. The structural drawings are the most useful documents at a job site during the time of erecting of the structural frame; therefore, it is required that they be accurate and informative. Buildings are not constructed from the engineering design calculations. It is essential that the engineer translate his or her calculations to a draftsperson in order to produce structural drawings that are sufficiently complete to permit the various tradespeople at the job site to work without expensive delays or extra costs. Architectural, mechanical, and electrical designs basically assume that the structural design, as depicted on the drawings, will match the building's fundamental configuration and purpose. However, it is not unusual to find that different engineering disciplines might require that their equipment simultaneously occupy the same space within the building. The structural engineer may not care that a beam must pass through an air duct, but will become concerned to find that a duct is required to pass through a beam, and thus reduce its capacity. On the other hand, the mechanical engineer's solution to this type of problem might be to recommend that all beams be limited to $7\frac{7}{32}$ in in depth just to allow space for the air ducts. The dilemma that results from the intersections of plumbing lines, electrical conduits, air ducts, or structural members should be resolved with a spirit of mutual cooperation. Also, it is best to address these interdisciplinary design problems in the office prior to the start of construction rather than at the job site where the options for a solution may be limited and also delay the progress of the work. In the case of wood structures, shrinkage and creep of lumber should be considered. Plumbing and electrical lines that are too rigidly attached to wall studs or joists can be fractured by the movement; therefore, some provision is usually made in the attachment hardware to anticipate this condition.

There are structural designers who sincerely believe that their work has been completed on a project at the time that the building permit is issued; unfortunately, this is not the reality of the situation. On an almost regular basis while the field work is in progress, the engineer will be confronted with questions and be required to give clarifications of the drawings. The amount of this kind of remedial work is to some degree directly related to the level of clarity of the information presented on the structural drawings. It is axiomatic that one extra hour spent in checking and improving the drawings at the office can save the engineer as much as four hours in explanations to support the work in the field. Wood-framed building design often requires a higher degree of drawing detail than other types of materials. The advantage in working with lumber as a structural material is that it offers a wider variety of possible solutions to on-site problems, and the material itself is inexpensive to fabricate.

The process of plan checking structural drawings that are necessary to obtain a building permit is not sufficiently satisfactory to guarantee the competency of the construction documents. The inclination of depending on the building department to check the plans for errors can lead to a false sense of security. These departments do not take responsibility for the design drawings, nor should they be required to do so. It is the plan checker's only duty to determine that the plans conform to the requirements of the governing building code. Whether the drawings are sufficiently informative or otherwise correct is not the building department's responsibility or concern. The building permit stamp as a rule reads only "that permission to construct is granted"; nothing is said about the feasibility of the design or the quality of the drawings. The engineer who relies on a building department plan checker to do part, or any, of his or her work is evading responsibility as the client's advocate and accepts the risk for harsh surprises. Inspection of the construction work in process is a good example of the role of a building department or other governing body. The damage caused by the 1994 Northridge, California, earthquake to wood-framed buildings could have been appreciably limited by more stringent inspection. Structural inspections made after the shock revealed many instances of inadequate building methods and materials. Also, the wide range of quality of framing workmanship indicated that the framing inspection criteria were not consistent.

The convenient organization and neatness of presentation of the structural calculations and drawings increase their level of comprehension for the plan checker. The practice of working "quick and dirty" may be expedient in the short term; however, it reflects on an engineer's professionalism and presents an opportunity for many other related future problems. Designs and drawings are judged on their ease of interpretation; if they are not clear or straightforward, they are almost automatically suspected of being incorrect.

There are four general possible sources of mistakes which can arise in the process of preparing structural drawings for wood-framed structures. The first possible source of mistakes can be traced to the quality of the architectural design drawings. It is very difficult for the engineer to produce high-quality structural drawings from incorrect or inadequate architectural designs. If the architectural design is not complete in scope or not specific, or gives dimensions that are either incomplete or incorrect, the structural drawings predictably will be equally deficient. Better communication during the design development phase of the work can modify this issue, but there can also be instances in which a candid approach may lead to serious professional confrontations. The use of wood as structural material may be economical; however, its stress capacity and modulus of elasticity are much less than steel, masonry, or concrete. Most codes impose restrictions on the use of wood either by fire rating or by the lower stress capacity. The use of plywood for floor diaphragms and seismic walls is particularly critical in that their sizes are restricted by a length to width ratio. This is done to limit the amplitude of movement. It will be shown in Chapter 7 that the lateral deflection of a structure is a factor in controlling wind or earthquake damage.

The second potential cause of mistakes on structural drawings can be attributed to the accuracy of the drawing dimensions. It is very frustrating for a tradesperson in the field to find an incorrect dimension or the lack of a dimension that is essential to the construction. A dimension problem at the job site is regarded as an inexcusable mistake and often leads to some animosity between the field workers and the design office. Also, to further aggravate the situation, this type of discrepancy is typically "discovered" on the day that the relevant work is being constructed, which indicates that no one on either side of the drawing board did any homework. It should have been anticipated. The most effective way to avoid this predicament is by a systematic method of cross-checking before the drawings are released to the field. If a dimension is not known or cannot be confirmed, it is better to leave the space on the drawing open; at least it will reduce the possibility of a field mistake and at the same time it will point to the existence of the problem. Accurate dimensions are critical to the rapidity of the execution of the site work. The idea that wood is an easily workable material may lead to a false sense of security. It is one thing to have to cut an extralong joist to size; however, if the joist is too short you have problem, especially if there is a large number of them. A study of the dimensions on drawings made by ancient Egyptians indicated that they were determined in the same manner as today. The original drawings of the tomb of Ramses IV are preserved on papyrus in the Museum of Turin. The plans are drawn to an approximate scale of 1 to 28 and have been verified by actual measurement at the "job site."

Incorrect details or the lack of referencing of details and section on the plans is the third source of confusion on structural drawings. There is no point in drawing a section or a detail unless it has a specific relevance or place of application on the plan, and the end user's attention is directed to it by a cross-reference number. A set of structural drawings may have all of the necessary information required for construction, but it must be conveniently interrelated by cross-referencing for the people in the field. A drawing of a section or of a detail has the power to communicate a large amount of information about the structure, such as the configuration, sizes of members, material strength, and the method of assembly. All of these graphic data must be interrelated on the plan by a number and by the sheet number on which they are located. The placement of foundation hardware such as anchor bolts and seismic holddowns on seismic walls may be correctly delineated by notes; however, experience indicates that this information should also be placed on the foundation plan. The concrete contractor may not be concerned with the structural hardware of the wood-framing contractor and will work independent of that situation. This is a real occurrence; it often occurs whenever subcontractors do not anticipate the other trades' work.

The fourth source of structural problems relates to clarity, or the lack thereof. Clarity may be defined as "precision of thought or expression." The total purpose in producing structural drawings is to ensure that the building gets constructed just as the engineer designed it. This would not be a challenge if there was total or absolute communication between the design office and the job site. However, this is not always the case; in actual fact it is more likely that field mistakes or site conditions will require revisions or clarifications from the engineer. Even though a contractor is ultimately accountable to the engineer for the quality of the work and materials of the construction, they may not be much better than the comprehension capacity of the workers who read the drawings. It should not be necessary for the tradespeople to have to guess the engineer's intent. It seems that questions are more prevalent at the start of the project. The contractor and tradespeople appreciate it when the engineer visits the job site, giving him or her the opportunity to closely monitor the degree of workmanship.

During the time that the building permit is being processed, the owner of the project will select a construction contractor, either by negotiation or by competitive bidding. Each of these methods has certain advantages. A negotiated price method of selecting a general contractor gives the owner a chance to discuss the project in detail to assure that the contractor's price is commensurate with the scope of the work expected; however, it will exclude the opportunity to obtain the lowest possible bid. Competitive bidding either by general contractors or by subcontractors offers the owner the latitude of purchasing the work for the lowest possible price. The value of a low bid very much depends on the quality of the field documents. Incomplete or nonspecific working drawings can create a situation in which the contractor can legitimately request a payment for extra work or to arbitrarily substitute less expensive materials. After a project has been completed and the costs are totaled, it may be found that with the added costs, the lowest bid was not to the owner's advantage. The engineer may be charged for these extra costs if they can be attributed to deficiencies in the engineer's design or drawings. Good communication between the design office and a contractor's field superintendent can serve to eliminate many difficulties and misunderstandings. Cooperation is an effective factor in eliminating or at least anticipating this type of problem.

A building is one of the few products that is consumed at the same place of its manufacture. Factory production technology provides specific constraints on both the quality of materials and the workmanship. Mass production methods have the advantages of carefully determining assembly line scheduling, testing, and the standardization of parts. Although the construction of a wood-framed building can be intricate and complicated, depending on its configuration, the same means of strict quality control and scheduling are not available to the contractor. The duty of a contractor's field superintendent is to complete the project on time within a fixed expense. The superintendent is ultimately charged with the responsibility for almost everything that transpires on the job. Authority and accountability derived from responsibility flow down from job superintendent to each successive level of field management. In many respects the chain of command is similar to a military organization. Depending on the size of the project, the superintendent can have a number of subordinates who are each assigned to monitor a particular phase of the work. It is quite important that a critical path method (CPM) time schedule for each subcontractor's work be established to expedite the progress of the construction. Calculated CPM dates such as early start, late start, early finish, and late finish can supply the superintendent the numerical data required to accurately determine the cumulative cost of the work to date, the timing of the work, and to fix the responsibility for delays and cost overruns. There are instances in which the contractor may want to increase the amount of labor or material for a specific subcontractor's task in order to adjust the time schedule or substitute another type of material to reduce either the cost of labor or the cost of materials. A current critical path schedule can assist the contractor in making these types of trade-off decisions. From this discussion of the functions and responsibilities of the engineer and the field superintendent, it can be seen that the successful completion of a project depends on mutual cooperation, skilled tradespeople, and a lot of meaningful communication (as opposed to the other kind). The field work versus the design office is not a recent challenge, the following is an inscription made by a public works engineer (circa 500 B.C.) upon an inspection of a job site. "There I found everybody in a depressed and sulky mood. They had abandoned all hope that the two opposite galleries of the tunnel would meet, as each of them had already been driven more than halfway through the mountain, and no junction had been achieved. As usual in such a case, the fault was again ascribed to the Engineer alone. I marked on the mountain ridge the exact position of the tunnel axis. I drew up plans and sections of the entire work. I then called the contractor and his men and began the excavation, in their presence, with the help of two shifts of experienced veterans. During the four years of my absence, the contractor and his supervisors had committed one error after the other. Each section of tunnel had departed from the straight line, always towards the right hand side, and if I had come later, Saldae would have two tunnels instead of one." This quotation may sound a bit contemporary; however, it can be verified in the book entitled, *Die Igenieurtechnik im Altertum* by C. Merckel, Berlin, 1899. Also, the ancient city of Saldae is in Algeria and has been renamed Wadi Saumman.

The drawings and structural calculations presented in the following chapters are based on three accepted control criteria for the design and construction of wood-framed buildings. The source of any specific design regulation or requirement will be designated in the explanatory narrative as the discourse progresses. The work that follows is primarily based on the 1991 edition of the *Uniform Building Code,* which is published by the International Conference of Building Officials. The *Uniform Building Code* will henceforth be indicated as UBC. The three chapters of the UBC that are most concerned with wood design and construction are Chapter 23, General Design Requirements; Chapter 25, Wood; and Chapter 29, Excavations and Foundations. Any reference to a section of the UBC will read as follows: UBC Section 2506(a), which in this particular instance refers to the subject Horizontal Member Design—Beam Span.

The second reference used is the 1991 edition of *National Design Specification for Wood Construction,* which will henceforth be indicated as NDS. Any reference to a section of the NDS will read as follows: NDS 6.3.7, which in this particular instance refers to the subject Beam Stability Factor.

The third reference source that will be used in the general commentary and explanations of this book is the book entitled *Timber Construction Manual* (3d ed.) published by the American Institute of Timber Construction. Any reference to this book will henceforth be indicated as AITC with page number, chapter, or example. It is imperative that the reader have copies of the above references so that he or she may fully comprehend the constraints and logic of wood design and construction. Much of the seismic design information presented in Chapter 7 has been researched in publications by the United States Federal Emergency Management Agency and the Building Seismic Council by the National Institute of Building Sciences.

2

Design Loads
and Forces

It is essential that each component or assembly of a structural frame be capable of resisting the predicted calculated design loads. The degree of strength of a structure is gaged by the allowable stress and deflection limits of the materials as specified in UBC Chapter 25. It is also necessary that the frame connections of the elementary parts of the structure have the capacity to transfer the load reactions to the succeeding support or resisting assembly. The nomenclature for each individual classification of load and force is customarily derived from their source or derivation. The two categories of vertical loads are *dead load* and *live load*. It is conventional to regard vertical forces as loads and lateral loads solely as forces. Loads and forces are essentially the same; that is, each is a vector consisting of magnitude and direction. In general, a vector that is classified as a load is defined by the fact that it only acts or reacts to gravity forces, and therefore its line of action is vertical. Also, gravitational loads are further differentiated as originating either from the dead weight of the structure or from an imposed active live weight resulting from the particular building occupancy. Force vectors, on the other hand, are imposed lateral loads which originate either from wind applied to the surface of the building or as an inertial response to seismic lateral movement of the structure.

Structural design is concerned with providing responsive physical constraints to an optimum combination of the dead load of the building plus the imposed live loads, wind loads, and seismic loads. UBC Section 2302 defines a dead load as the actual weight of the permanent parts of the structure; this definition includes the weights of the roof and floor materials, such as framing members, mechanical equipment, piping, electrical fixtures, walls, and ceilings. The codes make no provision for reduction of the unit dead load. Live loads are defined as the weight of anything within the building that is not considered to be permanently attached to or otherwise part of the structure. Unit dead loads and weights of building materials are tabulated in the last two pages of this chapter. These values are considered as a standard guideline in performing structural calculations. Weights or specific gravities of other types of materials that are not typically related to construction can be found in Chapter 6 of the *Manual of Steel Construction* published by the American Institute of Steel Construction.

In the process of performing the structural design of a building, the unit load expressed in lb/sq ft is used to calculate its magnitude and method of application. The load diagram configurations, such as those presented in Chapter 3, are derived by their aggregate tributary width or area. Uniformly distributed loads on a beam or a joist are calculated by the tributary width on each side of the member and are expressed in pounds per linear foot of length (lb/ft). The calculation of concentrated loads is based on the total tributary area to the point of application, and is expressed as pounds. The numerical values of both uniform and concentrated live loads to be supported by the members of a framing system depend on the specified use or the occupancy of the building. UBC Tables 23-A and 23-B (Appendix A) give a tabulation of the mandatory live loads for a variety of defined occupancies. Roof structural unit loads are specified on UBC Table 23-C (Appendix A). As previously stated, live loads are not permanent loads, and their magnitude can vary for certain tributary area sizes. As the area of support increases, the live load value can be determined by a statistical average. UBC Sections 2305 and 2306 present formulas generally used in calculating the amount of live load reduction permitted depending on the tributary area to be supported. Notice that UBC Table 23-C offers two alternative methods to calculate a roof live load; however, the building code also requires the use of the highest calculated live load value. It is assumed that this calculated live load will most accurately be commensurate with expected loading conditions. Oftentimes calculating a roof load to the least value may not accurately reflect the actual long-term loading situation. The designer should take into consideration that the building will be reroofed several times within its existence, and the new materials will be added to the present roofing, thus increasing the amount of dead load on the structure. On one occasion a bow-string trussed roof over a supermarket was reroofed; the contractor found it convenient to place all of the new materials at the center of the span at the top of the arch and then work outward in both directions. In this case not only was dead load of the roof structure increased, but it was added as a concentrated load at midspan, which increased the span moment by a factor greater than 2.

The problems created by added concentrated loads of equipment platforms or ventilation units on wood roofs can lead to damage or even failure of framing members. The two major design factors in this situation are the magnitude of the load and how the load is placed in its final position. The numerical value of the operating weight of the equipment is usually provided by the manufacturer; however, the designer should take into account the method of support and placing the unit; that is, the use of points of concentrated load as opposed to a uniformly distributed load platform on the equipment plan area. The designer should investigate the extra loads that could result from seismic or wind forces on the equipment. The method of placing roof-supported mechanical equipment can add a substantial amount of load to the structure which may not have been considered in the manufacturer's specification. The impact of dropping a heavy unit into place can significantly increase the load on the supporting members, depending on the height of drop. On one occasion the engineer required special-sized roof beams to support a platform for a heavy mechanical unit. However, since the contractor did not have a crane with a boom long enough to place the unit in its established location, it was placed at another position and then rolled to its final location, thereby damaging many of the lesser-sized members in the path of moving the unit.

Just as added roofing material can increase the dead load of a roof structure, so can the accumulation of a large volume of water. It is not unusual to read about situations in which large roof structural failures resulted from heavy water loads. Drainage of roof areas depends on an unencumbered surface slope to direct rainwater to the roof drains and overflow scuppers. One inch of water is equal to approximately 5.25 lb/sq ft of load. In order to prevent water from "ponding" on roof surfaces, the AITC recommends that wood roofs have a minimum slope of 0.25 in per foot to attain sufficient drainage. Experience indicates that this is only a minimum value; large-area roofs should have even greater slopes due to the higher possibility of collecting large amounts of water at the drainage points. Isolated ponding in small areas can be prevented by placing rafters and purlins with their crown side up, and by calculating the member deflection to be within the required limits specified in UBC Tables 23-D and 23-E. These requirements also apply to long-span roof beams. The AITC recommends that the beams have a minimum camber up at midspan of 1.5 times the calculated dead load deflection. These same criteria apply to roofs in regions where snow loads are probable. The density or load value of snow on a roof surface is set by local building officials. UBC Section 2305(d) permits snow load over 20 lb/sq ft and roof pitch greater than 20 degrees to be reduced by the formula used in Example 1, Sheet S-2, Case 4. Example 1, Sheet S-1, Case 1 is a demonstration of the calculation of live loads for a roof framed with rafters at intervals of 16 in o.c. Example 1, Sheet S-1, Case 2 is a demonstration of the roof live load for a panelized roof. Example 1, Sheet S-2, Case 3 is a demonstration of the roof live load reduction calculation for a uniformly distributed load of roof beam. Note that the purlins are spaced at 8 ft o.c. to accommodate the standard length of plywood panels. Also, the load on the supporting beam of the panelized framing system is applied as a continuous uniform load.

The ceilings of office buildings and in long corridors of apartment buildings are often constructed independent of the floor framing system to provide a chase for heating and ventilation ducts. The ceiling joists used to enclose this duct space are designed to support their own dead load, the weight of the mechanical ducts, plus a 10 lb/sq ft service access load, which is required by UBC Section 2104(d). There are times when it becomes necessary for a service mechanic to crawl through this space. The service access load will give some limited assurance that a person might not crash through a ceiling into an office or bedroom without an invitation. Ceiling design loads can challenge the engineer's judgment. It is difficult to predict the weight and location of suspended lighting fixtures or other types of hardware which could possibly be attached to a ceiling framing system. It is good practice to provide some reserve strength in the framing members to allow for such a contingency. Certain industries such as motion picture and television sound stages rely on ceiling or roof members for suspension of heavy scenery and lighting equipment. The standard method within the industry is to construct a wood rectangular grid system spaced approximately 30 to 36 in o.c. each way. The grid is designed to suspend a live load of 250 lb/sq ft. The entire system is supported at the ceiling level by the bottom chords of the roof trusses. Although the design load may seem excessive, judgment and experience indicate that there are instances in which it is quite realistic in areas where there is a high concentration of suspended equipment. Usually the lighting configuration is assembled on the stage floor and then hoisted into place. The number of suspension cables used, and their locations plus the impact of lifting can seriously overstress the support members. Also, since the grid live load exceeds 100 lb/sq ft, UBC Section 2312(e)1 requires that 25 percent of the load that exceeds 100 lb/sq ft is required in the design calculation of the seismic base shear of the building. Conditions of this type of loading may often occur in other types of manufacturing facilities in which hoists are suspended from roof framing beams. This does not present a problem as long as the beam is designed for the load. Concentrated loads of this type can overstress the beam in either bending when they are placed at midspan or in shear when they are placed close to the point of support. It is always good practice to check the deflection of a beam that may be required to suspend a concentrated load.

The geometry of roof plan configurations often requires that some members be designed for triangular-shaped load patterns. Roofs that have hip-and-valley members do not have a rectangular tributary width and therefore the loading pattern becomes a triangular figure. Roof valleys in particular allow a place for an extra accumulation of snow or rain; therefore, live reduction in these cases should be performed with some judgment. Example 1, Sheet S-3, Case 5, and Sheet S-4, Case 6 demonstrate the calculation of triangular-shaped loadings on roof members.

Floor dead loads are calculated in the same manner as roof dead loads; however, even though UBC Tables 23-A and 23-B specify numerical values of live loads, the engineer should make certain judgments in evaluating their classification and magnitude. An example of this concern can be found in UBC Section 2304(d), which classifies interior movable partitions of residences and offices as a uniform dead load equal to 20 lb/sq ft. It is quite possible that this additional load may prove to be unrealistic when it is calculated by dividing the total weight of all partitions by the enclosed floor plan area.

There are instances in which certain office equipment or machinery such as steel vaults, banks of filing cabinets, or large mainframe computers might be more accurately considered as dead load in view of their weight, method of support, and the duration on the floor. The live load classification of a floor area can make a major difference in the selected live load value. Quite often the use of heavy moving equipment in a factory or warehouse will require a design for a high unit live load. UBC Table 23-A offers light and heavy alternatives for several classifications of building occupancies. The design engineer should endeavor to use a live load that will most accurately reflect the actual use of the building. The determination of live loads can be a matter of judgment and experience in the interpretation of UBC Table 23-A. Reliance on the building code values may only solve the problem on paper; however, the design load may not reflect the reality of the use of the building. Building codes present only the best estimate of the expected minimum load. Example 2, Sheet S-1 demonstrates the methods of floor live load reduction for beams as specified in UBC Section 2306. Example 1 demonstrates the methods of calculating uniformly distributed loads.

Framing members may calculate to be within the allowable stresses for bending and shear as required by the UBC; however, the degree of deflection can also be a major factor in the design. The allowable limits of deflection for seasoned and unseasoned lumber as specified in UBC Tables 23-D and 23-E may be quite acceptable for ordinary conditions where the spans of joists and beams are relatively low, or when the anticipated live loads are acceptable. However, there are other cases in which spans may be unusually long or when the floor areas will experience a large amount of simultaneous foot traffic or when added marble floor surfaces may require more deflection control. The most unacceptable aspect of deflection is in cases where the floor vibration caused by normal foot traffic can be sensed at remote distances from the point of origin. Even though the structural design completely conforms to the building code requirements, this phenomenon tends to make people nervous. There are two primary approaches to effective deflection control. The first approach is to evaluate a level of acceptable deflection of the members, and then to convert it to a numerical control value. Floors that are covered with a 1-in-thick layer of marble plus a 1.5-in layer of concrete base may require a deflection control ratio of $L/490$ load (L = span length in inches). The value 490 represents a one-third increase over the live load value set in the UBC. The joists may either be increased in size to provide a larger moment of inertia of the member or they may be spaced at closer intervals to lower the tributary uniform load. The moment of inertia and the modulus of elasticity of the lumber are inversely proportional to the deflection. Therefore the second approach to the control of deflection is to set strict requirements for the modulus of elasticity of the framing lumber. Lumber that contains more than 15 percent moisture, or is said to be green, will have a reduced modulus of elasticity and thus will yield a high degree of deflection. On one occasion the contractor claimed that the lumber was so green that if it was stuck in the ground it would grow again.

Finally, there is one loading condition that frequently occurs on wood-framed buildings that is rarely calculated in the design process. Given an office building with floors designed for 50 lb/sq ft imposed live load plus a 20 lb/sq ft partition dead load as per code requirements, during construction the drywall contractor will use the open floor space to store a 3-ft-high stack of $\frac{5}{8}$-in-thick gypsum wallboard. Based upon 2.80 lb/sq ft, the imposed live load on the floor now becomes $3 \times (12/.625) \times 2.8 = 161.28$ lb/sq ft, which is 2.30 times greater than the design load. Also if the material is stacked at the midspan of the joists, the bending moment could be increased by a factor of 1.50. Something's got to give.

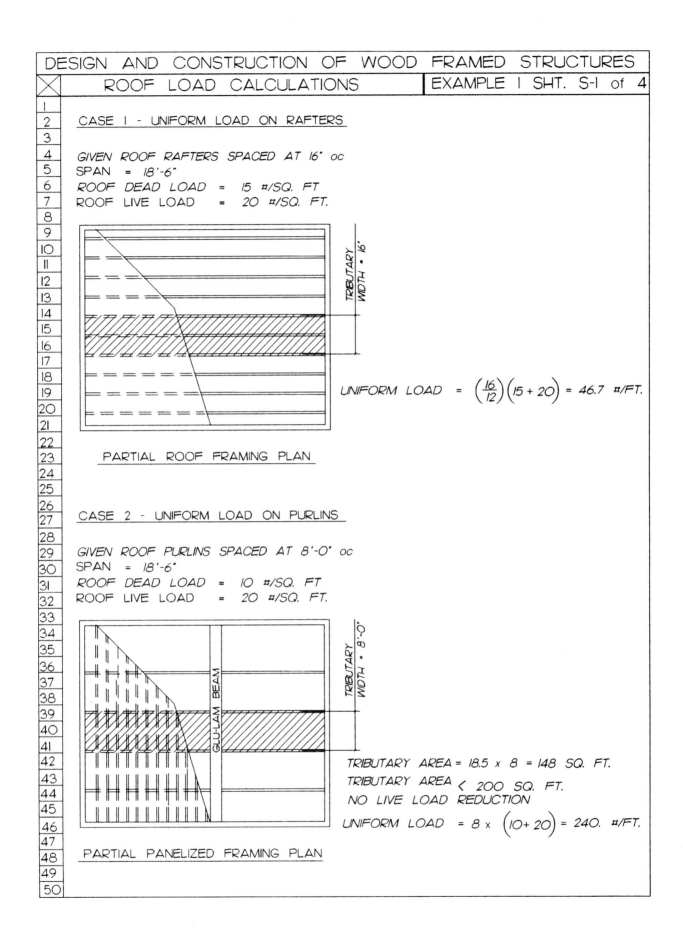

CASE 1 - UNIFORM LOAD ON RAFTERS

GIVEN ROOF RAFTERS SPACED AT 16" oc
SPAN = 18'-6"
ROOF DEAD LOAD = 15 #/SQ. FT
ROOF LIVE LOAD = 20 #/SQ. FT.

TRIBUTARY WIDTH = 16"

$$\text{UNIFORM LOAD} = \left(\frac{16}{12}\right)(15+20) = 46.7 \ \#/FT.$$

PARTIAL ROOF FRAMING PLAN

CASE 2 - UNIFORM LOAD ON PURLINS

GIVEN ROOF PURLINS SPACED AT 8'-0" oc
SPAN = 18'-6"
ROOF DEAD LOAD = 10 #/SQ. FT
ROOF LIVE LOAD = 20 #/SQ. FT.

TRIBUTARY WIDTH = 8'-0"

GLU-LAM BEAM

TRIBUTARY AREA = 18.5 x 8 = 148 SQ. FT.
TRIBUTARY AREA < 200 SQ. FT.
NO LIVE LOAD REDUCTION
$$\text{UNIFORM LOAD} = 8 \times (10+20) = 240. \ \#/FT.$$

PARTIAL PANELIZED FRAMING PLAN

CASE 3 - UNIFORM LOAD ON ROOF BEAM

GIVEN ROOF BEAMS SPACED AT 18'-0" oc
SPAN = 30'-0"
ROOF DEAD LOAD = 15 #/SQ. FT
ROOF LIVE LOAD = 20 #/SQ. FT.
FLAT ROOF

TRIBUTARY AREA = 18' x 30' = 540 sq. ft.

METHOD No. 1 - UBC TABLE No. 23-C
ROOF LIVE LOAD = 16 #/SQ. FT. √

METHOD No. 1 - UBC TABLE No. 23-C

$r = 0.08$

$R = 0.08 \left(540 - 150\right) = 31.2 \%$

UNIFORM LOAD = $18 \times \left(15 + 16\right)$ + BEAM = 600 #/FT.

CASE 4 - ROOF SNOW LOAD REDUCTION

GIVEN ROOF SNOW LOAD = 150 LBS./SQ. FT.
ROOF SLOPE = 6" VERTICAL TO 12" HORIZONTAL
ANGLE OF SLOPE = 26.56°

UBC SECTION 2305(d):

Snow loads in excess of 20 pounds per square foot may be reduced for each degree of pitch by R_s determined by the following formula:

$$R_s = \frac{S}{40} - \frac{1}{2}$$

R_s = Snow load reduction in pounds per square foot per degree of pitch over 20 degrees

S = Total snow load in pounds per square foot

$$R_s = \left(\frac{150}{40} - \frac{1}{2}\right) \times \left(26.56 - 20\right) = 21.32 \text{ #/sq. ft.}$$

SNOW LOAD = 150 - 21.32 = 128.68 #/sq. ft.

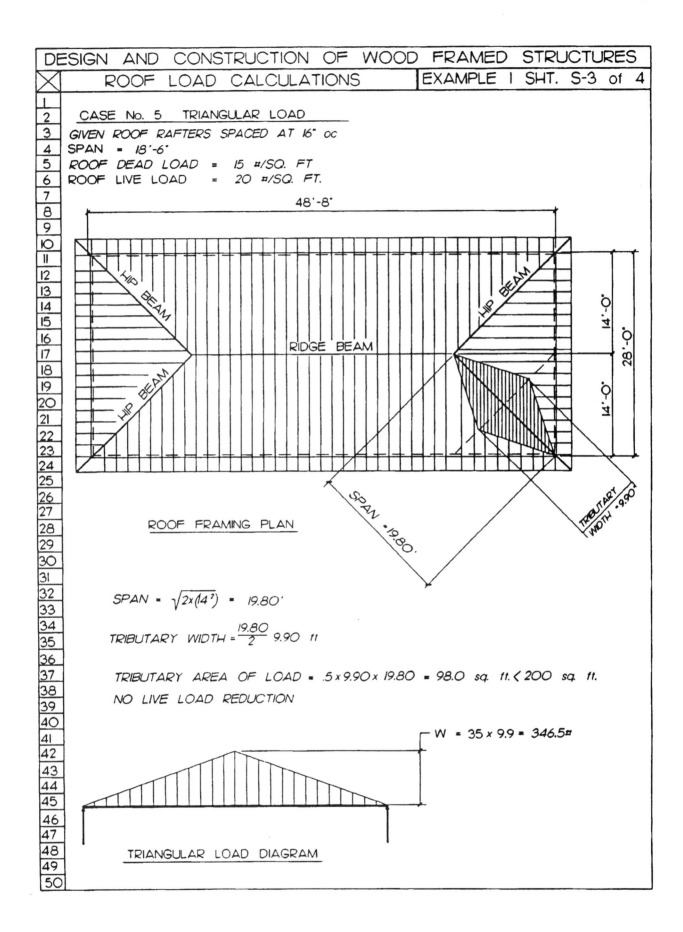

CASE No. 5 TRIANGULAR LOAD

GIVEN ROOF RAFTERS SPACED AT 16" oc

SPAN = 18'-6"

ROOF DEAD LOAD = 15 #/SQ. FT

ROOF LIVE LOAD = 20 #/SQ. FT.

48'-8"

14'-0"

28'-0"

14'-0"

HIP BEAM

HIP BEAM

HIP BEAM

RIDGE BEAM

HIP BEAM

SPAN = 19.80'

TRIBUTARY WIDTH = 9.90'

ROOF FRAMING PLAN

$$SPAN = \sqrt{2 \times (14^2)} = 19.80'$$

$$TRIBUTARY\ WIDTH = \frac{19.80}{2} = 9.90\ ft$$

TRIBUTARY AREA OF LOAD = .5 × 9.90 × 19.80 = 98.0 sq. ft. < 200 sq. ft.

NO LIVE LOAD REDUCTION

W = 35 × 9.9 = 346.5#

TRIANGULAR LOAD DIAGRAM

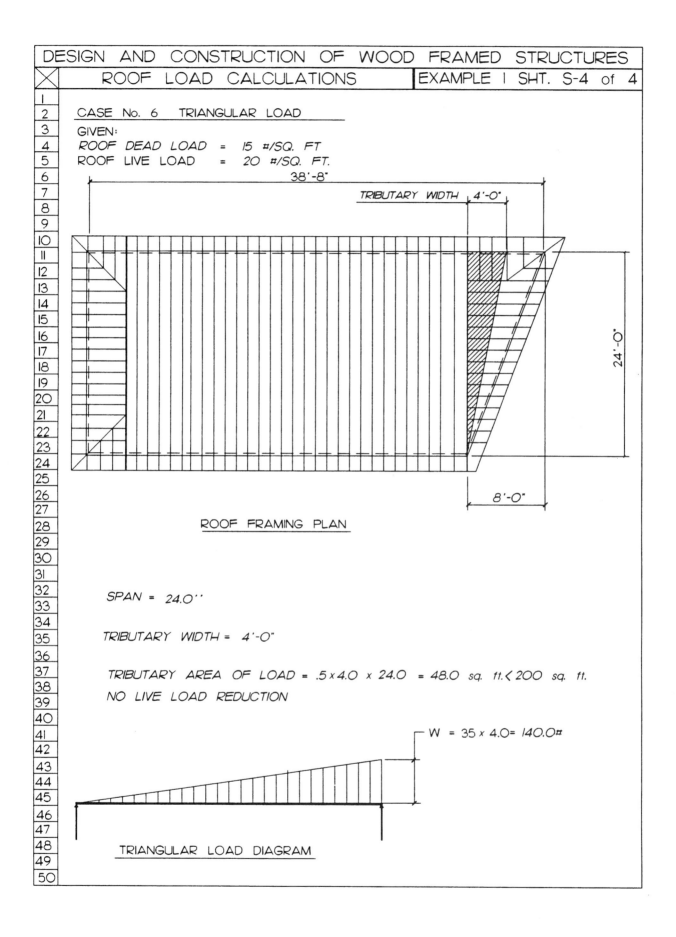

CASE No. 6   TRIANGULAR LOAD

GIVEN:
ROOF DEAD LOAD = 15 #/SQ. FT
ROOF LIVE LOAD   = 20 #/SQ. FT.

38'-8"

TRIBUTARY WIDTH   4'-0"

24'-0"

8'-0"

ROOF FRAMING PLAN

SPAN = 24.0''

TRIBUTARY WIDTH = 4'-0"

TRIBUTARY AREA OF LOAD = .5 x 4.0 x 24.0 = 48.0 sq. ft.< 200 sq. ft.
NO LIVE LOAD REDUCTION

W = 35 x 4.0= 140.0#

TRIANGULAR LOAD DIAGRAM

DESIGN AND CONSTRUCTION OF WOOD FRAMED STRUCTURES

FLOOR LIVE LOAD CALCULATIONS | EXAMPLE 2 SHT. S-1 of 1

CASE 1 - UNIFORM LOAD ON FLOOR BEAMS

GIVEN: AN OFFICE BUILDING FLOOR
BEAM SPAN = 36'-0"
TRIBUTARY WIDTH = 16'-0"

DESIGN LOADS:		
LIGHT WT. CONC.	=	13.3 #/sq ft
3/4" PLYWOOD	=	2.3
FLR. FRAMING	=	2.6
SUSPENDED CEILING	=	1.8
INSULATION	=	1.0
MISCELLANEOUS	=	1.0
DEAD LOAD	=	22.0
PARTITIONS	=	20.0
LIVE LOAD	=	50.0
TOTAL LOAD	=	92.0 #/sq ft

REFERENCE: UBC 2306, EQUATIONS 6-1 AND 6-2
R = REDUCTION PERCENT

EQ. 6-1 $R = r(A - 150)$
r = RATE OF REDUCTION = 0.80
A = TRIBUTARY AREA

TRIBUTARY AREA = 16.0 X 36 = 576 sq. ft.
LIVE LOAD REDUCTION:
EQ. No. 6-1 $R = .08\ (576 - 150) = 34.0\%$
LIVE LOAD = $50\ (1 - 0.34) = 33$ psf
UNIF. LOAD = 16.0(22 + 20 + 33) + BM = 1250 plf ← GOVERNS

EQ. 6-2 $R = 23.1\ (1 + D/L)$
D = UNIT DEAD LOAD
L = UNIT LIVE LOAD

$R = 23.1\ (1 + 42/50) = 42.5\%$

LIVE LOAD = $50 \times (1 - .425) = 28.75$ #/sq. ft.
PERCENT OF REDUCTION IS TOO HIGH - USE EQ. 6-1

NOTE: LIVE LOAD REDUCTION SHALL NOT EXCEED 40% IN GARAGES USED FOR THE STORAGE OF PRIVATE PLEASURE CARS HAVING A CAPACITY OF NOT MORE THAN NINE PASSENGERS PER VEHICLE.

WEIGHTS OF BUILDING MATERIALS

MATERIALS	WEIGHT LB. per Sq. Ft.	MATERIALS	WEIGHT LB. per Sq. Ft.
CIELINGS		PARTITIONS	
Channel suspended system	1	Clay Tile	
Lathing and plastering	See Partitions	3 in.	17
Acoustical fiber tile	1	4 in.	18
		6 in.	28
FLOORS		8 in.	34
Steel Deck	See Mfr.	10 in.	40
Concrete - Reinforced - 1 in.		Gypsum Block	
Stone	12.5	2 in.	9.5
Slag	11.5	3 in.	10.5
Lightweight	6 to 10	4 in.	12.5
Concrete - Plain - 1 in.		5 in.	14
Stone	12	6 in.	18.5
Slag	11	Wood Studs - 2 x 4's	
Lightweight	3 to 9	12 - 16 in. oc	2
Fills - 1 in.		Steel partitions	4
Gypsum	6	Plaster - 1 in.	
Sand	8	Cement	10
Cinders	4	Gypsum	5
Finishes		Lathing	
Terrazzo - 1 in.	13	Metal	0.5
Ceramic or Quarry Tile - 1 in.	10	Gypsum Board	2
Linoleum - 1/4 in.	1		
Mastic - 3/4 in.	9	WALLS	
Hardwood - 7/8 in.	4	Brick	
Softwood - 3/4 in.	2.5	4 in.	40
		8 in.	80
ROOFS		12 in.	120
Copper or Tin	1	Hollow Concrete Block (Heavy Aggregate)	
Corrugated steel	Check Gage		
3 - ply roofing	1	4 in.	30
3 - ply felt and gravel	5.5	6 in.	43
5 - ply felt and gravel	6	8 in.	55
Shingles		12 in.	80
Wood	2	Hollow Concrete Block (Light Aggregate)	
Asphalt	3		
Clay tile	9 to 14	4 in.	21
Slate - 1/4 in.	10	6 in.	30
Sheathing		8 in.	38
Wood - 3/4 in.		12 in.	55
Gypsum - 1 in.	3	Clay Tile (Load Bearing)	
Insulation - 1 in.	4		
Loose	0.5	4 in.	25
Poured in place	2	6 in.	30
Rigid	1.5	8 in.	33
		12 in.	45

COMPOSITION ROOFING

2 - 15# LAYERS + 90# CAP SHT	1.7	psf
3 - 15# LAYERS + 90# CAP SHT	2.2	psf
3 - 15# LAYERS + GRAVEL	5.6	psf
4 - 15# LAYERS + GRAVEL	6.0	psf
5 - 15# LAYERS + GRAVEL	6.5	psf
2" INSUL. MEMBRANE ASSEMB.	13.0	psf

FIR SHEATHING - BASED ON 36 pcf

3/8" PLYWOOD	1.1	psf
1/2" PLYWOOD	1.5	psf
5/8" PLYWOOD	1.8	psf
3/4" PLYWOOD	2.3	psf
11/8" PLYWOOD	3.4	psf
1" SHEATHING	2.3	psf
2" DECKING	4.3	psf
3" DECKING	7.0	psf
4" DECKING	9.3	psf

FLOORS

HARDWOOD - 1" NOM.	4.0	psf
CONCRETE - 1" THICK		
REGULAR	12.0	psf
LIGHTWEIGHT	6.0 to 10.0	psf
LINOLEUM OR SOFT TILE	1.5	psf
3/4" CERAMIC OR QUARRY TILE	10.0	psf
GYP-CRETE - 3/4" THICK	6.5	psf

WEIGHTS OF WOOD MEMBERS AS SPECIFIED IN THE CHART BELOW ARE BASED ON LUMBER WEIGHT OF 36 lbs./cu. ft.

WEIGHT OF FIR FRAMING MEMBERS

NOMINAL SIZE	JOIST SPACING oc		
	12" (psf)	16" (psf)	24" (psf)
2 X 4	1.4	1.1	0.7
2 X 6	2.2	1.7	1.1
2 X 8	2.9	2.2	1.5
2 X 10	3.7	2.8	1.9
2 X 12	4.4	3.3	2.2
2 X 14	5.2	3.9	2.6
4 X 6	5.0 plf		
4 X 8	6.8 plf	psf = lbs./sq. ft.	
4 X 10	8.6 plf	plf = lbs./linear ft.	
4 X 12	10.4 plf		
4 X 14	12.2 plf		

RIGID INSULATION

TEMLOCK - 1" THICK	1.2	psf
CORK	0.7	psf
GOLD BOND	1.5	psf
STYROFOAM	0.2	psf
FOAMGLASS	0.8	psf
RIGID FIBERGLASS	1.5	psf

MISCELLANEOUS FLOOR DECKING

POURED GYPSUM - 1" THICK	6.5	psf
VERMICULITE CONCRETE - 1" THICK	2.6	psf
CORRUGATED GALVANIZED STEEL		
16 GAGE	2.9	psf
20 GAGE	1.8	psf
22 GAGE	1.5	psf
24 GAGE	1.3	psf
ASPHALT SHINGLES	2.5	psf
WOOD SHINGLES	2.0	psf
CLAY TILE	9.0 to 14.0	psf

CEILINGS

ACOUSTIC FIBER TILE	1.0	psf
1/2" GYPSUM BOARD	2.2	psf
5/8" GYPSUM BOARD	2.8	psf
PLASTER - 1" THICK	8.0	psf
METAL SUSPENSION SYSTEM INCLUDING TILE	1.8	psf
WOOD SUSPENSION SYSTEM INCLUDING TILE	2.5	psf

ROLL ON or BATT INSULATION

ROCK WOOL - 1" THICK	0.2	psf
GLASS WOOL - 1" THICK	0.3	psf

WEIGHT OF SPRINKLER SYSTEMS plf

SIZE OF PIPE- in.	SCHEDULE 40, STD PIPE		SCHEDULE 10, THIN WALL	
	DRY	WET	DRY	WET
1	1.7	2.1	—	—
1 1/4	2.3	3.0	—	—
1 1/1/2	2.7	3.6	—	—
2	3.7	5.2	2.7	3.8
2 1/2	5.8	7.9	3.5	5.9
3	7.6	10.8	4.3	8.0
3 1/2	9.2	13.5	5.0	11.2
4	10.9	16.4	5.6	14.5
5	14.8	23.5	7.8	20.0
6	19.2	31.7	9.3	26.2
8	28.6	50.8	16.9	40.1
10	40.5	74.6	—	—

3

Design Methods

There are times in the course of the construction, when a carpenter will "estimate" the size of a wood beam rather than rely on an engineer's design calculation. It is difficult to comprehend why a person would take such a risk, especially if they have a limited knowledge of the subjects of strength of materials and structural design. Experience proves that whenever you shoot from the hip, you have more than a 50 percent chance of hitting your foot, or some other equally important appendage.

Chapter 22 of the UBC requires that buildings that are classified as Type V structures shall have a one-hour fire rating throughout. The UBC also requires that the fire-resistive requirements shall be as specified in Chapter 17 for various building occupancies. These two requirements allow the construction of three- and four-story wood-framed buildings. No distinction between post-and-beam and light-frame wood construction is made in this book, since they are essentially designed by the same mathematical procedures. In order to maintain a degree of uniformity in the design examples of this book, it was decided to use Douglas fir–larch as the framing material. The species of lumber and their stress grades vary for different geographical regions; however, it should be stated that other species of lumber could have been selected. UBC Chapter 25, Table 25-A-1 tabulates the allowable stress grade values for structural lumber for diverse species of wood and for a variety of uses. The allowable stress grade values in UBC Table 25-A-2 are for lumber machine stress-graded lumber. UBC Table 25-C-1 gives a tabulation of allowable stress grades of glued laminated beams and columns. These members are considered as a manufactured product and consist of various combinations of stress grades of structural lumber. The stress grade of a particular species of lumber that is specified in a building code does not represent an exact value. The procedure of evaluating lumber stress grade is done visually within specific limits and requirements of The West Coast Lumbermen's Association and the AITC. This method of stress determination is not regarded as exceptionally accurate; however, statistically it does yield a reliable criterion. A higher degree of grading accuracy is achieved by a machine testing procedure. Table 25-A-2 of the UBC and the *National Design Specifications Manual* (NDS) both offer tabulated allowable stress values of all species of lumber for specific uses in construction, this includes glued laminated wood members. Glued laminated members are fabricated under factory-controlled conditions for stress grade of lumber, adhesive materials, stress grade combinations of the members, moisture content, and quality of workmanship. Notice that the allowable stress grades of lumber in most categories are higher than those of sawn structural lumber. This is due to a comparatively high degree of quality control in production.

In view of the fact that wood is a natural substance, quality control factors for both use and manufacture are important in the determination of its capacity to resist superimposed loads. This fact requires that the reliability of structural lumbers be based on a rational standard in order to achieve a measurable degree of control in terms of species, size, use, and duration. The quality and strength of wood as a structural material are verified to the contractor and the building inspector by a grade mark certification made by a selected responsible control agency. The lumber should be protected against decay, moisture, and termite damage while it is stored prior to its use. Termites invade and eat the cellular material and thus diminish the structural capacity. Decay of lumber can be controlled by maintaining the internal moisture content to less than 20 percent. When the moisture content exceeds 25 percent of the material content, it becomes an important factor in controlling shrinkage and warping. Therefore members that are used for mudsills, ledgers, or that are in direct contact with concrete or masonry should be kiln-dried or chemically pressure treated to avoid termite infiltration. In conditions of this nature, some building codes permit the use of a naturally durable species of lumber such as redwood. Although exposed floors and attics are not in direct contact with moisture surfaces, they should have sufficient ventilation to prevent the accumulation of long-term interior moisture. The percent of moisture contained within the wood can vary depending on the exposed condition of its use. A change of moisture content can result in shrinking the size or configuration of the wood member. Also, placing heavy loads at critical points on a structural member for long periods can result in a reduction of the stress capacity of the lumber. UBC Section 2504.4(ii) permits the following allowable stress increases:

15 percent for 2 months' duration—snow loads

25 percent for 7 days—roof loads

33.3 percent for wind or seismic loads

100 percent for impact loads

NDS Table 4A presents recommended design adjustment factors of allowable stresses of structural lumber for various use conditions and durations. An example of a use condition related to the quality of the lumber can be found in the allowable shear stress increase permitted by the length of the splits on the wood member surface.

The unit allowable stresses and deflections of lumber are the criteria in structural calculations to determine member sizes of a building. The NDS Supplement presents tables for allowable stresses for both sawn lumber and glued laminated lumber for a comprehensive list of wood species and uses. The structural capacity of the member can be verified by its simultaneous resistance to bending stress, shear stress, and deformation or deflection resulting from externally applied loads and forces. Each of these major stress and strain considerations directly relates to the dimensions, the cross-section configuration, and the strength of the material of the member. The methods of analysis and design used for wood-framed buildings are the same as those used for buildings composed of other types of structural materials. It is assumed that the reader has an elementary understanding of the mechanics of statics and the principles of strength of structural materials; however, a brief review and explanation will serve to demonstrate the practical applications used for the design of wood-framed buildings. Analysis and design are two separate procedures, and before a structural analysis is started, it is necessary to know the shape and dimensions of the building plus the numerical magnitude, direction, and location of externally applied forces. The structural geometry of a building is delineated by the length of beams and columns, location of loads, size and shapes of members, and by the methods of connections. Chapter 2 demonstrates methods of calculation of gravity and externally applied loads on a building. Support of the various structural parts that comprise a wood frame is sequentially interactive; that is, starting from the top of the building and progressing down to the foundation, the roof and each floor level is supported by the columns, posts, and bearing walls of the next structural tier below. The task of the structural analysis procedure is to isolate the component parts of the building and their respective forces required for design or investigation. Analysis methodology uses the principles of engineering mechanics to derive a mathematical relationship of static or kinetic forces that may be externally applied to a rigid body. All of this assumes that the framing members are properly interconnected; otherwise, it is just a pile of lumber.

At this point, it is important to invoke certain definitions. A *force* is classified as a finite load having a magnitude and a direction which can change the state of linear or rotational motion of a rigid body to which it is applied. For the purposes of this book, a *rigid body* may be any part or assembly of a wood-framed building such as a beam, joist, wall assembly, or column. Forces are defined as vectors having both a numerical magnitude which is expressed in pounds, and a direction or line of action. It is customary to refer to vertical forces as "loads," and horizontal or lateral loads caused by wind or seismic encounters as lateral "forces." Also, although wind and seismic forces result from natural kinetic phenomena, they are treated as horizontal static forces in structural calculations. A force is diagrammed as a vector consisting of a line to represent magnitude and an arrow to indicate direction of its action. The drawings of the beam design diagrams on the following pages depict the conventional presentation for diagramming a force system. Notice that the algebraic sign convention indicates that vertical forces acting in the downward direction are calculated as a negative value, and conversely forces acting upward are calculated as a positive value. Lateral forces acting toward the right are assigned positive values, and forces acting toward the left are set as negative values.

An example of externally applied forces can be a combination of the weight of a cabinet placed at some point on the span of a beam plus the dead weight of the structure. The beam is supported by posts at each end, and it is assumed that its size and strength are sufficient to carry the total external load. In order for the beam to remain in its original position, the algebraic summation of forces reacting upward as post supports and the downward action of the beam load must equal zero. A state of equilibrium exists because the forces acting down (beam loads) are equal to the forces acting upward (post reactions). If the beam forces do not have an equal amount of vertical and horizontal reaction by the supporting members, it would move. To maintain the static condition of equilibrium of a system of forces on a rigid body, the summation of all of the force actions must be zero. This condition applies to forces acting in any combination of the vertical and horizontal directions.

In each case of a solution demonstration for the design formulas in this chapter or in the design examples presented in the following chapters, the summation of forces acting in any direction are equally resisted by the reactions of the building supports. Since there is no movement induced by the external loads, a condition of equilibrium exists. The geometry of the structure and the forces are considered to be mutually coplanar. The explanation diagrams are drawn on a two-dimensional plane established by x and y Cartesian coordinates. The drawings used for analysis and design in this book are diagrams of forces acting on a particular part or assembly of the structure. These diagrams are referred to as *free-body diagrams* because they differentiate between the forces that may be acting on other individual parts of the structure. The condition of equilibrium required to resist linear movement of a body in the x or y direction is mathematically expressed by the following equations:

$$\text{Summation of } F_x = 0$$

$$\text{Summation of } F_y = 0$$

Forces that may act in a third direction or coordinate (z) are not germane to the analysis or design of a structure in which the geometry is expressed only in x and y coordinates. Forces may be applied to a structure in any direction or angle; however, since the vector system is mutually coplanar and delineated by the same x and y coordinates, the forces must be resolved into their respective x and y components to solve the equations for F_x and F_y. In Case 1, Sheet 1, lines 4 to 12 demonstrate the trigonometric procedure used to resolve vectors into their horizontal and vertical components. The resistance of the vertical component of a force P applied to the beam at an angle is proportionately resisted by the support reactions. This diagram represents a condition that can be found in cases when the diagonal roof rafters exert a horizontal component (R_x) of force on the support. It is necessary to provide a horizontal element for lateral resistance to R_x to maintain horizontal equilibrium. The lateral forces calculated in Case 1, Sheet S-1 are often the result of sloped roof rafters. The designer should provide lateral resistance to this force as shown in Chapter 4, Example 5, Sheet S-1.

Equations of the summation of forces in the x and y directions determine reactions to constrain linear motion. However, as previously stated, the condition of equilibrium must also provide for resistance to rotation. The summation of moments about any point in the free-body system therefore must equal zero. Case 1, L 35 indicates that moments are calculated about the center line of the right-side support. A moment about any axis is defined as the magnitude of a force multiplied by its perpendicular distance to the line of direction of action. In Case 1 it can be seen that the moment resulting from R_x is equal to zero since the perpendicular distance of its line of action relative to the point of moments is equal to zero. Case 1 is an example of a calculation method in which rotation resistance is used to calculate a support reaction value. Case 2, Sheet S-2, L 41 demonstrates that the internal moment of the beam is calculated by taking moments about a point on the span. In view of the sign convention of forces and their respective distances about a selected point, in this instance $x = 7'-0''$, it can be seen that the internal bending moments are balanced by an equal but opposite moment. Moments rotating in a clockwise direction are designated as positive, while moments rotating in a counterclockwise direction are negative. The mathematical relationship between the internal moment of a beam and the shear can be verified by the principle that the algebraic summation of the area included under a shear diagram at any point in either direction from a point on the beam is equal to the internal moment at that point. This axiom can be verified by calculating the area of the shear diagram in either direction from a selected point of the beam. Also, it should be noted that the maximum internal bending moment on a beam span occurs at the point where $V = 0$; that is, at the point where it crosses the line from being a positive shear value to a negative shear value.

Building loads and their respective points of application on a beam or column are critical factors in calculating the magnitude and configuration of shear and moment diagrams necessary in performing either a design or an investigation procedure. The purpose of the structural design function is to ascertain a required size and shape of a structural part. Conversely, structural investigation of a known size member involves calculations to determine unit stresses and strain deformations at various points on the member. Structural design and investigation are alternate procedures used to verify that framing members comply with the conditions set by particular governing criteria or building code.

The strength of any engineering material is measured by an established constant ratio of the stress to its elastic strain. The numerical value of strain is defined as the amount a part will stretch or compress per inch of length as a result of tension or compressive forces. Stress is expressed in pounds per square inch on the cross-sectional area of the part. In 1678 Robert Hooke conceived that the strain of a material is directly proportional to its internal stress. The stress-strain ratio evaluates the structural adequacy for bending and shear of different types of structural materials. The proportional constant of the unit stress and unit strain or deformation for each particular material was first suggested by Thomas Young in 1802 and is referred to as *Young's modulus,* or as the *modulus of elasticity.* The designation and mathematical ratio for the modulus of elasticity is expressed in the equation given below.

$$E = \text{Stress/Strain} = \text{in per in of length}$$

The significance of the value of the modulus of elasticity in structural design is that whenever a member is stressed either in tension or compression, there will be a consequent proportional amount of strain, depending on the material. In the instance of a post, the axial load will compress its cross section with a resultant reduction of the length. After the axial load is removed, the post will resume its previous length, providing that the material has not been stressed past its elastic limit. The importance of the modulus of elasticity is that it provides a verifiable standard to set working stress values for bending, shear, tension, and compression for different species of lumber for particular uses. Design methods and the use of materials for wood-framed construction are discussed on the remaining pages of this chapter.

The equations used in the design cases in the following pages have been developed by mathematical static analysis methods. The scope of the number of design cases represents the most frequently encountered structural conditions. The first page of each case consists of a descriptive diagram of the loading condition, the resultant moment and shear diagrams, and the design formulas. The second page of Cases 1–19 consists of a numerical demonstration of the use of the formulas for a set of assumed or given values. It should be noted at this point that in every instance of calculating the deflection of a bending member, that it is multiplied by a factor of 1728 (12^3) to convert the result into inches. Also, it can be seen that the magnitude of the moment of inertia (I) and the modulus of elasticity (E) is inversely proportional to deflection. The physical properties of structural lumber are tabulated in Appendix B for both sawn and glued laminated lumber. Incremental increases in the depth of beams or joists can substantially reduce stresses and deflection since I is calculated by the fourth power of d (depth). The modulus of elasticity which denotes the stress to strain ratio of lumber directly correlates the quality of the wood material to stress and deflection. NDS Table 2.3.1 lists the parameter of design adjustment factors to be considered in the design of wood structures. The table specifies adjustment factors for moisture and temperature for the value of E used in the design of bending members. The design equations given in Case 20 for various wood posts and columns are demonstrated in design examples shown in Chapter 4.

EXAMPLE No. 1 - SIMPLE BEAM SUPPORTING A CONCENTRATED LOAD
RESOLVE THE CONCENTRATED LOAD P INTO X AND Y COMPONENTS

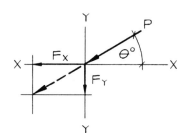

$$\sin \theta = \frac{P}{F_Y} \; ; \quad F_Y = P \times \sin \theta$$

$$\cos \theta = \frac{P}{F_X} \; ; \quad F_X = P \times \cos \theta$$

$$\therefore P = \sqrt{(F_X)^2 + (F_Y)^2}$$

$$\Sigma FX = O = R_X - F_X \; , \quad R_X = F_X$$

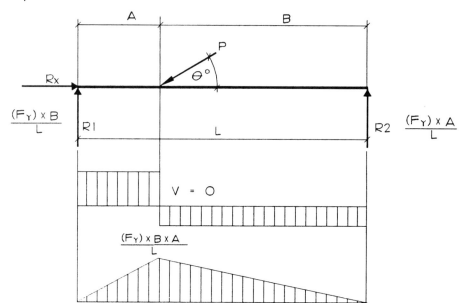

TO CALCULATE THE LEFT SIDE REACTION TAKE MOMENTS ABOUT R2

$$\Sigma M_{R2} = O = (F_Y) \times B - R1 \times L \; ; \quad R1 = \frac{(F_Y) \times B}{L}$$

TO CALCULATE THE RIGHT SIDE REACTION TAKE MOMENTS ABOUT R1

$$\Sigma M_{R1} = O = (F_Y) \times A - R2 \times L \; ; \quad R2 = \frac{(F_Y) \times A}{L}$$

MAXIMUM BENDING MOMENT OCCURS AT V = O

$$\text{MAX. MOMENT} = \frac{(F_Y) \times B \times A}{L} \quad \text{AT MID SPAN}$$

NOTE THAT THE BENDING MOMENT AT ANY POINT ON A SPAN IS
EQUAL TO THE AREA OF THE SHEAR DIAGRAM AT THAT POINT

EXAMPLE No. 2 - SIMPLE BEAM SUPPORTING A UNIFORM LOAD

TO CALCULATE THE LEFT SIDE REACTION TAKE MOMENTS ABOUT R2

$$M_y = 0 = R1 \times L - \frac{W \times L^2}{2} \qquad\qquad F_y = 0 = W \times L - R1 - R2$$

$$R1 = \frac{W \times L^2}{2 \times L} \qquad\qquad\qquad R2 = \frac{W \times L}{2}$$

$$R1 = \frac{W \times L}{2} \qquad\qquad\qquad R2 = R1$$

TO CALCULATE THE MID SPAN BENDING MOMENTS - TAKE MOMENTS AT POINT L/2

THE AREA OF THE SHEAR DIAGRAM IS EQUAL TO THE BENDING MOMENTS AT THAT POINT

$$\Sigma M_{MAX.} = W \times \left(\frac{L}{2}\right)^2 - L \times \left(\frac{W \times L}{2}\right)$$

AREA OF A RIGHT TRIANGLE

$$M_{MAX.} = \frac{W \times L^4}{4} - \frac{W \times L^2}{2}$$

$$AREA = \left(\frac{W \times L}{2}\right) \times \left(\frac{L}{4}\right) = \frac{W \times L^2}{8}$$

$$M_{MAX.} = \frac{W \times L^2}{8}$$

NOTE THAT THE MAX. MOMENT OCCURS AT POINT WHERE SHEAR = O

GIVEN: $L = 18'-0"$, $W = 250$ #/FT ;   BEAM SIZE 6 X 12 ; $\triangle_{ALLOW.} = \frac{L}{240}$

ALLOW. BEND. STRESS = 1250 psi, ALLOW. SHEAR STRESS = 85 psi $E = 1.6 \times 10^6$

$$AREA = 5.5 \times 11.25 = 61.87 \text{ in}^2, \qquad I = \frac{5.5 \times 11.25^2}{12} = 652.6 \text{ in}^4, \qquad S = \frac{5.5 \times 11.25^2}{6} = 116.0 \text{ in}^3$$

$$V = \frac{250 \times 18}{2} = 2250 \text{ #} \qquad M = \frac{250 \times 18^2}{8} = 10125 \text{ '#} \qquad f_b = \frac{M}{S} \qquad v = \frac{1.5 \times V}{A} \text{ (UBC Sec. 2506c)}$$

$$v = \frac{1.5 \times 2250}{61.87} = 54.55 \text{ psi} \qquad f_b = \frac{12 \times 10125}{116.0} = 1047.4 \text{ psi}$$

$$\triangle_{ALLOW.} = \frac{12 \times 18}{240} = 0.90 \text{ in.} \qquad \triangle = \frac{5 \times 18^4 \times 250 \times 1728}{384 \times 1.6 \times 10^6 \times 652.6} = 0.57 \text{ in.}$$

SIMPLE BEAM WITH A UNIFORM LOAD:

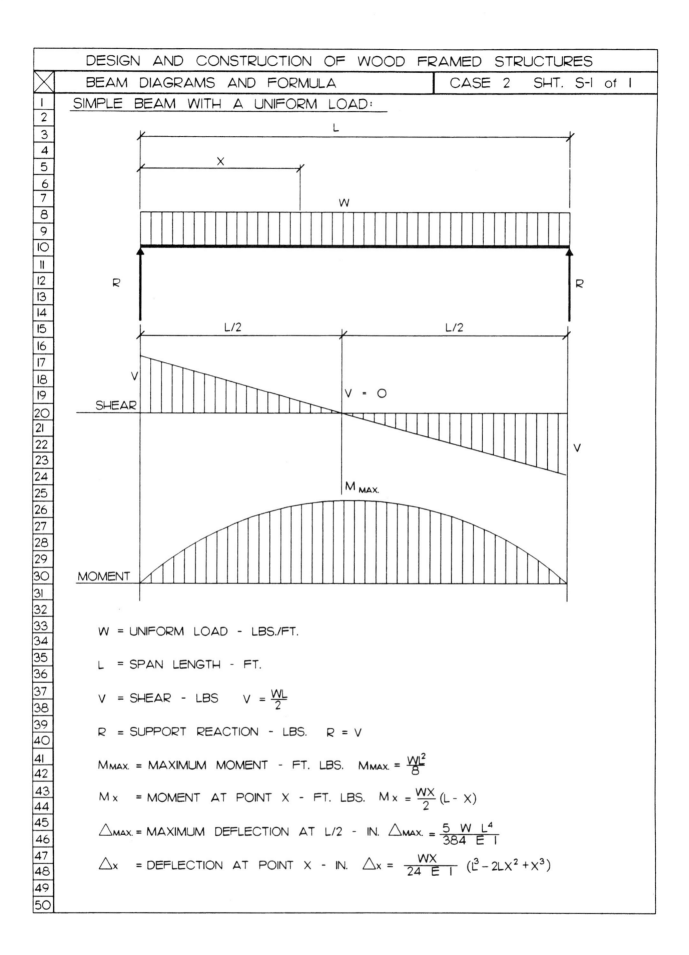

W = UNIFORM LOAD - LBS./FT.

L = SPAN LENGTH - FT.

V = SHEAR - LBS $V = \dfrac{WL}{2}$

R = SUPPORT REACTION - LBS.   R = V

$M_{MAX.}$ = MAXIMUM MOMENT - FT. LBS. $M_{MAX.} = \dfrac{WL^2}{8}$

M_x = MOMENT AT POINT X - FT. LBS. $M_x = \dfrac{WX}{2}(L - X)$

$\triangle_{MAX.}$ = MAXIMUM DEFLECTION AT L/2 - IN. $\triangle_{MAX.} = \dfrac{5\ W\ L^4}{384\ E\ I}$

$\triangle_x$ = DEFLECTION AT POINT X - IN. $\triangle_x = \dfrac{WX}{24\ E\ I}(L^3 - 2LX^2 + X^3)$

SIMPLE BEAM WITH A UNIFORM LOAD:

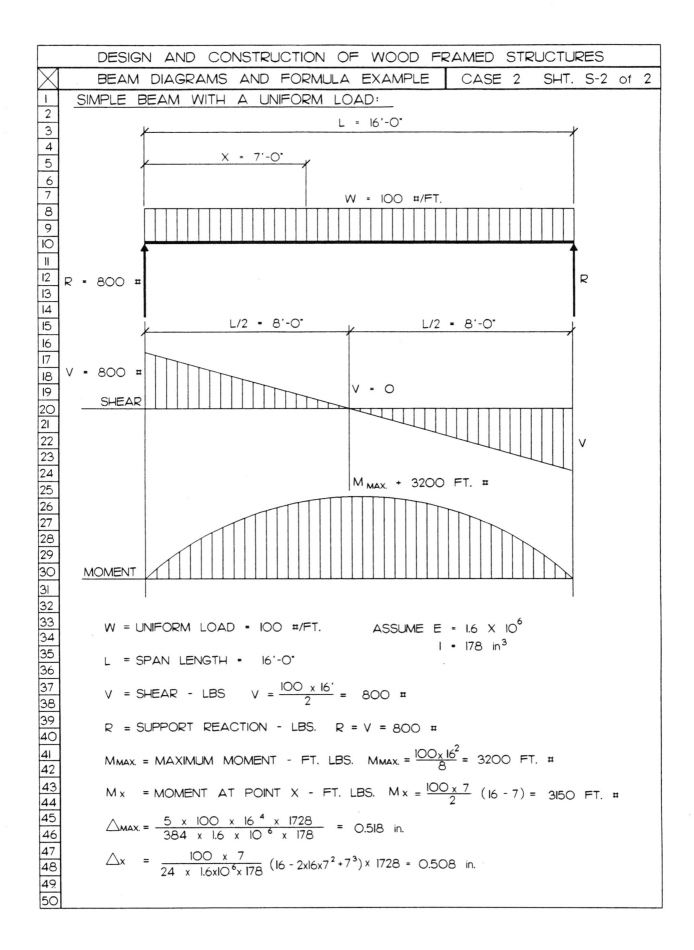

W = UNIFORM LOAD - 100 #/FT.   ASSUME E = 1.6 X 10^6

                                                                    I = 178 in^3

L = SPAN LENGTH - 16'-0"

V = SHEAR - LBS $V = \dfrac{100 \times 16'}{2} = 800$ #

R = SUPPORT REACTION - LBS.   R = V = 800 #

$M_{MAX.}$ = MAXIMUM MOMENT - FT. LBS. $M_{MAX.} = \dfrac{100 \times 16^2}{8} = 3200$ FT. #

M_x = MOMENT AT POINT X - FT. LBS. $M_x = \dfrac{100 \times 7}{2}(16 - 7) = 3150$ FT. #

$\triangle_{MAX.} = \dfrac{5 \times 100 \times 16^4 \times 1728}{384 \times 1.6 \times 10^6 \times 178} = 0.518$ in.

$\triangle_x = \dfrac{100 \times 7}{24 \times 1.6 \times 10^6 \times 178}(16 - 2 \times 16 \times 7^2 + 7^3) \times 1728 = 0.508$ in.

SIMPLE BEAM WITH A PARTIAL UNIFORM LOAD:

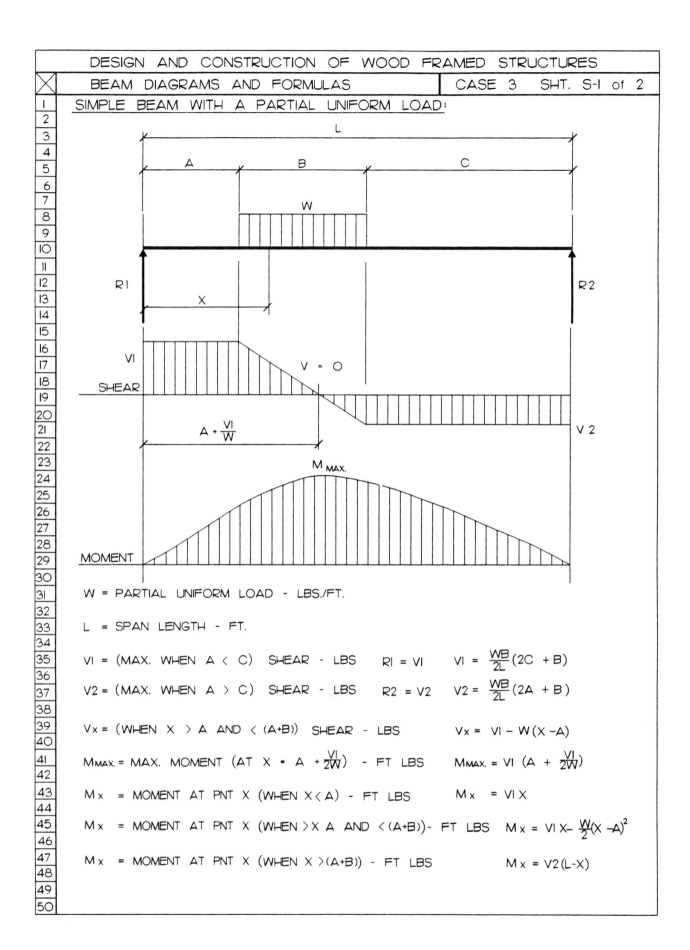

W = PARTIAL UNIFORM LOAD - LBS./FT.

L = SPAN LENGTH - FT.

V1 = (MAX. WHEN A < C) SHEAR - LBS   R1 = V1 $V1 = \dfrac{WB}{2L}(2C + B)$

V2 = (MAX. WHEN A > C) SHEAR - LBS   R2 = V2 $V2 = \dfrac{WB}{2L}(2A + B)$

Vx = (WHEN X > A AND < (A+B)) SHEAR - LBS $Vx = V1 - W(X - A)$

$M_{MAX.}$ = MAX. MOMENT $\left(\text{AT } X = A + \dfrac{V1}{2W}\right)$ - FT LBS $M_{MAX.} = V1\left(A + \dfrac{V1}{2W}\right)$

M_x = MOMENT AT PNT X (WHEN X < A) - FT LBS $M_x = V1\,X$

M_x = MOMENT AT PNT X (WHEN > X A AND < (A+B)) - FT LBS $M_x = V1\,X - \dfrac{W}{2}(X - A)^2$

M_x = MOMENT AT PNT X (WHEN X > (A+B)) - FT LBS $M_x = V2(L-X)$

SIMPLE BEAM WITH A PARTIAL UNIFORM LOAD:

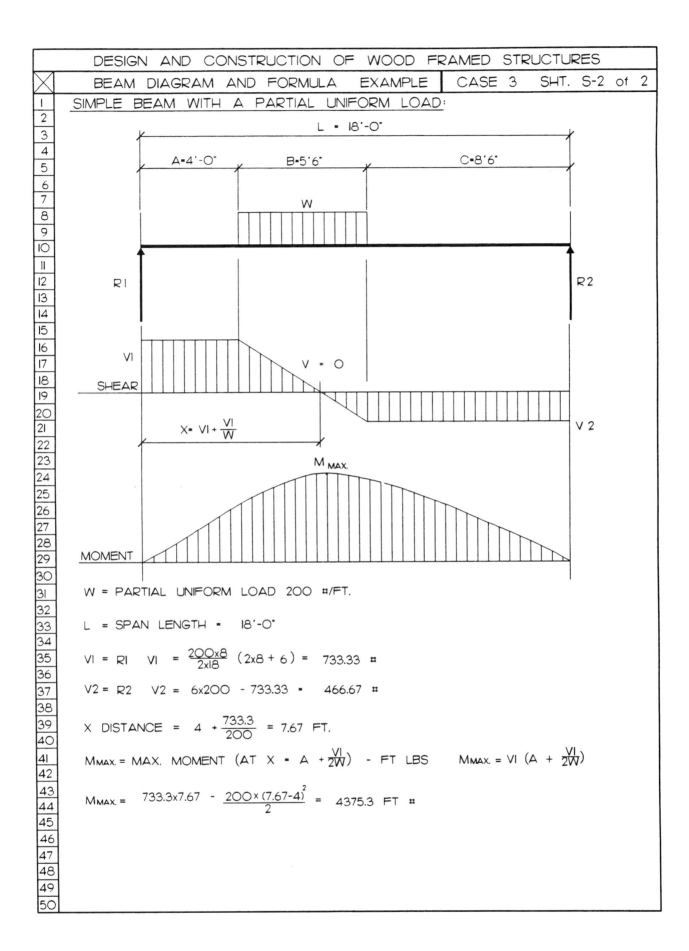

W = PARTIAL UNIFORM LOAD 200 #/FT.

L = SPAN LENGTH = 18'-0"

$V1 = R1 \quad V1 = \dfrac{200 \times 8}{2 \times 18}(2 \times 8 + 6) = 733.33 \ \#$

$V2 = R2 \quad V2 = 6 \times 200 - 733.33 = 466.67 \ \#$

$X \text{ DISTANCE} = 4 + \dfrac{733.3}{200} = 7.67 \ FT.$

$M_{MAX.} = \text{MAX. MOMENT (AT } X = A + \dfrac{V1}{2W}) - FT \ LBS \qquad M_{MAX.} = V1 \left(A + \dfrac{V1}{2W}\right)$

$M_{MAX.} = 733.3 \times 7.67 - \dfrac{200 \times (7.67-4)^2}{2} = 4375.3 \ FT \ \#$

SIMPLE BEAM WITH A PARTIAL UNIFORM LOAD AT ONE END OF THE BEAM:

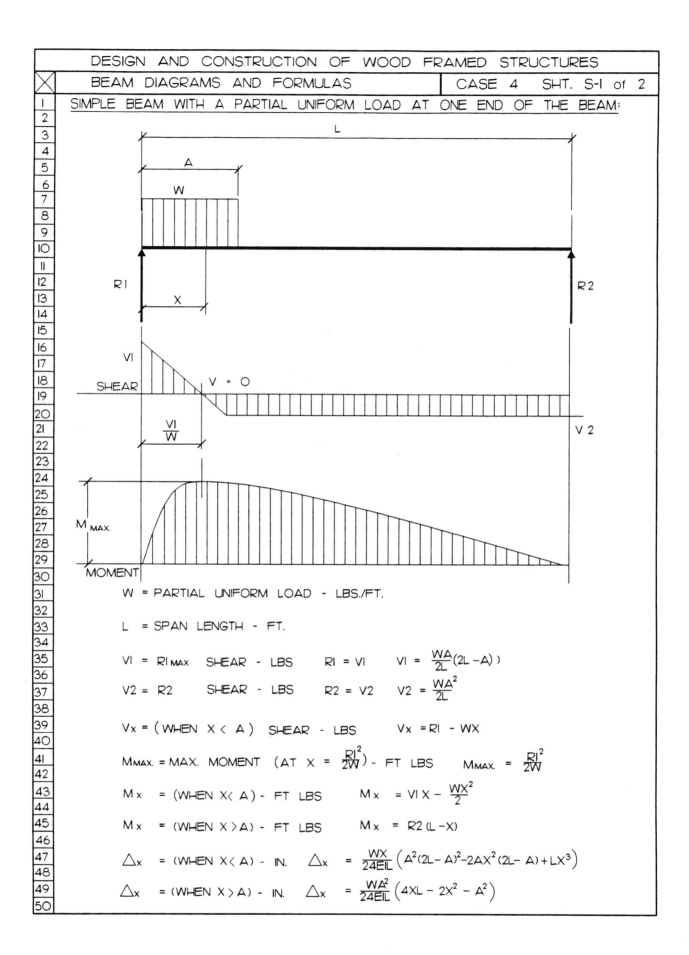

W = PARTIAL UNIFORM LOAD - LBS./FT.

L = SPAN LENGTH - FT.

$V1 = R1_{MAX}$ SHEAR - LBS $R1 = V1$ $V1 = \dfrac{WA}{2L}(2L-A))$

$V2 = R2$ SHEAR - LBS $R2 = V2$ $V2 = \dfrac{WA^2}{2L}$

$Vx = $ (WHEN $X < A$) SHEAR - LBS $Vx = R1 - WX$

$M_{MAX.} = $ MAX. MOMENT (AT $X = \dfrac{R1^2}{2W}$) - FT LBS $M_{MAX.} = \dfrac{R1^2}{2W}$

Mx = (WHEN $X < A$) - FT LBS Mx = $V1 X - \dfrac{WX^2}{2}$

Mx = (WHEN $X > A$) - FT LBS Mx = $R2 (L-X)$

$\triangle x$ = (WHEN $X < A$) - IN. $\triangle x$ = $\dfrac{WX}{24EIL}\left(A^2(2L-A)^2 - 2AX^2(2L-A) + LX^3 \right)$

$\triangle x$ = (WHEN $X > A$) - IN. $\triangle x$ = $\dfrac{WA^2}{24EIL}\left(4XL - 2X^2 - A^2 \right)$

SIMPLE BEAM WITH A PARTIAL UNIFORM LOAD AT ONE END OF THE BEAM:

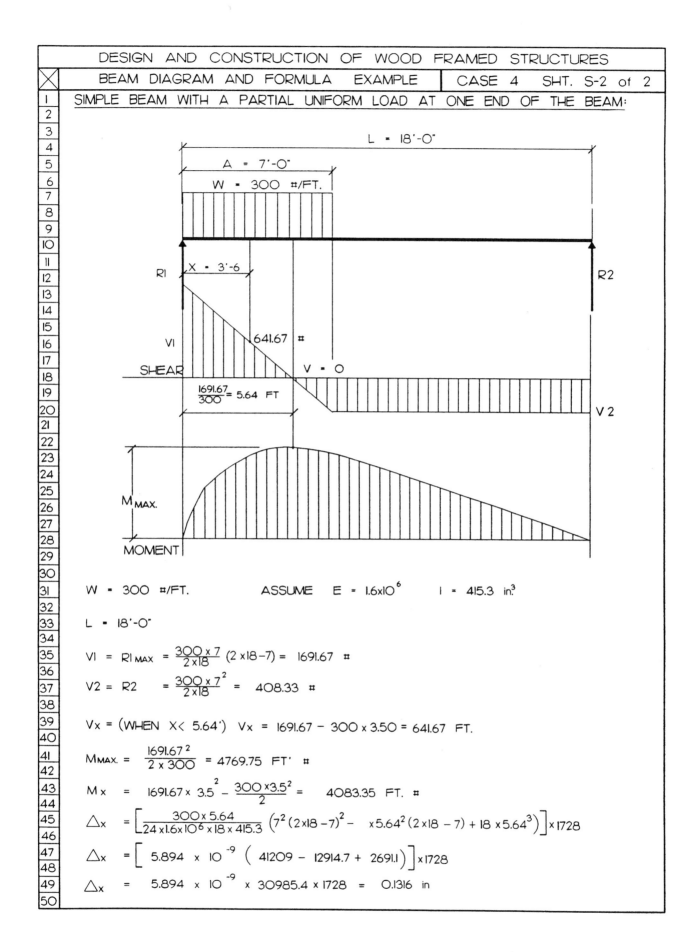

$W = 300$ #/FT.   ASSUME $E = 1.6 \times 10^6$ $I = 415.3$ in.³

$L = 18'-0"$

$V1 = R1_{MAX} = \dfrac{300 \times 7}{2 \times 18}(2 \times 18 - 7) = 1691.67$ #

$V2 = R2 = \dfrac{300 \times 7^2}{2 \times 18} = 408.33$ #

$Vx = $ (WHEN $X < 5.64'$) $Vx = 1691.67 - 300 \times 3.50 = 641.67$ FT.

$M_{MAX.} = \dfrac{1691.67^2}{2 \times 300} = 4769.75$ FT' #

$Mx = 1691.67 \times 3.5^2 - \dfrac{300 \times 3.5^2}{2} = 4083.35$ FT. #

$\triangle x = \left[\dfrac{300 \times 5.64}{24 \times 1.6 \times 10^6 \times 18 \times 415.3}\left(7^2(2 \times 18 - 7)^2 - x5.64^2(2 \times 18 - 7) + 18 \times 5.64^3\right)\right] \times 1728$

$\triangle x = \left[5.894 \times 10^{-9}\left(41209 - 12914.7 + 2691.1\right)\right] \times 1728$

$\triangle x = 5.894 \times 10^{-9} \times 30985.4 \times 1728 = 0.1316$ in

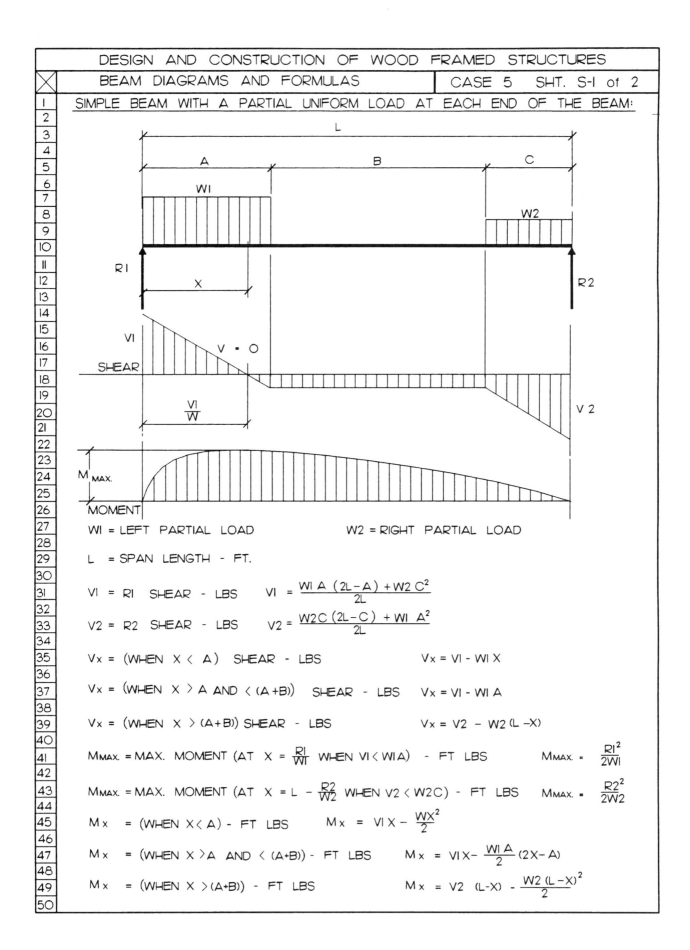

SIMPLE BEAM WITH A PARTIAL UNIFORM LOAD AT EACH END OF THE BEAM:

W1 = LEFT PARTIAL LOAD   W2 = RIGHT PARTIAL LOAD

L = SPAN LENGTH - FT.

V1 = R1 SHEAR - LBS $V1 = \dfrac{W1\,A\,(2L-A)+W2\,C^2}{2L}$

V2 = R2 SHEAR - LBS $V2 = \dfrac{W2\,C\,(2L-C)+W1\,A^2}{2L}$

Vx = (WHEN X < A) SHEAR - LBS $Vx = V1 - W1\,X$

Vx = (WHEN X > A AND < (A+B)) SHEAR - LBS $Vx = V1 - W1\,A$

Vx = (WHEN X > (A+B)) SHEAR - LBS $Vx = V2 - W2\,(L-X)$

$M_{MAX.}$ = MAX. MOMENT (AT X = $\dfrac{R1}{W1}$ WHEN V1 < W1A) - FT LBS $M_{MAX.} = \dfrac{R1^2}{2W1}$

$M_{MAX.}$ = MAX. MOMENT (AT X = L − $\dfrac{R2}{W2}$ WHEN V2 < W2C) - FT LBS $M_{MAX.} = \dfrac{R2^2}{2W2}$

Mx = (WHEN X < A) - FT LBS $Mx = V1\,X - \dfrac{Wx^2}{2}$

Mx = (WHEN X > A AND < (A+B)) - FT LBS $Mx = V1\,X - \dfrac{W1\,A}{2}(2X-A)$

Mx = (WHEN X > (A+B)) - FT LBS $Mx = V2\,(L-X) - \dfrac{W2\,(L-X)^2}{2}$

SIMPLE BEAM WITH A PARTIAL UNIFORM LOAD AT EACH END OF THE BEAM:

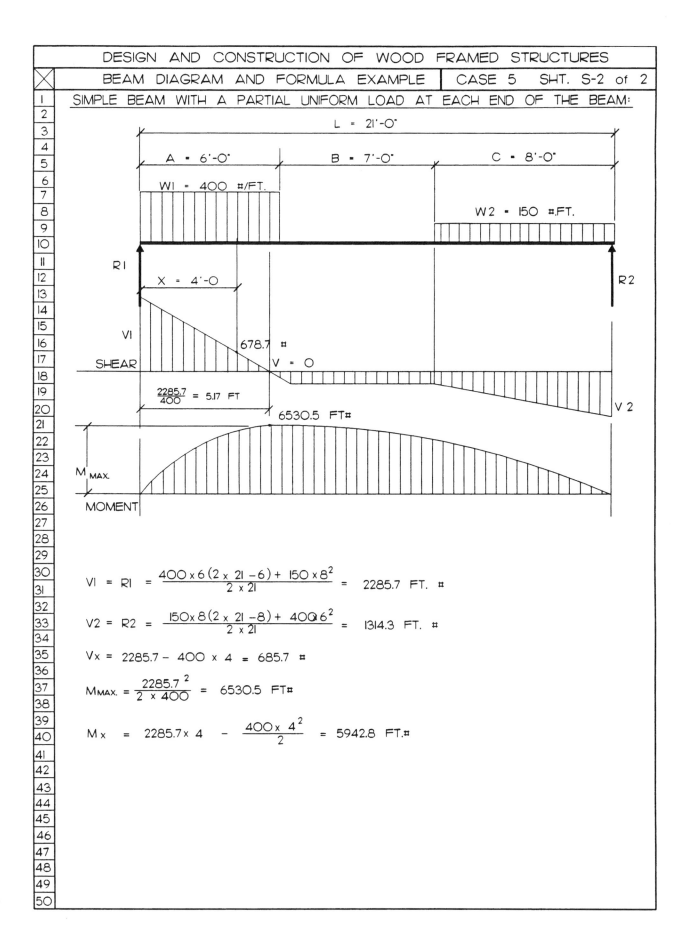

$$V_1 = R_1 = \frac{400 \times 6 (2 \times 21 - 6) + 150 \times 8^2}{2 \times 21} = 2285.7 \text{ FT. #}$$

$$V_2 = R_2 = \frac{150 \times 8 (2 \times 21 - 8) + 400 \times 6^2}{2 \times 21} = 1314.3 \text{ FT. #}$$

$$V_x = 2285.7 - 400 \times 4 = 685.7 \text{ #}$$

$$M_{MAX.} = \frac{2285.7^2}{2 \times 400} = 6530.5 \text{ FT#}$$

$$M_x = 2285.7 \times 4 - \frac{400 \times 4^2}{2} = 5942.8 \text{ FT.#}$$

SIMPLE BEAM WITH A RIGHT TRIANGULAR LOAD:

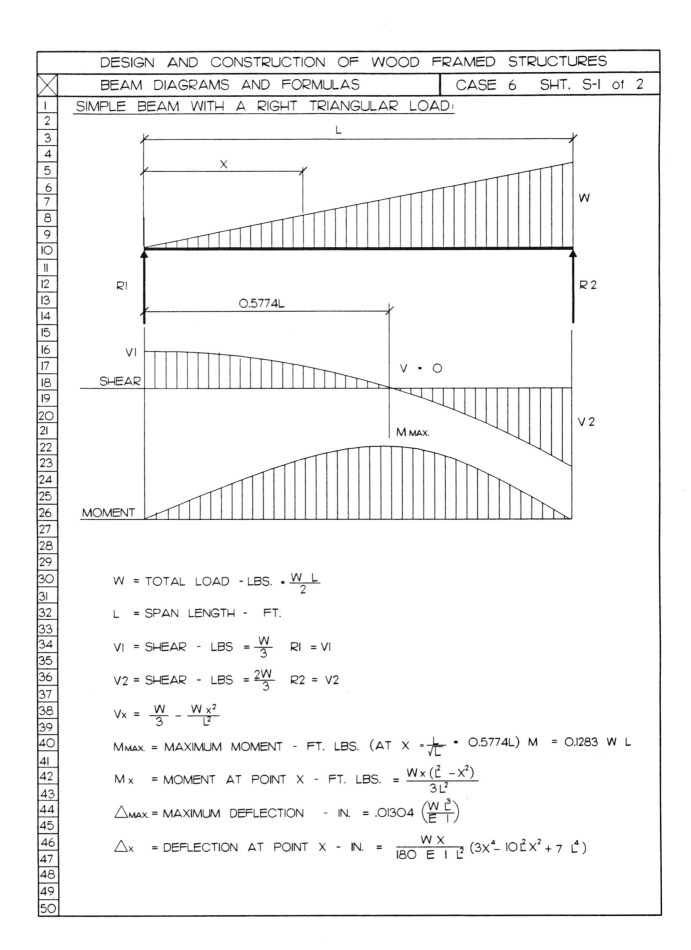

W = TOTAL LOAD - LBS. $= \dfrac{W\, L}{2}$

L = SPAN LENGTH - FT.

$V1$ = SHEAR - LBS $= \dfrac{W}{3}$ $R1 = V1$

$V2$ = SHEAR - LBS $= \dfrac{2W}{3}$ $R2 = V2$

$Vx = \dfrac{W}{3} - \dfrac{W\, x^2}{L^2}$

$M_{MAX.}$ = MAXIMUM MOMENT - FT. LBS. $\left(\text{AT } X = \dfrac{L}{\sqrt{L}} = 0.5774L\right)$ $M = 0.1283\ W\ L$

M_x = MOMENT AT POINT X - FT. LBS. $= \dfrac{W x\,(L^2 - x^2)}{3\,L^2}$

$\triangle_{MAX.}$ = MAXIMUM DEFLECTION - IN. $= .01304\left(\dfrac{W\, L^3}{E\ I}\right)$

$\triangle x$ = DEFLECTION AT POINT X - IN. $= \dfrac{W\, x}{180\ E\ I\ L^2}\left(3x^4 - 10\,L^2 x^2 + 7\ L^4\right)$

SIMPLE BEAM WITH A RIGHT TRIANGULAR LOAD:

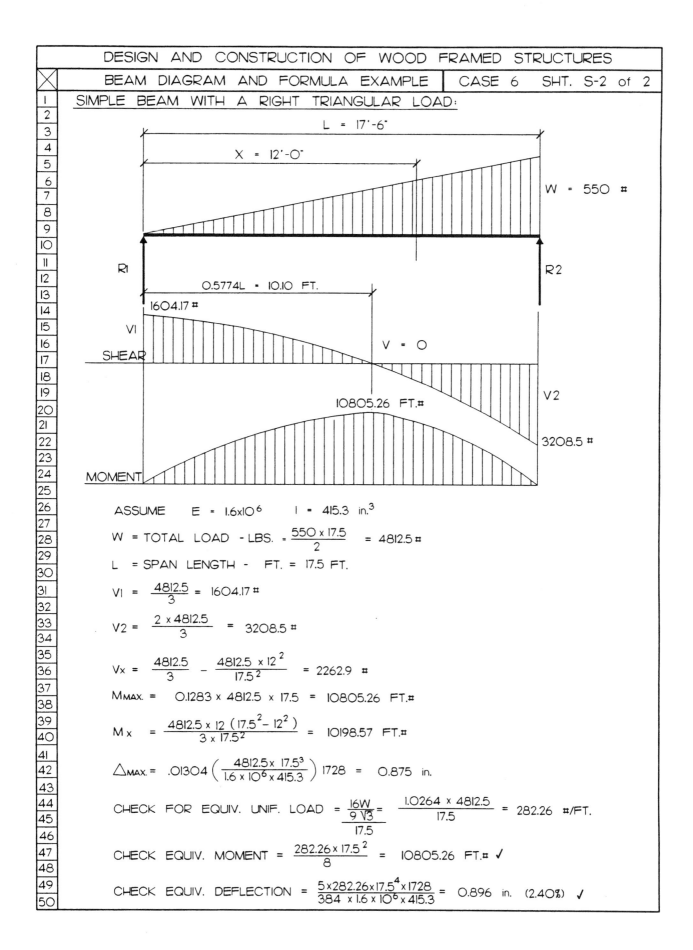

$L = 17'-6"$

$X = 12'-0"$

$W = 550$ #

R1   R2

$0.5774L = 10.10$ FT.

1604.17 #

V1

SHEAR $V = 0$

V2

10805.26 FT.#   3208.5 #

MOMENT

ASSUME $E = 1.6 \times 10^6$ $I = 415.3$ in.^{3}

$W = $ TOTAL LOAD - LBS. $= \dfrac{550 \times 17.5}{2} = 4812.5$ #

$L = $ SPAN LENGTH - FT. $= 17.5$ FT.

$V1 = \dfrac{4812.5}{3} = 1604.17$ #

$V2 = \dfrac{2 \times 4812.5}{3} = 3208.5$ #

$Vx = \dfrac{4812.5}{3} - \dfrac{4812.5 \times 12^2}{17.5^2} = 2262.9$ #

$M_{MAX.} = 0.1283 \times 4812.5 \times 17.5 = 10805.26$ FT.#

$M_x = \dfrac{4812.5 \times 12\,(17.5^2 - 12^2)}{3 \times 17.5^2} = 10198.57$ FT.#

$\triangle_{MAX.} = .01304 \left(\dfrac{4812.5 \times 17.5^3}{1.6 \times 10^6 \times 415.3} \right) 1728 = 0.875$ in.

CHECK FOR EQUIV. UNIF. LOAD $= \dfrac{16W}{9\sqrt{3}}{17.5} = \dfrac{1.0264 \times 4812.5}{17.5} = 282.26$ #/FT.

CHECK EQUIV. MOMENT $= \dfrac{282.26 \times 17.5^2}{8} = 10805.26$ FT.# ✓

CHECK EQUIV. DEFLECTION $= \dfrac{5 \times 282.26 \times 17.5^4 \times 1728}{384 \times 1.6 \times 10^6 \times 415.3} = 0.896$ in. (2.40%) ✓

SIMPLE BEAM WITH A CENTERED TRIANGULAR LOAD:

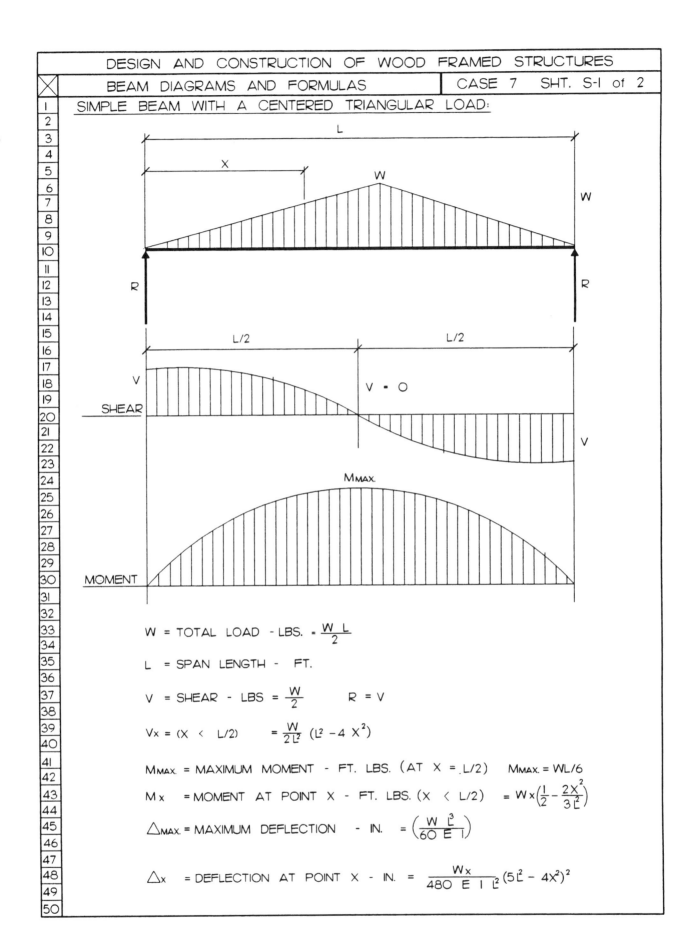

W = TOTAL LOAD - LBS. $= \dfrac{w\,L}{2}$

L = SPAN LENGTH - FT.

V = SHEAR - LBS $= \dfrac{W}{2}$ $R = V$

$V_x = (X < L/2) \qquad = \dfrac{W}{2\,L^2}\,(L^2 - 4\,X^2)$

$M_{MAX.}$ = MAXIMUM MOMENT - FT. LBS. (AT $X = L/2$) $M_{MAX.} = WL/6$

M_x = MOMENT AT POINT X - FT. LBS. $(X < L/2) = W x \left(\dfrac{1}{2} - \dfrac{2X^2}{3\,L^2}\right)$

$\triangle_{MAX.}$ = MAXIMUM DEFLECTION - IN. $= \left(\dfrac{W\,L^3}{60\,E\,I}\right)$

$\triangle_x$ = DEFLECTION AT POINT X - IN. $= \dfrac{Wx}{480\,E\,I\,L^2}\,(5\,L^2 - 4X^2)^2$

SIMPLE BEAM WITH A CENTERED TRIANGULAR LOAD:

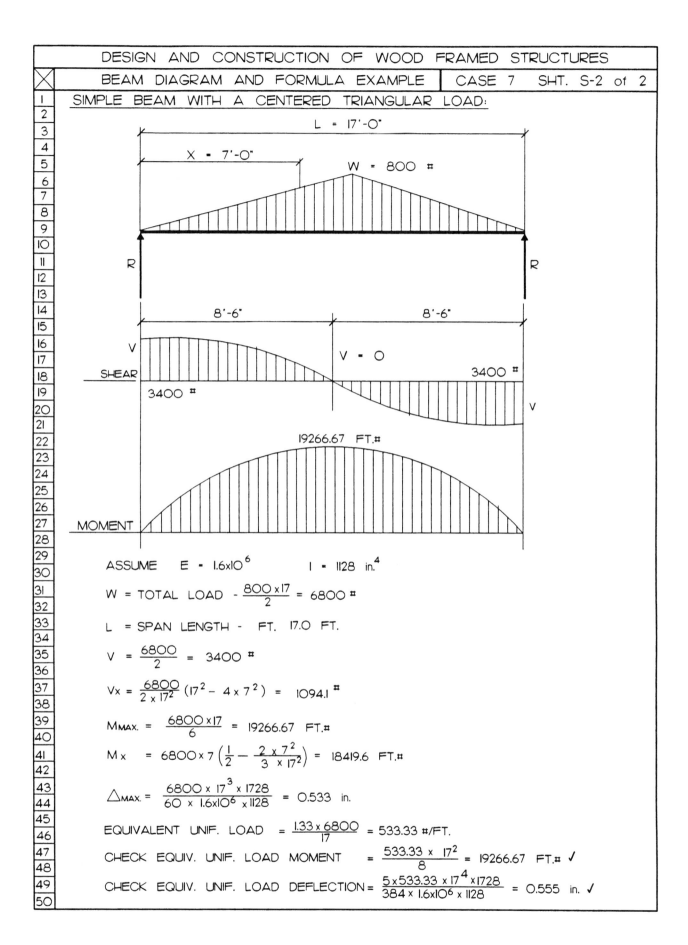

ASSUME $E = 1.6 \times 10^6$ $I = 1128$ in.^{4}

$W = $ TOTAL LOAD $- \dfrac{800 \times 17}{2} = 6800$ #

$L = $ SPAN LENGTH $-$ FT. 17.0 FT.

$V = \dfrac{6800}{2} = 3400$ #

$V_x = \dfrac{6800}{2 \times 17^2}(17^2 - 4 \times 7^2) = 1094.1$ #

$M_{MAX.} = \dfrac{6800 \times 17}{6} = 19266.67$ FT.#

$M_x = 6800 \times 7 \left(\dfrac{1}{2} - \dfrac{2 \times 7^2}{3 \times 17^2}\right) = 18419.6$ FT.#

$\triangle_{MAX.} = \dfrac{6800 \times 17^3 \times 1728}{60 \times 1.6 \times 10^6 \times 1128} = 0.533$ in.

EQUIVALENT UNIF. LOAD $= \dfrac{1.33 \times 6800}{17} = 533.33$ #/FT.

CHECK EQUIV. UNIF. LOAD MOMENT $= \dfrac{533.33 \times 17^2}{8} = 19266.67$ FT.# ✓

CHECK EQUIV. UNIF. LOAD DEFLECTION $= \dfrac{5 \times 533.33 \times 17^4 \times 1728}{384 \times 1.6 \times 10^6 \times 1128} = 0.555$ in. ✓

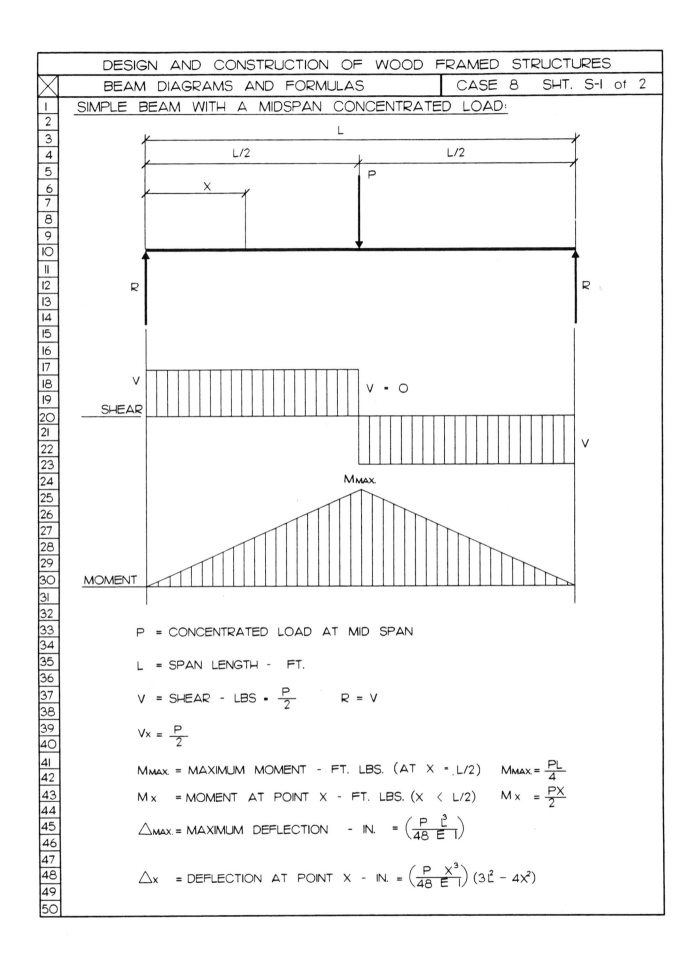

SIMPLE BEAM WITH A MIDSPAN CONCENTRATED LOAD:

P = CONCENTRATED LOAD AT MID SPAN

L = SPAN LENGTH - FT.

V = SHEAR - LBS. $= \dfrac{P}{2}$ R = V

$V_x = \dfrac{P}{2}$

$M_{MAX.}$ = MAXIMUM MOMENT - FT. LBS. (AT X = L/2) $M_{MAX.} = \dfrac{PL}{4}$

M_x = MOMENT AT POINT X - FT. LBS. (X < L/2) $M_x = \dfrac{PX}{2}$

$\triangle_{MAX.}$ = MAXIMUM DEFLECTION - IN. $= \left(\dfrac{P\ L^3}{48\ E\ I}\right)$

$\triangle_x$ = DEFLECTION AT POINT X - IN. $= \left(\dfrac{P\ X^3}{48\ E\ I}\right)(3L^2 - 4X^2)$

SIMPLE BEAM WITH A MIDSPAN CONCENTRATED LOAD AT MIDSPAN:

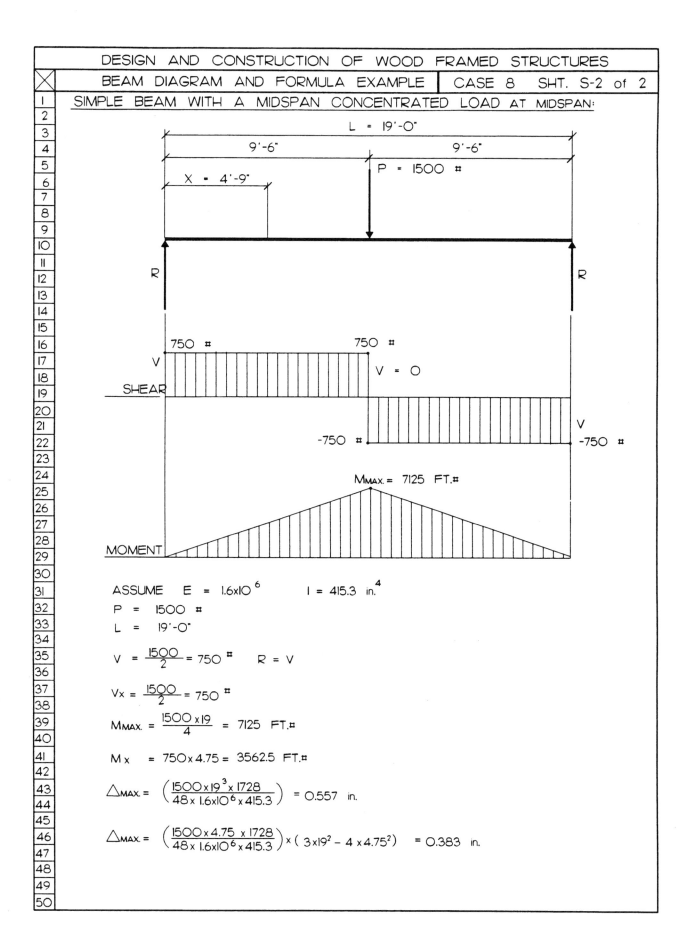

ASSUME $E = 1.6 \times 10^{6}$ $\qquad$ $I = 415.3$ in.^{4}

$P = 1500$ #

$L = 19'-0"$

$V = \dfrac{1500}{2} = 750$ # $\qquad R = V$

$Vx = \dfrac{1500}{2} = 750$ #

$M_{MAX.} = \dfrac{1500 \times 19}{4} = 7125$ FT.#

$Mx = 750 \times 4.75 = 3562.5$ FT.#

$\triangle_{MAX.} = \left(\dfrac{1500 \times 19^{3} \times 1728}{48 \times 1.6 \times 10^{6} \times 415.3} \right) = 0.557$ in.

$\triangle_{MAX.} = \left(\dfrac{1500 \times 4.75 \times 1728}{48 \times 1.6 \times 10^{6} \times 415.3} \right) \times (3 \times 19^{2} - 4 \times 4.75^{2}) = 0.383$ in.

SIMPLE BEAM WITH A CONCENTRATED LOAD AT ANY POINT ON THE SPAN

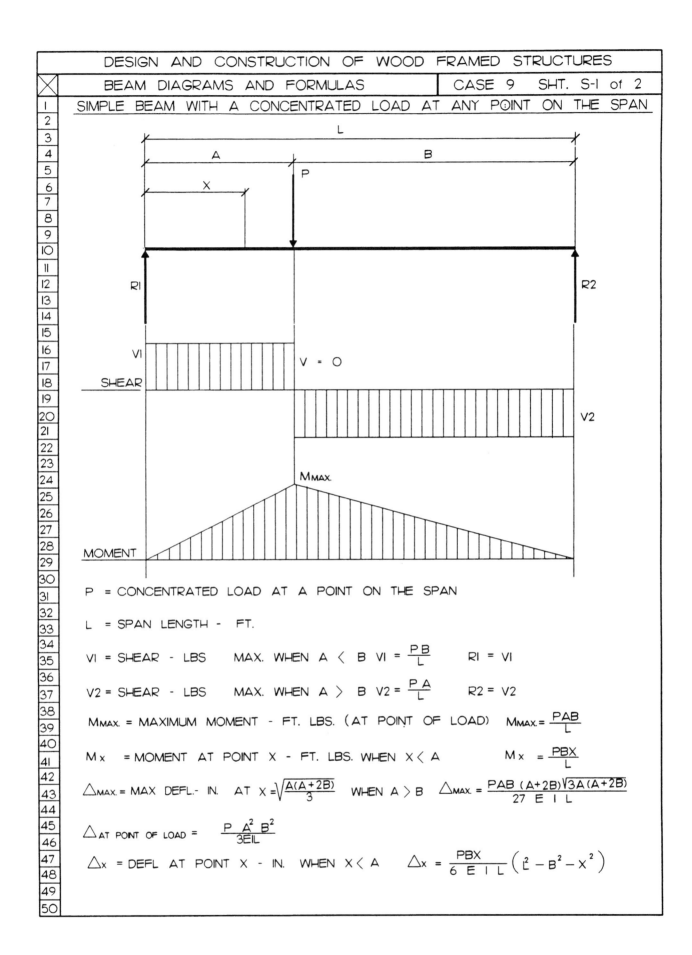

P = CONCENTRATED LOAD AT A POINT ON THE SPAN

L = SPAN LENGTH - FT.

V_1 = SHEAR - LBS   MAX. WHEN A $<$ B $V_1 = \dfrac{P B}{L}$ $R_1 = V_1$

V_2 = SHEAR - LBS   MAX. WHEN A $>$ B $V_2 = \dfrac{P A}{L}$ $R_2 = V_2$

$M_{MAX.}$ = MAXIMUM MOMENT - FT. LBS. (AT POINT OF LOAD) $M_{MAX.} = \dfrac{PAB}{L}$

M_x = MOMENT AT POINT X - FT. LBS. WHEN X $<$ A $M_x = \dfrac{PBX}{L}$

$\triangle_{MAX.}$ = MAX DEFL.- IN.   AT X $= \sqrt{\dfrac{A(A+2B)}{3}}$ WHEN A $>$ B $\triangle_{MAX.} = \dfrac{PAB\,(A+2B)\sqrt{3A\,(A+2B)}}{27\,E\,I\,L}$

$\triangle_{AT\ POINT\ OF\ LOAD} = \dfrac{P\,A^2\,B^2}{3EIL}$

$\triangle_x$ = DEFL AT POINT X - IN. WHEN X $<$ A $\triangle_x = \dfrac{PBX}{6\,E\,I\,L}\left(L^2 - B^2 - X^2\right)$

42 Design Methods

SIMPLE BEAM WITH A CONCENTRATED LOAD AT ANY POINT ON THE SPAN

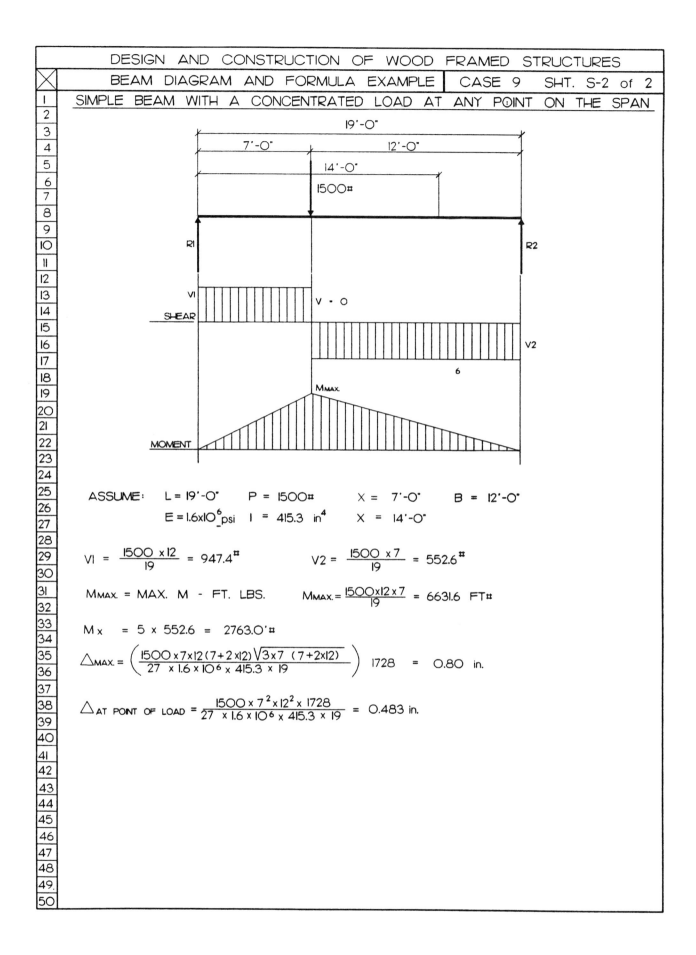

ASSUME: $L = 19'-0"$ $P = 1500\#$ $X = 7'-0"$ $B = 12'-0"$

$E = 1.6 \times 10^6$ psi $I = 415.3$ in^4 $X = 14'-0"$

$$V_1 = \frac{1500 \times 12}{19} = 947.4\#$$ $$V_2 = \frac{1500 \times 7}{19} = 552.6\#$$

$$M_{MAX.} = MAX.\ M - FT.\ LBS.$$ $$M_{MAX.} = \frac{1500 \times 12 \times 7}{19} = 6631.6\ FT\#$$

$$M_X = 5 \times 552.6 = 2763.0'\#$$

$$\triangle_{MAX.} = \left(\frac{1500 \times 7 \times 12\ (7 + 2 \times 12)\sqrt{3 \times 7\ (7 + 2 \times 12)}}{27 \times 1.6 \times 10^6 \times 415.3 \times 19} \right)\ 1728 = 0.80\ in.$$

$$\triangle_{AT\ POINT\ OF\ LOAD} = \frac{1500 \times 7^2 \times 12^2 \times 1728}{27 \times 1.6 \times 10^6 \times 415.3 \times 19} = 0.483\ in.$$

SIMPLE BEAM WITH EQUAL CONCENTRATED LOADS AT ONE THIRD POINTS:

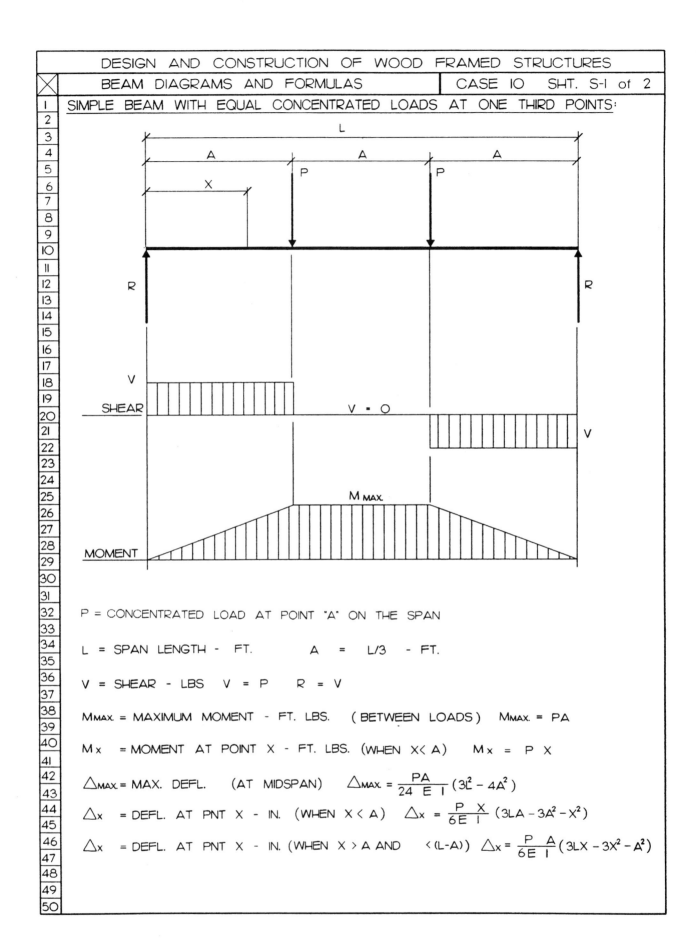

P = CONCENTRATED LOAD AT POINT "A" ON THE SPAN

L = SPAN LENGTH - FT.   A = L/3 - FT.

V = SHEAR - LBS   V = P   R = V

$M_{MAX.}$ = MAXIMUM MOMENT - FT. LBS.   (BETWEEN LOADS) $M_{MAX.}$ = PA

M_x = MOMENT AT POINT X - FT. LBS. (WHEN X< A) M_x = P X

$\triangle_{MAX.}$ = MAX. DEFL.   (AT MIDSPAN) $\triangle_{MAX.} = \dfrac{PA}{24\,E\,I}\,(3L^2 - 4A^2)$

$\triangle_x$ = DEFL. AT PNT X - IN. (WHEN X < A) $\triangle_x = \dfrac{P\,X}{6E\,I}\,(3LA - 3A^2 - X^2)$

$\triangle_x$ = DEFL. AT PNT X - IN. (WHEN X > A AND < (L-A)) $\triangle_x = \dfrac{P\,A}{6E\,I}\,(3LX - 3X^2 - A^2)$

44 Design Methods

SIMPLE BEAM WITH EQUAL CONCENTRATED LOADS AT ONE THIRD POINTS:

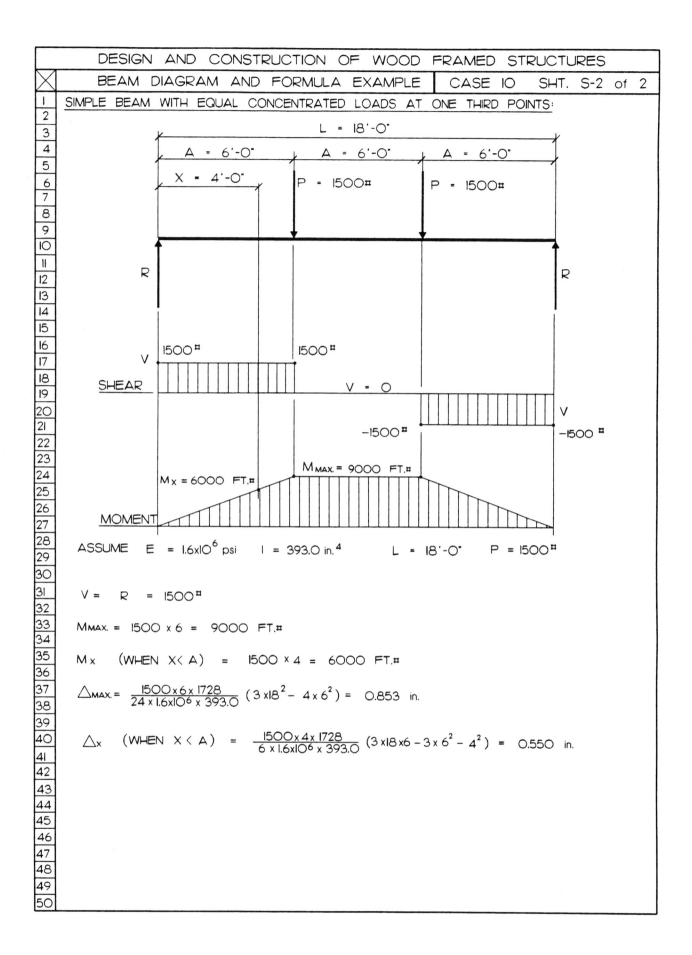

ASSUME   E = 1.6×10^6 psi   I = 393.0 in.^{4} L = 18'-0"   P = 1500$^\#$

V =   R   = 1500$^\#$

$M_{MAX.}$ = 1500 x 6 = 9000 FT.$^\#$

M_x (WHEN X< A)   =   1500 × 4 = 6000 FT.$^\#$

$\triangle_{MAX.} = \dfrac{1500 \times 6 \times 1728}{24 \times 1.6 \times 10^6 \times 393.0}\,(3 \times 18^2 - 4 \times 6^2) = 0.853$ in.

$\triangle_x$ (WHEN X < A) $= \dfrac{1500 \times 4 \times 1728}{6 \times 1.6 \times 10^6 \times 393.0}\,(3 \times 18 \times 6 - 3 \times 6^2 - 4^2) = 0.550$ in.

SIMPLE BEAM WITH TWO EQUAL CONCENTRATED LOADS UNEQUALLY PLACED:

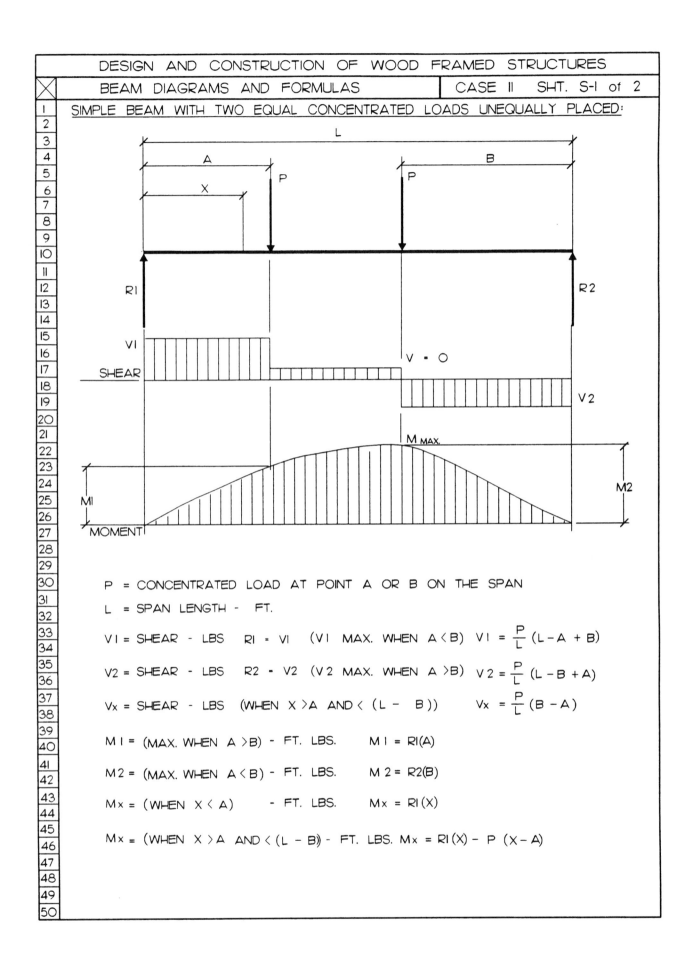

P = CONCENTRATED LOAD AT POINT A OR B ON THE SPAN

L = SPAN LENGTH - FT.

V1 = SHEAR - LBS   R1 = V1   (V1 MAX. WHEN A < B) $V1 = \dfrac{P}{L}(L - A + B)$

V2 = SHEAR - LBS   R2 = V2   (V2 MAX. WHEN A > B) $V2 = \dfrac{P}{L}(L - B + A)$

Vx = SHEAR - LBS   (WHEN X > A AND < (L - B)) $Vx = \dfrac{P}{L}(B - A)$

M1 = (MAX. WHEN A > B) - FT. LBS.   M1 = R1(A)

M2 = (MAX. WHEN A < B) - FT. LBS.   M2 = R2(B)

Mx = (WHEN X < A)   - FT. LBS.   Mx = R1(X)

Mx = (WHEN X > A AND < (L - B)) - FT. LBS. Mx = R1(X) - P(X - A)

SIMPLE BEAM WITH TWO UNEQUAL CONCENTRATED LOADS UNEQUALLY PLACED:

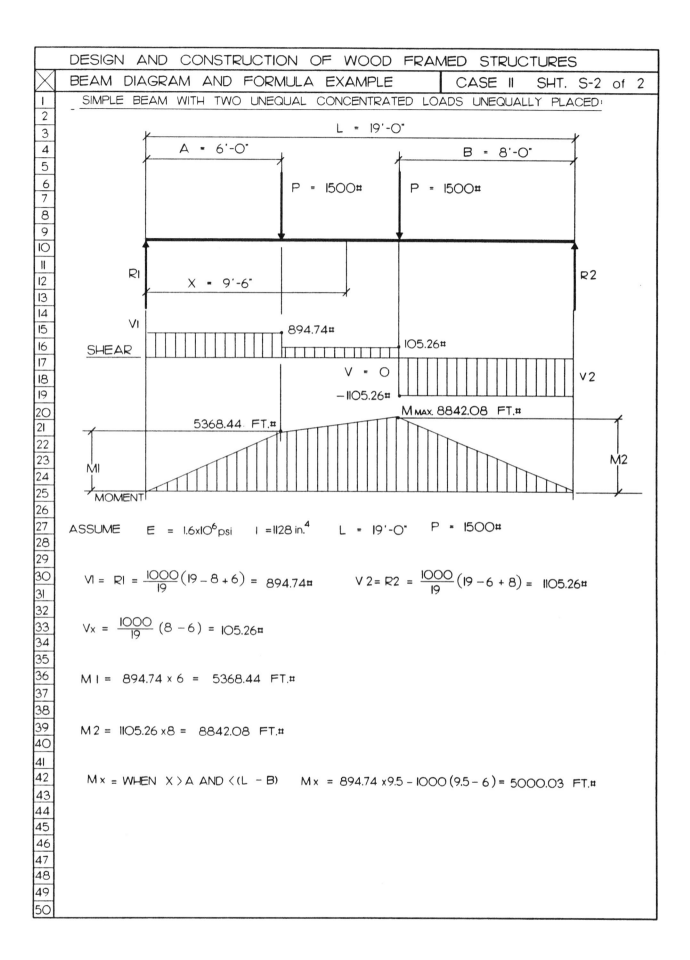

ASSUME $E = 1.6 \times 10^6$ psi $I = 1128$ in.^{4} $L = 19'\text{-}0"$ $P = 1500$#

$V_1 = R_1 = \dfrac{1000}{19}(19 - 8 + 6) = 894.74$# $V_2 = R_2 = \dfrac{1000}{19}(19 - 6 + 8) = 1105.26$#

$V_x = \dfrac{1000}{19}(8 - 6) = 105.26$#

$M_1 = 894.74 \times 6 = 5368.44$ FT.#

$M_2 = 1105.26 \times 8 = 8842.08$ FT.#

$M_x =$ WHEN $X > A$ AND $< (L - B)$ $M_x = 894.74 \times 9.5 - 1000(9.5 - 6) = 5000.03$ FT.#

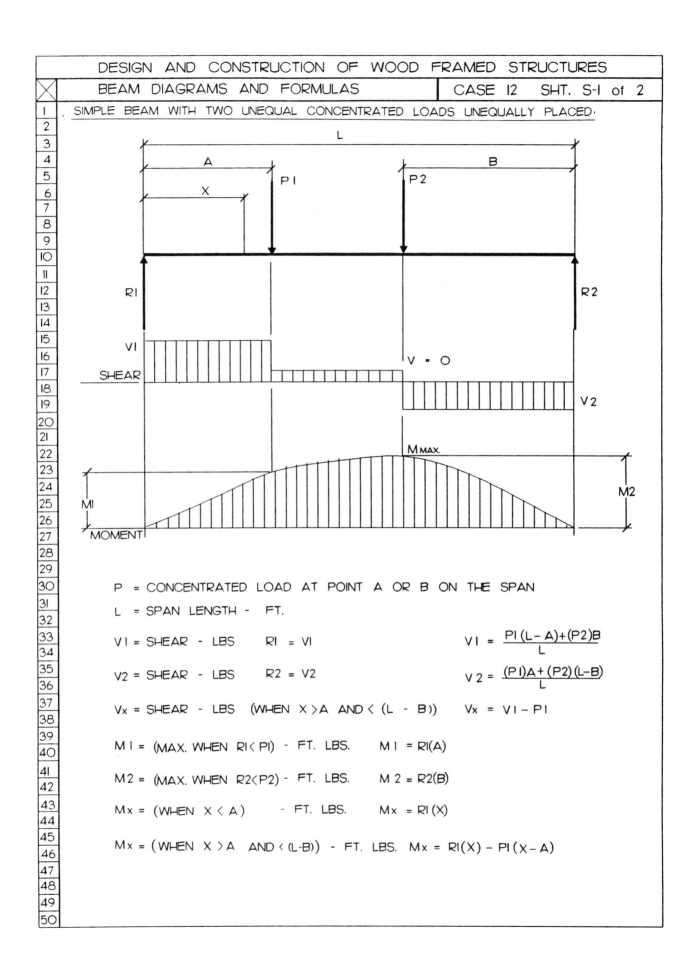

SIMPLE BEAM WITH TWO UNEQUAL CONCENTRATED LOADS UNEQUALLY PLACED.

P = CONCENTRATED LOAD AT POINT A OR B ON THE SPAN

L = SPAN LENGTH - FT.

$V1$ = SHEAR - LBS $R1 = V1$ $V1 = \dfrac{P1(L-A)+(P2)B}{L}$

$V2$ = SHEAR - LBS $R2 = V2$ $V2 = \dfrac{(P1)A+(P2)(L-B)}{L}$

Vx = SHEAR - LBS   (WHEN $X > A$ AND $< (L-B)$) $Vx = V1 - P1$

$M1$ = (MAX. WHEN $R1 < P1$) - FT. LBS. $M1 = R1(A)$

$M2$ = (MAX. WHEN $R2 < P2$) - FT. LBS. $M2 = R2(B)$

Mx = (WHEN $X < A$)   - FT. LBS. $Mx = R1(X)$

Mx = (WHEN $X > A$ AND $< (L-B)$) - FT. LBS. $Mx = R1(X) - P1(X-A)$

SIMPLE BEAM WITH TWO UNEQUAL CONCENTRATED LOADS UNEQUALLY PLACED:

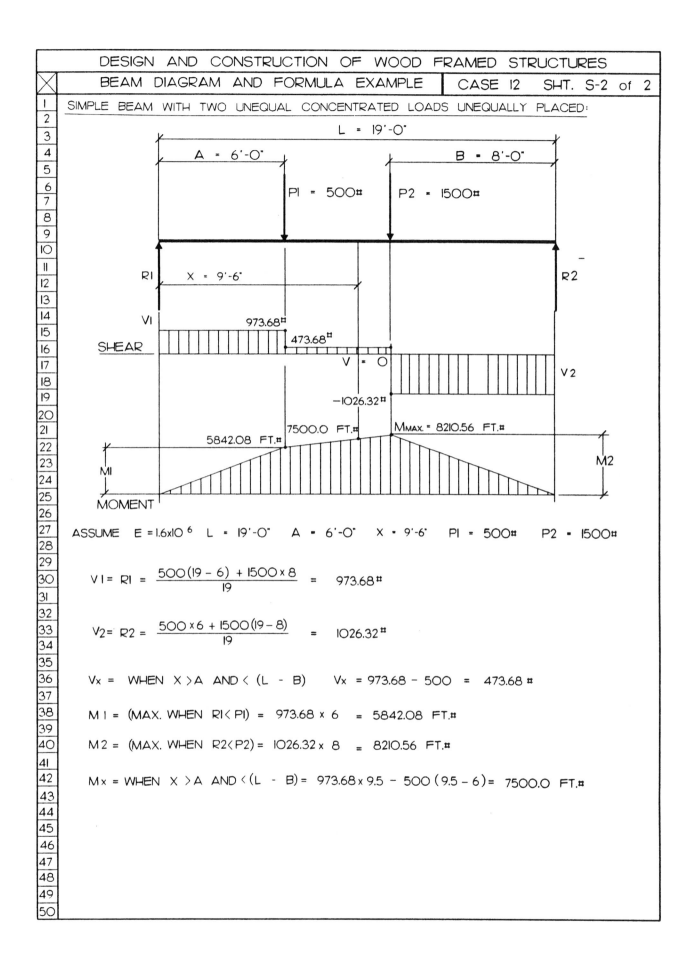

ASSUME E = 1.6x10^6 L = 19'-0" A = 6'-0" X = 9'-6" PI = 500# P2 = 1500#

$$V1 = R1 = \frac{500(19-6) + 1500 \times 8}{19} = 973.68\#$$

$$V2 = R2 = \frac{500 \times 6 + 1500(19-8)}{19} = 1026.32\#$$

Vx = WHEN X > A AND < (L - B)   Vx = 973.68 - 500 = 473.68#

M1 = (MAX. WHEN R1 < P1) = 973.68 x 6 = 5842.08 FT.#

M2 = (MAX. WHEN R2 < P2) = 1026.32 x 8 = 8210.56 FT.#

Mx = WHEN X > A AND < (L - B) = 973.68 x 9.5 - 500 (9.5 - 6) = 7500.0 FT.#

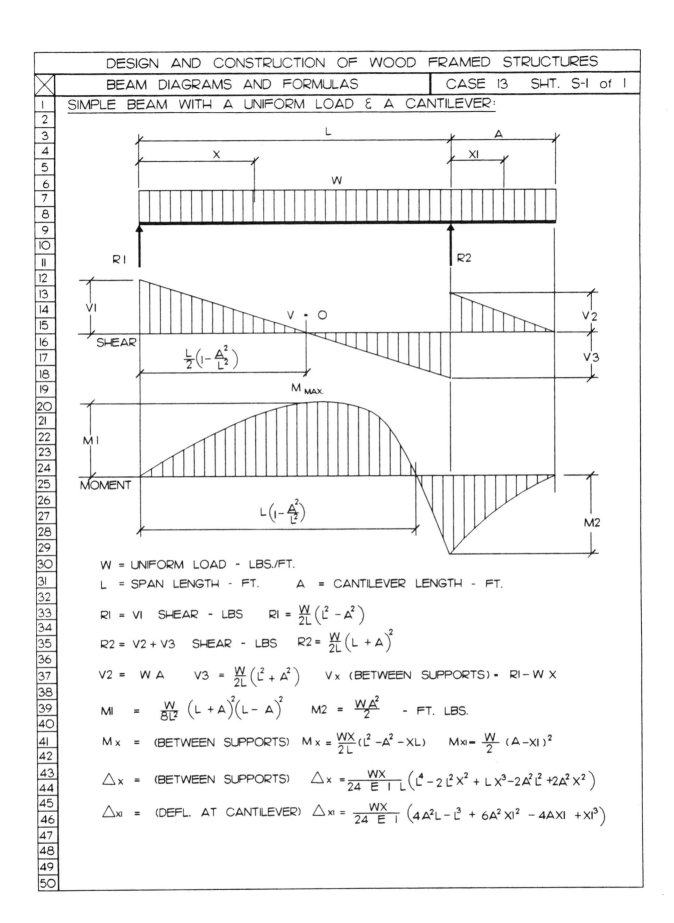

SIMPLE BEAM WITH A UNIFORM LOAD & A CANTILEVER:

W = UNIFORM LOAD - LBS./FT.

L = SPAN LENGTH - FT.   A = CANTILEVER LENGTH - FT.

R1 = V1 SHEAR - LBS $R1 = \dfrac{W}{2L}\left(L^2 - A^2\right)$

R2 = V2 + V3   SHEAR - LBS $R2 = \dfrac{W}{2L}\left(L + A\right)^2$

$V2 = WA$ $V3 = \dfrac{W}{2L}\left(L^2 + A^2\right)$ Vx (BETWEEN SUPPORTS) = $R1 - WX$

$M1 = \dfrac{W}{8L^2}\left(L + A\right)^2\left(L - A\right)^2$ $M2 = \dfrac{WA^2}{2}$ - FT. LBS.

Mx = (BETWEEN SUPPORTS) $Mx = \dfrac{WX}{2L}(L^2 - A^2 - XL)$ $Mx1 = \dfrac{W}{2}(A - X1)^2$

$\triangle x$ = (BETWEEN SUPPORTS) $\triangle x = \dfrac{WX}{24\,E\,I\,L}\left(L^4 - 2L^2X^2 + LX^3 - 2A^2L^2 + 2A^2X^2\right)$

$\triangle x1$ = (DEFL. AT CANTILEVER) $\triangle x1 = \dfrac{WX}{24\,E\,I}\left(4A^2L - L^3 + 6A^2X1^2 - 4AX1 + X1^3\right)$

SIMPLE BEAM WITH A UNIFORM LOAD & A CANTILEVER:

L = 19'-0" A = 6'-0"
X = 7'-0" XI = 3'-0"
W = 100 #/FT.

R1 R2

855.26 #
155.26 #
V = O
600 #
SHEAR
V1 V2 V3
1044.74 #

$M_{MAX.} = \frac{19}{2}\left(1 - \frac{6^2}{19^2}\right) = 8.55$ FT.

3647.37 FT.#
$M_{MAX.}$ 3657.38 FT.#
M1
MOMENT
M2

$INFLECT.\ PNT. = 19\left(1 - \frac{6^2}{19^2}\right) = 17.10$ FT.

1800 FT.#

ASSUME   L = 19'-0"   W = 100 #/FT.   A = 6'-0"   X = 7'-0"   XI = 3'-0"

$E = 1.6 \times 10^6$ psi   I = 178 in.^{4}

$$V1 = R1 = \frac{100}{2 \times 19}\left(19^2 - 6^2\right) = 855.26\text{ \#}$$

$$V2 + V3 = R2 = \frac{100}{2 \times 19}\left(19 + 6\right)^2 = 1644.74\text{ \#}$$

$$V2 = 100 \times 6 = 600\text{ \#} \qquad V3 = \frac{100}{2 \times 19}\left(19^2 + 6^2\right) = 1044.74\text{ \#} \qquad Vx = 855.26 - 100 \times 7 = 155.26\text{ \#}$$

$$M1 = \frac{100}{8 \times 19^2}\left(19 + 6\right)\left(19 - 6\right)^2 = 3657.38\text{ FT.\#} \qquad M2 = \frac{100 \times 6^2}{2} = 1800\text{ FT.\#}$$

$$Mx = \frac{100 \times 7}{2 \times 19}\left(19^2 - 7^2 - 6 \times 19\right) = 3647.37\text{ FT.\#} \qquad Mxi = \frac{100}{2}\left(6 - 3\right)^2 = 450.0\text{ FT.\#}$$

$$\triangle x = \frac{100 \times 7 \times 1728}{24 \times 1.6 \times 10^6 \times 178 \times 19}\left(19^4 - 2 \times 19^2 \times 7^2 + 19 \times 7^3 - 2 \times 6 \times 19^2 + 2 \times 6^2 \times 7^2\right) = 0.631\text{ in.}$$

$$\triangle xi = (DEFL.\ AT\ CANTILEVER) = \frac{100 \times 3 \times 1728}{24 \times 1.6 \times 10^6 \times 178}\left(4 \times 6^2 \times 19 - 19^3 + 6 + 6^2 \times 3^2 - 4 \times 6 \times 3 + 3^3\right) = 0.158\text{ in.}$$

CANTILEVER BEAM WITH A UNIFORM LOAD:

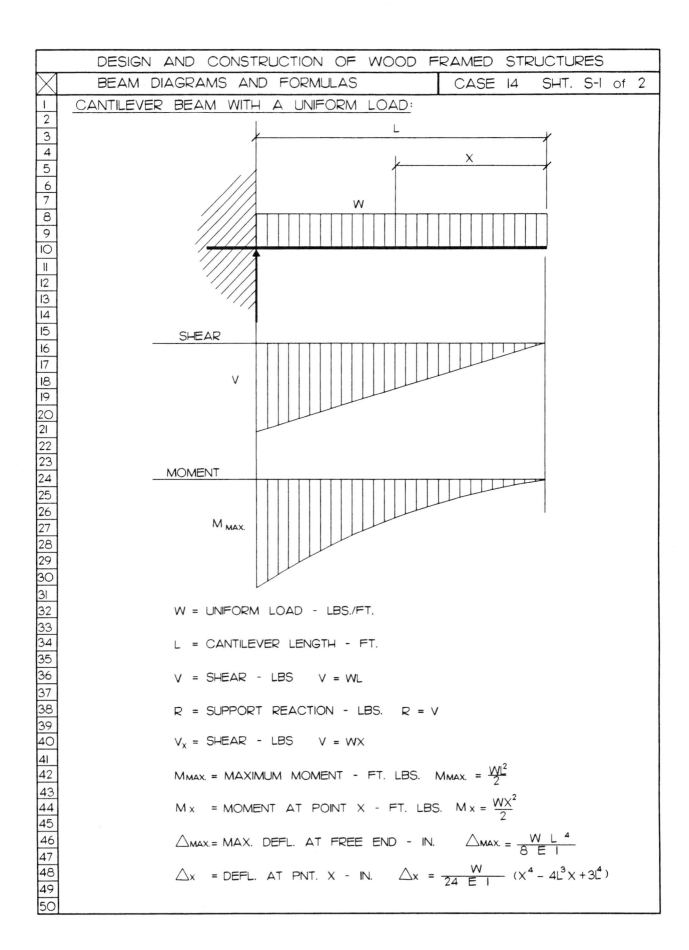

W = UNIFORM LOAD - LBS./FT.

L = CANTILEVER LENGTH - FT.

V = SHEAR - LBS $V = WL$

R = SUPPORT REACTION - LBS. $R = V$

V_x = SHEAR - LBS $V = WX$

$M_{MAX.}$ = MAXIMUM MOMENT - FT. LBS. $M_{MAX.} = \dfrac{WL^2}{2}$

M_x = MOMENT AT POINT X - FT. LBS. $M_x = \dfrac{WX^2}{2}$

$\triangle_{MAX.}$ = MAX. DEFL. AT FREE END - IN. $\triangle_{MAX.} = \dfrac{W L^4}{8 E I}$

$\triangle_x$ = DEFL. AT PNT. X - IN. $\triangle_x = \dfrac{W}{24 E I}(x^4 - 4L^3 X + 3L^4)$

CANTILEVER BEAM WITH A UNIFORM LOAD:

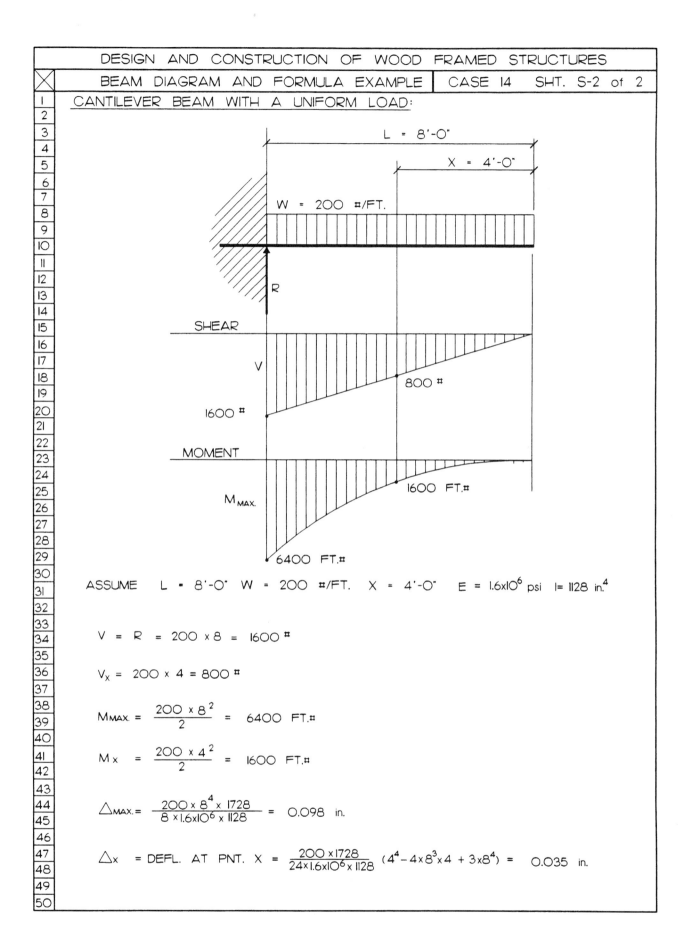

ASSUME $\quad$ L = 8'-0" $\quad$ W = 200 #/FT. $\quad$ X = 4'-0" $\quad$ E = 1.6x10^6 psi $\quad$ I= 1128 in.^{4}

$$V = R = 200 \times 8 = 1600 \text{ \#}$$

$$V_x = 200 \times 4 = 800 \text{ \#}$$

$$M_{MAX.} = \frac{200 \times 8^2}{2} = 6400 \text{ FT.\#}$$

$$M_x = \frac{200 \times 4^2}{2} = 1600 \text{ FT.\#}$$

$$\triangle_{MAX.} = \frac{200 \times 8^4 \times 1728}{8 \times 1.6x10^6 \times 1128} = 0.098 \text{ in.}$$

$$\triangle_x = \text{DEFL. AT PNT. X} = \frac{200 \times 1728}{24 \times 1.6x10^6 \times 1128} (4^4 - 4 \times 8^3 \times 4 + 3 \times 8^4) = 0.035 \text{ in.}$$

CANTILEVER BEAM WITH A TRIANGULAR LOAD:

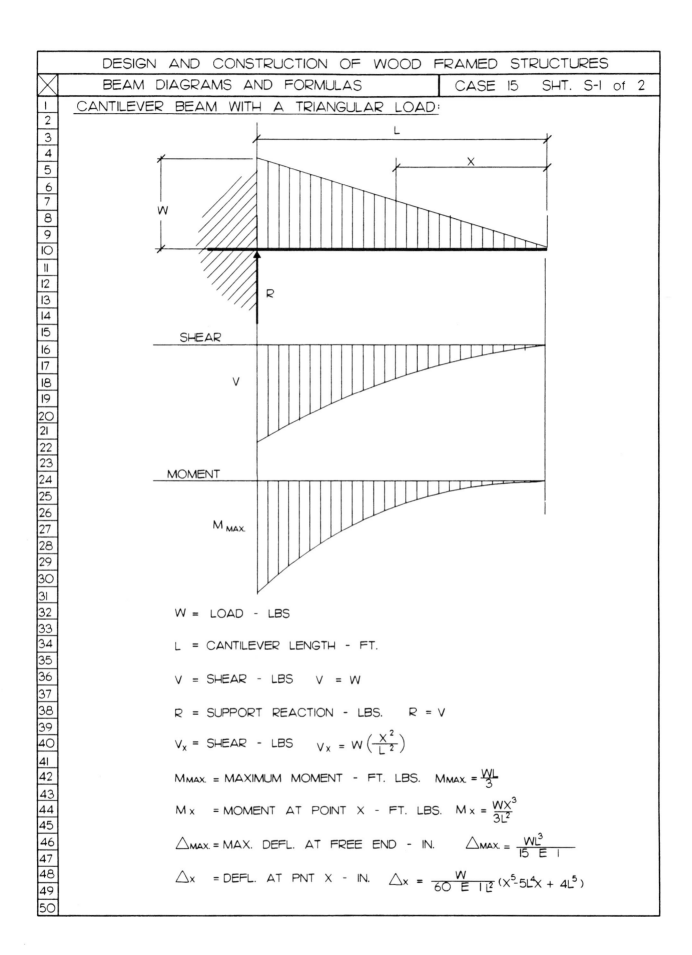

W = LOAD - LBS

L = CANTILEVER LENGTH - FT.

V = SHEAR - LBS   V = W

R = SUPPORT REACTION - LBS.   R = V

V_x = SHEAR - LBS $V_x = W\left(\dfrac{X^2}{L^2}\right)$

$M_{MAX.}$ = MAXIMUM MOMENT - FT. LBS. $M_{MAX.} = \dfrac{WL}{3}$

M_x = MOMENT AT POINT X - FT. LBS. $M_x = \dfrac{WX^3}{3L^2}$

$\triangle_{MAX.}$ = MAX. DEFL. AT FREE END - IN. $\triangle_{MAX.} = \dfrac{WL^3}{15\ E\ I}$

$\triangle_x$ = DEFL. AT PNT X - IN. $\triangle_x = \dfrac{W}{60\ E\ I L^2}(X^5 - 5L^4 X + 4L^5)$

CANTILEVER BEAM WITH A TRIANGULAR LOAD:

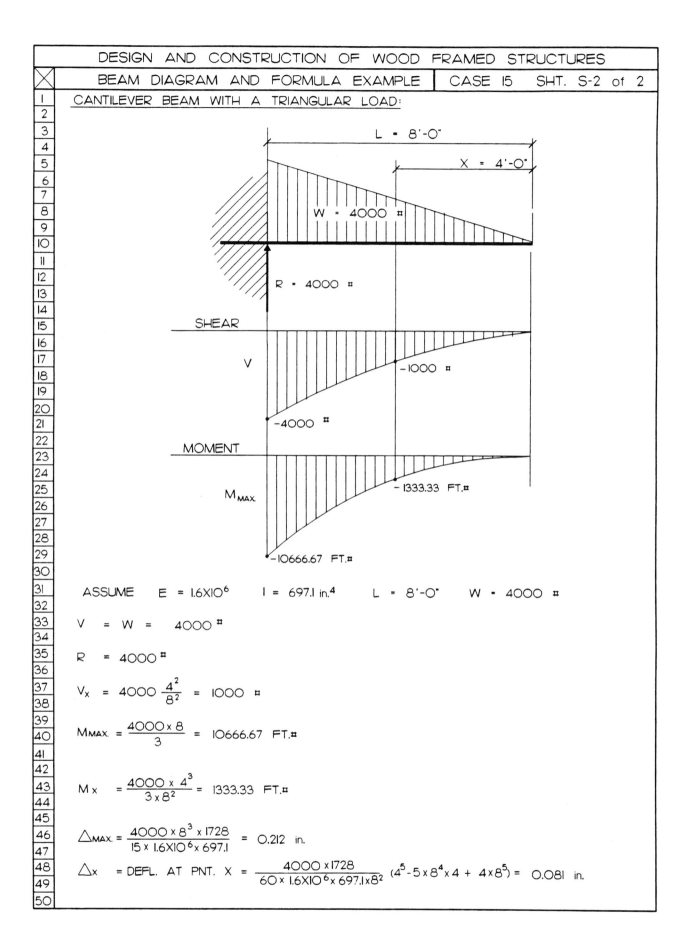

ASSUME $E = 1.6 \times 10^6$ $I = 697.1$ in.^{4} $L = 8'\text{-}0"$ $W = 4000$ #

$V = W = 4000$ #

$R = 4000$ #

$V_x = 4000 \dfrac{4^2}{8^2} = 1000$ #

$M_{MAX.} = \dfrac{4000 \times 8}{3} = 10666.67$ FT.#

$M_x = \dfrac{4000 \times 4^3}{3 \times 8^2} = 1333.33$ FT.#

$\triangle_{MAX.} = \dfrac{4000 \times 8^3 \times 1728}{15 \times 1.6 \times 10^6 \times 697.1} = 0.212$ in.

$\triangle_x = $ DEFL. AT PNT. X $= \dfrac{4000 \times 1728}{60 \times 1.6 \times 10^6 \times 697.1 \times 8^2}(4^5 - 5 \times 8^4 \times 4 + 4 \times 8^5) = 0.081$ in.

CANTILEVER BEAM WITH A CONCENTRATED LOAD AT ANY POINT:

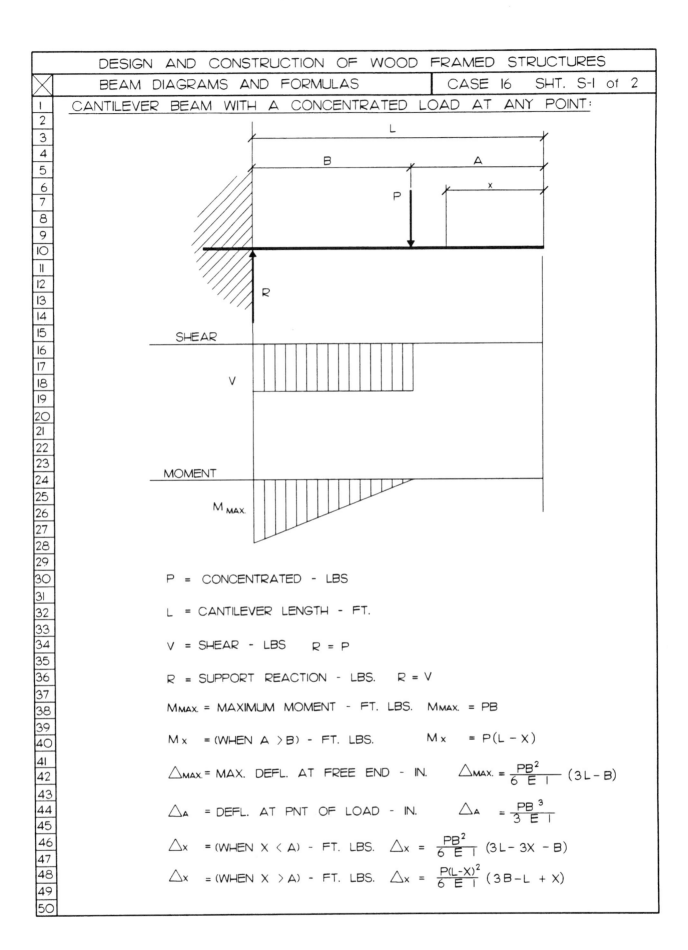

P = CONCENTRATED - LBS

L = CANTILEVER LENGTH - FT.

V = SHEAR - LBS R = P

R = SUPPORT REACTION - LBS. R = V

$M_{MAX.}$ = MAXIMUM MOMENT - FT. LBS. $M_{MAX.}$ = PB

M_x = (WHEN $A > B$) - FT. LBS. M_x = $P(L - X)$

$\triangle_{MAX.}$ = MAX. DEFL. AT FREE END - IN. $\triangle_{MAX.}$ = $\dfrac{PB^2}{6EI}(3L - B)$

$\triangle_A$ = DEFL. AT PNT OF LOAD - IN. $\triangle_A$ = $\dfrac{PB^3}{3EI}$

$\triangle_x$ = (WHEN $X < A$) - FT. LBS. $\triangle_x$ = $\dfrac{PB^2}{6EI}(3L - 3X - B)$

$\triangle_x$ = (WHEN $X > A$) - FT. LBS. $\triangle_x$ = $\dfrac{P(L-X)^2}{6EI}(3B - L + X)$

CANTILEVER BEAM WITH A CONCENTRATED LOAD AT ANY POINT:

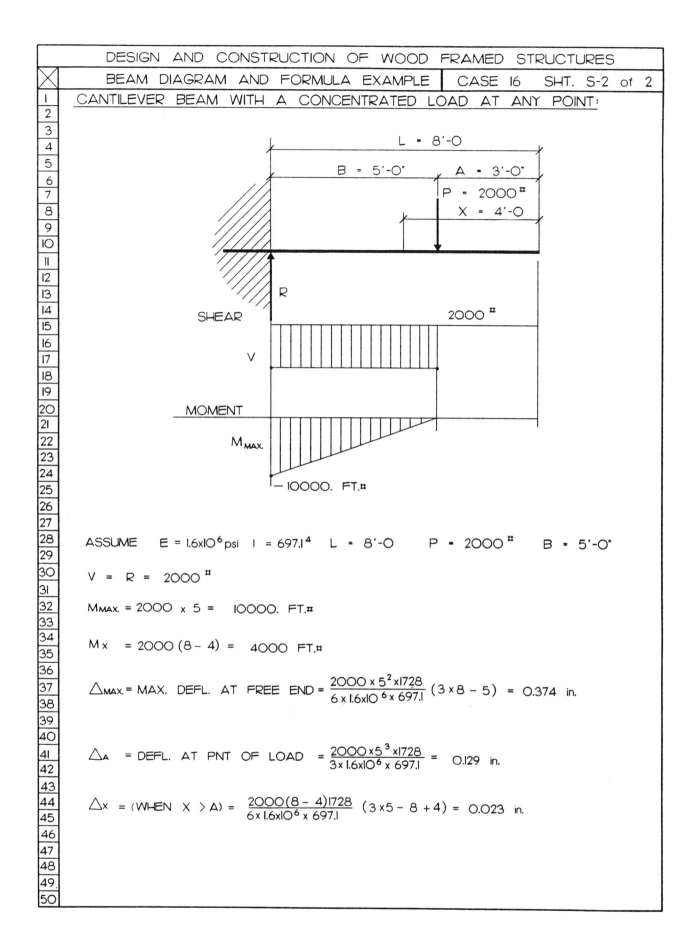

ASSUME $E = 1.6 \times 10^6$ psi $I = 697.1^4$ $L = 8'-0$ $P = 2000^{\#}$ $B = 5'-0"$

$V = R = 2000^{\#}$

$M_{MAX.} = 2000 \times 5 = 10000.$ FT.$^{\#}$

$M_x = 2000(8-4) = 4000$ FT.$^{\#}$

$\triangle_{MAX.} = $ MAX. DEFL. AT FREE END $= \dfrac{2000 \times 5^2 \times 1728}{6 \times 1.6 \times 10^6 \times 697.1}(3 \times 8 - 5) = 0.374$ in.

$\triangle_A = $ DEFL. AT PNT OF LOAD $= \dfrac{2000 \times 5^3 \times 1728}{3 \times 1.6 \times 10^6 \times 697.1} = 0.129$ in.

$\triangle_x = $ (WHEN $X > A$) $= \dfrac{2000(8-4)1728}{6 \times 1.6 \times 10^6 \times 697.1}(3 \times 5 - 8 + 4) = 0.023$ in.

CANTILEVER BEAM WITH A CONCENTRATED LOAD AT FREE END:

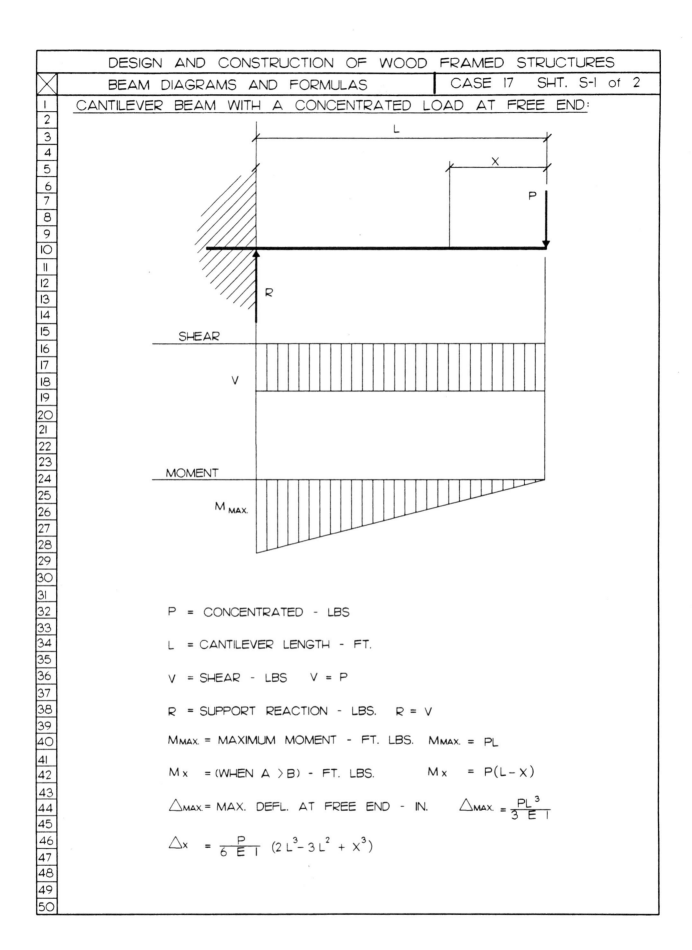

P = CONCENTRATED - LBS

L = CANTILEVER LENGTH - FT.

V = SHEAR - LBS $V = P$

R = SUPPORT REACTION - LBS. $R = V$

$M_{MAX.}$ = MAXIMUM MOMENT - FT. LBS. $M_{MAX.} = PL$

M_x = (WHEN A > B) - FT. LBS. $M_x = P(L - X)$

$\triangle_{MAX.}$ = MAX. DEFL. AT FREE END - IN. $\triangle_{MAX.} = \dfrac{PL^3}{3 E I}$

$\triangle_x = \dfrac{P}{6 E I} (2 L^3 - 3 L^2 + X^3)$

CANTILEVER BEAM WITH A CONCENTRATED LOAD AT FREE END:

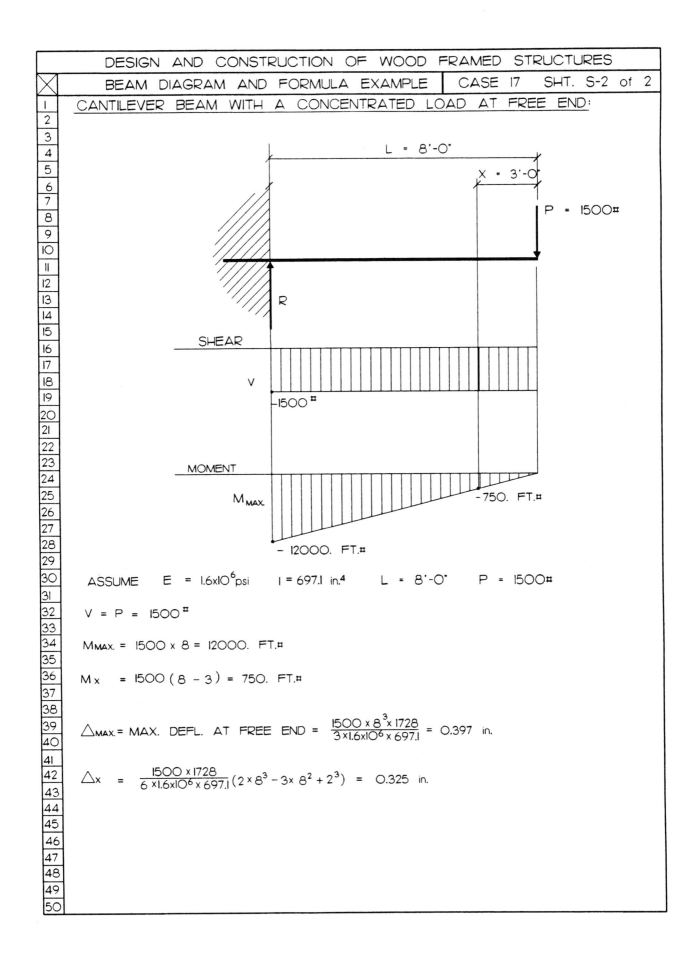

ASSUME $E = 1.6 \times 10^6$ psi $I = 697.1$ in.^{4} L = 8'-0"   P = 1500#

$V = P = 1500$#

$M_{MAX.} = 1500 \times 8 = 12000.$ FT.#

$M_x = 1500(8 - 3) = 750.$ FT.#

$\triangle_{MAX.} = $ MAX. DEFL. AT FREE END $= \dfrac{1500 \times 8^3 \times 1728}{3 \times 1.6 \times 10^6 \times 697.1} = 0.397$ in.

$\triangle_x = \dfrac{1500 \times 1728}{6 \times 1.6 \times 10^6 \times 697.1}(2 \times 8^3 - 3x \times 8^2 + 2^3) = 0.325$ in.

BEAM AND CANTILEVER WITH A UNIFORM LOAD

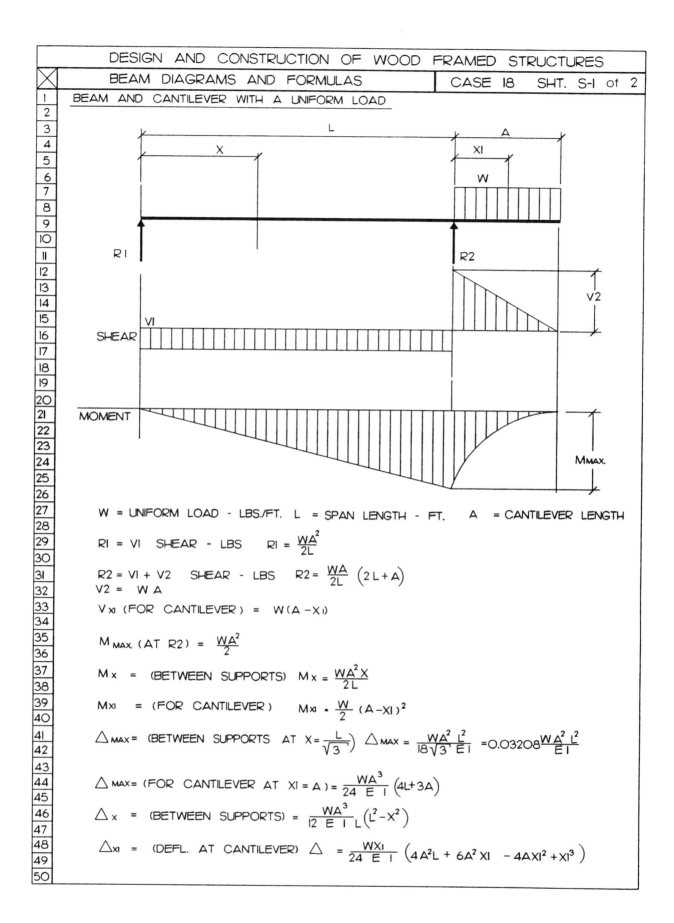

W = UNIFORM LOAD - LBS./FT. L = SPAN LENGTH - FT. A = CANTILEVER LENGTH

$R1 = V1$ SHEAR - LBS $R1 = \dfrac{WA^2}{2L}$

$R2 = V1 + V2$ SHEAR - LBS $R2 = \dfrac{WA}{2L}(2L+A)$

$V2 = WA$

V_{X1} (FOR CANTILEVER) $= W(A-X_1)$

$M_{MAX.}$ (AT R2) $= \dfrac{WA^2}{2}$

M_X = (BETWEEN SUPPORTS) $M_X = \dfrac{WA^2 X}{2L}$

M_{X1} = (FOR CANTILEVER) $M_{X1} = \dfrac{W}{2}(A-X_1)^2$

$\triangle_{MAX}$ = (BETWEEN SUPPORTS AT $X = \dfrac{L}{\sqrt{3}}$) $\triangle_{MAX} = \dfrac{WA^2 L^2}{18\sqrt{3} \, EI} = 0.03208 \dfrac{WA^2 L^2}{EI}$

$\triangle_{MAX}$ = (FOR CANTILEVER AT $X_1 = A$) $= \dfrac{WA^3}{24 \, EI}(4L+3A)$

$\triangle_X$ = (BETWEEN SUPPORTS) $= \dfrac{WA^3}{12 \, EIL}(L^2-X^2)$

$\triangle_{X1}$ = (DEFL. AT CANTILEVER) $\triangle = \dfrac{WX_1}{24 \, EI}(4A^2 L + 6A^2 X_1 - 4AX_1^2 + X_1^3)$

BEAM AND CANTILEVER WITH UNIFORM LOAD

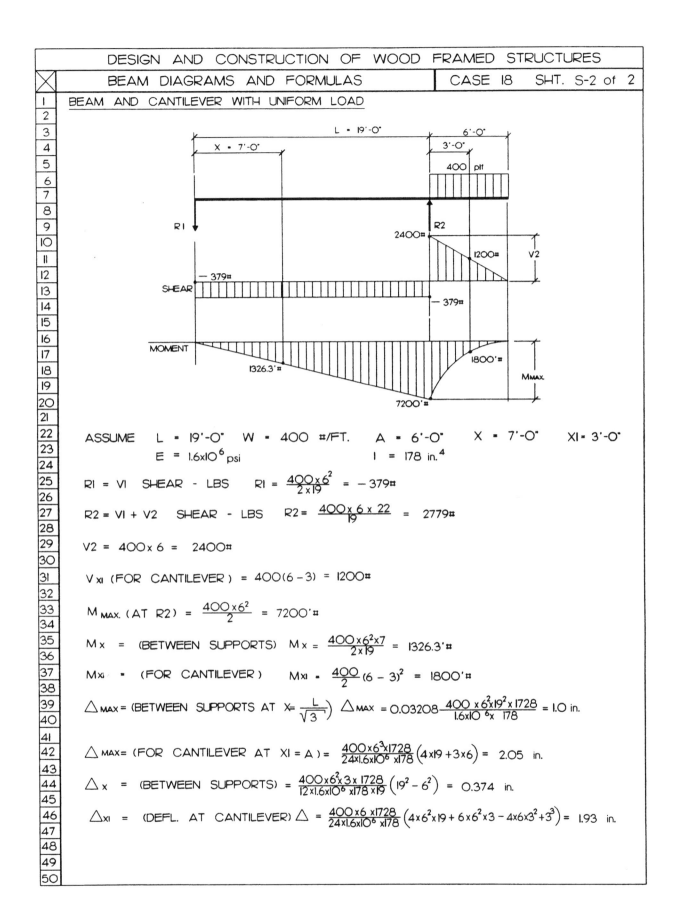

ASSUME   L = 19'-0"   W = 400 #/FT.   A = 6'-0"   X = 7'-0"   X1 = 3'-0"

E = 1.6x10^6 psi   I = 178 in.^{4}

R1 = V1   SHEAR - LBS   R1 = $\dfrac{400 \times 6^2}{2 \times 19}$ = -379#

R2 = V1 + V2   SHEAR - LBS   R2 = $\dfrac{400 \times 6 \times 22}{19}$ = 2779#

V2 = 400 x 6 = 2400#

V$_{X1}$ (FOR CANTILEVER) = 400(6 - 3) = 1200#

M$_{MAX.}$ (AT R2) = $\dfrac{400 \times 6^2}{2}$ = 7200'#

M$_X$ = (BETWEEN SUPPORTS) M$_X$ = $\dfrac{400 \times 6^2 \times 7}{2 \times 19}$ = 1326.3'#

M$_{X1}$ = (FOR CANTILEVER)   M$_{X1}$ = $\dfrac{400}{2}$ (6 - 3)^2 = 1800'#

$\triangle$$_{MAX}$ = (BETWEEN SUPPORTS AT X = $\dfrac{L}{\sqrt{3}}$) $\triangle$$_{MAX}$ = 0.03208 $\dfrac{400 \times 6^2 \times 19^2 \times 1728}{1.6 \times 10^6 \times 178}$ = 1.0 in.

$\triangle$$_{MAX}$ = (FOR CANTILEVER AT X1 = A) = $\dfrac{400 \times 6^3 \times 1728}{24 \times 1.6 \times 10^6 \times 178}$ (4 x 19 + 3 x 6) = 2.05 in.

$\triangle$$_X$ = (BETWEEN SUPPORTS) = $\dfrac{400 \times 6^2 \times 3 \times 1728}{12 \times 1.6 \times 10^6 \times 178 \times 19}$ (19^2 - 6^2) = 0.374 in.

$\triangle$$_{X1}$ = (DEFL. AT CANTILEVER) $\triangle$ = $\dfrac{400 \times 6 \times 1728}{24 \times 1.6 \times 10^6 \times 178}$ (4 x 6^2 x 19 + 6 x 6^2 x 3 - 4 x 6 x 3^2 + 3^3) = 1.93 in.

Design Methods **61**

BEAM AND CANTILEVER WITH A CONCENTRATED LOAD

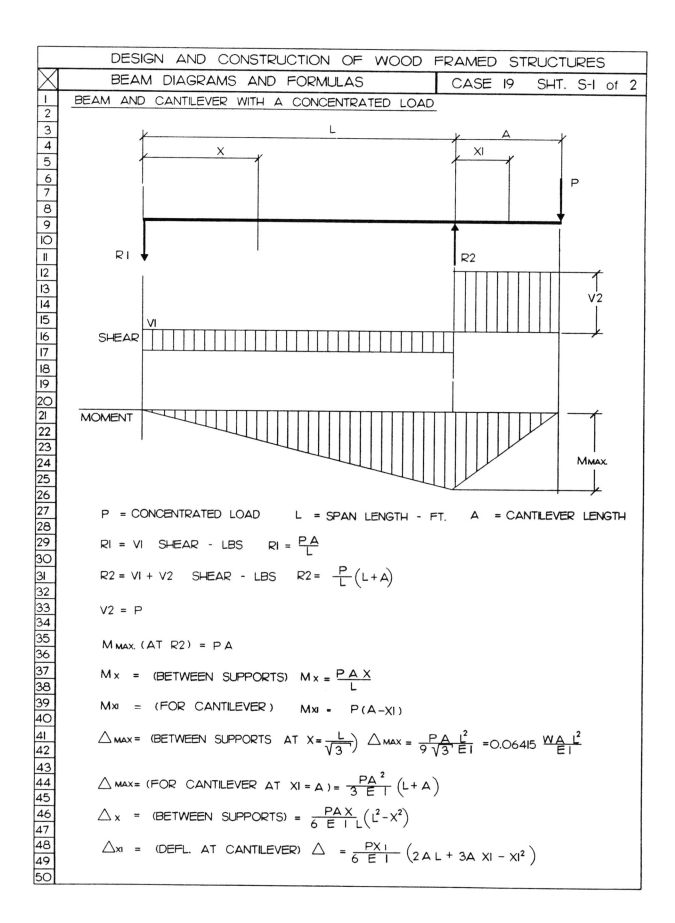

P = CONCENTRATED LOAD L = SPAN LENGTH - FT. A = CANTILEVER LENGTH

$R1 = V1$ SHEAR - LBS $R1 = \dfrac{PA}{L}$

$R2 = V1 + V2$ SHEAR - LBS $R2 = \dfrac{P}{L}(L+A)$

$V2 = P$

$M_{MAX.} (AT\ R2) = PA$

M_X = (BETWEEN SUPPORTS) $M_X = \dfrac{PAX}{L}$

M_{X1} = (FOR CANTILEVER) $M_{X1} = P(A-X1)$

$\triangle_{MAX}$ = (BETWEEN SUPPORTS AT $X = \dfrac{L}{\sqrt{3}}$) $\triangle_{MAX} = \dfrac{PA}{9\sqrt{3}}\dfrac{L^2}{EI} = 0.06415\dfrac{WA}{EI}L^2$

$\triangle_{MAX}$ = (FOR CANTILEVER AT $X1 = A$) $= \dfrac{PA^2}{3\ EI}(L+A)$

$\triangle_X$ = (BETWEEN SUPPORTS) $= \dfrac{PAX}{6\ EIL}(L^2-X^2)$

$\triangle_{X1}$ = (DEFL. AT CANTILEVER) $\triangle = \dfrac{PX1}{6\ EI}(2AL + 3A\ X1 - X1^2)$

BEAM AND CANTILEVER WITH A CONCENTRATED LOAD

$P = 500\#$ ⠀⠀⠀⠀ $L = 19'\text{-}0"$ ⠀⠀⠀⠀ $A = 6'\text{-}0"$

$R1 = V1$ ⠀ SHEAR - LBS ⠀ $R1 = \dfrac{500 \times 6}{19} = 157.9\#$

$R2 = V1 + V2$ ⠀ SHEAR - LBS ⠀ $R2 = \dfrac{500}{19}\left(19 + 6\right) = 557.9\#$

$V2 = 500\#$

$M_{MAX.} (AT\ R2) = 500 \times 6 = 3000'\#$

$M_x = $ (BETWEEN SUPPORTS) ⠀ $M_x = \dfrac{500 \times 7 \times 6}{19} = 1105.3'\#$

$M_{x1} = $ (FOR CANTILEVER) ⠀ $M_{x1} = 500\left(6 - 3\right) = 1500'\#$

$\triangle_{MAX} = $ (BETWEEN SUPPORTS AT $X = \dfrac{L}{\sqrt{3}}$) ⠀ $\triangle_{MAX} = 0.06415 \times \dfrac{500 \times 6 \times 19^2 \times 1728}{1.6 \times 10^6 \times 178} = 0.122$ in.

$\triangle_{MAX} = $ (FOR CANTILEVER AT $X1 = A$) $= \dfrac{500 \times 6^2 \times 1728}{3 \times 1.6 \times 10^6 \times 178}\left(19 + 6\right) = 0.910$ in.

$\triangle_x = $ (BETWEEN SUPPORTS) $= \dfrac{500 \times 6 \times 7 \times 1728}{6 \times 1.6 \times 10^6 \times 178 \times 19}\left(19^2 - 7^2\right) = 0.349$ in.

$\triangle_{x1} = $ (DEFL. AT CANTILEVER) $\triangle = \dfrac{500 \times 3 \times 1728}{6 \times 1.6 \times 10^6 \times 178}\left(2 \times 6 \times 19 + 3 \times 6 \times 3 - 3^2\right) = 0.505$ in.

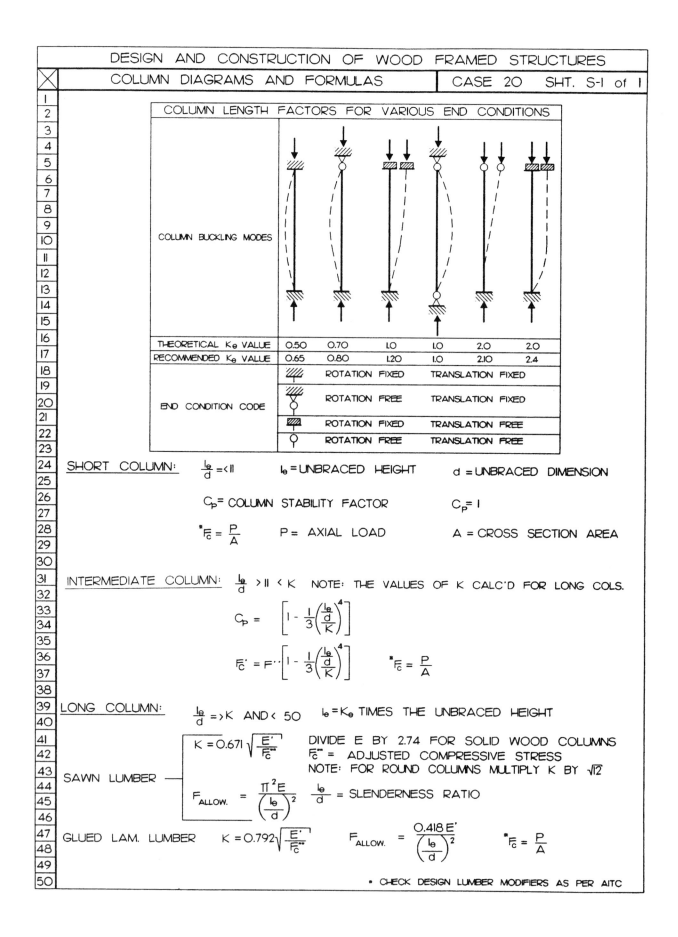

COLUMN LENGTH FACTORS FOR VARIOUS END CONDITIONS

THEORETICAL K_e VALUE	0.50	0.70	1.0	1.0	2.0	2.0
RECOMMENDED K_e VALUE	0.65	0.80	1.20	1.0	2.10	2.4

END CONDITION CODE

▨	ROTATION FIXED	TRANSLATION FIXED
⊙	ROTATION FREE	TRANSLATION FIXED
▨	ROTATION FIXED	TRANSLATION FREE
○	ROTATION FREE	TRANSLATION FREE

SHORT COLUMN: $\dfrac{l_e}{d} = < 11$ l_e = UNBRACED HEIGHT d = UNBRACED DIMENSION

C_P = COLUMN STABILITY FACTOR $C_P = 1$

*$F_c = \dfrac{P}{A}$ P = AXIAL LOAD A = CROSS SECTION AREA

INTERMEDIATE COLUMN: $\dfrac{l_e}{d} > 11 < K$ NOTE: THE VALUES OF K CALC'D FOR LONG COLS.

$$C_P = \left[1 - \frac{1}{3}\left(\frac{\frac{l_e}{d}}{K}\right)^4\right]$$

$$F_c' = F^{\cdot\cdot}\left[1 - \frac{1}{3}\left(\frac{\frac{l_e}{d}}{K}\right)^4\right] \qquad {}^*F_c = \frac{P}{A}$$

LONG COLUMN: $\dfrac{l_e}{d} = > K$ AND < 50 $l_e = K_e$ TIMES THE UNBRACED HEIGHT

SAWN LUMBER

$$K = 0.671\sqrt{\frac{E'}{F_c^{\cdot\cdot\cdot}}}$$

DIVIDE E BY 2.74 FOR SOLID WOOD COLUMNS
$F_c^{\cdot\cdot}$ = ADJUSTED COMPRESSIVE STRESS
NOTE: FOR ROUND COLUMNS MULTIPLY K BY $\sqrt{12}$

$$F_{ALLOW.} = \frac{\pi^2 E}{\left(\frac{l_e}{d}\right)^2} \qquad \frac{l_e}{d} = \text{SLENDERNESS RATIO}$$

GLUED LAM. LUMBER $K = 0.792\sqrt{\dfrac{E'}{F_c^{\cdot\cdot}}}$ $F_{ALLOW.} = \dfrac{0.418\,E'}{\left(\frac{l_e}{d}\right)^2}$ ${}^*F_c = \dfrac{P}{A}$

• CHECK DESIGN LUMBER MODIFIERS AS PER AITC

4

Design Examples

Dimensions, applied loads, material specifications, and the function of a member are the four prime categories of data required to design a structure. Dimensional data may include such information as the span of a beam or joist, the height of a column, and the width and depth of a member. The configuration of a structure is delineated by its dimensions, such as the unbraced height of studs or posts, the clear span of beams or joists, and cross-sectional sizes and shapes. The purpose of a structural component is to support the applied loads. It is necessary for the designer to know the type, magnitude, and application of all loads to be resisted. Loads that are derived from various live load criteria may allow for certain adjusted design stresses. Also, the method and point of application of a load can make a substantial difference in the design moment of the member. It should be noted that the development of applied loads is presented in each example, since their evaluation is basic to the definition of the problem. Simply knowing the span and the load on a beam is not sufficient information for an insightful designer to make any judgment that would constitute bona fide solution of a problem. Material specifications are used to determine the allowable working stress limits for which the design is performed. The function of the member as part of the structure can also determine the allowable working stresses and the permitted stress adjustments. The strengths of the materials used in the examples of this chapter are accessed from UBC Tables 25-A and 25-C for allowable working stresses for various types of structural lumber. For the sake of consistency, the examples use values specified for Douglas fir–larch.

This chapter consists of a series of examples of structural designs or investigations of wood beams and columns. The examples were devised to demonstrate a point concerning a particular design condition such as loads and allowable stresses. The equations, formulas, and methods that are used in this chapter have been demonstrated in the cases presented in Chapter 3. Each prototype is designated by an example number and a sheet number. In several instances, two or more cases will be presented within one example; when this occurs, the example designation will also include the respective case number. When an example consists of only one case, no separate case number will be given. The object of the commentary of the design examples that follows is to focus on a unique design procedure. The numbers in the left-hand margin of the calculation page are used to direct the reader's attention to a specific point under consideration. An example of a line number designation may be L10.

EXAMPLE 1 S-1

Design loads are itemized as tabulated in Chapter 2. The roof live load is derived from UBC Table 25-C. Span and spacing of the rafters are given design conditions. The uniform load is calculated as 16 in o.c. = 1.33 ft tributary width. The lumber used is classified as "seasoned lumber"; therefore UBC Table 23-E allows $K = 0.50$ for determining the amount of load used in calculating the total load deflection as per UBC Table 23-D. Lines 13 and 15 use a value of 1.25 in the calculation of section modulus and area required. UBC Section 2504, Duration of Load, permits a 25 percent increase in working stress for intermittent loading conditions. Lines 30 to 41 diagram the shear adjustment for shear load at a 45 degree angle from the face of the support. There are instances in which the unit allowable shear stress is critical in the design. This situation usually occurs for short-span beams with high vertical loads. The UBC makes an allowance for this condition by specifying shear stress increases depending on the quality of the lumber. UBC Table 25-A-1, subscript note 8 presents tabulated values of "shear stress modification factors."

EXAMPLE 2 S-1

L1 to L10 demonstrate the method of calculating the rafter uniform load. Notice that L28 to L33 use a duration factor of 1.25 in the denominator to determine the required section modulus and area. The roof span of 17 ft 10 in is determined as the projected horizontal distance between supports. L1 to L10 calculation of the ceiling load includes a 10 lb/sq ft live load.

EXAMPLE 3 S-1

The roof clear span of 15 ft 6 in is determined as the projected horizontal distance between supports. The slope of the roof members supporting vertical load creates a horizontal force component at the wall plate line.

EXAMPLE 4 S-1

L1 to L10 demonstrate the calculation and reduction for a snow load. The lumber used is classified as "unseasoned lumber"; therefore UBC Table 23-E allows $K = 1.0$ for determining the amount of load used in calculating the total load deflection as per UBC Table 23-D. The slope of the roof members supporting vertical load creates a horizontal force component at the wall plate line.

EXAMPLE 5 S-1

The ceiling joists of this example are used to resist the horizontal force component shown in Examples 3 and 4. Design loads are itemized as tabulated in Chapter 2. Slope angle of the rafters equals 26.6 degrees. Span of the ridge beam is a given design condition. The lumber used is classified as "seasoned lumber"; therefore, UBC Table 23-E allows $K = 0.50$ for determining the amount of load used in calculating the total load deflection as per UBC Table 23-D. L5 shows the calculation of the tributary area of the roof supported by the ridge beam. UBC Table 23-C specifies a roof live load equal to 14 lb/sq ft for slope greater than 4 to 12 and tributary area over 200 sq ft. The bending and shear stresses used in the calculations on L29 and L32 are increased by a factor of 25 percent for intermittent loads as specified in UBC 2504. The horizontal thrust resulting from the slope of the roof rafters is resisted in tension by the ceiling joists. It is important to connect the rafters to the ceiling joists at the exterior wall double plates to resist the tension.

EXAMPLE 6 S-1

Design loads are itemized as tabulated in Chapter 2. Slope angle of the hip beam equals 26.6 degrees. The span of the hip beam is a given design condition. The triangular shape of the loading plan is shown on the roof plan. The roof live load is set at 16 lb/sq ft as per UBC Table 23-C. The lumber used is classified as "seasoned lumber"; therefore, UBC Table 23-E allows $K = 0.50$ for determining the amount of load used in calculating the total load deflection as per UBC Table 23-D.

EXAMPLE 7 S-1

The calculations investigate the deflection of the rafters. Case 1 calculates the bending and shear for a total load on the span and a dead load on the cantilever. Case 2 checks the cantilever deflection. The roof is considered as being flat. The cantilever total load is reduced by the weight of the interior plaster ceiling. The value of P represents the weight of the fascia wall support at the end of the cantilever. The clear span and cantilever are given design conditions. The bending and shear stresses used in the calculations are increased by a factor of 25 percent for intermittent loads.

EXAMPLE 8 S-1

The plan on the page is a diagram of a partial plan of a panelized roof system. Notice that the purlin member spacing is 4 ft 0 in o.c. The roof is constructed by shop fabricating 4 ft × 8 ft plywood panels with 2 × 4 stiffener joists spaced at 24 in o.c. The prefabricated panels are placed and nailed to the 4 × purlins which are supported by the glued laminated roof beams. In view of the fact that the roof is relatively flat, it is important to calculate the purlin and beam deflections to prevent water ponding.

EXAMPLE 9 S-1

L1 to L15 calculate the roof live load and the allowable reduction based on tributary area supported. L20 to L26 demonstrate glued laminated beam calculations as outlined in NDS Part V. C_f = the size factor, C_s = slenderness factor, l_e = effective length. L46 shows that the dead load deflection is increased by a factor of 1.5 as per UBC requirements for minimum camber.

EXAMPLE 10 S-1

L1 to L15 calculate the roof live load and the allowable reduction based on tributary area supported. L20 to L26 demonstrate glued laminated beam calculations as outlined in NDS Part V. C_f = the size factor, C_s = slenderness factor, l_e = effective length, C_k = concentrated load factor. L47 shows that the dead load deflection is increased by a factor of 1.5 as per UBC requirements for minimum camber.

EXAMPLE 11 S-1

L1 to L15 calculate the roof live load and the allowable reduction based on tributary area supported. L20 to L26 demonstrate glued laminated beam calculations as outlined in NDS Part V. C_f = the size factor, C_s = slenderness factor, l_e = effective length, C_k = concentrated load factor. L47 shows that the dead load deflection is increased by a factor of 1.5 as per UBC requirements for minimum camber. The ends of glued laminated beams are often sloped to facilitate roof drainage at the point where they are connected to side walls. S-2, L30 to L45 demonstrate the calculation for the taper of the beam at the support.

EXAMPLE 12 S-1

L2 to L11 tabulate the design loads. Notice that a partition load of 20 lb/sq ft is used as an additional dead load for the partitions that may occur in the joist area. Case 2 checks the joists spaced at 12 in o.c.

EXAMPLE 13 S-1

Case 3 checks the joists at 16 in o.c. with a 1-in-thick hardwood floor in lieu of lightweight concrete. L30 to L43 show a diagram for the equivalent length of span for the calculation of the shear value used to determine the cross-sectional area required.

EXAMPLE 14 S-1

L2 to L11 tabulate the design loads. Notice that a partition load of 20 lb/sq ft is used as an additional dead load for the partitions that may occur in the joist area. The floor joists support a concentrated load imposed by a stud wall supporting part of the roof structure. Notice that the maximum moment occurs at the point where the shear is equal to zero.

EXAMPLE 15 S-1

L15 to L25 present a cross section of a floor and ceiling assembly. The floor supports a 1-in-thick bed of concrete and a 1 in layer of floor marble. Floors that support marble or brittle tile surfaces should be designed with extra care for deflection. Deflection can be limited by designing to a limit of $\frac{1}{490}$.

EXAMPLE 16 S-1

The design of wood floors used to support automobile parking loads requires a live load of 50 lb/sq ft. S-1, L9 shows a 25 percent impact. This value equals the load set by the American Association of State Highway Officials. There is some question concerning the automobile imposing a uniformly distributed load. Sheet S-2 demonstrates a calculation for the automobile wheel loads applied as concentrated loads. Interaction of span and load variables indicates that both Case 1 and Case 2 should be checked.

EXAMPLE 17 S-1

Case 1 investigates the joists with total load on the span and dead load only on the balcony cantilever. Case 2 investigates the joists with total load on the span and on the balcony cantilever. Case 3 investigates the joists with dead load only on the span and a total load on the balcony cantilever. Notice that the span dead load resists uplift at the left-side support.

EXAMPLE 18 S-1

This calculation presents a demonstration of floor joists supported by a series of evenly spaced posts and girders. The UBC requires that a space of 18 in be maintained between the existing grade and the bottom of the framing joists. Case 2 demonstrates the design of the support girders.

EXAMPLE 19 S-1

Case 1 is a calculation of a floor joist for an office building. The joist is designed for a uniform load only. Cases 2 and 3 on S-2 design the joist with a combination of the uniform load and a required concentrated load applied at midspan. Cases 2 and 3 calculate the maximum bending moment at the midspan. Case 4 places the concentrated load at the edge of the left support to determine the maximum shear. The table at the bottom of Sheet S-3 tabulates the moments and shear values for each design case. Notice that the placement of the concentrated load substantially increases the design moment and shear.

EXAMPLES 20, 21, AND 22

These examples demonstrate the methods of design and investigation of glued laminated beams used for roofs and floors. The live load reduction methods are shown for both types of loading; the required stress adjustment factors are also calculated for uniformly loaded beams.

EXAMPLE 23

Demonstrates the column load calculations with the live load reductions for roof and floor loads. Columns are designed in Case 1 as short columns, while Case 2 shows the column design for the same load as an intermediate column.

FLAT ROOF RAFTERS | EXAMPLE 1 SHT. S-1 of 1

DESIGN LOADS:

GRAVEL	=	3.4 #/sq ft
3 PLY ROOFING	=	2.3
1/2" PLYWOOD	=	1.5
FRAMING	=	2.8
PLASTER CEILING	=	8.0
MISCELLANEOUS	=	1.0
DEAD LOAD	=	19.0
LIVE LOAD - RESIDENCE	=	20.0
TOTAL LOAD	=	39.0 #/sq ft

CLEAR SPAN = 17'-10"

SPACING = 16" oc

UNIF. LOAD = (16/12) × 39 = 52 plf

SEASONED LUMBER K = 0.50

DEFLECTION LOAD = 1.33 (20 + .5 X 19) = 39 plf

$$M = \frac{52 \times 17.83^2}{8} = 2066.4\ '\#$$

$$S_{REQ'D} = \frac{12 \times 2066.4}{1450} = 13.68\ in^3$$

$$V = \frac{52 \times 15.83}{2} = 411.6\ \#$$

$$A_{REQ'D} = \frac{1.5 \times 411.6}{95} = 3.46\ in^2$$

$$\text{ALLOW. } \triangle = \frac{12 \times 17.83}{360} = 0.594$$

$$I_{REQ'D} = \frac{5 \times 39 \times 17.83^4 \times 1728}{384 \times 1.6 \times 10^6 \times .594} = 93.86\ in^4$$

TRY 2 X 10's @ 16" oc $A = 13.88\ in^2$ $I = 98.93\ in^4$ $S = 21.39\ in^3$

$$\text{ALLOW. } \triangle = \frac{12 \times 17.83}{240} = 0.89\ in$$

$$\triangle = \frac{5 \times 39 \times 17.83^4 \times 1728}{384 \times 1.6 \times 10^6 \times 98.93} = 0.526\ in\ \checkmark$$

$$\triangle = \frac{5 \times 80 \times 17.83^4 \times 1728}{384 \times 1.6 \times 10^6 \times 307.5} = 0.38\ in < 0.59\ in.$$

$$\text{TOTAL LOAD DEFL. } \triangle = \frac{5 \times 52 \times 17.83^4 \times 1728}{384 \times 1.6 \times 10^6 \times 98.93} = 0.747\ in$$

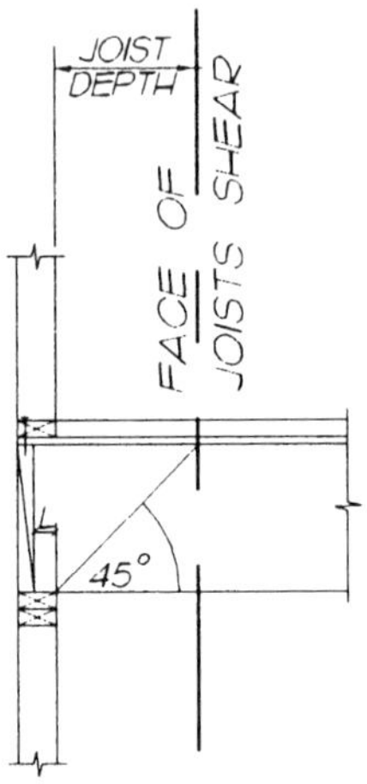

RE-CHECK SHEAR CALCULATION

SHEAR SPAN = 17.83-(2 X .83) = 16.17"

$$\text{SHEAR} = \frac{52 \times 16.17}{2} = 315.5\ \#$$

JOIST REACTION = 52 X 17.83 X 0.5 = 463.58 #

BEARING AREA:

L = 3.5 - 1.5 = 2" W = WIDTH OF JOIST

A = 2 X 1.5 = 3 sq in

$$\text{BEARING STRESS} = \frac{463.58}{3} = 154.53\ psi$$

RAFTER DESIGN LOADS:

LT. WT. CONC. TILE	=	9.0 #/sq ft
5/8" PLYWOOD	=	1.8
FRAMING	=	2.8
MISCELLANEOUS	=	1.0
DEAD LOAD	=	14.6
LIVE LOAD	=	20.0
TOTAL LOAD	=	34.6 #/sq ft

CEILING JOIST DESIGN LOADS:

INSULATION	=	1.50 #/sq ft
FRAMING	=	2.8
5/8" GYP. BOARD	=	2.8
MISCELLANEOUS	=	1.0
DEAD LOAD	=	8.10 SAY 8.0
LIVE LOAD	=	10.0
TOTAL LOAD	=	18.0 #/sq ft

RAFTER CLEAR SPAN = 17'-10"
SPACING = 16" oc
RFTR UNIF LD = (16/12) X 34.6 = 46 plf
F_B = 1450 psi F_V = 95 psi   E = 1.6x10^6 psi

CEILING JOIST CLEAR SPAN = 21'-4"
UNSEASONED LUMBER   K = 1
CEIL. JST. UNIF. LD. = (16/12) X18 = 24 plf

RAFTER DESIGN:

$$M = \frac{46 \times 17.83^2}{8} = 1828'\#$$

$$S_{REQD} = \frac{12 \times 1828}{1.25 \times 1450} = 12.1 \ in^3$$

$$V = \frac{46 \times 16.5}{2} = 379.50\#$$

$$A_{REQD} = \frac{1.5 \times 379.5}{1.25 \times 95} = 4.80 \ in^2$$

$$\triangle_{ALLOW.} = \frac{12 \times 17.83}{240} = 0.89 \ in$$

$$I_{REQD} = \frac{5 \times 46 \times 17.83^4 \times 1728}{384 \times 1.6 \times 10^6 \times .89} = 73.5 \ in^4$$

USE 2 X 10's Ø 16" oc   A = 13.88 in^2 I = 98.93 in^4 S = 21.39 in^3

$$f = \frac{12 \times 1828}{21.39} = 820.4 \ psi \ \checkmark$$

$$V = \frac{1.5 \times 379.5}{13.88} = 41.0 \ psi \ \checkmark$$

CEILING JOIST DESIGN: $M = \frac{24 \times 21.33^2}{8} = 1364.9'\#$ $V = \frac{24 \times 20.5}{2} = 246.2\#$

$$\triangle_{ALLOW.} = \frac{12 \times 21.33}{360} = 0.71 \ in$$ TRY 2 X 10's Ø 16" oc

$$\triangle = \frac{5 \times 24 \times 21.33^4 \times 1728}{384 \times 1.6 \times 10^6 \times 98.93} = 0.0706 \ in \ \checkmark$$

$$f = \frac{12 \times 1364.9}{21.39} = 765.7 \ psi \ \checkmark$$

$$V = \frac{1.5 \times 246.2}{13.88} = 26.6 \ psi \ \checkmark$$

RAFTER DESIGN LOADS:

CONCRETE TILE	=	10.0 #/sq ft
5/8" PLYWOOD	=	1.8
FRAMING	=	2.7
INSULATION	=	1.5
CEILING	=	8.0
MISCELLANEOUS	=	1.0
DEAD LOAD	=	25.0
LIVE LOAD	=	16.0
TOTAL LOAD		41.0 #/sq ft
	=	

RFTR CLEAR SPAN = 15'-8" LESS 6" = 15'-2"

SPACING = 16" oc

RFTR UNIF LD = (16/12) X 41.0 = 54.7 SAY 55. plf

UNSEASONED LUMBER   K = 1

F_B = 1450 psi F_V = 95 psi   E = 1.6x10⁶ psi

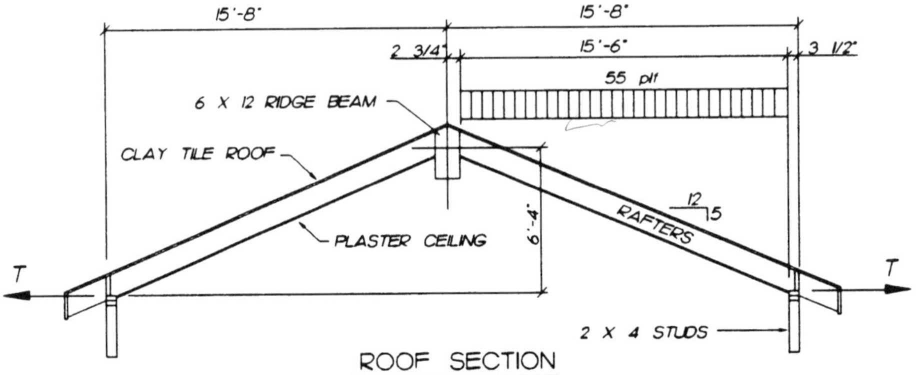

ROOF SECTION

RAFTER DESIGN:

$$M = \frac{55 \times 15.5^2}{8} = 1651.7 \, '\#$$ $$S_{REQD} = \frac{12 \times 1651.7}{1.25 \times 1450} = 10.9 \, in^3$$

$$V = \frac{55 \times 14.17}{2} = 389.60\#$$ $$A_{REQD} = \frac{1.5 \times 389.6}{1.25 \times 95} = 4.9 \, in^2$$

$$\triangle_{ALLOW.} = \frac{12 \times 15.50}{240} = 0.775 \, in$$ $$I_{REQD} = \frac{5 \times 55 \times 15.5^4 \times 1728}{384 \times 1.6 \times 10^6 \times .775} = 57.6 \, in^3$$

TRY 2 X 10's @ 16" oc   A = 13.88 in²   I = 98.93 in⁴   S = 21.39 in³

$$\triangle_{ALLOW.} = \frac{12 \times 15.50}{240} = 0.775 \, in$$ $$\triangle = \frac{5 \times 55 \times 15.5^4 \times 1728}{384 \times 1.6 \times 10^6 \times 98.93} = 0.451 \, in \checkmark$$

$$f = \frac{12 \times 1651.7}{21.39} = 926.6 \, psi \checkmark$$

RECHECK V - L = 15.5' - $\frac{(2 \times 9.25)}{12}$ = 14.0' $V = \frac{55 \times 14}{2} = 385\#$ $V = \frac{1.5 \times 385}{13.88} = 21.4 \, psi \checkmark$

CALC. HORIZ. THRUST T AT EACH SIDE:

$$T = \frac{55 \times (2 \times 15.5)^2}{8 \times 6.33} = 1043.7 \, \#/JST$$ OR 1043.7/1.33 = 782.8 #/ft.

USE 2 X 10's @ 16" oc

RAFTER DESIGN LOADS:

CONCRETE TILE	=	10.0 #/sq ft
5/8" PLYWOOD	=	1.8
FRAMING	=	2.7
INSULATION	=	1.5
CEILING	=	8.0
MISCELLANEOUS	=	1.0
DEAD LOAD	=	25.0
SNOW LOAD	=	45.0
TOTAL LOAD	=	70 #/sq ft

RFTR CLEAR SPAN = 17'-6" LESS 6" = 17'-0"

$SNOW = 50.0$ psf $R_s = \left[\dfrac{50}{40} - \dfrac{1}{2}\right] \times (26.6-20) = 5$ %

SNOW LOAD = $50 \times (1-0.50) = 45.$ psf

SPACING = 16" oc   UNSEASONED LUMBER   K = 1

RFTR UNIF LD = $(16/12) \times 70.0 = 93.$ plf

$F_B = 1450$ psi $F_V = 95$ psi $E = 1.6 \times 10^6$ psi

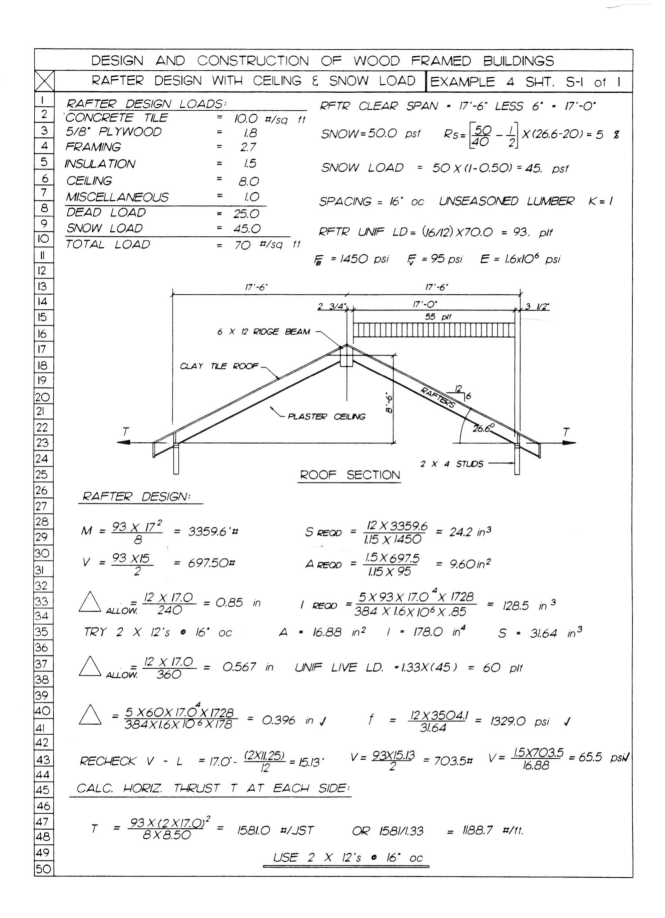

ROOF SECTION

RAFTER DESIGN:

$M = \dfrac{93 \times 17^2}{8} = 3359.6$ '# $S_{REQD} = \dfrac{12 \times 3359.6}{1.15 \times 1450} = 24.2$ in³

$V = \dfrac{93 \times 15}{2} = 697.50$ # $A_{REQD} = \dfrac{1.5 \times 697.5}{1.15 \times 95} = 9.60$ in²

$\triangle_{ALLOW.} = \dfrac{12 \times 17.0}{240} = 0.85$ in $I_{REQD} = \dfrac{5 \times 93 \times 17.0^4 \times 1728}{384 \times 1.6 \times 10^6 \times .85} = 128.5$ in³

TRY 2 X 12's @ 16" oc   A = 16.88 in²   I = 178.0 in⁴   S = 31.64 in³

$\triangle_{ALLOW.} = \dfrac{12 \times 17.0}{360} = 0.567$ in   UNIF LIVE LD. = $1.33 \times (45) = 60$ plf

$\triangle = \dfrac{5 \times 60 \times 17.0^4 \times 1728}{384 \times 1.6 \times 10^6 \times 178} = 0.396$ in ✓ $f = \dfrac{12 \times 3504.1}{31.64} = 1329.0$ psi ✓

RECHECK V - L = $17.0' - \dfrac{(2 \times 11.25)}{12} = 15.13'$ $V = \dfrac{93 \times 15.13}{2} = 703.5$ # $V = \dfrac{1.5 \times 703.5}{16.88} = 65.5$ psi✓

CALC. HORIZ. THRUST T AT EACH SIDE:

$T = \dfrac{93 \times (2 \times 17.0)^2}{8 \times 8.50} = 1581.0$ #/JST   OR 1581/1.33 = 1188.7 #/ft.

USE 2 X 12's @ 16" oc

1	
2	

RAFTER DESIGN LOADS:

WOOD SHINGLES	=	2.0	#/sq ft
1/2" PLYWOOD	=	1.5	
FRAMING	=	3.0	
INSULATION	=	1.5	
MISCELLANEOUS	=	1.0	
DEAD LOAD	=	9.0	
LIVE LOAD	=	14.0	
TOTAL LOAD	=	23.0	#/sq ft

RIDGE BEAM CLEAR SPAN = 18'-0"

TRIBUTARY WIDTH = 18'-0"   SEASONED LUMBER

SUPPORTED AREA = 18 X 18 = 324 sq. ft.

UBC SEC. 2306 EQ. (6-1)

$R = 0.60 \times (324 - 150) = 10.4\%$

$LIVE\ LD = 14 \times (1 - .104) = 12.50\ psf$

UBC TABLE No. 23-C LIVE LOAD = 14 psf ✓

$F_B = 1450\ psi \quad F_V = 95\ psi \quad E = 1.6 \times 10^6\ psi$

TOTAL UNIFORM LOAD = 18 X 23 + BEAM = 435 plf

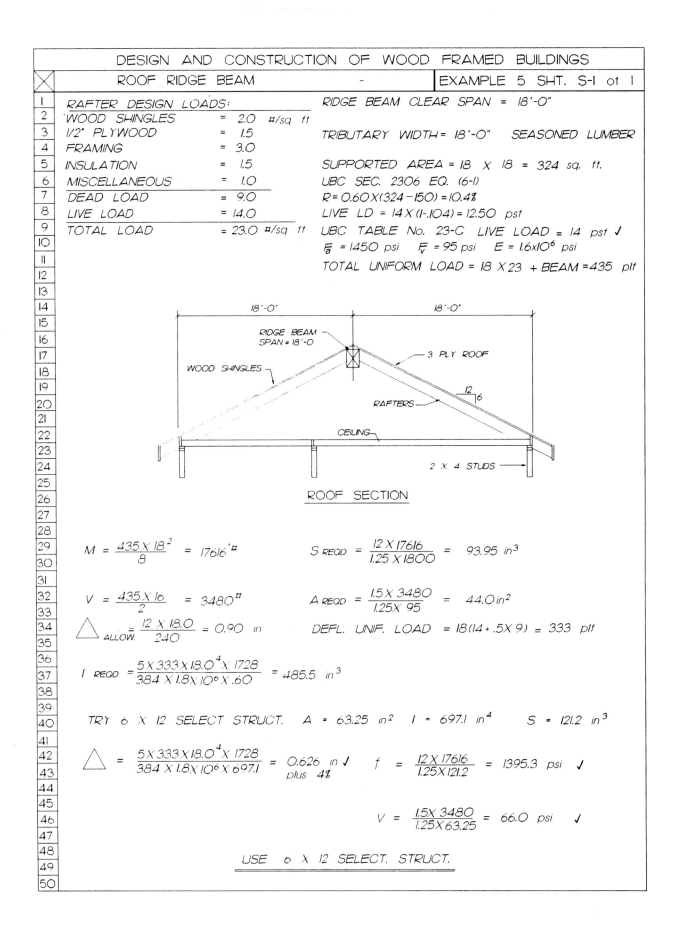

ROOF SECTION

$$M = \frac{435 \times 18^2}{8} = 17616\ '^{\#}$$

$$S_{REQD} = \frac{12 \times 17616}{1.25 \times 1800} = 93.95\ in^3$$

$$V = \frac{435 \times 16}{2} = 3480^{\#}$$

$$A_{REQD} = \frac{1.5 \times 3480}{1.25 \times 95} = 44.0\ in^2$$

$$\triangle_{ALLOW.} = \frac{12 \times 18.0}{240} = 0.90\ in$$

DEFL. UNIF. LOAD = 18(14 + .5 X 9) = 333 plf

$$I_{REQD} = \frac{5 \times 333 \times 18.0^4 \times 1728}{384 \times 1.8 \times 10^6 \times .60} = 485.5\ in^3$$

TRY 6 X 12 SELECT STRUCT.   A = 63.25 in² I = 697.1 in⁴   S = 121.2 in³

$$\triangle = \frac{5 \times 333 \times 18.0^4 \times 1728}{384 \times 1.8 \times 10^6 \times 697.1} = 0.626\ in\ ✓$$
plus 4%

$$f = \frac{12 \times 17616}{1.25 \times 121.2} = 1395.3\ psi\ ✓$$

$$V = \frac{1.5 \times 3480}{1.25 \times 63.25} = 66.0\ psi\ ✓$$

USE 6 X 12 SELECT. STRUCT.

DESIGN AND CONSTRUCTION OF WOOD FRAMED BUILDINGS

| | ROOF HIP BEAM | EXAMPLE 6 SHT. S-1 of 1 |

RAFTER DESIGN LOADS:

1.
2. WOOD SHINGLES = 2.0 #/sq ft
3. 1/2" PLYWOOD = 1.5
4. FRAMING = 3.0
5. INSULATION = 1.5
6. MISCELLANEOUS = 1.0
7. DEAD LOAD = 9.0
8. LIVE LOAD = 16.0
9. TOTAL LOAD = 25.0 #/sq ft

HIP BEAM CLEAR SPAN = 18'-0"
TRIBUTARY WIDTH = 12'-0"   SEASONED LUMBER

SUPPORTED AREA = 18 X 12 X .5 = 108 sq. ft.

UBC TABLE No. 23-C LIVE LOAD = 16 psf

MAX. UNIFORM LOAD = 12 X 25 = 300 plf

$F_B = 1250$ psi $F_V = 85$ psi $E = 1.6 \times 10^6$ psi

ROOF PLAN

ROOF SECTION

$$W = \frac{300 \times 18}{2} = 2700^{\#} \qquad R_1 = R_2 = \frac{2700}{2} = 1350^{\#}$$

$$M = \frac{2700 \times 18}{6} = 8100'^{\#}$$

$$S_{REQD} = \frac{12 \times 8100}{1.25 \times 1250} = 62.2 \ in^3$$

$$V = 1350 - \left(\frac{300}{9}\right) = 1316.7^{\#}$$

$$A_{REQD} = \frac{1.5 \times 1316.7}{1.25 \times 85} = 18.6 \ in^2$$

$$\triangle_{ALLOW.} = \frac{12 \times 18.0}{360} = 0.60 \ in$$

$$DEFL. \ EQUIV. \ UNIF \ LD = \frac{4 \ W_{LL}}{3 \times 18}$$

$$DEFL. \ EQUIV. \ LIVE \ LD = \frac{4 \times 16 \times 12 \times 18 \times .5}{3 \times 18} = 128 \ plf$$

$$I_{REQD} = \frac{5 \times 128 \times 18.0^4 \times 1728}{384 \times 1.8 \times 10^6 \times .60} = 280.0 \ in^3$$

TRY 4 X 12 DF No. 2   A = 39.38 in^2 I = 415.3 in^4 S = 73.83 in^3

CONVERT W = 2700# TO A UNIF. LOAD

$$\triangle = \frac{5 \times 128 \times 18.0^4 \times 1728}{384 \times 1.6 \times 10^6 \times 415.3} = 0.455 \ in \checkmark$$

$$UNIF. \ LD = \frac{4 \times 2700}{3 \times 18} = 200 \ plf \ (TOTAL \ LD)$$

$$f = \frac{12 \times 8100}{78.33} = 1240.9 \ psi \ \checkmark$$

$$RECHECK \ MOMENT = \frac{200 \times 18^2}{8} = 8100'^{\#} \ \checkmark$$

$$V = \frac{1.5 \times 1316.7}{39.38} = 50.2 \ psi \ \checkmark$$

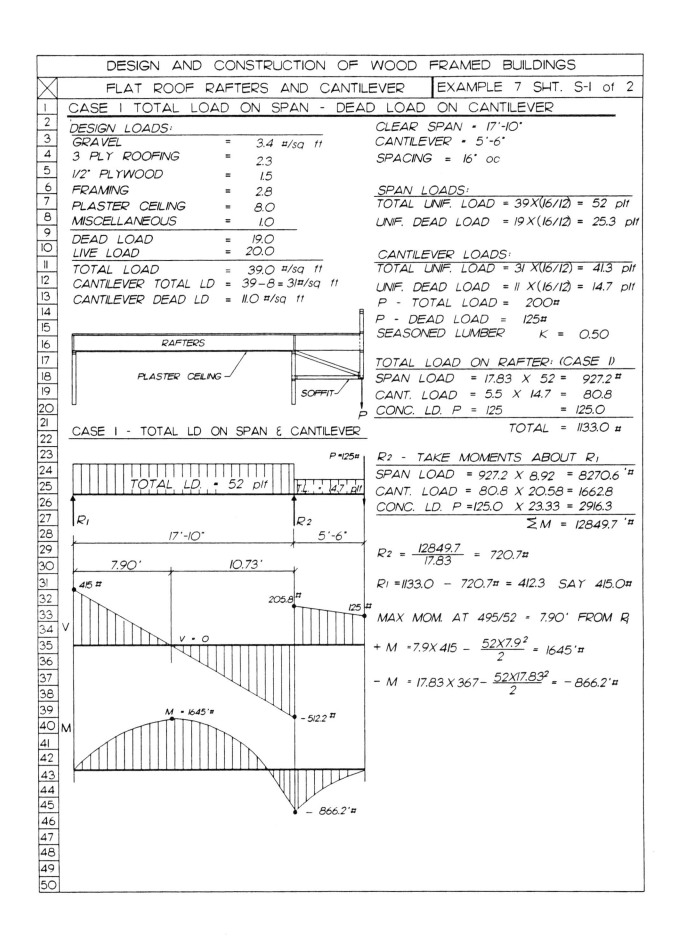

CASE I TOTAL LOAD ON SPAN - DEAD LOAD ON CANTILEVER

DESIGN LOADS:

GRAVEL	=	3.4 #/sq ft
3 PLY ROOFING	=	2.3
1/2" PLYWOOD	=	1.5
FRAMING	=	2.8
PLASTER CEILING	=	8.0
MISCELLANEOUS	=	1.0
DEAD LOAD	=	19.0
LIVE LOAD	=	20.0
TOTAL LOAD	=	39.0 #/sq ft
CANTILEVER TOTAL LD	=	39 − 8 = 31 #/sq ft
CANTILEVER DEAD LD	=	11.0 #/sq ft

RAFTERS

PLASTER CEILING

SOFFIT

P

CASE I - TOTAL LD ON SPAN & CANTILEVER

P = 125#

TOTAL LD. = 52 plf   T.L. = 14.7 plf

R₁   R₂

17'-10"   5'-6"

7.90'   10.73'

415 #

205.8 #   125 #

V   v = 0

M = 1645'#   − 512.2 #

M

− 866.2'#

CLEAR SPAN = 17'-10"
CANTILEVER = 5'-6"
SPACING = 16" oc

SPAN LOADS:
TOTAL UNIF. LOAD = 39 X (16/12) = 52 plf
UNIF. DEAD LOAD = 19 X (16/12) = 25.3 plf

CANTILEVER LOADS:
TOTAL UNIF. LOAD = 31 X (16/12) = 41.3 plf
UNIF. DEAD LOAD = 11 X (16/12) = 14.7 plf
P - TOTAL LOAD = 200#
P - DEAD LOAD = 125#
SEASONED LUMBER   K = 0.50

TOTAL LOAD ON RAFTER: (CASE I)

SPAN LOAD	= 17.83 X 52 =	927.2#
CANT. LOAD	= 5.5 X 14.7 =	80.8
CONC. LD. P = 125	=	125.0
	TOTAL =	1133.0 #

R₂ - TAKE MOMENTS ABOUT R₁

SPAN LOAD	= 927.2 X 8.92 =	8270.6 '#
CANT. LOAD	= 80.8 X 20.58 =	1662.8
CONC. LD. P = 125.0	X 23.33 =	2916.3
	$\sum$M =	12849.7 '#

$R_2 = \dfrac{12849.7}{17.83} = 720.7$#

$R_1 = 1133.0 - 720.7$# $= 412.3$ SAY 415.0#

MAX MOM. AT 495/52 = 7.90' FROM R₁

$+ M = 7.9 X 415 - \dfrac{52 X 7.9^2}{2} = 1645$'#

$- M = 17.83 X 367 - \dfrac{52 X 17.83^2}{2} = -866.2$#

CASE 2 TOTAL LOAD ON SPAN - TOTAL LOAD ON CANTILEVER

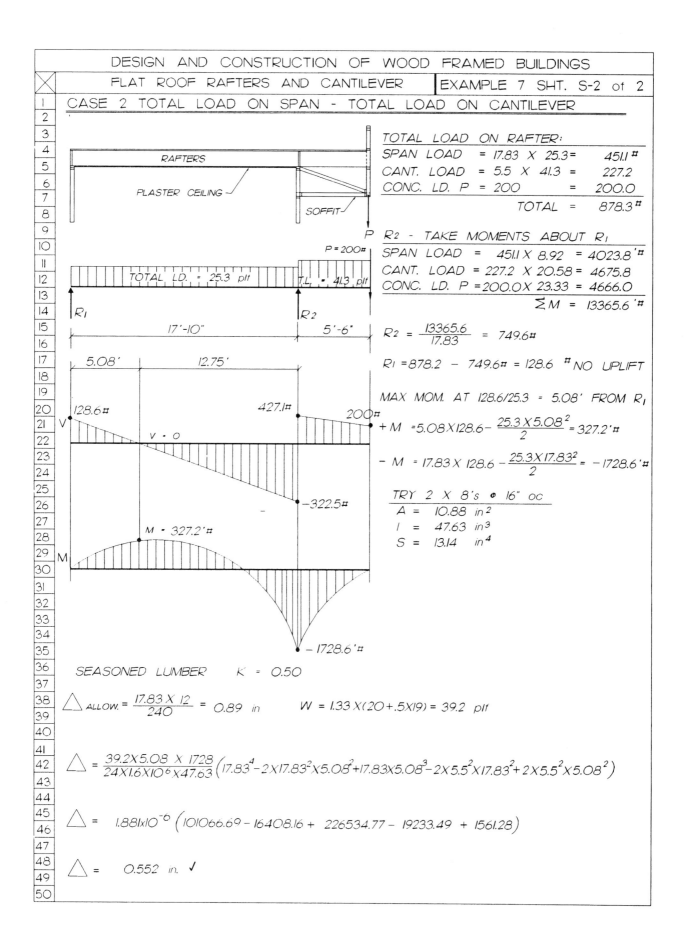

TOTAL LOAD ON RAFTER:

SPAN LOAD = 17.83 X 25.3 = 451.1 #

CANT. LOAD = 5.5 X 41.3 = 227.2

CONC. LD. P = 200 = 200.0

TOTAL = 878.3 #

R_2 - TAKE MOMENTS ABOUT R_1

SPAN LOAD = 451.1 X 8.92 = 4023.8 '#

CANT. LOAD = 227.2 X 20.58 = 4675.8

CONC. LD. P = 200.0 X 23.33 = 4666.0

ΣM = 13365.6 '#

$R_2 = \dfrac{13365.6}{17.83} = 749.6$#

$R_1 = 878.2 - 749.6$# $= 128.6$ # NO UPLIFT

MAX MOM. AT 128.6/25.3 = 5.08' FROM R_1

$+ M = 5.08 \times 128.6 - \dfrac{25.3 \times 5.08^2}{2} = 327.2'$#

$- M = 17.83 \times 128.6 - \dfrac{25.3 \times 17.83^2}{2} = -1728.6'$#

TRY 2 X 8's @ 16" oc

A = 10.88 in^2

I = 47.63 in^3

S = 13.14 in^4

SEASONED LUMBER   K = 0.50

$\triangle_{ALLOW.} = \dfrac{17.83 \times 12}{240} = 0.89$ in $W = 1.33 \times (20 + .5 \times 19) = 39.2$ plf

$\triangle = \dfrac{39.2 \times 5.08 \times 1728}{24 \times 1.6 \times 10^6 \times 47.63} \left(17.83^4 - 2 \times 17.83^2 \times 5.08^2 + 17.83 \times 5.08^3 - 2 \times 5.5^2 \times 17.83^2 + 2 \times 5.5^2 \times 5.08^2\right)$

$\triangle = 1.881 \times 10^{-6} \left(101066.69 - 16408.16 + 226534.77 - 19233.49 + 1561.28\right)$

$\triangle = 0.552$ in. ✓

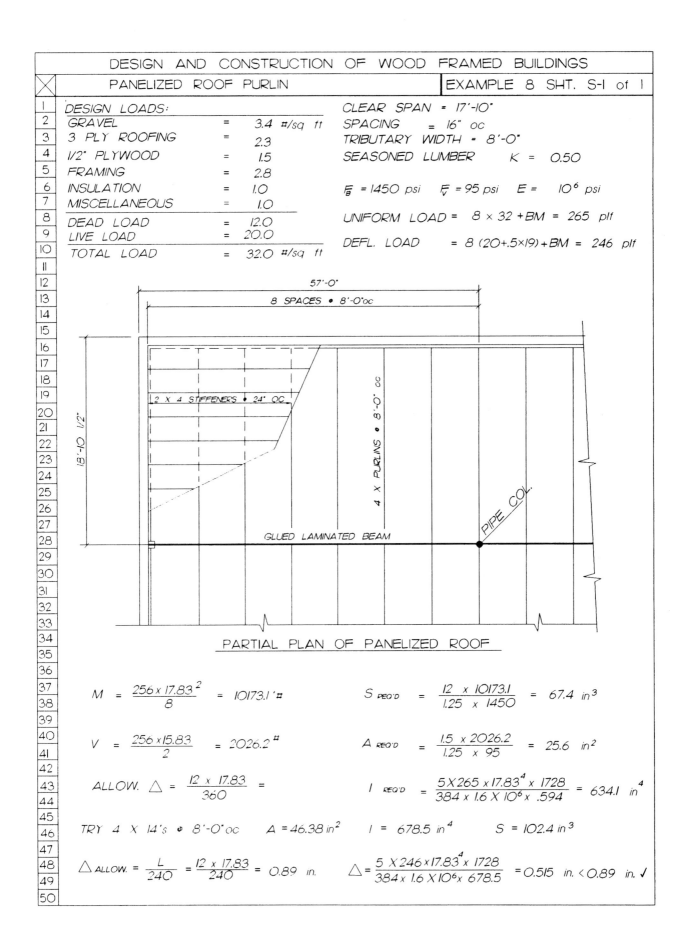

	DESIGN LOADS:		
2	GRAVEL	=	3.4 #/sq ft
3	3 PLY ROOFING	=	2.3
4	1/2" PLYWOOD	=	1.5
5	FRAMING	=	2.8
6	INSULATION	=	1.0
7	MISCELLANEOUS	=	1.0
8	DEAD LOAD	=	12.0
9	LIVE LOAD	=	20.0
10	TOTAL LOAD	=	32.0 #/sq ft

CLEAR SPAN = 17'-10"
SPACING = 16" oc
TRIBUTARY WIDTH = 8'-0"
SEASONED LUMBER   K = 0.50

$F_B = 1450$ psi $F_V = 95$ psi $E = 10^6$ psi

UNIFORM LOAD = $8 \times 32 + BM = 265$ plf

DEFL. LOAD = $8(20+.5\times19)+BM = 246$ plf

57'-0"

8 SPACES • 8'-0"oc

2 X 4 STIFFENERS • 24" OC

18'-10 1/2"

4 X PURLINS • 8'-0" oc

GLUED LAMINATED BEAM

PIPE COL.

PARTIAL PLAN OF PANELIZED ROOF

$$M = \frac{256 \times 17.83^2}{8} = 10173.1 \text{ '#}$$

$$S_{REQ'D} = \frac{12 \times 10173.1}{1.25 \times 1450} = 67.4 \text{ in}^3$$

$$V = \frac{256 \times 15.83}{2} = 2026.2 \text{ #}$$

$$A_{REQ'D} = \frac{1.5 \times 2026.2}{1.25 \times 95} = 25.6 \text{ in}^2$$

$$ALLOW. \triangle = \frac{12 \times 17.83}{360} =$$

$$I_{REQ'D} = \frac{5 \times 265 \times 17.83^4 \times 1728}{384 \times 1.6 \times 10^6 \times .594} = 634.1 \text{ in}^4$$

TRY 4 X 14's • 8'-0" oc $A = 46.38 \text{ in}^2$ $I = 678.5 \text{ in}^4$ $S = 102.4 \text{ in}^3$

$$\triangle_{ALLOW.} = \frac{L}{240} = \frac{12 \times 17.83}{240} = 0.89 \text{ in.}$$

$$\triangle = \frac{5 \times 246 \times 17.83^4 \times 1728}{384 \times 1.6 \times 10^6 \times 678.5} = 0.515 \text{ in.} < 0.89 \text{ in.} \checkmark$$

PANELIZED ROOF GLUED LAMINATED BEAM | EXAMPLE 9 SHT. S-1 of 1

DESIGN LOADS:

GRAVEL	=	3.4 #/sq ft
3 PLY ROOFING	=	2.3
1/2" PLYWOOD	=	1.5
FRAMING	=	2.8
INSULATION	=	1.0
MISCELLANEOUS	=	1.0
DEAD LOAD	=	12.0
LIVE LOAD	=	20.0
TOTAL LOAD	=	32.0 #/sq ft

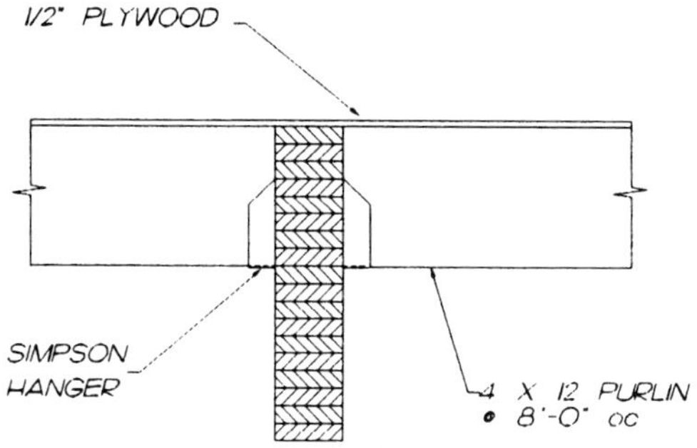

1/2" PLYWOOD
SIMPSON HANGER
4 X 12 PURLIN @ 8'-0" oc

BEAM SECTION

CLEAR SPAN = 56'-0"

TRIBUTARY WIDTH = 17'-10"

SEASONED LUMBER K = 0.50

LUMBER DESIGNATION 24-V8 DF/DF

F_B = 2400psi F_V = 165psi $E = 1.8 \times 10^6$ psi

INTERIOR BEAMS - DRY CONDITION

TRIBUTARY AREA = 17.83 × 56 = 998.5 sq. ft.

LIVE LOAD REDUCTION:

UBC METHOD 1, LIVE LOAD = 12 psf

METHOD 2, % = .08 (998.5 − 150) = 67.9%

USE LIVE LOAD = 12 psf

UNIF. LOAD = 17.83 × 24 + BM = 475 plf

DEFL. LOAD = 17.83 (12 + .5 × 12) + BM = 370 plf

TRY A GLU - LAM BM 8 3/4" X 28 1/2"

19 LAMINATIONS DEPTH = 28.5 in. C_F = 0.91

$A = 249.4\ in^2$ $I = 16{,}880\ in^4$ $S = 1184\ in^3$

CHECK $C_F = \sqrt[1/9]{\dfrac{12}{28.5}} = 0.908$ FOR UNIFORM LOAD

CHECK BEAM SLENDERNESS $C_S = \sqrt{\dfrac{l_e \times d}{b^2}}$

$l_e = 1.92 \times 8 \times 12 = 184.3$

$C_S = \sqrt{\dfrac{184.3 \times 28.5}{8.75^2}} = 8.28 < 10.0$ ✓

$M = \dfrac{475 \times 57^2}{8} = 192909.4'\#$

$S_{REQ'D} = \dfrac{12 \times 192909.4}{1.25 \times .914 \times 2400} = 844.2\ in^3$

$V = \dfrac{475 \times 52.5}{2} = 12468.8\#$

$A_{REQ'D} = \dfrac{1.5 \times 12468.8}{1.25 \times .914 \times 165} = 99.2\ in^2$

$\Delta_{ALLOW.} = \dfrac{L}{240} = \dfrac{12 \times 57}{240} = 2.85$ in.

$\Delta = \dfrac{5 \times 370 \times 57^4 \times 1728}{384 \times 1.8 \times 10^6 \times 11070} = 2.89$ in. ✓

UNIFORM DEAD LOAD = 17.83 × 12 + BM = 260 plf

$\Delta_{DEAD\ LOAD} = \dfrac{5 \times 260 \times 57^4 \times 1728}{384 \times 1.8 \times 10^6 \times 16880} = 2.03$ in

CAMBER = 1.5 × 2.03 = 3.0 in.

USE GLU LAM BEAM 8 3/4 in X 28 1/2 CAMBER UP 3" AT MIDSPAN

DESIGN LOADS:

GRAVEL	=	3.4 #/sq ft
3 PLY ROOFING	=	2.3
1/2" PLYWOOD	=	1.5
FRAMING	=	2.8
INSULATION	=	1.0
MISCELLANEOUS	=	1.0
DEAD LOAD	=	12.0
LIVE LOAD	=	20.0
TOTAL LOAD	=	32.0 #/sq ft

CLEAR SPAN = 40'-0"
TRIBUTARY WIDTH = 8'-0"
SEASONED LUMBER   K = 0.50
LUMBER DESIGNATION 24-V8 DF/DF

$F_B = 2400 psi$ $F_V = 165 psi$ $E = 1.8 \times 10^6 psi$

INTERIOR BEAMS - DRY CONDITION
TRIBUTARY AREA = 8.0 × 40 = 320.0 sq. ft.

LIVE LOAD REDUCTION:

UBC METHOD 1, LIVE LOAD = 16 psf

METHOD 2, % = .08 (320 − 150) = 13.6%

USE LIVE LOAD = 16 psf

UNIF. LOAD = 8.0 × 24 + BM = 240 plf

DEFL. LOAD = 8.0 (12 + .5 × 16) + BM = 200 plf

TRY A GLU - LAM BM 8 3/4" X 28 1/2"

19 LAMINATIONS   DEPTH = 28.5 in. $C_F = 0.91$

$A = 249.4 in^2$ $I = 16,880 in^4$ $S = 1184 in^3$

CHECK $C_F = \sqrt[1/9]{\dfrac{12}{28.5}} = 0.908$ FOR UNIFORM LOAD

CHECK BEAM SLENDERNESS $C_S = \sqrt{\dfrac{l_e \times d}{b^2}}$

$l_e = 1.61 \times 20 \times 12 = 386.4$ $C_S = \sqrt{\dfrac{386.4 \times 28.5}{8.75^2}} = 12.0 > 10.0$

$C_K = 0.811x \sqrt{\dfrac{E}{F_b}} = 0.811x \sqrt{\dfrac{1.8 \times 10^6}{2400}} = 22.21$

DIMENSION: 40'-0", with 20'-0" + 20'-0"

BEAM

DEAD LOAD = 8,200#
LIVE LOAD = 7,080#
TOTAL LOAD = 15,280#

$M = \dfrac{240 \times 40^2}{8} + \dfrac{15280 \times 40}{4} = 200,800'\#$

$F' = C_F \times F_B$ $F' = 0.908 \times 2400 = 2179$ psi

$V = \dfrac{240 \times 40}{2} + \dfrac{15280}{2} = 12,440\#$

IF $C_S > 10.0$ AND $< C_K$ THEN:

$S_{REQ'D} = \dfrac{12 \times 200,800}{1.25 \times 2117.1} = 910.5 \ in^3$

$F'' = F' \left[1 - \dfrac{1}{3} \left(\dfrac{C_S}{C_K} \right)^4 \right] = 2179 \left[1 - \dfrac{1}{3} \left(\dfrac{12.0}{22.21} \right)^4 \right]$

$A_{REQ'D} = \dfrac{1.5 \times 12,440}{1.25 \times .914 \times 165} = 99.4 \ in^2$

$F'' = 2117.1$ psi

$\triangle_{ALLOW.} = \dfrac{L}{240} = \dfrac{12 \times 40}{240} = 2.00$ in. $\triangle_{LIVE \ LD.} = \dfrac{L}{360} = \dfrac{12 \times 40}{360} = 1.33$ in.

$\triangle_{ALLOW.} = \dfrac{5 \times 200 \times 40^4 \times 1728}{384 \times 1.8 \times 10^6 \times 11070} + \dfrac{.5 \times 8200 \times 40^3 \times 1728}{48 \times 1.8 \times 10^6 \times 11070} = 0.578 + 0.474 = 1.052$ in. ✓

$\triangle_{LIVE \ LD.} = \dfrac{5 \times 160 \times 40^4 \times 1728}{384 \times 1.8 \times 10^6 \times 11070} + \dfrac{7080 \times 40^3 \times 1728}{48 \times 1.8 \times 10^6 \times 11070} = 0.462 + 0.799 = 1.261$ in. ✓

$\triangle_{DEAD \ LD.} = \dfrac{5 \times 96 \times 40^4 \times 1728}{384 \times 1.8 \times 10^6 \times 11070} + \dfrac{8200 \times 40^3 \times 1728}{48 \times 1.8 \times 10^6 \times 11070} = 0.277 + 0.948 = 1.225$ in.

CAMBER = 1.5 × 1.225 = 1.84 in.

USE GLU LAM BEAM 8 3/4 in X 28 1/2   CAMBER UP 2" AT MIDSPAN

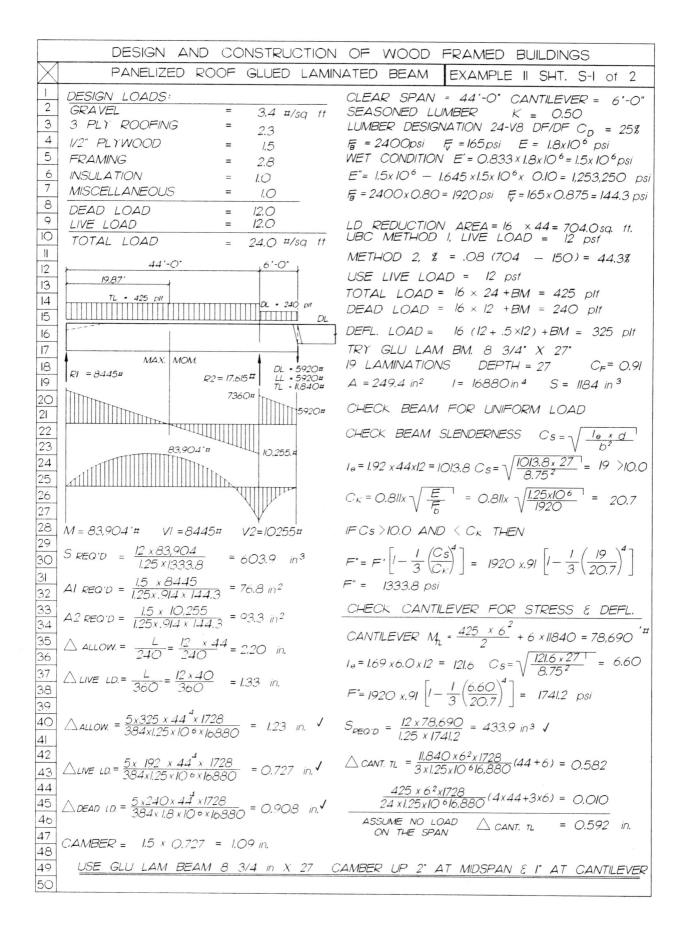

DESIGN LOADS:

GRAVEL	=	3.4 #/sq ft
3 PLY ROOFING	=	2.3
1/2" PLYWOOD	=	1.5
FRAMING	=	2.8
INSULATION	=	1.0
MISCELLANEOUS	=	1.0
DEAD LOAD	=	12.0
LIVE LOAD	=	12.0
TOTAL LOAD	=	24.0 #/sq ft

$M = 83,904'$# $V1 = 8445$# $V2 = 10255$#

$S_{REQ'D} = \dfrac{12 \times 83,904}{1.25 \times 1333.8} = 603.9\ in^3$

$A1_{REQ'D} = \dfrac{1.5 \times 8445}{1.25 \times .914 \times 144.3} = 76.8\ in^2$

$A2_{REQ'D} = \dfrac{1.5 \times 10,255}{1.25 \times .914 \times 144.3} = 93.3\ in^2$

$\triangle\ ALLOW. = \dfrac{L}{240} = \dfrac{12 \times 44}{240} = 2.20\ in.$

$\triangle\ LIVE\ LD. = \dfrac{L}{360} = \dfrac{12 \times 40}{360} = 1.33\ in.$

$\triangle_{ALLOW.} = \dfrac{5 \times 325 \times 44^4 \times 1728}{384 \times 1.25 \times 10^6 \times 16880} = 1.23\ in.\ ✓$

$\triangle_{LIVE\ LD.} = \dfrac{5 \times 192 \times 44^4 \times 1728}{384 \times 1.25 \times 10^6 \times 16880} = 0.727\ in.✓$

$\triangle_{DEAD\ LD.} = \dfrac{5 \times 240 \times 44^4 \times 1728}{384 \times 1.8 \times 10^6 \times 16880} = 0.908\ in.✓$

$CAMBER = 1.5 \times 0.727 = 1.09\ in.$

USE GLU LAM BEAM 8 3/4 in X 27   CAMBER UP 2" AT MIDSPAN & 1" AT CANTILEVER

CLEAR SPAN = 44'-0" CANTILEVER = 6'-0"
SEASONED LUMBER   K = 0.50
LUMBER DESIGNATION 24-V8 DF/DF $C_D = 25\%$
$F_B = 2400\,psi$ $F_V = 165\,psi$ $E = 1.8 \times 10^6\ psi$
WET CONDITION $E' = 0.833 \times 1.8 \times 10^6 = 1.5 \times 10^6\,psi$
$E'' = 1.5 \times 10^6 - 1.645 \times 1.5 \times 10^6 \times 0.10 = 1,253,250\ psi$
$F_B = 2400 \times 0.80 = 1920\,psi$ $F_V = 165 \times 0.875 = 144.3\,psi$

LD REDUCTION AREA = $16 \times 44 = 704.0$ sq. ft.
UBC METHOD I, LIVE LOAD = 12 psf

METHOD 2, $\% = .08(704 - 150) = 44.3\%$

USE LIVE LOAD = 12 psf
TOTAL LOAD = $16 \times 24 + BM = 425\ plf$
DEAD LOAD = $16 \times 12 + BM = 240\ plf$

DEFL. LOAD = $16(12 + .5 \times 12) + BM = 325\ plf$
TRY GLU LAM BM. 8 3/4" X 27"
19 LAMINATIONS   DEPTH = 27 $C_F = 0.91$
$A = 249.4\ in^2$ $I = 16880\ in^4$ $S = 1184\ in^3$

CHECK BEAM FOR UNIFORM LOAD

CHECK BEAM SLENDERNESS $C_S = \sqrt{\dfrac{l_e \times d}{b^2}}$

$l_e = 1.92 \times 44 \times 12 = 1013.8$ $C_S = \sqrt{\dfrac{1013.8 \times 27}{8.75^2}} = 19 > 10.0$

$C_K = 0.811 \times \sqrt{\dfrac{E}{F_b}} = 0.811 \times \sqrt{\dfrac{1.25 \times 10^6}{1920}} = 20.7$

IF $C_S > 10.0$ AND $< C_K$ THEN

$F'' = F' \left[1 - \dfrac{1}{3}\left(\dfrac{C_S}{C_K}\right)^4\right] = 1920 \times .91 \left[1 - \dfrac{1}{3}\left(\dfrac{19}{20.7}\right)^4\right]$

$F'' = 1333.8\ psi$

CHECK CANTILEVER FOR STRESS & DEFL.

$CANTILEVER\ M_{TL} = \dfrac{425 \times 6^2}{2} + 6 \times 11840 = 78,690'$#

$l_e = 1.69 \times 6.0 \times 12 = 121.6$ $C_S = \sqrt{\dfrac{121.6 \times 27}{8.75^2}} = 6.60$

$F'' = 1920 \times .91 \left[1 - \dfrac{1}{3}\left(\dfrac{6.60}{20.7}\right)^4\right] = 1741.2\ psi$

$S_{REQ'D} = \dfrac{12 \times 78,690}{1.25 \times 1741.2} = 433.9\ in^3\ ✓$

$\triangle_{CANT.\ TL} = \dfrac{11,840 \times 6^2 \times 1728}{3 \times 1.25 \times 10^6\,16,880}(44+6) = 0.582$

$\dfrac{425 \times 6^2 \times 1728}{24 \times 1.25 \times 10^6\,16,880}(4 \times 44 + 3 \times 6) = 0.010$

ASSUME NO LOAD $\triangle_{CANT.\ TL} = 0.592\ in.$
ON THE SPAN

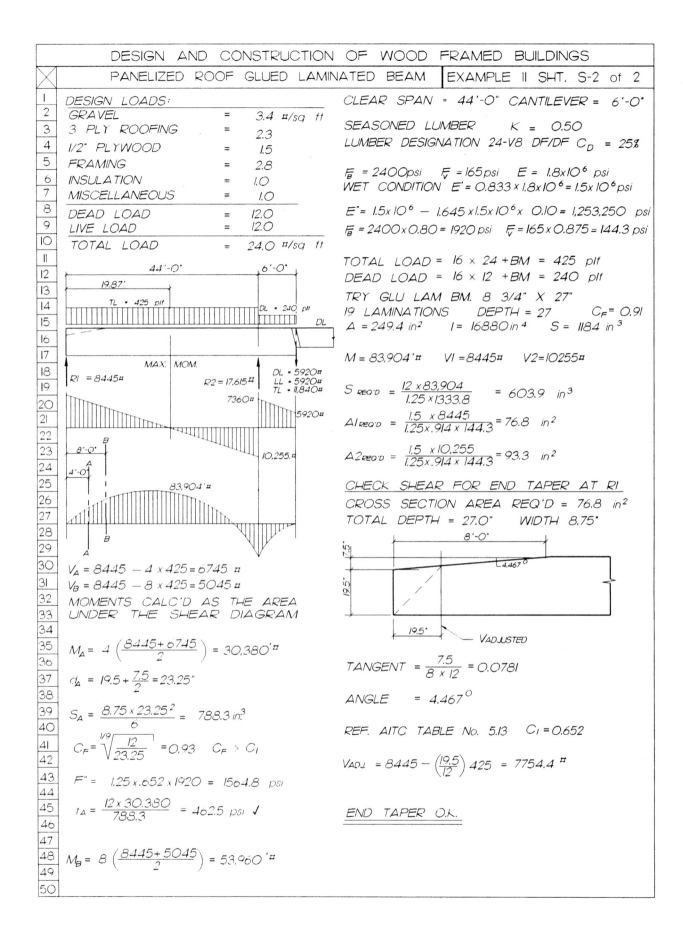

DESIGN LOADS:

GRAVEL	=	3.4 #/sq ft
3 PLY ROOFING	=	2.3
1/2" PLYWOOD	=	1.5
FRAMING	=	2.8
INSULATION	=	1.0
MISCELLANEOUS	=	1.0
DEAD LOAD	=	12.0
LIVE LOAD	=	12.0
TOTAL LOAD	=	24.0 #/sq ft

$V_A = 8445 - 4 \times 425 = 6745$ #

$V_B = 8445 - 8 \times 425 = 5045$ #

MOMENTS CALC'D AS THE AREA UNDER THE SHEAR DIAGRAM

$M_A = 4 \left(\dfrac{8445 + 6745}{2} \right) = 30,380$ '#

$d_A = 19.5 + \dfrac{7.5}{2} = 23.25$"

$S_A = \dfrac{8.75 \times 23.25^2}{6} = 788.3$ in³

$C_F = \sqrt[1/9]{\dfrac{12}{23.25}} = 0.93 \quad C_F > C_i$

$F'' = 1.25 \times .652 \times 1920 = 1564.8$ psi

$t_A = \dfrac{12 \times 30.380}{788.3} = 462.5$ psi ✓

$M_B = 8 \left(\dfrac{8445 + 5045}{2} \right) = 53,960$ '#

CLEAR SPAN = 44'-0" CANTILEVER = 6'-0"

SEASONED LUMBER $\quad K = 0.50$

LUMBER DESIGNATION 24-V8 DF/DF $C_D = 25\%$

$F_B = 2400$ psi $\quad F_V = 165$ psi $\quad E = 1.8 \times 10^6$ psi

WET CONDITION $E' = 0.833 \times 1.8 \times 10^6 = 1.5 \times 10^6$ psi

$E'' = 1.5 \times 10^6 - 1.645 \times 1.5 \times 10^6 \times 0.10 = 1,253,250$ psi

$F_B = 2400 \times 0.80 = 1920$ psi $\quad F_V = 165 \times 0.875 = 144.3$ psi

TOTAL LOAD = $16 \times 24 + BM = 425$ plf

DEAD LOAD = $16 \times 12 + BM = 240$ plf

TRY GLU LAM BM. 8 3/4" X 27"

19 LAMINATIONS $\quad$ DEPTH = 27" $\quad C_F = 0.91$

$A = 249.4$ in² $\quad I = 16880$ in⁴ $\quad S = 1184$ in³

$M = 83,904$ '# $\quad V1 = 8445$ # $\quad V2 = 10255$ #

$S_{REQ'D} = \dfrac{12 \times 83,904}{1.25 \times 1333.8} = 603.9$ in³

$A1_{REQ'D} = \dfrac{1.5 \times 8445}{1.25 \times .914 \times 144.3} = 76.8$ in²

$A2_{REQ'D} = \dfrac{1.5 \times 10,255}{1.25 \times .914 \times 144.3} = 93.3$ in²

CHECK SHEAR FOR END TAPER AT R1

CROSS SECTION AREA REQ'D = 76.8 in²

TOTAL DEPTH = 27.0" $\quad$ WIDTH 8.75"

TANGENT $= \dfrac{7.5}{8 \times 12} = 0.0781$

ANGLE $= 4.467°$

REF. AITC TABLE No. 5.13 $\quad C_i = 0.652$

$V_{ADJ} = 8445 - \left(\dfrac{19.5}{12} \right) 425 = 7754.4$ #

END TAPER O.K.

CASE 1

DESIGN LOADS:

LIGHT WEIGHT CONC.	=	13.7	#/sq ft
3/4" PLYWOOD	=	2.3	
FRAMING	=	4.4	
CEILING	=	2.8	
MISCELLANEOUS	=	1.0	
DEAD LOAD	=	24.2	
PARTITIONS	=	20.0	
LIVE LOAD - RESIDENCE	=	40.0	
TOTAL LOAD	=	84.2	#/sq ft

CLEAR SPAN = 17'-10"

SPACING = 16" oc

UNIFORM LOAD = (16/12) × 84.2 = 112. plf

UNSEASONED LUMBER K = 1

$$M = \frac{112 \times 17.83^2}{8} = 4450.7'\# \qquad S_{REQ'D} = \frac{12 \times 4450.7}{1450} = 36.8 \ in^3$$

$$V = \frac{112 \times 15.83}{2} = 886.5^\# \qquad A_{REQ'D} = \frac{1.5 \times 886.5}{95} = 14. \ in^2$$

$$ALLOW. \ \triangle = \frac{12 \times 17.83}{240} = 0.89 \ in. \qquad I_{REQ'D} = \frac{5 \times 112 \times 17.83^4 \times 1728}{384 \times 1.6 \times 10^6 \times .89} = 178.85 \ in^4$$

$$TRY \ 2 \ X \ 14's \ @ \ 16" \ oc \ (BF = 1.75 \ /sq \ ft) \qquad I = \frac{1.5 \times 13.5^3}{12} = 307.5 \ in^4$$

$$LIVE \ LOAD \ DEFL. \quad W = 1.33(20 + 40) = 80 \ plf \qquad \triangle = \frac{L}{360} = \frac{12 \times 17.83}{360} = 0.59 \ in.$$

$$\triangle = \frac{5 \times 80 \times 17.83^4 \times 1728}{384 \times 1.6 \times 10^6 \times 307.5} = 0.38 \ in < 0.59 \ in.$$

$$TOTAL \ LOAD \ DEFL. \qquad \triangle = \frac{5 \times 112 \times 17.83^4 \times 1728}{384 \times 1.6 \times 10^6 \times 307.5} = 0.52 \ in$$

CASE 2

CHECK 2 X 12's @ 12" oc SPACED AT 12" oc   UNIF. LOAD = 84 #/ft

$$M = \frac{84 \times 17.83^2}{8} = 23338.0'\# \qquad S_{REQ'D} = \frac{12 \times 3338.0}{1450} = 27.6 \ in^3$$

$$V = \frac{84 \times 15.83}{2} = 664.8^\# \qquad A_{REQ'D} = \frac{1.5 \times 664.8}{95} = 10.5 \ in^2$$

$$ALLOW. \ \triangle = \frac{12 \times 17.83}{240} = 0.89 \ in. \qquad I_{REQ'D} = \frac{5 \times 84 \times 17.83^4 \times 1728}{384 \times 1.6 \times 10^6 \times .89} = 133.9 \ in^4$$

$$TRY \ 2 \ X \ 12's \ @ \ 16" \ oc \ (BF = 2.0 \ /sq \ ft) \qquad I = \frac{1.5 \times 11.5^3}{12} = 190.1 \ in^4$$

$$LIVE \ LOAD \ DEFL. \quad W = (20 + 40) = 60 \ plf \qquad \triangle = \frac{L}{360} = \frac{12 \times 17.83}{360} = 0.59 \ in.$$

$$\triangle = \frac{5 \times 60 \times 17.83^4 \times 1728}{384 \times 1.6 \times 10^6 \times 190.1} = 0.35 \ in < 0.59 \ in.$$

$$TOTAL \ LOAD \ DEFL. \qquad \triangle = \frac{5 \times 84 \times 17.83^4 \times 1728}{384 \times 1.6 \times 10^6 \times 307.5} = 0..63 \ in$$

DESIGN AND CONSTRUCTION OF WOOD FRAMED BUILDINGS

RESIDENTIAL FLOOR JOIST DESIGN | EXAMPLE 13 SHT. S-1 of 1

CASE 3

DESIGN LOADS:

1" HARDWOOD FLR.	=	4.0 #/sq ft
3/4" PLYWOOD	=	2.3
FRAMING	=	4.4
CEILING	=	2.8
MISCELLANEOUS	=	1.0
DEAD LOAD	=	14.5
PARTITIONS	=	20.0
LIVE LOAD - RESIDENCE	=	40.0
TOTAL LOAD	=	74.5 #/sq ft

CLEAR SPAN = 17'-10"

SPACING = 16" oc

UNIF. LOAD = (16/12) × 74.5 = 99.3 SAY 100 plf

SEASONED LUMBER K = 0.50

$W_\triangle = 1.33\,(60 + .5 \times 14.5) = 89.4$ plf

$$M = \frac{100 \times 17.83^2}{8} = 3973.9\ '\#$$

$$S_{REQ'D} = \frac{12 \times 3973.9}{1450} = 32.9\ in^3$$

$$V = \frac{100 \times 15.83}{2} = 791.5\ \#$$

$$A_{REQ'D} = \frac{1.5 \times 791.5}{95} = 12.5\ in^2$$

$$\text{ALLOW. } \triangle = \frac{12 \times 17.83}{240} = 0.89\ in.$$

$$I_{REQ'D} = \frac{5 \times 89.4 \times 17.83^4 \times 1728}{384 \times 1.6 \times 10^6 \times .89} = 142.8\ in^4$$

TRY 2 X 12's @ 16" oc (BF = 1.50/sq ft)

$$I = \frac{1.5 \times 11.5^3}{12} = 190.1\ in^4$$

LIVE LOAD DEFL. W = 1.33(20 + 40) = 80 plf

$$\triangle = \frac{L}{360} = \frac{12 \times 17.83}{360} = 0.59\ in.$$

$$\triangle = \frac{5 \times 80 \times 17.83^4 \times 1728}{384 \times 1.6 \times 10^6 \times 307.5} = 0.38\ in < 0.59\ in.$$

TOTAL LOAD DEFL. $\triangle = \dfrac{5 \times 100 \times 17.83^4 \times 1728}{384 \times 1.6 \times 10^6 \times 307.5} = 0.46$ in

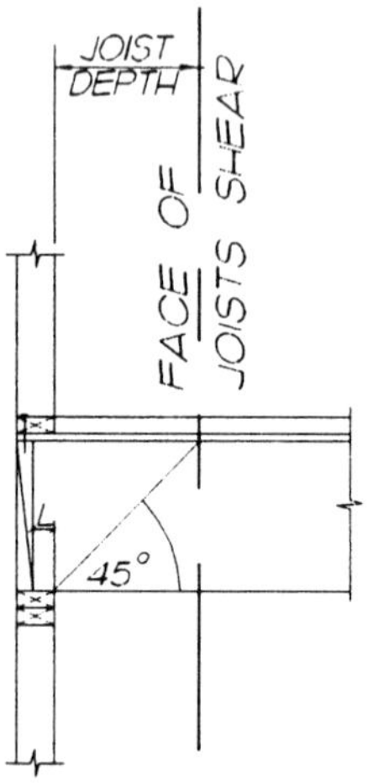

CASE 1 SHEAR CALCULATION

SHEAR = 1.33 X 84.2 X (17.83 - 2X1.0) = 886.5#

JOIST REACTION = 1.33 X 84.2 X 17.83 X 0.5 = 998.35 #

BEARING AREA:

L = 3.5 - 1.5 = 2" W = WIDTH OF JOIST

A = 2 X 1.5 = 3 sq in

$$\text{BEARING STRESS} = \frac{998.35}{3} = 332.78\ psi$$

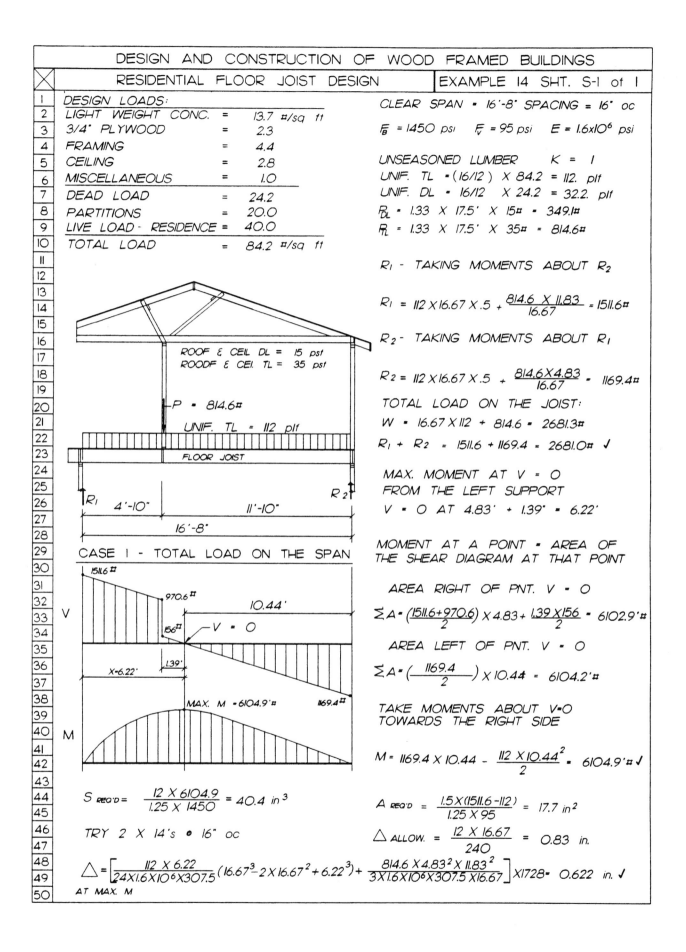

	DESIGN LOADS:
1	
2	LIGHT WEIGHT CONC. = 13.7 #/sq ft
3	3/4" PLYWOOD = 2.3
4	FRAMING = 4.4
5	CEILING = 2.8
6	MISCELLANEOUS = 1.0
7	DEAD LOAD = 24.2
8	PARTITIONS = 20.0
9	LIVE LOAD - RESIDENCE = 40.0
10	TOTAL LOAD = 84.2 #/sq ft

CLEAR SPAN = 16'-8" SPACING = 16" oc

$F_B = 1450$ psi $\quad F_V = 95$ psi $\quad E = 1.6 \times 10^6$ psi

UNSEASONED LUMBER $\quad K = 1$

UNIF. TL = (16/12) X 84.2 = 112. plf

UNIF. DL = 16/12 X 24.2 = 32.2. plf

P_{DL} = 1.33 X 17.5' X 15# = 349.1#

P_{TL} = 1.33 X 17.5' X 35# = 814.6#

R_1 - TAKING MOMENTS ABOUT R_2

$R_1 = 112 \times 16.67 \times .5 + \dfrac{814.6 \times 11.83}{16.67} = 1511.6\#$

R_2 - TAKING MOMENTS ABOUT R_1

$R_2 = 112 \times 16.67 \times .5 + \dfrac{814.6 \times 4.83}{16.67} = 1169.4\#$

TOTAL LOAD ON THE JOIST:

W = 16.67 X 112 + 814.6 = 2681.3#

$R_1 + R_2$ = 1511.6 + 1169.4 = 2681.0# ✓

ROOF & CEIL DL = 15 psf
ROODF & CEI. TL = 35 psf

P = 814.6#

UNIF. TL = 112 plf

FLOOR JOIST

R_1 4'-10" 11'-10" R_2

16'-8"

CASE 1 - TOTAL LOAD ON THE SPAN

MAX. MOMENT AT V = 0
FROM THE LEFT SUPPORT

V = 0 AT 4.83' + 1.39' = 6.22'

MOMENT AT A POINT = AREA OF
THE SHEAR DIAGRAM AT THAT POINT

AREA RIGHT OF PNT. V = 0

$\sum A = \dfrac{(1511.6+970.6)}{2} \times 4.83 + \dfrac{1.39 \times 156}{2} = 6102.9'\#$

AREA LEFT OF PNT. V = 0

$\sum A = \left(\dfrac{1169.4}{2}\right) \times 10.44 = 6104.2'\#$

TAKE MOMENTS ABOUT V=0
TOWARDS THE RIGHT SIDE

$M = 1169.4 \times 10.44 - \dfrac{112 \times 10.44^2}{2} = 6104.9'\#$ ✓

1511.6#
970.6#
10.44'
V
156# — V = 0
X=6.22' 1.39'
MAX. M = 6104.9'#   1169.4#
M

$S_{REQ'D} = \dfrac{12 \times 6104.9}{1.25 \times 1450} = 40.4$ in³

$A_{REQ'D} = \dfrac{1.5 \times (1511.6 - 112)}{1.25 \times 95} = 17.7$ in²

TRY 2 X 14's @ 16" oc

$\triangle_{ALLOW.} = \dfrac{12 \times 16.67}{240} = 0.83$ in.

$\triangle = \left[\dfrac{112 \times 6.22}{24 \times 1.6 \times 10^6 \times 307.5}(16.67^3 - 2 \times 16.67^2 + 6.22^3) + \dfrac{814.6 \times 4.83^2 \times 11.83^2}{3 \times 1.6 \times 10^6 \times 307.5 \times 16.67}\right] \times 1728 = 0.622$ in. ✓

AT MAX. M

CASE 1

DESIGN LOADS:

1" THICK CONCRETE	=	12.0 #/sq ft
1" MARBLE	=	15.0
1" PLYWOOD	=	2.5
FRAMING	=	4.5
PLASTER CEILING	=	8.0
MISCELLANEOUS	=	1.0
DEAD LOAD	=	43.0
PARTITIONS	=	20.0
LIVE LOAD - RESIDENCE =		40.0
TOTAL LOAD	=	103.0 #/sq ft

CLEAR SPAN = 16'-6"

$F_B = 1450$ psi $F_V = 95$ psi $E = 1.6 \times 10^6$ psi

SPACING = 12" oc

UNIFORM LOAD = 103.0 plf

DEFL. LOAD = $40 + 20 + .5 \times 43 = 81.5$ plf

SEASONED LUMBER $K = 0.50$

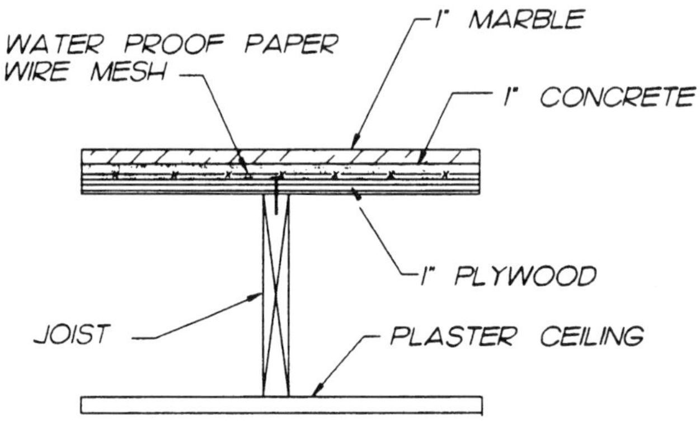

WATER PROOF PAPER
WIRE MESH
1" MARBLE
1" CONCRETE
1" PLYWOOD
JOIST
PLASTER CEILING

JOIST & FLOOR SECTION

$$M = \frac{112 \times 16.50^2}{8} = 3505.2\ '\# \qquad S_{REQ'D} = \frac{12 \times 3505.2}{1450} = 29.0\ in^3$$

$$V = \frac{112 \times 14.50}{2} = 746.8\ \# \qquad A_{REQ'D} = \frac{1.5 \times 746.8}{95} = 11.8\ in^2$$

$$\triangle_{ALLOW.} = \frac{12 \times 16.50}{360} = 0.55\ in. \qquad I_{REQ'D} = \frac{5 \times 81.5 \times 16.5^4 \times 1728}{384 \times 1.6 \times 10^6 \times .55} = 150.3\ in^4$$

TRY 2 X 12's @ 12" oc

$$\text{TOTAL LOAD DEFL.} \qquad \triangle = \frac{5 \times 103 \times 16.5^4 \times 1728}{384 \times 1.6 \times 10^6 \times 190.1} = 0.57\ in \quad + 2\% \quad \checkmark$$

USE 2 X 12's @ 12" oc

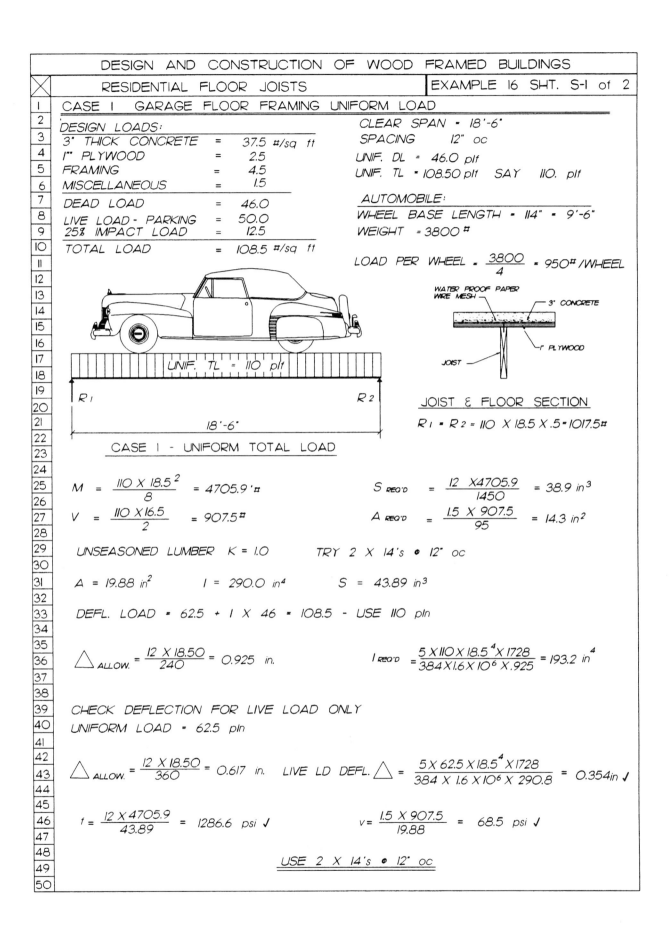

1	CASE 1 GARAGE FLOOR FRAMING UNIFORM LOAD
2	
3	DESIGN LOADS:
4	3" THICK CONCRETE = 37.5 #/sq ft
5	1" PLYWOOD = 2.5
6	FRAMING = 4.5
7	MISCELLANEOUS = 1.5

CLEAR SPAN = 18'-6"
SPACING 12" oc

UNIF. DL = 46.0 plf
UNIF. TL = 108.50 plf SAY 110. plf

DESIGN LOADS:
3" THICK CONCRETE = 37.5 #/sq ft
1" PLYWOOD = 2.5
FRAMING = 4.5
MISCELLANEOUS = 1.5

DEAD LOAD = 46.0
LIVE LOAD - PARKING = 50.0
25% IMPACT LOAD = 12.5

TOTAL LOAD = 108.5 #/sq ft

AUTOMOBILE:
WHEEL BASE LENGTH = 114" = 9'-6"
WEIGHT = 3800 #

$$LOAD \ PER \ WHEEL = \frac{3800}{4} = 950 \ \#/WHEEL$$

WATER PROOF PAPER
WIRE MESH
3" CONCRETE
1" PLYWOOD
JOIST

UNIF. TL = 110 plf

R_1 R_2

18'-6"

JOIST & FLOOR SECTION

$R_1 = R_2 = 110 \times 18.5 \times .5 = 1017.5 \#$

CASE 1 - UNIFORM TOTAL LOAD

$$M = \frac{110 \times 18.5^2}{8} = 4705.9 \ '\#$$

$$S_{REQ'D} = \frac{12 \times 4705.9}{1450} = 38.9 \ in^3$$

$$V = \frac{110 \times 16.5}{2} = 907.5 \#$$

$$A_{REQ'D} = \frac{1.5 \times 907.5}{95} = 14.3 \ in^2$$

UNSEASONED LUMBER K = 1.0   TRY 2 X 14's @ 12" oc

$A = 19.88 \ in^2$ $I = 290.0 \ in^4$ $S = 43.89 \ in^3$

DEFL. LOAD = 62.5 + 1 X 46 = 108.5 - USE 110 pln

$$\triangle_{ALLOW.} = \frac{12 \times 18.50}{240} = 0.925 \ in.$$

$$I_{REQ'D} = \frac{5 \times 110 \times 18.5^4 \times 1728}{384 \times 1.6 \times 10^6 \times .925} = 193.2 \ in^4$$

CHECK DEFLECTION FOR LIVE LOAD ONLY

UNIFORM LOAD = 62.5 pln

$$\triangle_{ALLOW.} = \frac{12 \times 18.50}{360} = 0.617 \ in.$$ LIVE LD DEFL. $$\triangle = \frac{5 \times 62.5 \times 18.5^4 \times 1728}{384 \times 1.6 \times 10^6 \times 290.8} = 0.354 in \checkmark$$

$$f = \frac{12 \times 4705.9}{43.89} = 1286.6 \ psi \checkmark$$ $$v = \frac{1.5 \times 907.5}{19.88} = 68.5 \ psi \checkmark$$

USE 2 X 14's @ 12" oc

CASE 2   DEAD LOAD PLUS WHEEL LOAD

DESIGN LOADS:

3" THICK CONCRETE	=	37.5 #/sq ft
1" PLYWOOD	=	2.5
FRAMING	=	4.5
MISCELLANEOUS	=	1.5
DEAD LOAD	=	46.0 #/sq ft

CLEAR SPAN = 18'-6"
SPACING = 12" oc
UNIF. DL = 46 plf
AUTOMOBILE:
WHEEL BASE LENGTH = 114" = 9'-6"
=
LOAD / WHEEL = 950 #

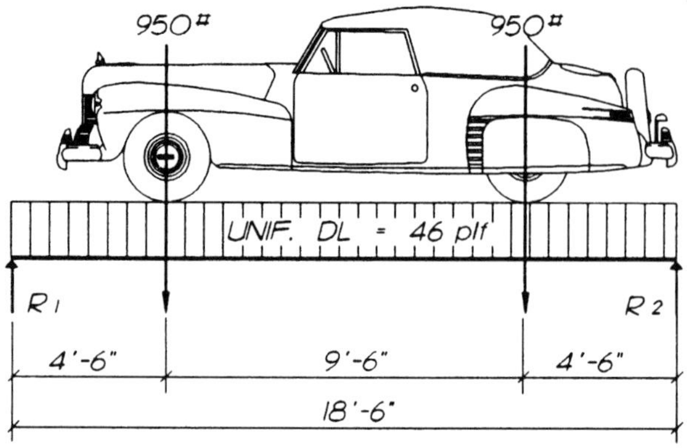

$R_1 = R_2 = 18.5 \times 46 \times .5 + 950 = 1375.5$ #

MAXIMUM MOM. OCCURS AT MIDSPAN

M. MAX = AREA OF SHEAR DIAGRAM

950#   950#

UNIF. DL = 46 plf

R1   R2

4'-6"   9'-6"   4'-6"

18'-6"

AREA TOWARDS LEFT SIDE:

$A = \left(\dfrac{1375.5 + 1168.5}{2}\right) \times 4.5 + \dfrac{218.5 \times 4.75}{2}$

AREA = 6242.9'#

AREA = MAX. MOMENT, CHECK BY TAKING MOMENTS AT THE MIDSPAN TOWARDS THE RT. SIDE

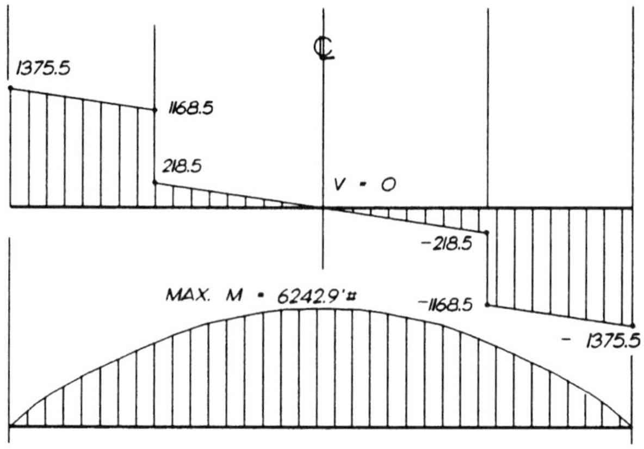

CASE 2 -   UNIF. DEAD LOAD + WHEEL LOADS

1375.5

1168.5

218.5

v = 0

−218.5

MAX. M = 6242.9'#   −1168.5

− 1375.5

$M = 1375.5 \times 9.25 - \dfrac{46 \times 9.25^2}{2} - 950 \times 4.75$

$M = 12723.4 - 1967.9 - 4512.5 = 6242.9'$# ✓

$V = 1375.5 - 46 = 1329.5$ #

UNSEASONED LUMBER   K = 1.0

$A = 19.88$ in^2 $I = 290.8$ in^4

$S = 43.89$ in^3

$S_{REQ'D} = \dfrac{12 \times 6242.9}{1450} = 41.67$ in^3

$A_{REQ'D} = \dfrac{1.5 \times 1329.5}{95} = 21.0$ in^2

$\triangle_{ALLOW.} = \dfrac{12 \times 18.50}{240} = 0.925$ in.

$\triangle = \dfrac{5 \times 46 \times 18.5^4 \times 1728}{384 \times 1.6 \times 10^6 \times 290.8} + \dfrac{950 \times 4.5 \times (3 \times 18.5^2 - 4 \times 4.5^2) \times 1728}{24 \times 1.6 \times 10^6 \times 290.8} = 0.261 + 0.626 = 0.887$ in ✓

$f = \dfrac{12 \times 4105.4}{43.89} = 1122.5$ psi ✓ $v = \dfrac{1.5 \times 854.5}{19.88} = 64.5$ psi ✓

USE 2 X 14's @ 12" oc

CASE 1 TOTAL LOAD ON SPAN — DEAD LOAD ON CANTILEVER

DESIGN LOADS — JOIST SPAN:

LIGHT WEIGHT CONC.	=	13.7 #/sq ft
3/4" PLYWOOD	=	2.3
FRAMING	=	4.4
CEILING	=	2.8
MISCELLANEOUS	=	1.0
DEAD LOAD	=	24.2
PARTITIONS	=	20.0
LIVE LOAD - RESIDENCE	=	40.0
TOTAL LOAD	=	84.2 #/sq ft

DESIGN LOADS — BALCONY CANTILEVER:

3/4" PLYWOOD	=	2.3
FRAMING	=	4.4
SOFFIT	=	8.0
MISCELLANEOUS	=	1.3
DEAD LOAD	=	16.0
LIVE LOAD - RES. BALC.	=	60.0
TOTAL LOAD	=	76.0 #/sq ft

CLEAR SPAN = 17'-4"

SPACING = 16" oc

TOTAL LOAD = (16/12) X 84.2 = 112. plf

DEAD LOAD = (16/12) X 16 = 21.3 SAY 22 plf

R_2 - CALC. MOMENTS ABOUT R_1

$$R_2 = \left(\frac{22 \times 5.5 \times 20.08 + 17.33 \times 112 \times 8.68}{17.33}\right)$$

$R_2 = 1110.7$ #

LOAD ON THE BEAM = 17.33 X 112 + 5.5 X 22
LOAD ON THE BEAM = 2062.0 #

$R_1 = 2062.0$ # $- 1110.7$ # $= 951.3$ SAY 952 #
MAX MOM. AT 952/112 = 8.50' FROM R_1

CALC. MOMENTS TOWARD THE LEFT

$$M = 8.5 \times 952 - \frac{112 \times 8.5^2}{2} = 4046 \text{'\#}$$

AREA OF SHEAR TOWARD LEFT SIDE

$$AREA = \frac{8.50 \times 952}{2} = 4046 \text{'\#}$$

$V_{MAX.} = 989.3 - 112 = 877.3$ #

CANTILEVER $M_{DEAD\ LD.} = -\frac{22 \times 5.5^2}{2} = -332.8$ '#

UNSEASONED LUMBER $\kappa = 1.0$

TRY 2 X 12's @ 16" oc $A = 16.88$ in^2 $I = 178.0$ in^4 $S = 31.64$ in^3

$f = \frac{12 \times 4046}{31.64} = 1534.5$ psi (+6%) $v = \frac{1.5 \times 877.3}{16.88} = 78.0$ psi ✓ $\triangle_{ALLOW.} = \frac{12 \times 17.33}{240} = 0.87$ in.

$$\triangle = \frac{112 \times 8.5 \times 1728}{24 \times 1.6 \times 10^6 \times 178} \times (17.33^3 - 2 \times 17.33 \times 8.5^2 + 8.5^3) = 0.80 \text{ in } ✓$$

$\triangle_{ALLOW.} = \frac{12 \times 17.33}{360} = 0.578$ in. $W_\triangle = 1.33 \times 60 = 90$ plf

$$\triangle = \frac{112 \times 8.5 \times 1728}{24 \times 1.6 \times 10^6 \times 178} \times (17.33^3 - 2 \times 17.33 \times 8.5^2 + 8.5^3) = 0.64 \text{ in } \text{TOO HIGH}$$

CASE 2 - TOTAL LOAD ON SPAN AND CANTILEVER

DESIGN LOADS - JOIST SPAN:

LIGHT WEIGHT CONC.	=	13.7 #/sq ft
3/4" PLYWOOD	=	2.3
FRAMING	=	4.4
CEILING	=	2.8
MISCELLANEOUS	=	1.0
DEAD LOAD	=	24.2
PARTITIONS	=	20.0
LIVE LOAD - RESIDENCE	=	40.0
TOTAL LOAD	=	84.2 #/sq ft

DESIGN LOADS - BALCONY CANTILEVER:

3/4" PLYWOOD	=	2.3
FRAMING	=	4.4
SOFFIT	=	8.0
MISCELLANEOUS	=	1.3
DEAD LOAD	=	16.0
LIVE LOAD - RES. BALC.	=	60.0
TOTAL LOAD	=	76.0 #/sq ft

CLEAR SPAN = 17'-4"
BALCONY CANTILEVER = 5'-6"
SPACING = 16" oc

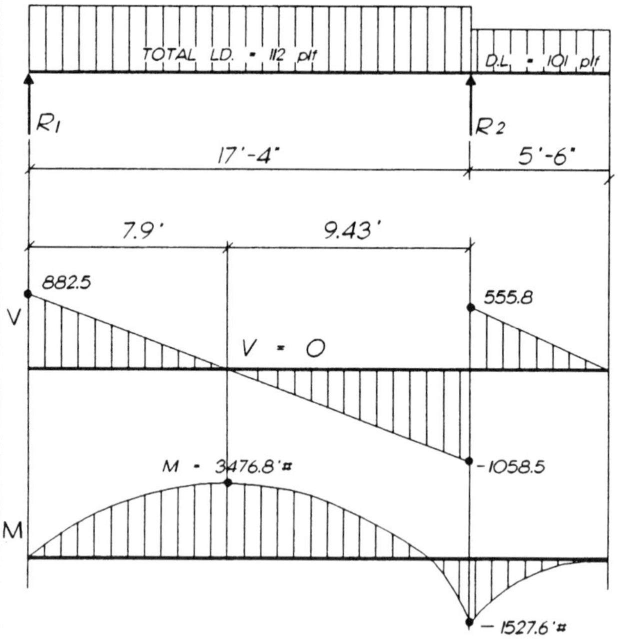

TOTAL LD SPAN = (16/12) X 84.2 = 112. plf

TOTAL LD CANT. = 16/12) X 76 = 101. plf

R2 - TAKE MOMENTS ABOUT R1

$$R_2 = \frac{(101 \times 5.5 \times 20.08 + 17.33 \times 112 \times 8.67)}{17.33}$$

R2 = 1614.3#

LOAD ON THE BEAM = 17.33 X 112 + 5.5 X 101
LOAD ON THE BEAM = 2496.8#

R1 = 2062.0# - 1110.7# = 882.5#

MAX. MOM AT 882.5/112 = 7.9' FROM R1

TAKING MOM. TOWARD THE LEFT @ V=0

$$M = 882.5 \times 7.9 - \frac{112 \times 7.9^2}{2} = = 3476.8'\#$$

AREA OF SHEAR TOWARD LEFT SIDE

$$AREA = \frac{882.5 \times 7.9}{2} = 3485.8'\# \approx 3476.8'\#$$

V MAX. = 1058.5 - 112 = 946.5#

CANTILEVER $M_{TOTAL\ LD.} = \frac{101 \times 5.5^2}{2} = -1527.6'\#$

UNSEASONED LUMBER K = 1.0
TRY 2 X 12's @ 16" oc   A = 16.88 in²   I = 178.0 in⁴   S = 31.64 in³

$f = \frac{12 \times 3476.7}{31.64} = 1318.6$ psi ✓ $v = \frac{1.5 \times 1058.5}{16.88} = 94.1$ psi ✓   △ ALLOW. $= \frac{12 \times 17.33}{240} = 0.87$ in.

$\triangle = \frac{112 \times 7.9 \times 1728}{24 \times 1.6 \times 10^6 \times 178} \times (17.33^3 - 2 \times 17.33 \times 7.9^2 + 7.9^3) = 0.79$ in ✓

△ ALLOW. $= \frac{12 \times 17.33}{360} = 0.578$ in. $W_\triangle = 1.33 \times 60 = 90$ plf

△ ALLOW. = (90/112) X .79 = 0.635 in.   TOO HIGH SPACING AT 16" oc

CASE 3 - DEAD LOAD ON SPAN AND TOTAL LOAD ON CANTILEVER

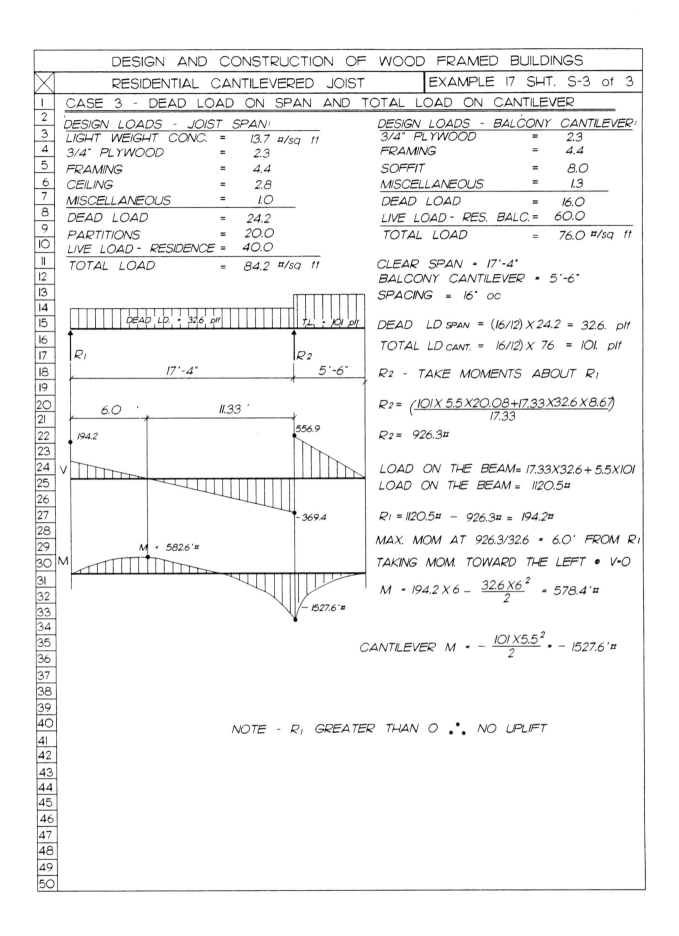

DESIGN LOADS - JOIST SPAN:

LIGHT WEIGHT CONC.	=	13.7 #/sq ft
3/4" PLYWOOD	=	2.3
FRAMING	=	4.4
CEILING	=	2.8
MISCELLANEOUS	=	1.0
DEAD LOAD	=	24.2
PARTITIONS	=	20.0
LIVE LOAD - RESIDENCE =		40.0
TOTAL LOAD	=	84.2 #/sq ft

DESIGN LOADS - BALCONY CANTILEVER:

3/4" PLYWOOD	=	2.3
FRAMING	=	4.4
SOFFIT	=	8.0
MISCELLANEOUS	=	1.3
DEAD LOAD	=	16.0
LIVE LOAD - RES. BALC. =		60.0
TOTAL LOAD	=	76.0 #/sq ft

CLEAR SPAN = 17'-4"
BALCONY CANTILEVER = 5'-6"
SPACING = 16" oc

DEAD LD SPAN = (16/12) X 24.2 = 32.6. plf

TOTAL LD CANT. = 16/12 X 76 = 101. plf

R_2 - TAKE MOMENTS ABOUT R_1

$$R_2 = \frac{(101 \times 5.5 \times 20.08 + 17.33 \times 32.6 \times 8.67)}{17.33}$$

$R_2 = 926.3\#$

LOAD ON THE BEAM = 17.33 X 32.6 + 5.5 X 101
LOAD ON THE BEAM = 1120.5#

$R_1 = 1120.5\# - 926.3\# = 194.2\#$

MAX. MOM AT 926.3/32.6 = 6.0' FROM R_1

TAKING MOM. TOWARD THE LEFT @ V=0

$$M = 194.2 \times 6 - \frac{32.6 \times 6^2}{2} = 578.4'\#$$

$$\text{CANTILEVER } M = -\frac{101 \times 5.5^2}{2} = -1527.6'\#$$

NOTE - R_1 GREATER THAN 0 ∴ NO UPLIFT

CASE 1

DESIGN LOADS:

3/4" PLYWOOD	=	2.3 #/sq ft
FRAMING	=	4.4
MISCELLANEOUS	=	1.0
DEAD LOAD	=	7.7
PARTITIONS	=	20.0
LIVE LOAD - RESIDENCE =		40.0
TOTAL LOAD	=	67.7 #/sq ft

CLEAR SPAN = 6'-6"

SPACING = 16" oc

UNIFORM LOAD = (16/12) ×67.7 = 90.0. plf

UNSEASONED LUMBER   K = 1.0

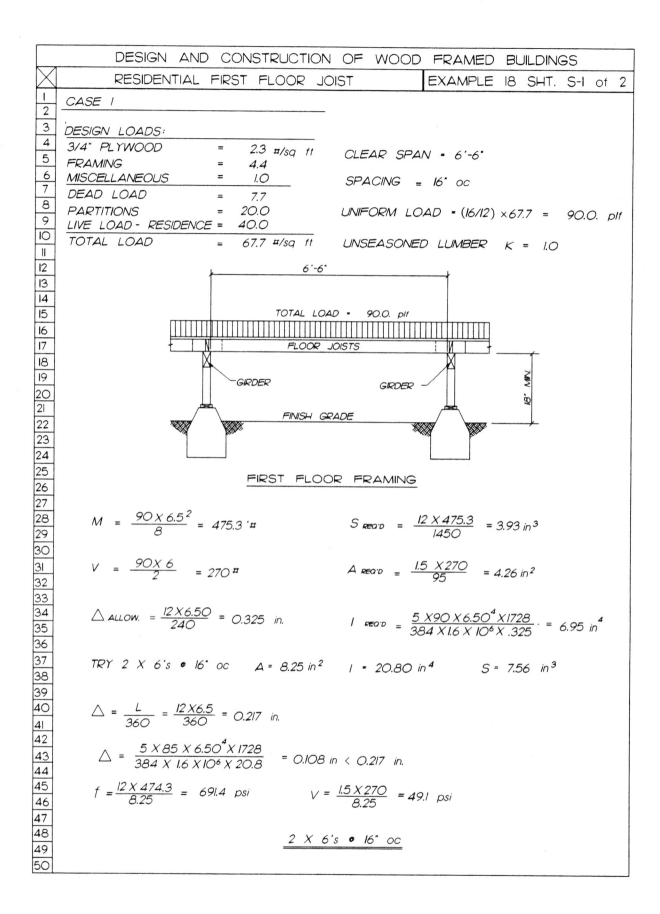

FIRST FLOOR FRAMING

$$M = \frac{90 \times 6.5^2}{8} = 475.3 \text{ '\#}$$

$$S_{REQ'D} = \frac{12 \times 475.3}{1450} = 3.93 \text{ in}^3$$

$$V = \frac{90 \times 6}{2} = 270 \text{\#}$$

$$A_{REQ'D} = \frac{1.5 \times 270}{95} = 4.26 \text{ in}^2$$

$$\triangle_{ALLOW.} = \frac{12 \times 6.50}{240} = 0.325 \text{ in.}$$

$$I_{REQ'D} = \frac{5 \times 90 \times 6.50^4 \times 1728}{384 \times 1.6 \times 10^6 \times .325} = 6.95 \text{ in}^4$$

TRY 2 X 6's @ 16" oc $A = 8.25 \text{ in}^2$ $I = 20.80 \text{ in}^4$ $S = 7.56 \text{ in}^3$

$$\triangle = \frac{L}{360} = \frac{12 \times 6.5}{360} = 0.217 \text{ in.}$$

$$\triangle = \frac{5 \times 85 \times 6.50^4 \times 1728}{384 \times 1.6 \times 10^6 \times 20.8} = 0.108 \text{ in} < 0.217 \text{ in.}$$

$$f = \frac{12 \times 474.3}{8.25} = 691.4 \text{ psi}$$

$$V = \frac{1.5 \times 270}{8.25} = 49.1 \text{ psi}$$

2 X 6's @ 16" oc

CASE 2

DESIGN LOADS:

3/4" PLYWOOD	=	2.3	#/sq ft
FRAMING	=	4.4	
MISCELLANEOUS	=	1.0	
DEAD LOAD	=	7.7	
PARTITIONS	=	20.0	
LIVE LOAD - RESIDENCE =	40.0	
TOTAL LOAD	=	67.7	#/sq ft

CLEAR SPAN = 6'-0"

SPACING = 6'-6" oc

UNIFORM LOAD = 6.5 X 67.7 = 440.0. plf

UNSEASONED LUMBER K = 1.0

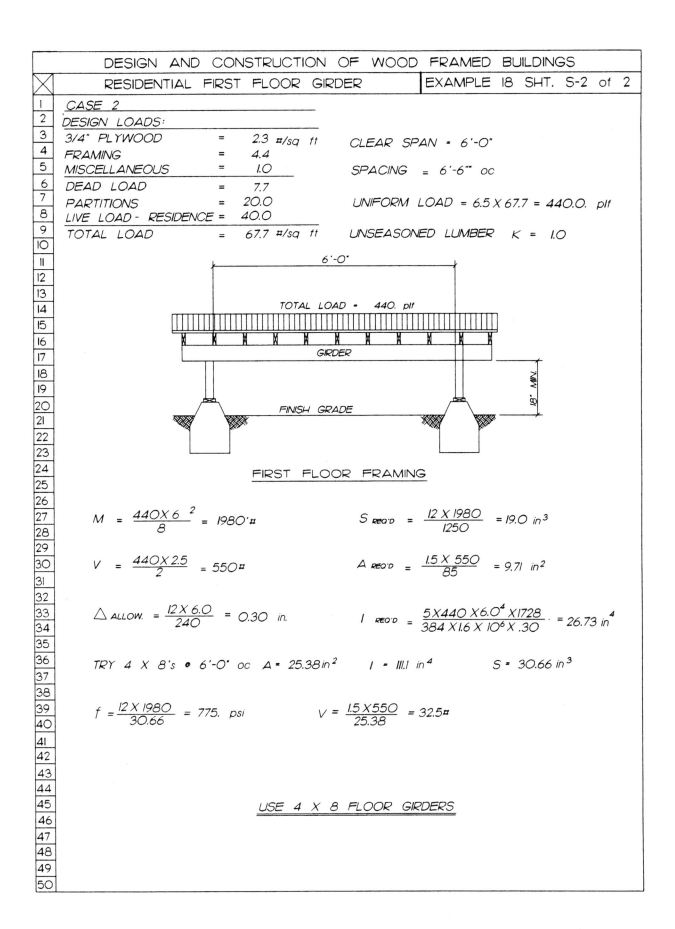

6'-0"

TOTAL LOAD = 440. plf

GIRDER

FINISH GRADE

18" MIN.

FIRST FLOOR FRAMING

$$M = \frac{440 \times 6^2}{8} = 1980' \#$$

$$S_{REQ'D} = \frac{12 \times 1980}{1250} = 19.0 \ in^3$$

$$V = \frac{440 \times 2.5}{2} = 550 \#$$

$$A_{REQ'D} = \frac{1.5 \times 550}{85} = 9.71 \ in^2$$

$$\triangle_{ALLOW.} = \frac{12 \times 6.0}{240} = 0.30 \ in.$$

$$I_{REQ'D} = \frac{5 \times 440 \times 6.0^4 \times 1728}{384 \times 1.6 \times 10^6 \times .30} = 26.73 \ in^4$$

TRY 4 X 8's @ 6'-0" oc A = 25.38 in^2 I = 111.1 in^4 S = 30.66 in^3

$$f = \frac{12 \times 1980}{30.66} = 775. \ psi$$

$$V = \frac{1.5 \times 550}{25.38} = 32.5 \#$$

USE 4 X 8 FLOOR GIRDERS

CASE 1

DESIGN LOADS:

LIGHT WEIGHT CONC.	=	13.7 #/sq ft
3/4" PLYWOOD	=	2.3
FRAMING	=	4.4
CEILING	=	2.8
MISCELLANEOUS	=	1.0
DEAD LOAD	=	24.2
PARTITIONS	=	20.0
LIVE LOAD - OFFICE	=	50.0
TOTAL LOAD	=	94.2 #/sq ft

CLEAR SPAN = 17'-6"

SPACING = 16" oc

UNIFORM LOAD = $(16/12) \times 94.2 = 126.$ plf

UNSEASONED LUMBER K = 1.0

CONCENTRATED LOAD = 2000 #/2.5 sq ft

$R_1 = R_2 = 126 \times 17.5 \times .5 = 1102.5$ #

$W_\triangle = 1.33 \times (70 + 24.2) = 126.$ plf

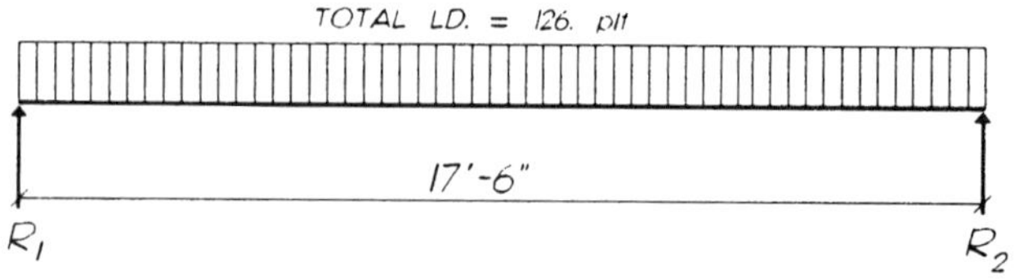

TOTAL LD. = 126. plf

17'-6"

R_1 R_2

$$M = \frac{126 \times 17.50^2}{8} = 4823.4 \ '\#$$

$$S_{REQ'D} = \frac{12 \times 4823.4}{1450} = 39.9 \ in^3$$

$$V = \frac{126 \times 15.50}{2} = 976.5 \ \#$$

$$A_{REQ'D} = \frac{1.5 \times 976.5}{95} = 15.4 \ in^2$$

$$ALLOW. \ \triangle = \frac{12 \times 17.50}{240} = 0.88 \ in.$$

$$I_{REQ'D} = \frac{5 \times 95.9 \times 17.5^4 \times 1728}{384 \times 1.6 \times 10^6 \times .88} = 188.84 \ in^4$$

TRY 2 X 14's @ 16" oc

$A = 19.88 \ in.^2$ $I = 290.0 \ in.^4$ $S = 43.89 \ in.^3$

LIVE LOAD DEFL. $W = 1.33 \times (20 + 50) = 93$ plf $\triangle = \frac{L}{360} = \frac{12 \times 17.50}{360} = 0.58$ in.

$$\triangle = \frac{5 \times 93 \times 17.5^4 \times 1728}{384 \times 1.6 \times 10^6 \times 290.0} = 0.423 \ in < 0.58 \ in.$$

TOTAL LOAD DEFL. $\triangle = \dfrac{5 \times 126 \times 17.5^4 \times 1728}{384 \times 1.6 \times 10^6 \times 290.0} = 0.57$ in

CASE 2

CLEAR SPAN = 17'-6"   SPACING = 16" oc   UNSEASONED LUMBER   K = 1.0

W DEAD LD = (16/12) × 24.2 = 32.2 plf   CONCENTRATED LOAD = 2000 #/2.5 sq ft

CONVERT CONCENTRATED LOAD TO PARTIAL UNIFORM LOAD

W CONCENTRATED LOAD = (12/16) × (2000 / 2.5^2) = 426. plf

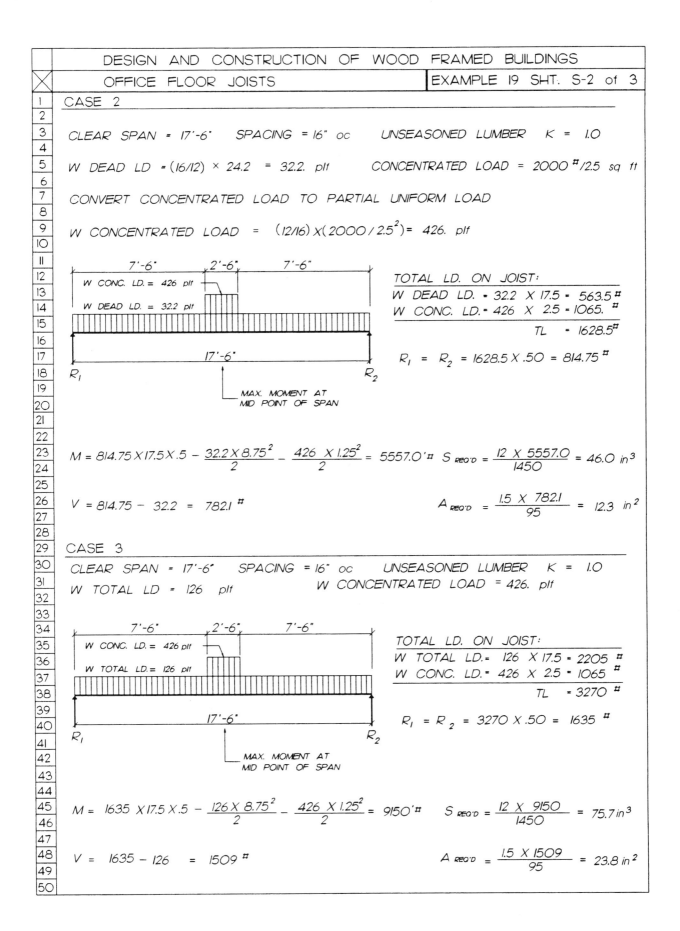

TOTAL LD. ON JOIST:
W DEAD LD. = 32.2 X 17.5 = 563.5 #
W CONC. LD. = 426 X 2.5 = 1065. #
                              TL = 1628.5 #

$R_1 = R_2$ = 1628.5 X .50 = 814.75 #

$M = 814.75 \times 17.5 \times .5 - \dfrac{32.2 \times 8.75^2}{2} - \dfrac{426 \times 1.25^2}{2} = 5557.0\text{'}\#$ $S_{REQ'D} = \dfrac{12 \times 5557.0}{1450} = 46.0\ in^3$

$V = 814.75 - 32.2 = 782.1\ \#$ $A_{REQ'D} = \dfrac{1.5 \times 782.1}{95} = 12.3\ in^2$

CASE 3

CLEAR SPAN = 17'-6"   SPACING = 16" oc   UNSEASONED LUMBER   K = 1.0

W TOTAL LD = 126 plf   W CONCENTRATED LOAD = 426. plf

TOTAL LD. ON JOIST:
W TOTAL LD. = 126 X 17.5 = 2205 #
W CONC. LD. = 426 X 2.5 = 1065. #
                              TL = 3270 #

$R_1 = R_2$ = 3270 X .50 = 1635 #

$M = 1635 \times 17.5 \times .5 - \dfrac{126 \times 8.75^2}{2} - \dfrac{426 \times 1.25^2}{2} = 9150\text{'}\#$ $S_{REQ'D} = \dfrac{12 \times 9150}{1450} = 75.7\ in^3$

$V = 1635 - 126 = 1509\ \#$ $A_{REQ'D} = \dfrac{1.5 \times 1509}{95} = 23.8\ in^2$

CASE 4

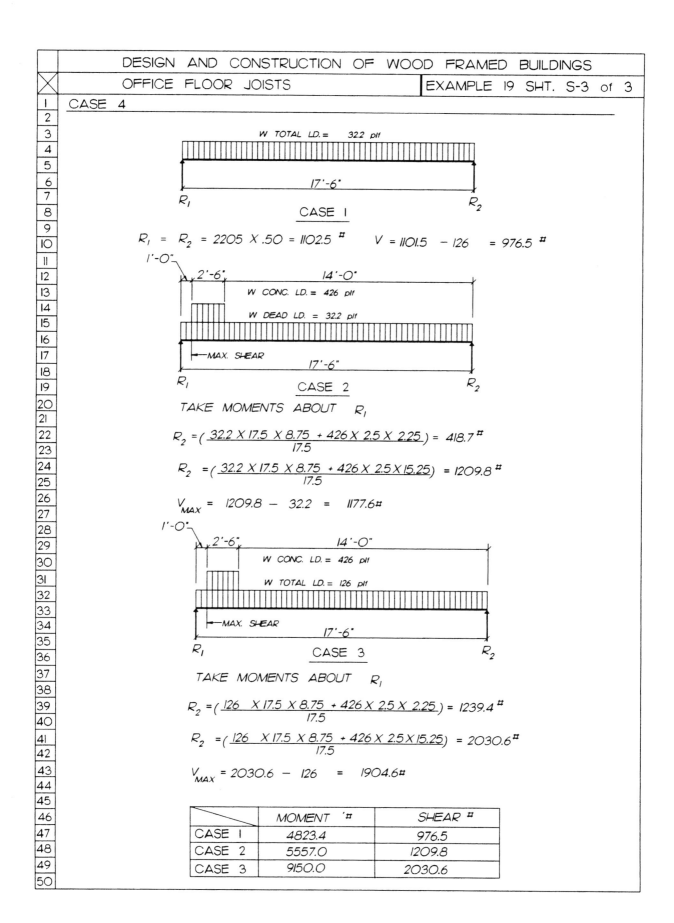

CASE 1

$R_1 = R_2 = 2205 \times .50 = 1102.5^{\#}$ $V = 1101.5 - 126 = 976.5^{\#}$

CASE 2

TAKE MOMENTS ABOUT R_1

$R_2 = \left(\dfrac{32.2 \times 17.5 \times 8.75 + 426 \times 2.5 \times 2.25}{17.5} \right) = 418.7^{\#}$

$R_2 = \left(\dfrac{32.2 \times 17.5 \times 8.75 + 426 \times 2.5 \times 15.25}{17.5} \right) = 1209.8^{\#}$

$V_{MAX} = 1209.8 - 32.2 = 1177.6^{\#}$

CASE 3

TAKE MOMENTS ABOUT R_1

$R_2 = \left(\dfrac{126 \times 17.5 \times 8.75 + 426 \times 2.5 \times 2.25}{17.5} \right) = 1239.4^{\#}$

$R_2 = \left(\dfrac{126 \times 17.5 \times 8.75 + 426 \times 2.5 \times 15.25}{17.5} \right) = 2030.6^{\#}$

$V_{MAX} = 2030.6 - 126 = 1904.6^{\#}$

	MOMENT '$^{\#}$	SHEAR $^{\#}$
CASE 1	4823.4	976.5
CASE 2	5557.0	1209.8
CASE 3	9150.0	2030.6

CASE   No. 1

DETERMINE THE REQUIRED SIZE OF A FLOOR JOIST FOR AN OFFICE FLOOR
CLEAR SPAN = 17'-8"   SPACING = 16" oc

DESIGN LOADS

1.5" LT. WT. CONC.	= 13.0 psf	ALLOWABLE BENDING STRESS	= 1450 psi
3/4" PLYWOOD	= 2.3	ALLOWABLE SHEAR STRESS	= 95 psi
FRAMING	= 3.9	MODULUS OF ELASTICITY - E	= 1.6 x 10^6 psi
CEILING	= 2.8		
MISCELLANEOUS	= 1.0		

UNIFORM LOAD $= \left(\dfrac{16}{12}\right) \times 93 = 126.7$ SAY 124 plf

DEAD LOAD	= 23.0 psf	
PARTITIONS	= 20.0	
LIVE LOAD	= 50.0	
TOTAL LOAD	= 93.0 psf	

CONCENTRATED LD AT MIDSPAN $= \dfrac{2000}{2.5^2} = 320$ psf

ACTUAL CONC. LD. = 320 x 1.33 x 2.5 = 1064#

$M = \dfrac{124 \times 17.67^2}{8} + \dfrac{1064 \times 17.67}{4} = 9539.8 '#$ SECTION MODULUS REQ'D. $= \dfrac{12 \times 9539.8}{1450} = 78.95$ in.^{3}

$V = \dfrac{124 \times 17.67}{2} + \dfrac{1064}{2} = 1627.5#$ CROSS SECTION AREA REQ'D. $= \dfrac{1.5 \times 1627.5}{95} = 17.13$ in.^{2}

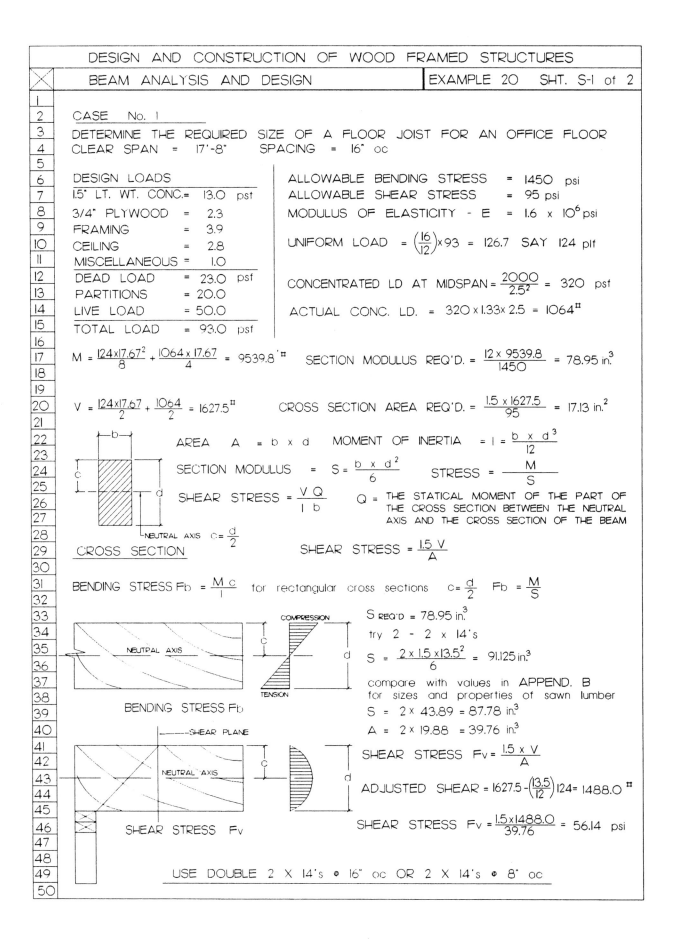

AREA   A = b x d   MOMENT OF INERTIA $= I = \dfrac{b \times d^3}{12}$

SECTION MODULUS $= S = \dfrac{b \times d^2}{6}$ STRESS $= \dfrac{M}{S}$

SHEAR STRESS $= \dfrac{V Q}{I b}$ Q = THE STATICAL MOMENT OF THE PART OF THE CROSS SECTION BETWEEN THE NEUTRAL AXIS AND THE CROSS SECTION OF THE BEAM

NEUTRAL AXIS c = $\dfrac{d}{2}$

CROSS SECTION   SHEAR STRESS $= \dfrac{1.5 V}{A}$

BENDING STRESS Fb $= \dfrac{M c}{I}$ for rectangular cross sections   c = $\dfrac{d}{2}$ Fb $= \dfrac{M}{S}$

COMPRESSION

NEUTRAL AXIS

TENSION

BENDING STRESS Fb

S REQ'D = 78.95 in.^{3}

try 2 - 2 x 14's

$S = \dfrac{2 \times 1.5 \times 13.5^2}{6} = 91.125$ in.^{3}

compare with values in APPEND. B
for sizes and properties of sawn lumber
S = 2 x 43.89 = 87.78 in.^{3}
A = 2 x 19.88 = 39.76 in.^{3}

SHEAR PLANE

NEUTRAL AXIS

SHEAR STRESS Fv

SHEAR STRESS Fv $= \dfrac{1.5 \times V}{A}$

ADJUSTED SHEAR $= 1627.5 - \left(\dfrac{13.5}{12}\right) 124 = 1488.0$ #

SHEAR STRESS Fv $= \dfrac{1.5 \times 1488.0}{39.76} = 56.14$ psi

USE DOUBLE 2 X 14's @ 16" oc OR 2 X 14's @ 8" oc

CASE No. 2

INVESTIGATE THE VERTICAL DEFLECTION OF THE FLOOR JOISTS DESIGNED IN EXAMPLE I - ALL GIVEN AND CALCULATED DATA TO REMAIN THE SAME

FLOOR JOISTS ARE DOUBLE 2 X 14's @ 16" oc   SPAN = 17'-8"   SEASONED LUMBER

$I = 2 \times 290.0 = 580.0 \, in.^4$ $E = 1.7 \times 10^6$ $K = 1$

TOTAL UNIFORM LOAD = 124 plf   UNIFORM LIVE LOAD = $1.33 \times 70 = 93.1$ plf

CONCENTRATED LOAD = $1064^{\#}$

ALLOWABLE LIVE LOAD DEFLECTION = $\dfrac{12 \times 17.67}{360}$ = 0.59 in.

ALLOWABLE TOTAL LOAD DEFLECTION = $\dfrac{12 \times 17.67}{240}$ = 0.88 in.

$$\triangle_{MAX.} = \frac{5WL}{384EI} + \frac{PL^3}{48EI}$$

$$\triangle_{LL.} = \frac{5 \times 93.1 \times 17.67^4 \times 1728}{384 \times 1.7 \times 10^6 \times 580} + \frac{1064 \times 17.67^3 \times 1728}{48 \times 1.7 \times 10^6 \times 580} = 0.203 + 0.228 = 0.431 \text{ in. } \checkmark$$

$$\triangle_{TL.} = \frac{5 \times 124 \times 17.67^4 \times 1728}{384 \times 1.7 \times 10^6 \times 580} + \frac{1064 \times 17.67^3 \times 1728}{48 \times 1.7 \times 10^6 \times 580} = 0.271 + 0.215 = 0.486 \text{ in. } \checkmark$$

CASE No. 3

CHECK FLOOR JOISTS DESIGNED IN EXAMPLE No. I FOR GLUED LAMINATED JOISTS F_b = 2400 psi F_v = 165 psi   MODULUS OF ELASTICITY = 1.8×10^6

GLUED LAMINATED LUMBER COMBINATION SYMBOL 24FE6

BENDING MOMENT = $9539.8^{'\#}$ ADJUSTED SHEAR = $1488^{\#}$

SECTION MOD. REQ'D. = $\dfrac{12 \times 9539.8}{2400}$ = 47.7 $in.^3$

CROSS SECTION AREA REQ'D = $\dfrac{1.5 \times 1488}{165}$ = 13.5 in^2

CHECK GLUED LAMINATED JOIST 2 1/8" X 15 I = 597.7 in^4

$$\triangle_{LL.} = \frac{5 \times 93.1 \times 17.67^4 \times 1728}{384 \times 1.8 \times 10^6 \times 597.7} + \frac{1064 \times 17.67^3 \times 1728}{48 \times 1.8 \times 10^6 \times 597.7} = 0.190 + 0.196 = 0.386 \text{ in. } \checkmark$$

$$\triangle_{TL.} = \frac{5 \times 124 \times 17.67^4 \times 1728}{384 \times 1.8 \times 10^6 \times 597.7} + \frac{1064 \times 17.67^3 \times 1728}{48 \times 1.8 \times 10^6 \times 597.7} = 0.253 + 0.196 = 0.449 \text{ in. } \checkmark$$

USE GLU LAM JOIST 2 1/8" X 15" @ 16" oc

CASE No. 1

DESIGN A ROOF BEAM   SPAN = 38'-0   TRIBUTARY WIDTH = 20'-0"

GLUED LAMINATED COMBINATION SYMBOL 24EI   MOD. ELASTICITY = 1.8×10^6

F_s = 2400 psi F_v = 165 psi   TRIBUTARY AREA = 38 x 20 = 760 sq. ft.

LIVE LOAD REDUCTION:

REF. UBC TABLE No. 23-C

METHOD 1 - LIVE LOAD = 12psf

METHOD 2 - % REDUCTION   R = r(A - 150) =   0.08(760 - 150) = 56.8 % LIMIT = 40%

LIVE LOAD = 20 X (1 - 0.4) = 12 psf ✓

ROOF LOADS

ROOFING & GRAVEL	=	5.60 psf
1/2" THICK PLYWOOD	=	1.50
RAFTERS (2X8's @ 16)	=	2.20
INSULATION	=	0.20
SPRINKLERS	=	5.20
ELECTRICAL	=	0.50
MISCELLANEOUS	=	1.00
DEAD LOAD	=	16.20
LIVE LOAD	=	12.00
TOTAL LOAD	=	28.20 psf

UNIFORM TOTAL LOAD = 20 x 28.2 + 30 = 594 plf

UNIFORM DEAD LOAD = 20 x 16.2 + 30 = 354 plf

$$M = \frac{594 \times 38^2}{8} = 107217 \text{ '}^{\#}$$

estimated depth of beam = 24"

$$V = \frac{(38 - 2 \times 2)594}{2} = 10098 ^{\#}$$

REF. UBC

2504.4 - ALLOW. INCREASE FOR LOAD DURATION = 25%

2504.5 SIZE FACTOR ADJUSTMENT FOR GLU LAM BEAMS

$C_F = (12/D)^{1/9}$ D - DEPTH OF BEAM

ESTIMATED DEPTH OF BEAM = 24" $C_F = (12/24)^{1/9} = 0.926$

ALLOWABLE BENDING STRESS = 0.926 x 1.25 x 2400 = 2777.6 psi

SECTION MODULUS REQ'D. = $\frac{12 \times 107217}{2777.6}$ = 463.2 $in.^3$ $S = \frac{bxd^2}{6}$ or $d = \sqrt{\frac{6 \times S}{b}}$

assume b = 5 1/8" $d = \sqrt{\frac{6 \times 463.2}{5.125}}$ = 23.29 in   TRY BEAM 5 1/8" X 24"

CROSS SECTION AREA - A = 123.0 $in.^2$ MOMENT OF INERTIA - I = 5904 $in.^4$

$$t_v = \frac{1.5 \times 10098}{123.0 \times 1.25} = 98.5 \text{ psi} < 165 \text{ psi}$$

SLOPE ROOF = 1/4 in./ft. MIN.   ALLOW. TOTAL LOAD DEFL. = $\frac{12 \times 38}{240}$ = 1.90 in.

$$\triangle = \frac{5 \times 594 \times 38^4 \times 1728}{384 \times 1.8 \times 10^6 \times 5904} = 2.62 \text{ in. } 38\% \text{ OVER}$$

CHECK BEAM 5 1/8" X 27"   A = 138.38 $in.^2$ I = 8406.3 $in.^4$

$$\triangle = \frac{5 \times 594 \times 38^4 \times 1728}{384 \times 1.8 \times 10^6 \times 8406.3} = 1.83 \text{ in.}$$

AITC RECOMMENDS CAMBER = 1.5 x DEAD LOAD DEFLECTION

CAMBER = $1.5 \left(\frac{354}{594} \right) 1.83$ = 1.10 in.

USE GLU - LAM BEAM 5 1/8" X 27" CAMBER UP 1.25"

OFFICE FLOOR GLUED LAMINATED BEAM | EXAMPLE 22 SHT. S-1 of 1

DESIGN LOADS:

LIGHT WT. CONC.	=	13.3 #/sq ft
3/4" PLYWOOD	=	2.3
2 X 14 @ 24	=	2.6
SUSPENDED CEILING	=	1.8
INSULATION	=	1.0
MISCELLANEOUS	=	1.0
DEAD LOAD	=	22.0
PARTITIONS	=	20.0
LIVE LOAD	=	50.0
TOTAL LOAD	=	92.0 #/sq ft

CLEAR SPAN = 36'-0"

TRIBUTARY WIDTH = 16'-0"

SEASONED LUMBER K = 0.50

LUMBER DESIGNATION 24-V8 DF/DF

F_B = 2400psi F_V = 165psi $E = 1.8 \times 10^6$ psi

INTERIOR BEAMS - DRY CONDITION

TRIBUTARY AREA = 16.0 × 36 = 576 sq. ft.

LIVE LOAD REDUCTION:

PER CENT REDUCT. = .08 (576 − 150) = 34.0%

LIVE LOAD = 50 (1 − 0.34) = 33 psf

UNIF. LOAD = 16.0(22 + 20 + 33) + BM = 1250 plf

DEFL. LOAD = 16.0(42 + .5 × 33) + BM = 985 plf

3/4" PLYWOOD
SIMPSON HANGER
2 X 12's @ 24" oc

BEAM SECTION

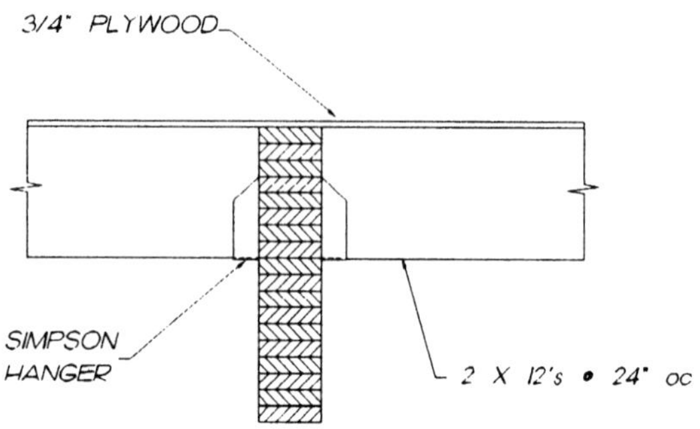

TRY A GLU - LAM BM 8 3/4 X 28

19 LAMINATIONS DEPTH = 27.5 in. C_F = 0.91

$A = 249.4\ in^2$ $I = 16{,}880\ in^4$ $S = 1184\ in^3$

CHECK $C_F = \sqrt[1/9]{\frac{12}{28.5}} = 0.908$ FOR UNIFORM LOAD

CHECK BEAM SLENDERNESS $C_S = \sqrt{\frac{l_e \times d}{b^2}}$

$l_e = 1.92 \times 24 = 46$

$C_S = \sqrt{\frac{46 \times 28.5}{8.75^2}} = 4.14 < 10.0$ ✓

INTERMEDIATE LENGTH BEAM

$M = \frac{1250 \times 36^2}{8} = 202{,}500.0$#

$S_{REQ'D} = \frac{12 \times 202{,}500.0}{.914 \times 2400} = 1107.8\ in^3$

$V = \frac{1250 \times 31.25}{2} = 19{,}531.2$ #

$A_{REQ'D} = \frac{1.5 \times 19{,}531.2}{.914 \times 165} = 194.3\ in^2$

$\Delta_{ALLOW} = \frac{L}{240} = \frac{12 \times 36}{240} = 1.80$ in.

$\Delta = \frac{5 \times 985 \times 36^4 \times 1728}{384 \times 1.8 \times 10^6 \times 16880} = 1.225$ in. ✓

UNIFORM DEAD LOAD = 16 × 44 + BM = 750 plf

$\Delta_{DEAD\ LOAD} = \frac{5 \times 750 \times 36^4 \times 1728}{384 \times 1.8 \times 10^6 \times 16880} = 0.933$ in

CAMBER = 1.5 × .933 = 1.50 in.

USE GLU LAM BEAM 8 3/4 in X 28 1/2 CAMBER UP AT MIDSPAN 1.50 in.

DESIGN AND CONSTRUCTION OF WOOD FRAMED BUILDINGS

WOOD COLUMNS — EXAMPLE 23 SHT. S-1 of 1

ROOF LOADS:

GRAVEL	=	3.3 #/sq ft
ROOFING	=	3.2
1/2" PLYWOOD	=	1.5
FRAMING	=	2.2
INSULATION	=	1.8
SUSPENDED CEILING	=	1.0
MISCELLANEOUS	=	1.0
DEAD LOAD	=	14.0
LIVE LOAD	=	20.0
TOTAL LOAD	=	34.0 #/sq ft

FLOOR LOADS:

LIGHT WT. CONC.	=	13.3 #/sq ft
3/4" PLYWOOD	=	2.3
2 X 14 @ 24	=	2.6
SUSPENDED CEILING	=	1.8
INSULATION	=	1.0
MISCELLANEOUS	=	1.0
DEAD LOAD	=	22.0
PARTITIONS	=	20.0
LIVE LOAD	=	50.0
TOTAL LOAD	=	92.0 #/sq ft

CLEAR SPAN = 36'-0"

TRIBUTARY WIDTH = 16'-0"

SEASONED LUMBER DRY CONDITION

GLU LAM DESIGNATION 24-V8 DF/DF

$F_B = 2400$ psi $F_V = 165$ psi $F_C = 1650$ psi $E = 1.8 \times 10^6$ psi

TRIBUTARY AREA = 16.0 × 36 = 576 sq. ft.

ROOF LIVE LOAD REDUCTION:

METHOD No. 1, LIVE LOAD = 16 psf

UNIF. ROOF LOAD = 16.0 (14 + 16) + BM = 525 plf

ROOF LIVE LOAD REDUCTION:

METHOD No. 2, % = .08 (576 − 150) = 34.0%

LIVE LOAD = 50 (1 − 0.34) = 33.0 psf

UNIF. FLR. LOAD = 16.0 (22 + 33 + 20) + BM = 1250 plf

CASE 1 - SHORT COLUMN - HT. = 6'-8"

BEAM POST LOAD - 2nd TO 1st FLR. = 36 x .5 (525 + 1250) = 31,950#

$K_e = 1.0$ HT. = 6'-8" 8x8 POST AREA = 56.25 sq. in.

$\frac{l_e}{d} = \frac{1 \times 12 \times 6.67}{7.5} = 10.67 < 11$ $F_c = \frac{31{,}950}{56.25} = 568.0$ psi ✓

CASE 2 - INTERMEDIATE COLUMN - HT. = 12'-0"

BEAM POST LOAD - 2nd TO 1st FLR. = 31,950#

$K_e = 1.0$ HT. = 12'-0" 8x8 POST AREA = 56.25 sq. in.

$\frac{l_e}{d} = \frac{1 \times 12 \times 12}{7.5} = 19.20 > 11 < 50$

$F_c = \frac{31{,}950}{56.25} = 568.0$ psi ✓

5

Construction Details

The structural strength of a building is partially dependent on the capacity of its component parts to resist dead loads and externally applied live loads. However, the endurance of the entire structure also relies on the adequacy of its connections to sequentially transfer loads and forces to the subsequent supporting members. Individual parts of the structure may satisfy all design requirements, but it is equally consequential that the connections be sufficiently strong to allow the total structure to work as a complete assembly. The methods and strength of connection are critical to the degree of structural capacity of the building.

Although wood-framed buildings are considered to be flexible structures as compared to those constructed with steel, masonry, or concrete, the connections should be designed to constrain independent movement of associated structural elements. This requirement is particularly critical in the design of resistance to wind or seismic lateral forces. The plane surfaces of roofs, floors, and walls are designed as resistance diaphragms to lateral forces. The horizontal roof and floor diaphragms must be connected to the vertical shear walls to integrate the structure and thus facilitate a uniform distribution of the forces.

The detail drawings presented in this chapter demonstrate recommended standard methods of framing connections for a variety of conditions. The engineer may calculate the required resistance strength of a connection and thereby specify it to be constructed in some way other than as shown in this chapter. An example of this instance can be demonstrated in Fig. 5.2b, which shows the blocking connected to the double 2 × 4 wall plate with 16d toe nails spaced at 8 in o.c.

Calculations might indicate that the floor connection to the shear wall requires greater resistance, and that metal hardware is required. Standard methods and details should not be used arbitrarily. It is always good practice to check the structural strength of a detail to determine if it can resist the expected loads and forces. This principle applies to all aspects of structural design. A good rule to follow is to

"Mistrust the obvious." A structural detail on a drawing may meet all design require-ments; however, its working capacity depends to some degree on the quality of the workmanship in the field. The structural design may end up being not much better than the least skilled or motivated person at the job site. Deficiencies of this nature can be controlled by careful field inspection of the work as it progresses.

The general nomenclature of framing members is given in Fig. 5.1a and Fig. 5.1b elevations of interior and exterior wood-framed walls. The studs are usually spaced at 16 in o.c.; however, there are instances when the calculation of the com-bined stress of vertical load and wind load may require spacing at 12 in o.c. UBC Table 25-R-3 specifies the allowable stud heights for bearing and nonbearing walls. The studs may exceed the heights listed in the code table, providing a design cal-culation is made for the vertical and horizontal loads. Exterior wall studs that sup-port more than two stories require structural calculation.

The mudsill shown in Fig. 5.2c is in contact with concrete and therefore is required to be either redwood or pressure-treated lumber. The anchor bolt size and spacing is not specified, since it must be calculated to resist lateral forces act-ing parallel to the wall. Figure 5.2d uses a plywood gusset plate to connect the ceiling joists to the roof rafters. The gusset plate connects the rafters to the ceiling joists so that the horizontal load component of the roof sloped rafters can be resisted by ceiling joists. Also, notice that a Simpson A35 metal clip is used to con-nect the roof plywood diaphragm to the shear wall.

Figures 5.3 and 5.3a show that the first floor joists are supported by cripple studs the required 18 in clear above the finished grade. Cripple studs are limited to a height of 4 ft 0 in unless specially calculated. It is good practice to apply ply-wood to cripple studs because they tend to move outward from seismic forces.

Figures 5.4b and 5.4c represent the connection of a wood stud wall to a floor that is framed with the floor joists spanning parallel to the wall. It is good practice to add blocking between the wall and the first adjacent joist to provide a positive connection between the floor and the wall.

Figures 5.5 and 5.6 present framing details using Trus Joist I-type cross-sectional shape. Notice this type of joist uses an end closure piece in lieu of blacking, and that the bottom flange of the I section is nailed through to the double 2 × 4 plate.

Figure 5.7 presents the wall section of a one-story structure. The roof rafters lap the wall studs and are supported by a 1 × 4 in let-in strip. The mudsill is raised above the concrete slab on grade. This type design is usually used for a residential detached garage.

Figures 5.8 to 5.12 present interior wall sections showing roof and floor support for a variety of configurations. The addition of a Simpson strap across the ridge of the sloped roof ensures that it will react as an uninterrupted diaphragm. Also, note that the floor joists in Fig. 5.9 are continuously blocked at 8 ft 0 in o.c. as per UBC Section 2505(h).

Figures 5.13 and 5.14 show detail methods of connecting walls at the top dou-ble 2 × 4 plate to maintain continuity in transmitting lateral forces in shear walls. The double plate splice presented in Fig. 5.13 is a standard method of lapping the 2 × 4's.

Figures 5.15 and 5.16 show a support system for wood-framed first floors that are supported to the existing grade. The stability of the floor depends on placing blocking between the floor joists as shown in Fig. 5.15. The codes do not usually require the diagonal bracing shown in Fig. 5.16. Recent inspections of damage caused by the Northridge earthquake indicated that first floors suffered severe damage as a result of lateral movement. The lack of horizontal stability permitted the cripple studs at the perimeter wall to move, and thus diminish the seismic resistance of the exterior wall stucco.

Figures 5.17 to 5.37 present framing details for Trus Joist L-type framing mem-bers. It is recommended that this type of floor or roof joist be used with considera-tion for floor deflection and vibration. Figures 5.38 to 5.64 present framing details for Trus Joist I-type framing members. This type of framing is rapidly increasing in the framing of floors and roofs since it offers certain advantages over comparable sawn lumber sizes. The material is fabricated with kiln-dried lumber and with manufacturing quality control. The increases in spans, spacing, and erection reflect significant cost reduction in both labor and material.

Figure 5.65 presents the method of constructing corners of wood stud walls. Notice that the double 2 × 4 plates are cross-lapped at the top of the wall. Figure 5.66 recommends a double Simpson strap at the top corner of a wood stud wall. These straps are capable of maintaining the wall corner in the event of random movement caused by seismic forces.

Figure 5.67 presents a detail of a wood stud wall intersection. Inspection of seismic damage to wood-framed buildings after the Northridge earthquake indicated that many of the interior shear walls and partitions perpendicular to exterior and interior shear walls separated at their intersection. It is recommended that the walls be connected with Simpson A35-type hardware to achieve a more uniform distribution of the lateral force.

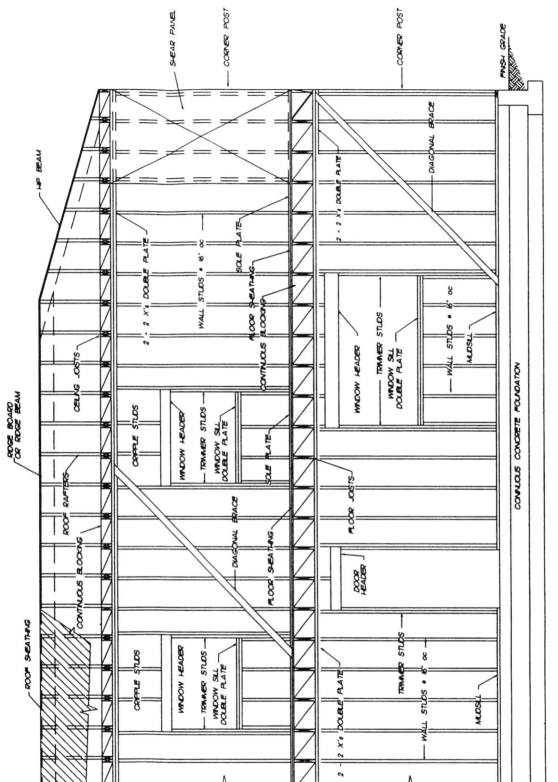

TYPICAL EXTERIOR WALL FRAMING ELEVATION

Fig. 5.1a

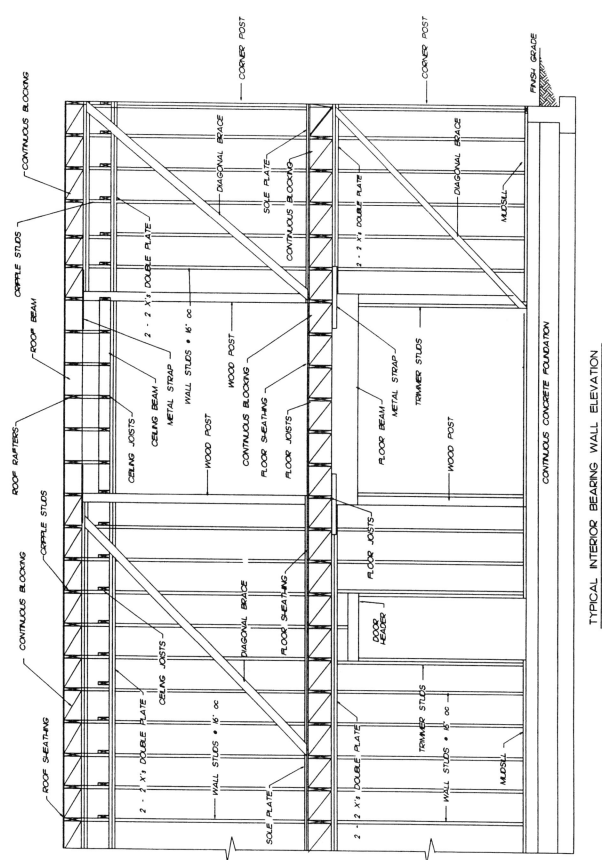

TYPICAL INTERIOR BEARING WALL ELEVATION

Fig. 5.1b

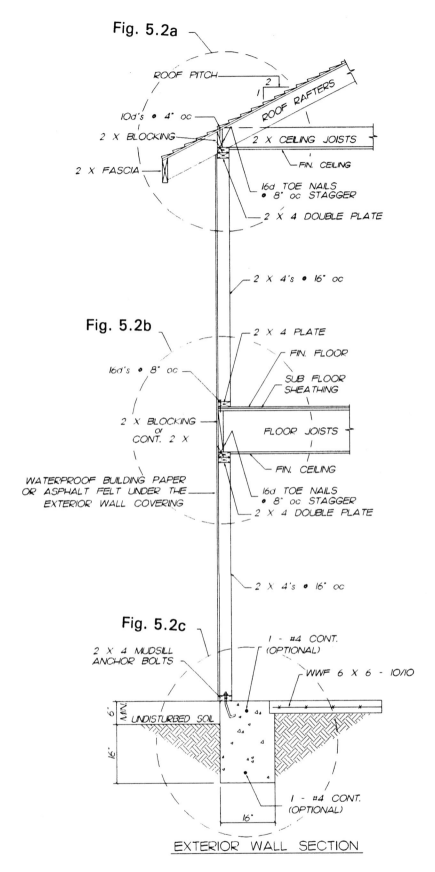

Fig. 5.2a

ROOF PITCH

ROOF RAFTERS

10d's • 4" oc

2 X BLOCKING

2 X FASCIA

2 X CEILING JOISTS

FIN. CEILING

16d TOE NAILS • 8" oc STAGGER

2 X 4 DOUBLE PLATE

2 X 4's • 16" oc

Fig. 5.2b

2 X 4 PLATE

FIN. FLOOR

16d's • 8" oc

SUB FLOOR SHEATHING

2 X BLOCKING or CONT. 2 X

FLOOR JOISTS

FIN. CEILING

WATERPROOF BUILDING PAPER OR ASPHALT FELT UNDER THE EXTERIOR WALL COVERING

16d TOE NAILS • 8" oc STAGGER

2 X 4 DOUBLE PLATE

2 X 4's • 16" oc

Fig. 5.2c

2 X 4 MUDSILL ANCHOR BOLTS

1 - #4 CONT. (OPTIONAL)

WWF 6 X 6 - 10/10

6" MIN.

UNDISTURBED SOIL

16"

1 - #4 CONT. (OPTIONAL)

16"

EXTERIOR WALL SECTION

Fig. 5.2

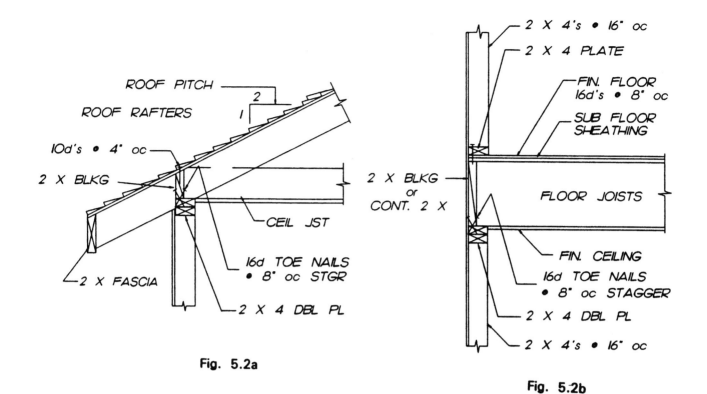

ROOF PITCH

ROOF RAFTERS

2

1

10d's • 4" oc

2 X BLKG

2 X FASCIA

CEIL JST

16d TOE NAILS • 8" oc STGR

2 X 4 DBL PL

Fig. 5.2a

2 X 4's • 16" oc

2 X 4 PLATE

FIN. FLOOR 16d's • 8" oc

SUB FLOOR SHEATHING

2 X BLKG or CONT. 2 X

FLOOR JOISTS

FIN. CEILING

16d TOE NAILS • 8" oc STAGGER

2 X 4 DBL PL

2 X 4's • 16" oc

Fig. 5.2b

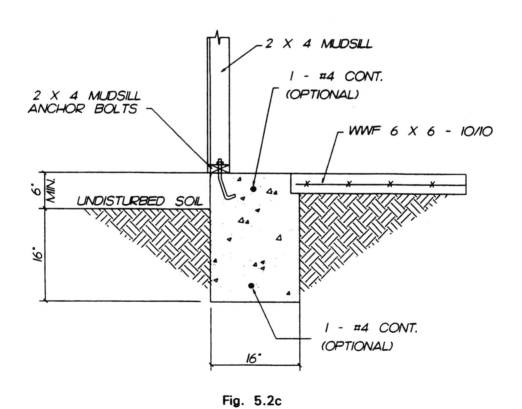

2 X 4 MUDSILL

1 - #4 CONT. (OPTIONAL)

2 X 4 MUDSILL ANCHOR BOLTS

WWF 6 X 6 - 10/10

6" MIN.

UNDISTURBED SOIL

16"

1 - #4 CONT. (OPTIONAL)

16"

Fig. 5.2c

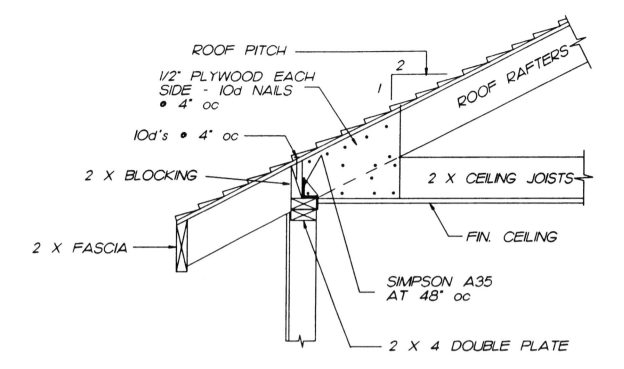

ROOF PITCH

1/2" PLYWOOD EACH
SIDE - 10d NAILS
● 4" oc

10d's ● 4" oc

2 X BLOCKING

2 X FASCIA

ROOF RAFTERS

2 X CEILING JOISTS

FIN. CEILING

SIMPSON A35
AT 48" oc

2 X 4 DOUBLE PLATE

Fig. 5.2d

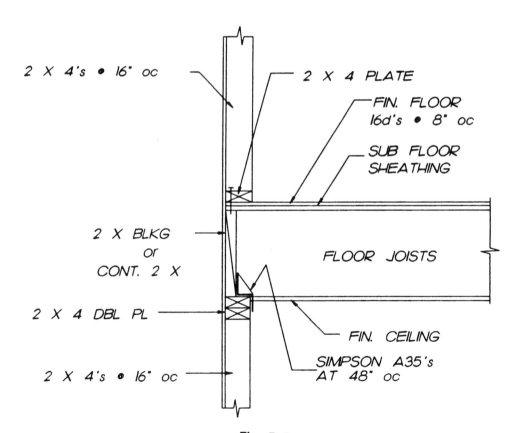

2 X 4's ● 16" oc

2 X 4 PLATE

FIN. FLOOR
16d's ● 8" oc

SUB FLOOR
SHEATHING

2 X BLKG
or
CONT. 2 X

FLOOR JOISTS

2 X 4 DBL PL

FIN. CEILING

SIMPSON A35's
AT 48" oc

2 X 4's ● 16" oc

Fig. 5.2e

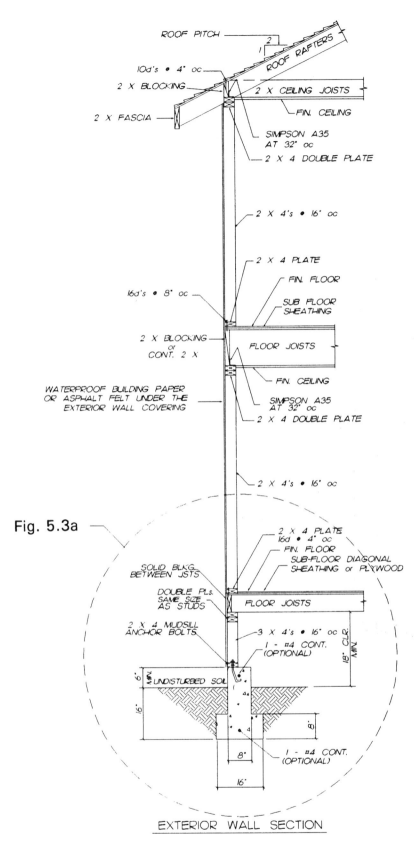

ROOF PITCH

2 / 1

ROOF RAFTERS

10d's • 4" oc

2 X BLOCKING

2 X CEILING JOISTS

FIN. CEILING

2 X FASCIA

SIMPSON A35
AT 32" oc

2 X 4 DOUBLE PLATE

2 X 4's • 16" oc

2 X 4 PLATE

FIN. FLOOR

SUB FLOOR
SHEATHING

16d's • 8" oc

2 X BLOCKING
or
CONT. 2 X

FLOOR JOISTS

FIN. CEILING

WATERPROOF BUILDING PAPER
OR ASPHALT FELT UNDER THE
EXTERIOR WALL COVERING

SIMPSON A35
AT 32" oc

2 X 4 DOUBLE PLATE

2 X 4's • 16" oc

Fig. 5.3a

2 X 4 PLATE
16d • 4" oc

FIN. FLOOR

SUB-FLOOR DIAGONAL
SHEATHING or PLYWOOD

SOLID BLKG.
BETWEEN JSTS

DOUBLE PLs.
SAME SIZE
AS STUDS

FLOOR JOISTS

2 X 4 MUDSILL
ANCHOR BOLTS

3 X 4's • 16" oc

1 - #4 CONT.
(OPTIONAL)

18" CLR.
MIN.

6" MIN.

UNDISTURBED SOIL

16"

1 - #4 CONT.
(OPTIONAL)

8'

8"

16"

EXTERIOR WALL SECTION

Fig. 5.3

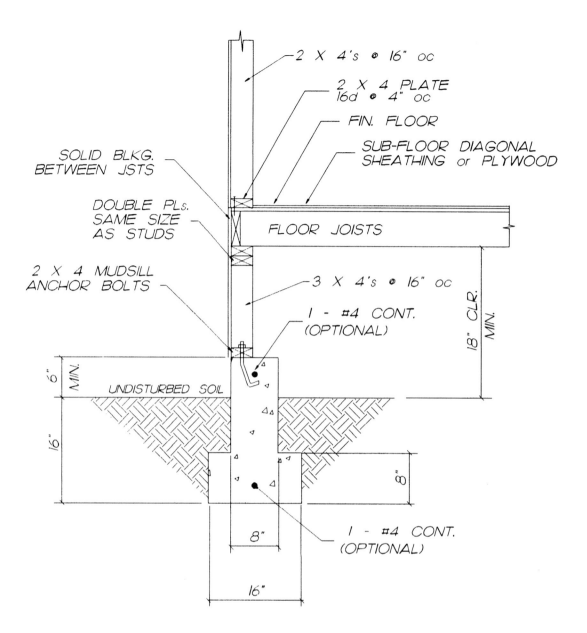

Fig. 5.3a

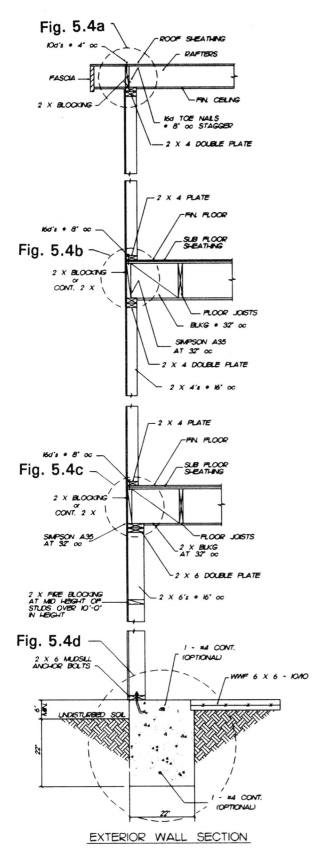

Fig. 5.4a

ROOF SHEATHING

RAFTERS

10d's @ 4" oc

FASCIA

FIN. CEILING

2 X BLOCKING

16d TOE NAILS
@ 8" oc STAGGER

2 X 4 DOUBLE PLATE

2 X 4 PLATE

FIN. FLOOR

SUB FLOOR
SHEATHING

16d's @ 8" oc

Fig. 5.4b

2 X BLOCKING
or
CONT. 2 X

FLOOR JOISTS

BLKG @ 32" oc

SIMPSON A35
AT 32" oc

2 X 4 DOUBLE PLATE

2 X 4's @ 16" oc

2 X 4 PLATE

FIN. FLOOR

SUB FLOOR
SHEATHING

16d's @ 8" oc

Fig. 5.4c

2 X BLOCKING
or
CONT. 2 X

FLOOR JOISTS

SIMPSON A35
AT 32" oc

2 X BLKG
AT 32" oc

2 X 6 DOUBLE PLATE

2 X FIRE BLOCKING
AT MID HEIGHT OF
STUDS OVER 10'-0"
IN HEIGHT

2 X 6's @ 16" oc

Fig. 5.4d

1 - #4 CONT.
(OPTIONAL)

2 X 6 MUDSILL
ANCHOR BOLTS

WWF 6 X 6 - 10/10

6" MIN.

UNDISTURBED SOIL

22"

1 - #4 CONT.
(OPTIONAL)

22"

EXTERIOR WALL SECTION

Fig. 5.4

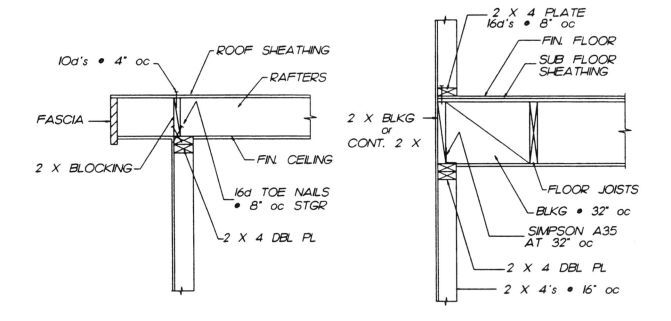

Fig. 5.4a

Fig. 5.4b

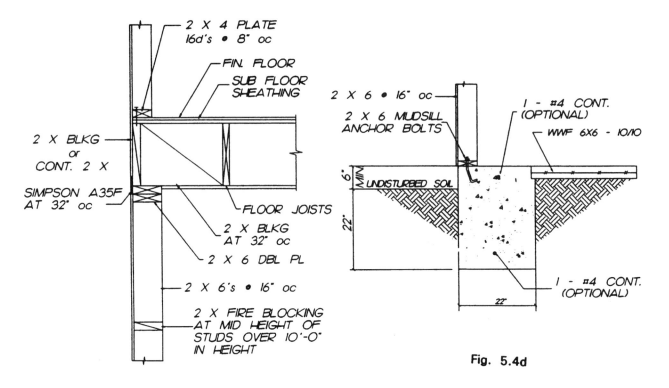

Fig. 5.4c

Fig. 5.4d

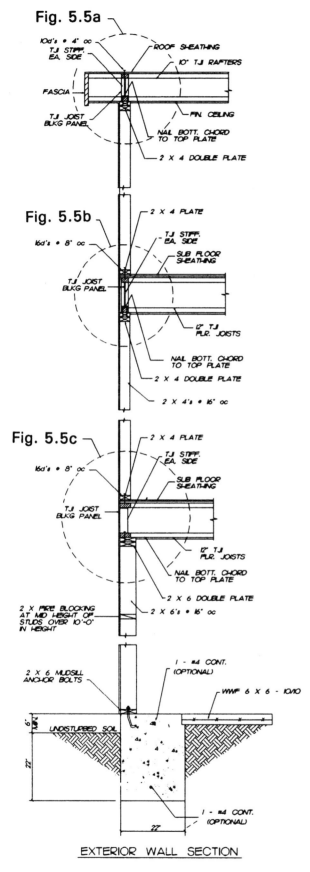

Fig. 5.5a

10d's @ 4" oc
TJI STIFF.
EA. SIDE

ROOF SHEATHING

10" TJI RAFTERS

FASCIA

FIN. CEILING

TJI JOIST
BLKG PANEL

NAIL BOTT. CHORD
TO TOP PLATE

2 X 4 DOUBLE PLATE

Fig. 5.5b

2 X 4 PLATE

16d's @ 8" oc

TJI STIFF.
EA. SIDE

SUB FLOOR
SHEATHING

TJI JOIST
BLKG PANEL

12" TJI
FLR. JOISTS

NAIL BOTT. CHORD
TO TOP PLATE

2 X 4 DOUBLE PLATE

2 X 4's @ 16" oc

Fig. 5.5c

2 X 4 PLATE

16d's @ 8" oc

TJI STIFF.
EA. SIDE

SUB FLOOR
SHEATHING

TJI JOIST
BLKG PANEL

12" TJI
FLR. JOISTS

NAIL BOTT. CHORD
TO TOP PLATE

2 X 6 DOUBLE PLATE

2 X 6's @ 16" oc

2 X FIRE BLOCKING
AT MID HEIGHT OF
STUDS OVER 10'-0"
IN HEIGHT

2 X 6 MUDSILL
ANCHOR BOLTS

1 - #4 CONT.
(OPTIONAL)

WWF 6 X 6 - 10/10

6"
MIN.

UNDISTURBED SOIL

22"

1 - #4 CONT.
(OPTIONAL)

22"

EXTERIOR WALL SECTION

Fig. 5.5

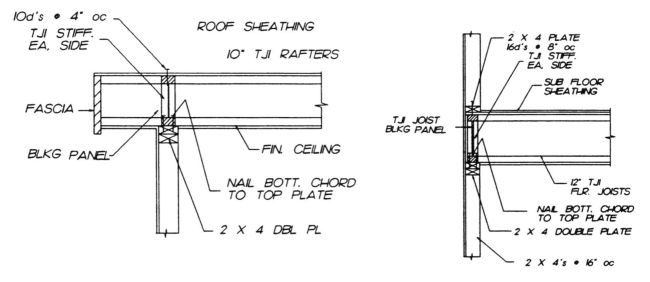

Fig. 5.5a

Fig. 5.5b

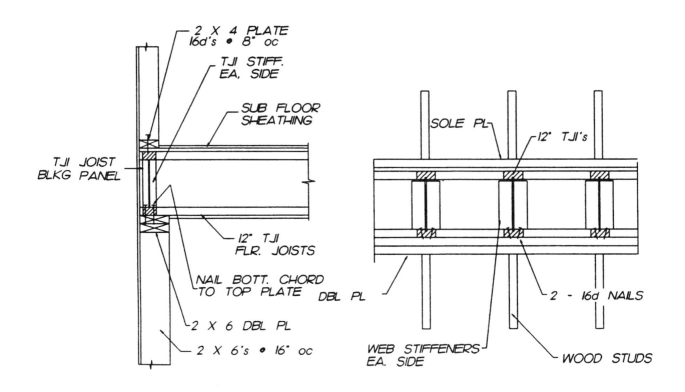

Fig. 5.5c

Fig. 5.5d

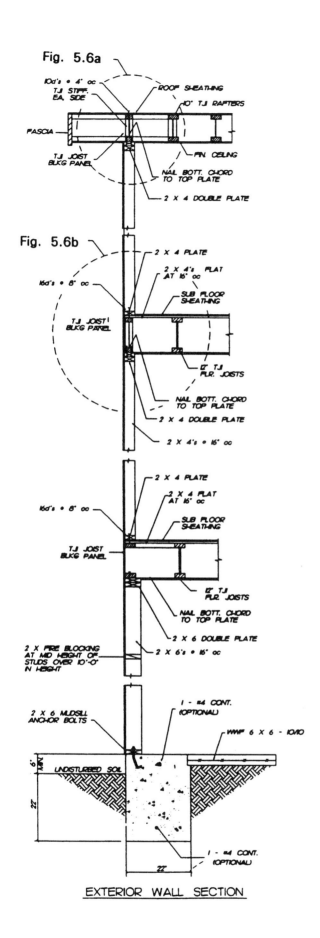

Fig. 5.6a

10d's @ 4" oc
TJ STIFF. EA. SIDE
ROOF SHEATHING
10" TJ RAFTERS
FASCIA
TJ JOIST BLKG PANEL
FIN. CEILING
NAIL BOTT. CHORD TO TOP PLATE
2 X 4 DOUBLE PLATE

Fig. 5.6b

2 X 4 PLATE
2 X 4's FLAT AT 16" oc
SUB FLOOR SHEATHING
16d's @ 8" oc
TJ JOIST BLKG PANEL
12" TJ FLR. JOISTS
NAIL BOTT. CHORD TO TOP PLATE
2 X 4 DOUBLE PLATE
2 X 4's @ 16" oc

2 X 4 PLATE
2 X 4 FLAT AT 16" oc
SUB FLOOR SHEATHING
16d's @ 8" oc
TJ JOIST BLKG PANEL
12" TJ FLR. JOISTS
NAIL BOTT. CHORD TO TOP PLATE
2 X 6 DOUBLE PLATE
2 X 6's @ 16" oc
2 X FIRE BLOCKING AT MID HEIGHT OF STUDS OVER 10'-0" IN HEIGHT

2 X 6 MUDSILL ANCHOR BOLTS
1 - #4 CONT. (OPTIONAL)
WWF 6 X 6 - 10/10
6" MIN.
UNDISTURBED SOIL
22"
1 - #4 CONT. (OPTIONAL)
22"

EXTERIOR WALL SECTION

Fig. 5.6

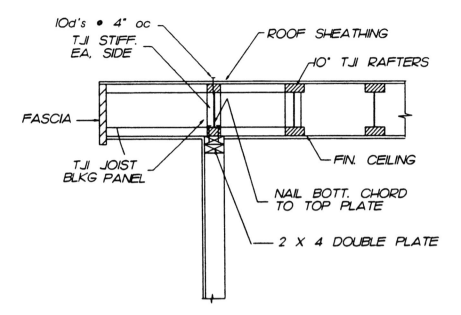

10d's ● 4" oc
TJI STIFF.
EA. SIDE

ROOF SHEATHING

10" TJI RAFTERS

FASCIA

FIN. CEILING

TJI JOIST
BLKG PANEL

NAIL BOTT. CHORD
TO TOP PLATE

2 X 4 DOUBLE PLATE

Fig. 5.6a

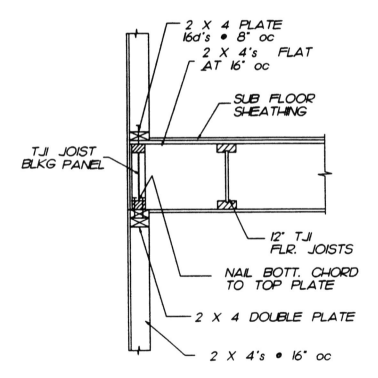

2 X 4 PLATE
16d's ● 8" oc
2 X 4's FLAT
AT 16" oc

SUB FLOOR
SHEATHING

TJI JOIST
BLKG PANEL

12" TJI
FLR. JOISTS

NAIL BOTT. CHORD
TO TOP PLATE

2 X 4 DOUBLE PLATE

2 X 4's ● 16" oc

Fig. 5.6b

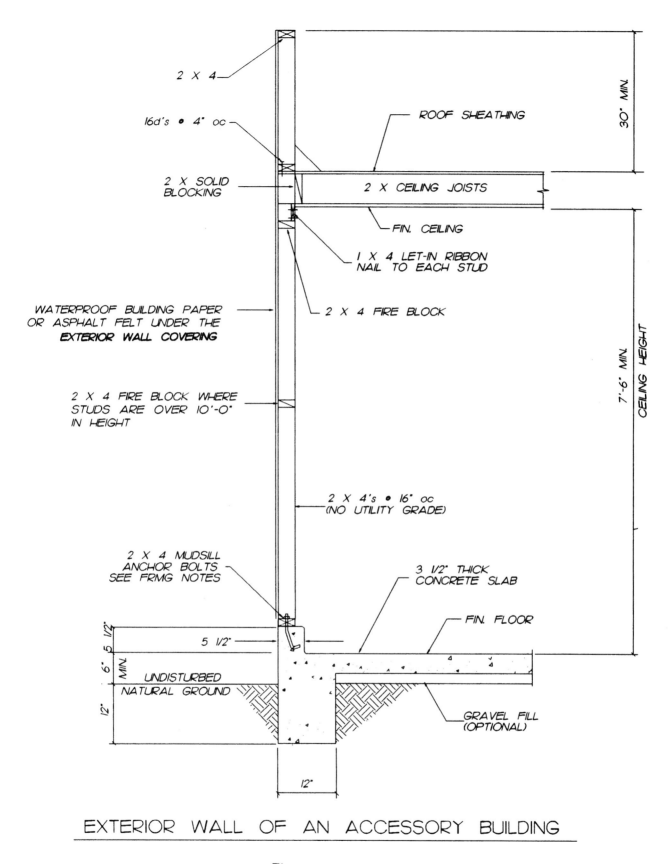

2 X 4

16d's @ 4" oc

2 X SOLID
BLOCKING

ROOF SHEATHING

2 X CEILING JOISTS

FIN. CEILING

1 X 4 LET-IN RIBBON
NAIL TO EACH STUD

2 X 4 FIRE BLOCK

WATERPROOF BUILDING PAPER
OR ASPHALT FELT UNDER THE
EXTERIOR WALL COVERING

2 X 4 FIRE BLOCK WHERE
STUDS ARE OVER 10'-0"
IN HEIGHT

2 X 4's @ 16" oc
(NO UTILITY GRADE)

2 X 4 MUDSILL
ANCHOR BOLTS
SEE FRMG NOTES

3 1/2" THICK
CONCRETE SLAB

FIN. FLOOR

5 1/2"

UNDISTURBED
NATURAL GROUND

GRAVEL FILL
(OPTIONAL)

5 1/2"

6" MIN.

12"

12"

30" MIN.

7'-6" MIN. CEILING HEIGHT

EXTERIOR WALL OF AN ACCESSORY BUILDING

Fig. 5.7

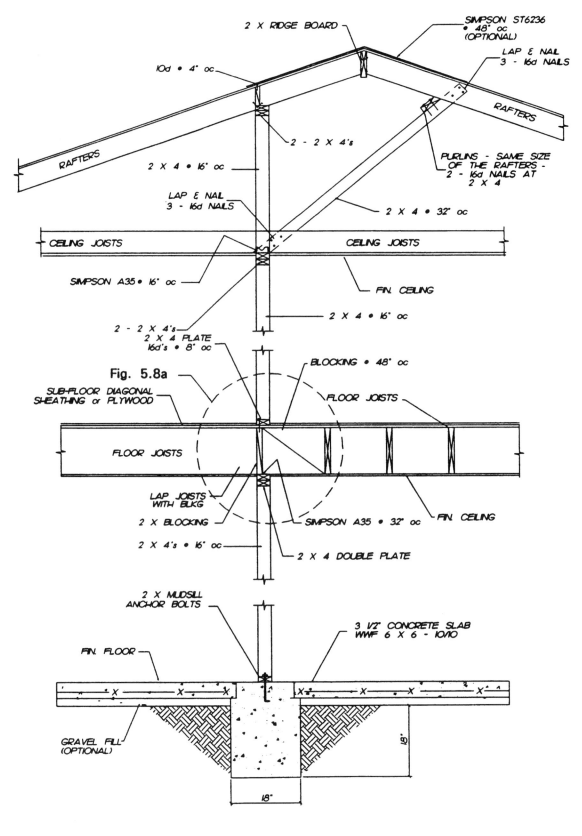

2 X RIDGE BOARD

SIMPSON ST6236
● 48" oc
(OPTIONAL)

LAP & NAIL
3 - 16d NAILS

10d ● 4" oc

RAFTERS

RAFTERS

2 - 2 X 4's

2 X 4 ● 16" oc

PURLINS - SAME SIZE
OF THE RAFTERS -
2 - 16d NAILS AT
2 X 4

LAP & NAIL
3 - 16d NAILS

2 X 4 ● 32" oc

CEILING JOISTS

CEILING JOISTS

SIMPSON A35 ● 16" oc

FIN. CEILING

2 - 2 X 4's

2 X 4 ● 16" oc

2 X 4 PLATE
16d's ● 8" oc

Fig. 5.8a

BLOCKING ● 48" oc

SUB-FLOOR DIAGONAL
SHEATHING or PLYWOOD

FLOOR JOISTS

FLOOR JOISTS

LAP JOISTS
WITH BLKG

2 X BLOCKING

2 X 4's ● 16" oc

SIMPSON A35 ● 32" oc

FIN. CEILING

2 X 4 DOUBLE PLATE

2 X MUDSILL
ANCHOR BOLTS

3 1/2" CONCRETE SLAB
WWF 6 X 6 - 10/10

FIN. FLOOR

GRAVEL FILL
(OPTIONAL)

18"

18"

INTERIOR WALL SECTION

Fig. 5.8

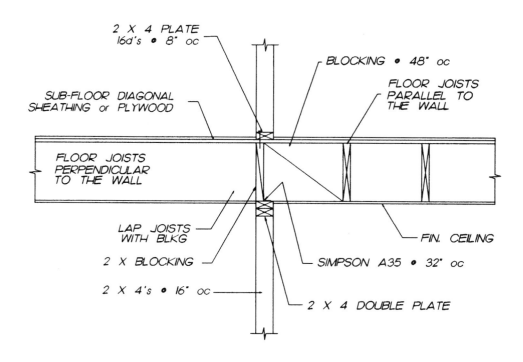

2 X 4 PLATE
16d's @ 8" oc

BLOCKING @ 48" oc

FLOOR JOISTS
PARALLEL TO
THE WALL

SUB-FLOOR DIAGONAL
SHEATHING or PLYWOOD

FLOOR JOISTS
PERPENDICULAR
TO THE WALL

LAP JOISTS
WITH BLKG

2 X BLOCKING

2 X 4's @ 16" oc

FIN. CEILING

SIMPSON A35 @ 32" oc

2 X 4 DOUBLE PLATE

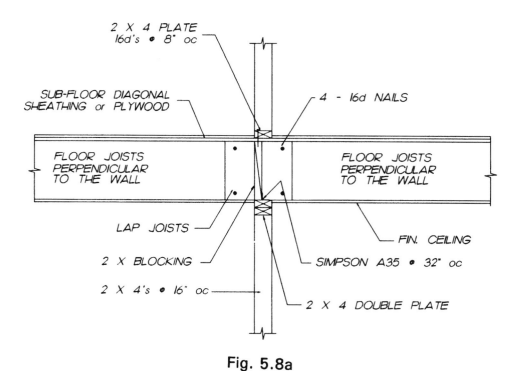

2 X 4 PLATE
16d's @ 8" oc

4 - 16d NAILS

SUB-FLOOR DIAGONAL
SHEATHING or PLYWOOD

FLOOR JOISTS
PERPENDICULAR
TO THE WALL

FLOOR JOISTS
PERPENDICULAR
TO THE WALL

LAP JOISTS

2 X BLOCKING

2 X 4's @ 16" oc

FIN. CEILING

SIMPSON A35 @ 32" oc

2 X 4 DOUBLE PLATE

Fig. 5.8a

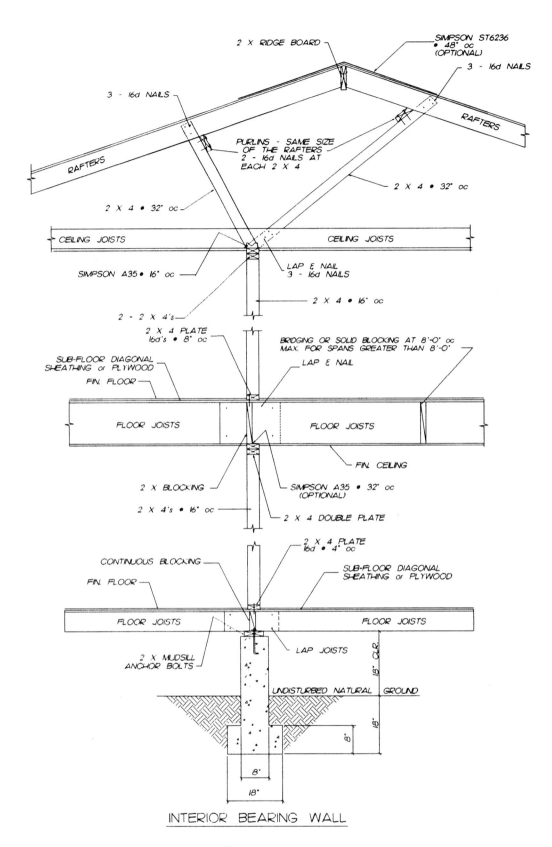

2 X RIDGE BOARD

SIMPSON ST6236
● 48" oc
(OPTIONAL)

3 - 16d NAILS

3 - 16d NAILS

RAFTERS

RAFTERS

PURLINS - SAME SIZE
OF THE RAFTERS -
2 - 16d NAILS AT
EACH 2 X 4

2 X 4 ● 32" oc

2 X 4 ● 32" oc

CEILING JOISTS

CEILING JOISTS

SIMPSON A35 ● 16" oc

LAP & NAIL
3 - 16d NAILS

2 - 2 X 4's

2 X 4 ● 16" oc

2 X 4 PLATE
16d's ● 8" oc

BRIDGING OR SOLID BLOCKING AT 8'-0" oc
MAX. FOR SPANS GREATER THAN 8'-0"

SUB-FLOOR DIAGONAL
SHEATHING or PLYWOOD

LAP & NAIL

FIN. FLOOR

FLOOR JOISTS

FLOOR JOISTS

FIN. CEILING

2 X BLOCKING

SIMPSON A35 ● 32" oc
(OPTIONAL)

2 X 4's ● 16" oc

2 X 4 DOUBLE PLATE

2 X 4 PLATE
16d ● 4" oc

CONTINUOUS BLOCKING

SUB-FLOOR DIAGONAL
SHEATHING or PLYWOOD

FIN. FLOOR

FLOOR JOISTS

FLOOR JOISTS

18" CLR

2 X MUDSILL
ANCHOR BOLTS

LAP JOISTS

UNDISTURBED NATURAL GROUND

18"

8"

8"

18"

INTERIOR BEARING WALL

Fig. 5.9

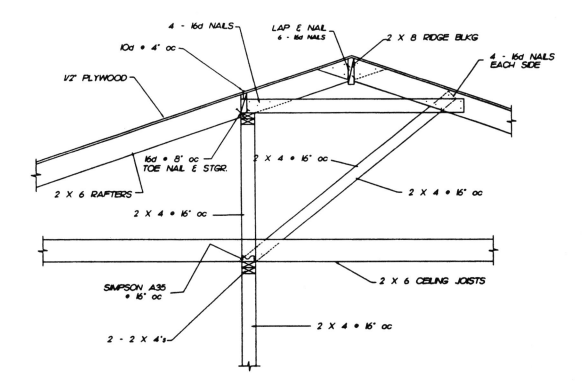

Fig. 5.10a

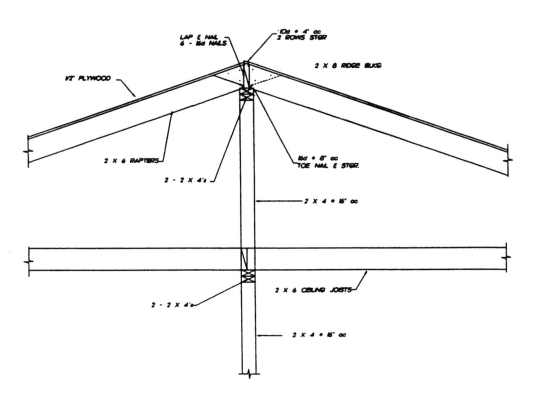

Fig. 5.10b

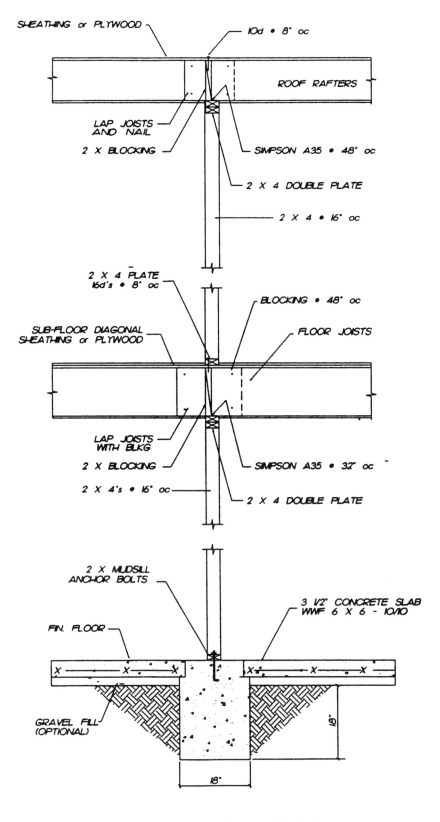

SHEATHING or PLYWOOD

10d • 8" oc

ROOF RAFTERS

LAP JOISTS AND NAIL

2 X BLOCKING

SIMPSON A35 • 48" oc

2 X 4 DOUBLE PLATE

2 X 4 • 16" oc

2 X 4 PLATE
16d's • 8" oc

BLOCKING • 48" oc

SUB-FLOOR DIAGONAL
SHEATHING or PLYWOOD

FLOOR JOISTS

LAP JOISTS WITH BLKG

2 X BLOCKING

SIMPSON A35 • 32" oc

2 X 4's • 16" oc

2 X 4 DOUBLE PLATE

2 X MUDSILL
ANCHOR BOLTS

3 1/2" CONCRETE SLAB
WWF 6 X 6 - 10/10

FIN. FLOOR

GRAVEL FILL
(OPTIONAL)

18"

18"

INTERIOR WALL SECTION

Fig. 5.11

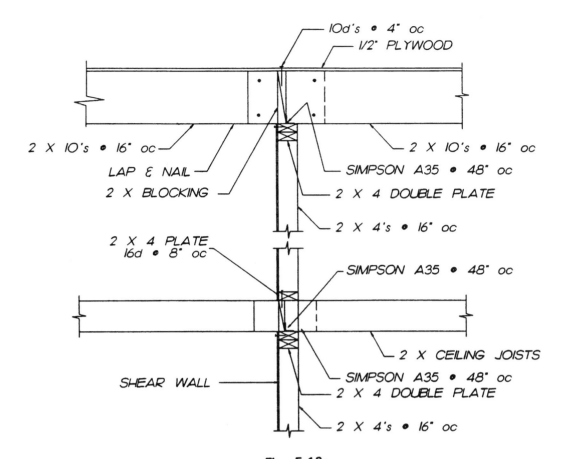

Fig. 5.12a

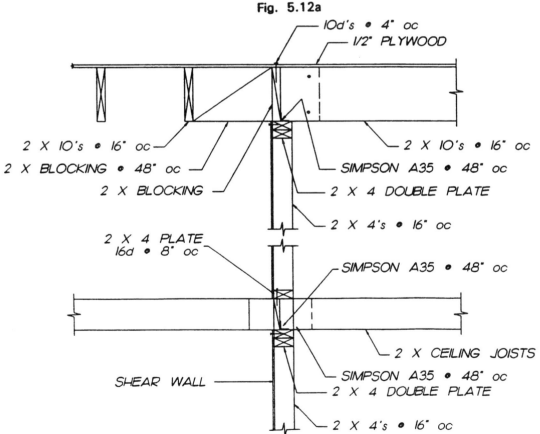

Fig. 5.12b

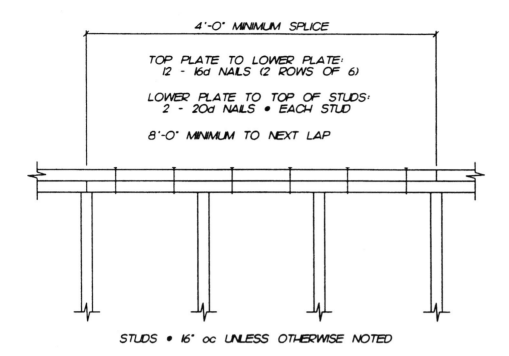

4'-0" MINIMUM SPLICE

TOP PLATE TO LOWER PLATE:
12 - 16d NAILS (2 ROWS OF 6)

LOWER PLATE TO TOP OF STUDS:
2 - 20d NAILS • EACH STUD

8'-0" MINIMUM TO NEXT LAP

STUDS • 16" oc UNLESS OTHERWISE NOTED

Fig. 5.13

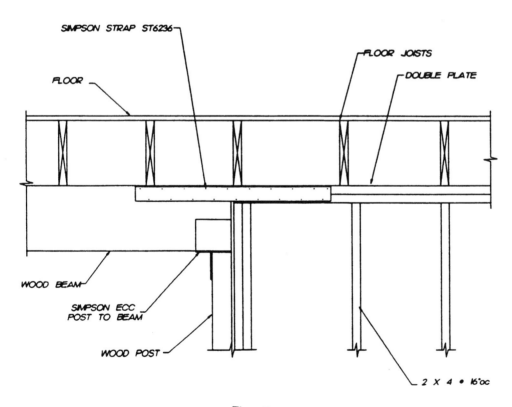

SIMPSON STRAP ST6236

FLOOR JOISTS

DOUBLE PLATE

FLOOR

WOOD BEAM

SIMPSON ECC
POST TO BEAM

WOOD POST

2 X 4 • 16"oc

Fig. 5.14

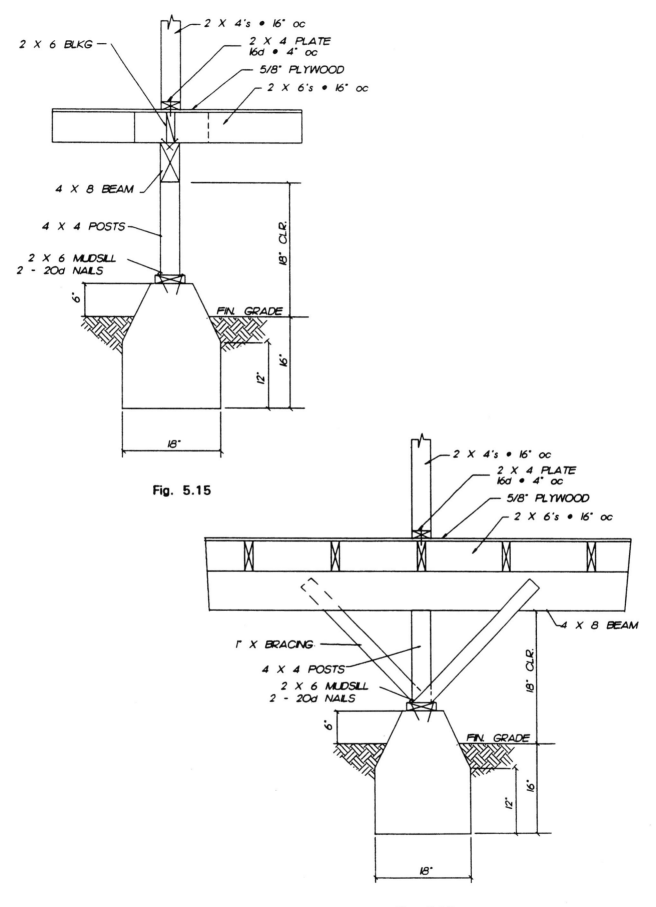

2 X 4's • 16" oc
2 X 4 PLATE 16d • 4" oc
5/8" PLYWOOD
2 X 6's • 16" oc
2 X 6 BLKG
4 X 8 BEAM
4 X 4 POSTS
2 X 6 MUDSILL 2 - 20d NAILS
18" CLR.
6"
FIN. GRADE
16"
12"
18"

Fig. 5.15

2 X 4's • 16" oc
2 X 4 PLATE 16d • 4" oc
5/8" PLYWOOD
2 X 6's • 16" oc
4 X 8 BEAM
1" X BRACING
4 X 4 POSTS
2 X 6 MUDSILL 2 - 20d NAILS
18" CLR.
6"
FIN. GRADE
16"
12"
18"

Fig. 5.16

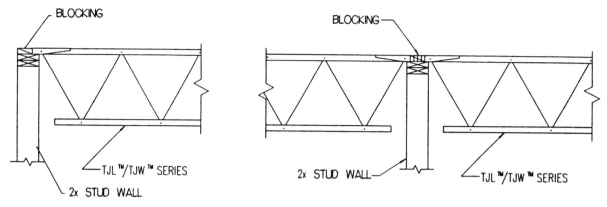

BLOCKING

TJL™/TJW™ SERIES

2x STUD WALL

Fig. 5.17

BLOCKING

2x STUD WALL

TJL™/TJW™ SERIES

Fig. 5.18

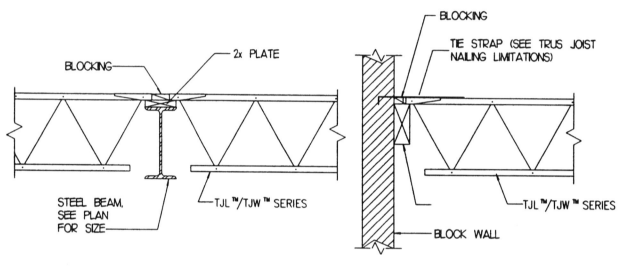

BLOCKING

2x PLATE

STEEL BEAM,
SEE PLAN
FOR SIZE

TJL™/TJW™ SERIES

Fig. 5.19

BLOCKING

TIE STRAP (SEE TRUS JOIST
NAILING LIMITATIONS)

TJL™/TJW™ SERIES

BLOCK WALL

Fig. 5.20

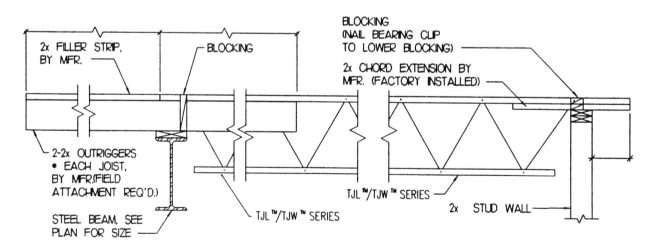

2x FILLER STRIP,
BY MFR.

BLOCKING

2-2x OUTRIGGERS
• EACH JOIST,
BY MFR.(FIELD
ATTACHMENT REQ'D.)

STEEL BEAM, SEE
PLAN FOR SIZE

TJL™/TJW™ SERIES

BLOCKING
(NAIL BEARING CLIP
TO LOWER BLOCKING)

2x CHORD EXTENSION BY
MFR. (FACTORY INSTALLED)

TJL™/TJW™ SERIES

2x STUD WALL

Fig. 5.21

Fig. 5.22

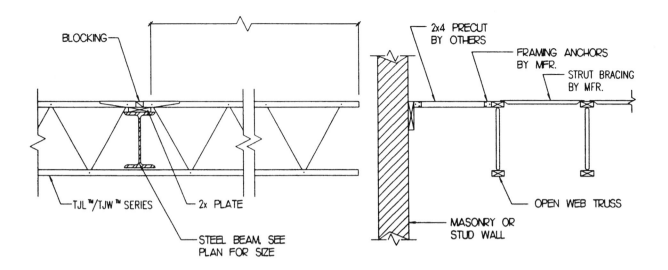

BLOCKING

TJL™/TJW™ SERIES

2x PLATE

STEEL BEAM, SEE
PLAN FOR SIZE

2x4 PRECUT
BY OTHERS

FRAMING ANCHORS
BY MFR.

STRUT BRACING
BY MFR.

OPEN WEB TRUSS

MASONRY OR
STUD WALL

Fig. 5.23   Fig. 5.24

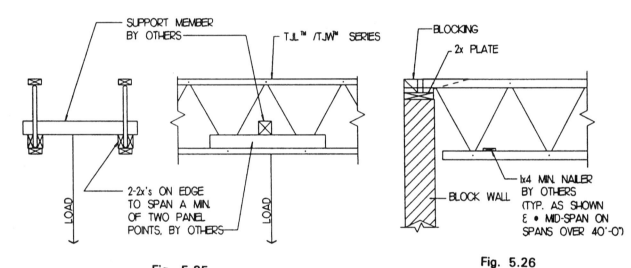

SUPPORT MEMBER
BY OTHERS

TJL™/TJW™ SERIES

2-2x's ON EDGE
TO SPAN A MIN.
OF TWO PANEL
POINTS, BY OTHERS

LOAD

LOAD

BLOCKING

2x PLATE

BLOCK WALL

1x4 MIN. NAILER
BY OTHERS
(TYP. AS SHOWN
& • MID-SPAN ON
SPANS OVER 40'-0")

Fig. 5.25   Fig. 5.26

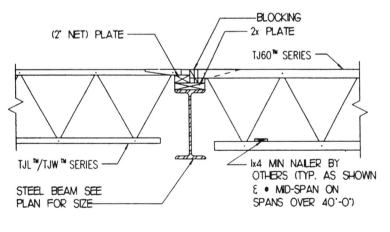

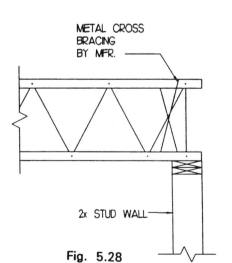

(2" NET) PLATE

BLOCKING

2x PLATE

TJ60™ SERIES

TJL™/TJW™ SERIES

STEEL BEAM SEE
PLAN FOR SIZE

1x4 MIN NAILER BY
OTHERS (TYP. AS SHOWN
& • MID-SPAN ON
SPANS OVER 40'-0")

METAL CROSS
BRACING
BY MFR.

2x STUD WALL

Fig. 5.27   Fig. 5.28

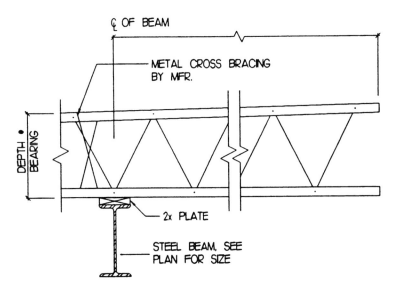

Fig. 5.29

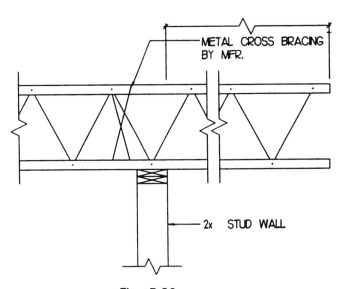

Fig. 5.30

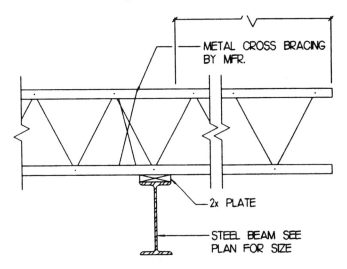

Fig. 5.31

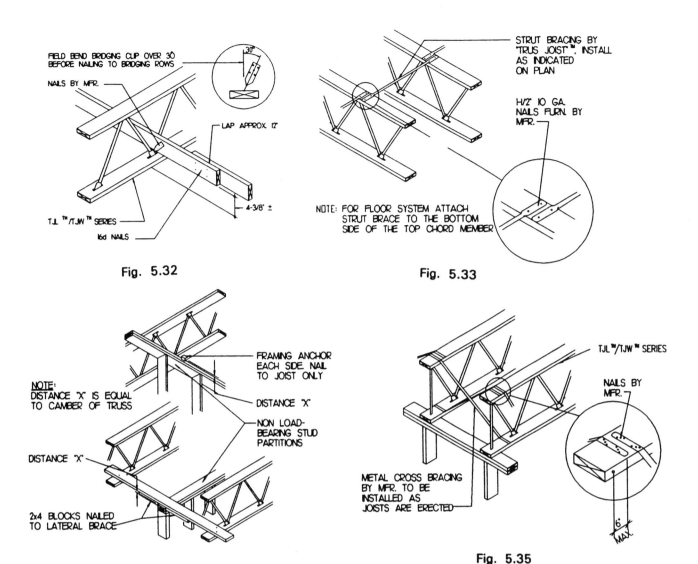

FIELD BEND BRIDGING CLIP OVER 30°
BEFORE NAILING TO BRIDGING ROWS

NAILS BY MFR.

30°

LAP APPROX. 12"

TJL ™/TJW ™ SERIES

16d NAILS

4-3/8" ±

Fig. 5.32

STRUT BRACING BY
"TRUS JOIST". INSTALL
AS INDICATED
ON PLAN

H/2" 10 GA.
NAILS FURN. BY
MFR.

NOTE: FOR FLOOR SYSTEM ATTACH
STRUT BRACE TO THE BOTTOM
SIDE OF THE TOP CHORD MEMBER

Fig. 5.33

NOTE:
DISTANCE "X" IS EQUAL
TO CAMBER OF TRUSS

DISTANCE "X"

2x4 BLOCKS NAILED
TO LATERAL BRACE

FRAMING ANCHOR
EACH SIDE NAIL
TO JOIST ONLY

DISTANCE "X"

NON LOAD-
BEARING STUD
PARTITIONS

Fig. 5.34

TJL ™/TJW ™ SERIES

NAILS BY
MFR.

METAL CROSS BRACING
BY MFR. TO BE
INSTALLED AS
JOISTS ARE ERECTED

6"
MAX.

Fig. 5.35

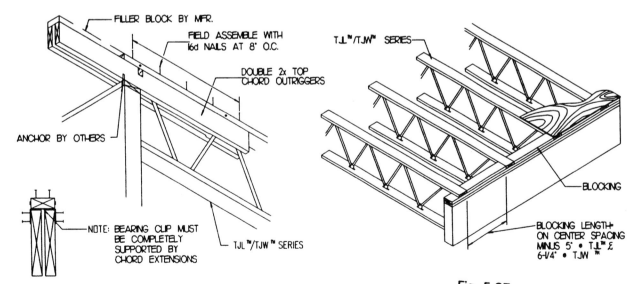

FILLER BLOCK BY MFR.

FIELD ASSEMBLE WITH
16d NAILS AT 8" O.C.

DOUBLE 2x TOP
CHORD OUTRIGGERS

ANCHOR BY OTHERS

NOTE: BEARING CLIP MUST
BE COMPLETELY
SUPPORTED BY
CHORD EXTENSIONS

TJL ™/TJW ™ SERIES

Fig. 5.36

TJL ™/TJW ™ SERIES

BLOCKING

BLOCKING LENGTH=
ON CENTER SPACING
MINUS 5" • TJL ™ £
6-1/4" • TJW ™

Fig. 5.37

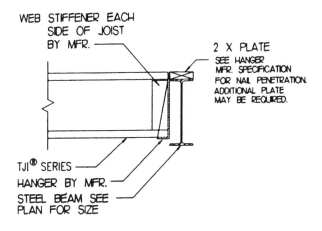

WEB STIFFENER EACH SIDE OF JOIST BY MFR.

2 X PLATE
SEE HANGER MFR. SPECIFICATION FOR NAIL PENETRATION. ADDITIONAL PLATE MAY BE REQUIRED.

TJI® SERIES

HANGER BY MFR.

STEEL BEAM SEE PLAN FOR SIZE

Fig. 5.38

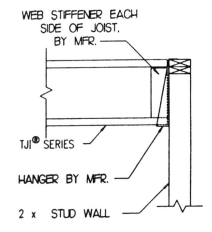

WEB STIFFENER EACH SIDE OF JOIST, BY MFR.

TJI® SERIES

HANGER BY MFR.

2 x STUD WALL

Fig. 5.39

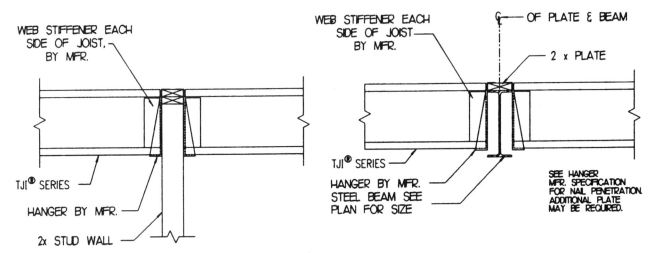

WEB STIFFENER EACH SIDE OF JOIST, BY MFR.

TJI® SERIES

HANGER BY MFR.

2x STUD WALL

Fig. 5.40

℄ OF PLATE & BEAM

2 x PLATE

WEB STIFFENER EACH SIDE OF JOIST BY MFR.

TJI® SERIES

HANGER BY MFR.

STEEL BEAM SEE PLAN FOR SIZE

SEE HANGER MFR. SPECIFICATION FOR NAIL PENETRATION. ADDITIONAL PLATE MAY BE REQUIRED.

Fig. 5.41

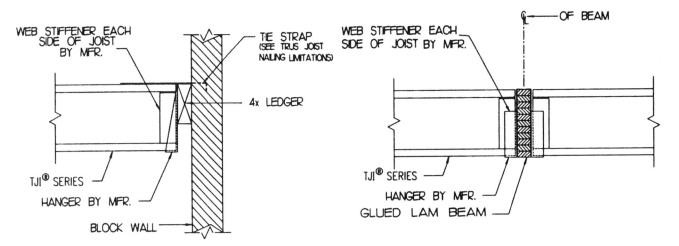

WEB STIFFENER EACH SIDE OF JOIST BY MFR.

TIE STRAP (SEE TRUS JOIST NAILING LIMITATIONS)

4x LEDGER

TJI® SERIES

HANGER BY MFR.

BLOCK WALL

Fig. 5.42

℄ OF BEAM

WEB STIFFENER EACH SIDE OF JOIST BY MFR.

TJI® SERIES

HANGER BY MFR.

GLUED LAM BEAM

Fig. 5.43

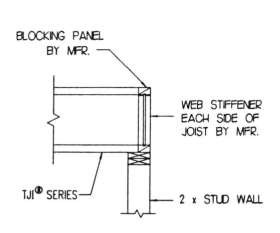

Fig. 5.44

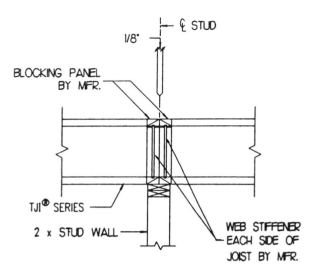

Fig. 5.45

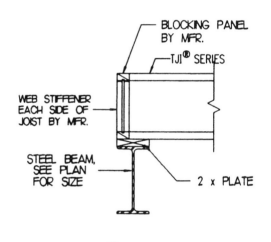

Fig. 5.46

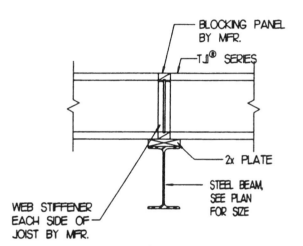

Fig. 5.47

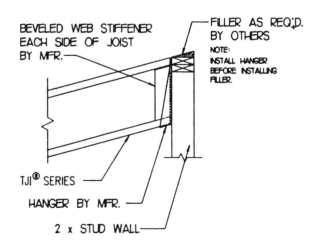

Fig. 5.48

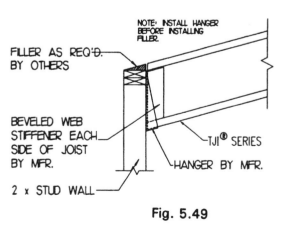

Fig. 5.49

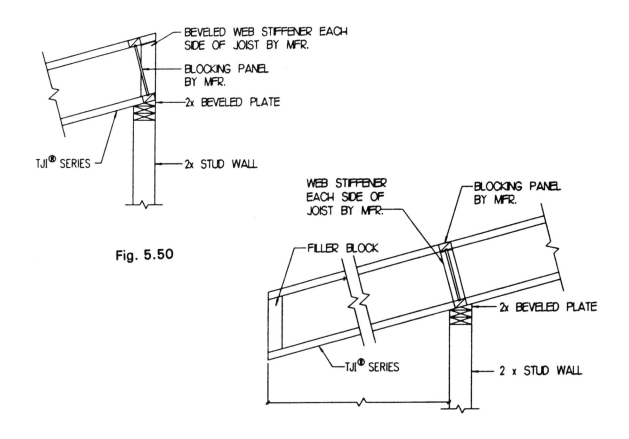

BEVELED WEB STIFFENER EACH SIDE OF JOIST BY MFR.

BLOCKING PANEL BY MFR.

2x BEVELED PLATE

2x STUD WALL

TJI® SERIES

Fig. 5.50

WEB STIFFENER EACH SIDE OF JOIST BY MFR.

BLOCKING PANEL BY MFR.

FILLER BLOCK

2x BEVELED PLATE

TJI® SERIES

2 x STUD WALL

Fig. 5.51

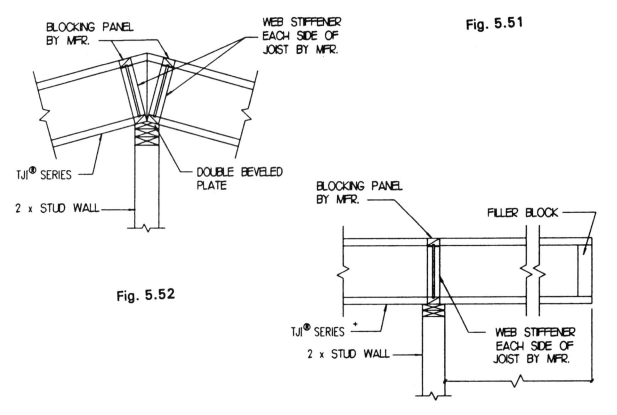

BLOCKING PANEL BY MFR.

WEB STIFFENER EACH SIDE OF JOIST BY MFR.

TJI® SERIES

DOUBLE BEVELED PLATE

2 x STUD WALL

Fig. 5.52

BLOCKING PANEL BY MFR.

FILLER BLOCK

TJI® SERIES

2 x STUD WALL

WEB STIFFENER EACH SIDE OF JOIST BY MFR.

Fig. 5.53

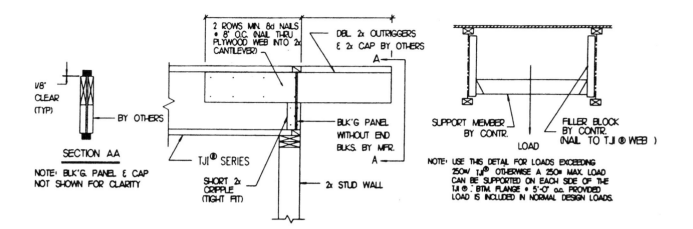

Section AA

1/8" CLEAR (TYP)

BY OTHERS

NOTE: BLK'G. PANEL & CAP NOT SHOWN FOR CLARITY

2 ROWS MIN. 8d NAILS @ 8" O.C. (NAIL THRU PLYWOOD WEB INTO 2x CANTILEVER)

DBL. 2x OUTRIGGERS & 2x CAP BY OTHERS

A

BLK'G PANEL WITHOUT END BLKS. BY MFR.

A

TJI® SERIES

SHORT 2x CRIPPLE (TIGHT FIT)

2x STUD WALL

Fig. 5.54

SUPPORT MEMBER BY CONTR.

LOAD

FILLER BLOCK BY CONTR. (NAIL TO TJI® WEB)

NOTE: USE THIS DETAIL FOR LOADS EXCEEDING 250# TJI® OTHERWISE A 250# MAX. LOAD CAN BE SUPPORTED ON EACH SIDE OF THE TJI® BTM. FLANGE @ 5'-0" o.c. PROVIDED LOAD IS INCLUDED IN NORMAL DESIGN LOADS.

Fig. 5.55

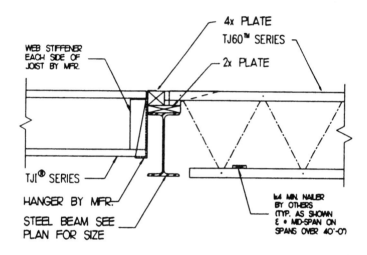

WEB STIFFENER EACH SIDE OF JOIST BY MFR.

4x PLATE

TJ60™ SERIES

2x PLATE

TJI® SERIES

HANGER BY MFR.

STEEL BEAM SEE PLAN FOR SIZE

1x4 MIN. NAILER BY OTHERS (TYP. AS SHOWN & @ MID-SPAN ON SPANS OVER 40'-0")

Fig. 5.56

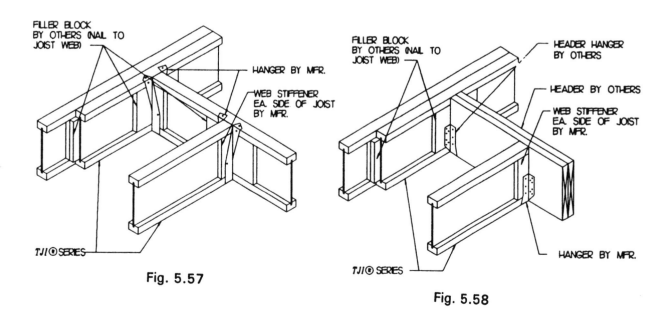

FILLER BLOCK BY OTHERS (NAIL TO JOIST WEB)

HANGER BY MFR.

WEB STIFFENER EA. SIDE OF JOIST BY MFR.

TJI® SERIES

Fig. 5.57

FILLER BLOCK BY OTHERS (NAIL TO JOIST WEB)

HEADER HANGER BY OTHERS

HEADER BY OTHERS

WEB STIFFENER EA. SIDE OF JOIST BY MFR.

HANGER BY MFR.

TJI® SERIES

Fig. 5.58

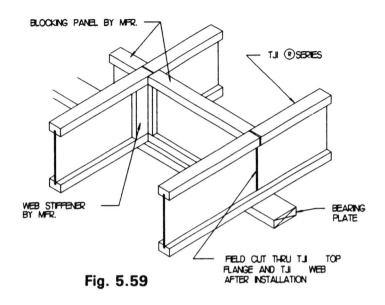

BLOCKING PANEL BY MFR.

TJI ®SERIES

WEB STIFFENER
BY MFR.

BEARING
PLATE

FIELD CUT THRU TJI TOP
FLANGE AND TJI WEB
AFTER INSTALLATION

Fig. 5.59

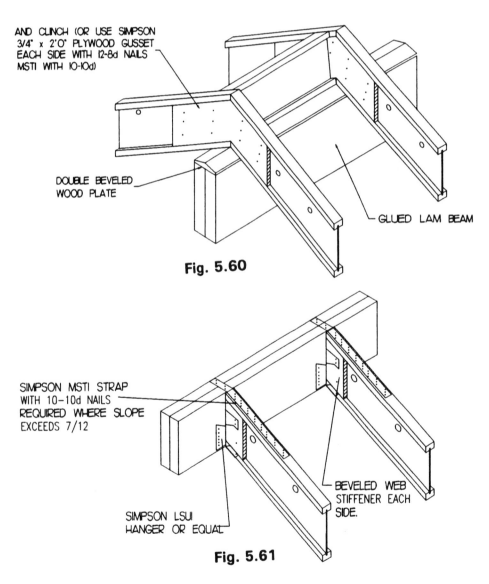

AND CLINCH (OR USE SIMPSON
3/4" x 2'0" PLYWOOD GUSSET
EACH SIDE WITH 12-8d NAILS
MSTI WITH 10-10d)

DOUBLE BEVELED
WOOD PLATE

GLUED LAM BEAM

Fig. 5.60

SIMPSON MSTI STRAP
WITH 10-10d NAILS
REQUIRED WHERE SLOPE
EXCEEDS 7/12

BEVELED WEB
STIFFENER EACH
SIDE.

SIMPSON LSUI
HANGER OR EQUAL

Fig. 5.61

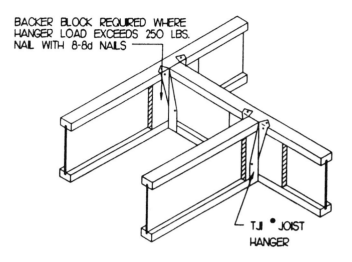

BACKER BLOCK REQUIRED WHERE
HANGER LOAD EXCEEDS 250 LBS.
NAIL WITH 8-8d NAILS

TJI • JOIST
HANGER

Fig. 5.62

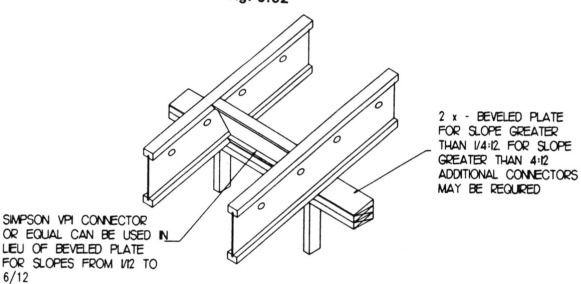

2 x - BEVELED PLATE
FOR SLOPE GREATER
THAN 1/4:12. FOR SLOPE
GREATER THAN 4:12
ADDITIONAL CONNECTORS
MAY BE REQUIRED

SIMPSON VPI CONNECTOR
OR EQUAL CAN BE USED IN
LIEU OF BEVELED PLATE
FOR SLOPES FROM 1/12 TO
6/12

Fig. 5.63

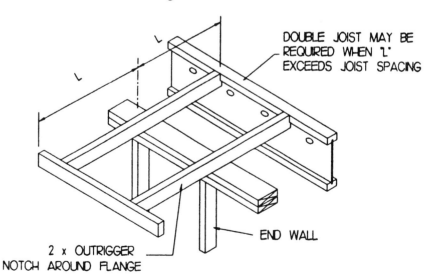

DOUBLE JOIST MAY BE
REQUIRED WHEN 'L'
EXCEEDS JOIST SPACING

END WALL

2 x OUTRIGGER
NOTCH AROUND FLANGE

Fig. 5.64

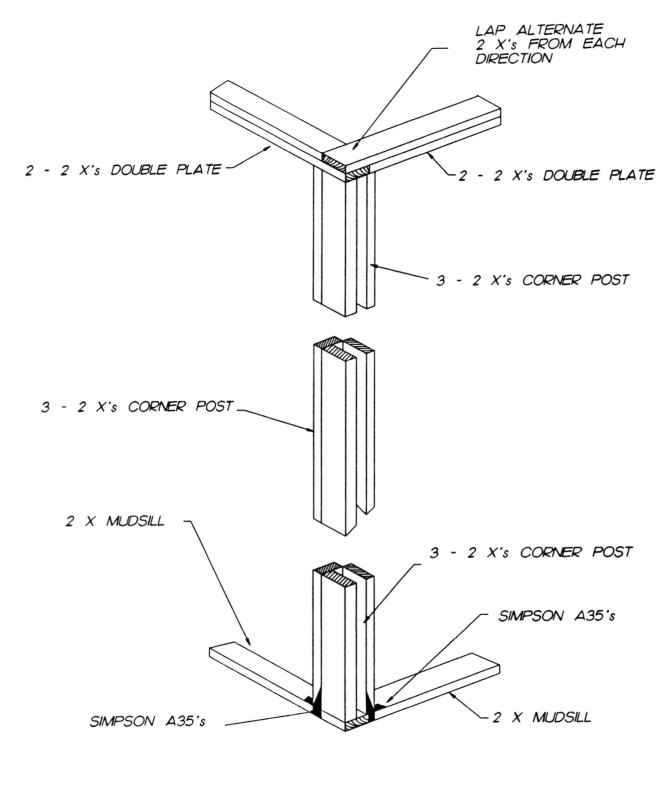

LAP ALTERNATE
2 X's FROM EACH
DIRECTION

2 - 2 X's DOUBLE PLATE

2 - 2 X's DOUBLE PLATE

3 - 2 X's CORNER POST

3 - 2 X's CORNER POST

2 X MUDSILL

3 - 2 X's CORNER POST

SIMPSON A35's

SIMPSON A35's

2 X MUDSILL

STUD WALL CORNER

Fig. 5.65

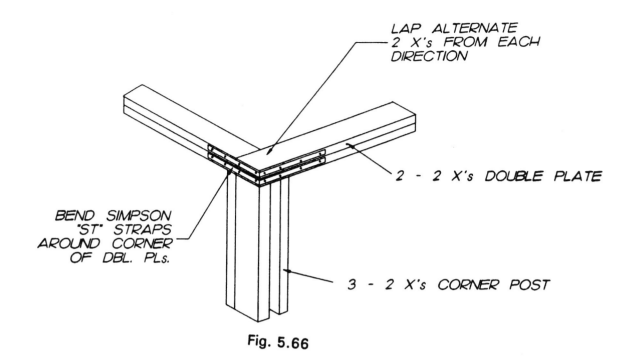

LAP ALTERNATE
2 X's FROM EACH
DIRECTION

2 - 2 X's DOUBLE PLATE

BEND SIMPSON
"ST" STRAPS
AROUND CORNER
OF DBL. PLs.

3 - 2 X's CORNER POST

Fig. 5.66

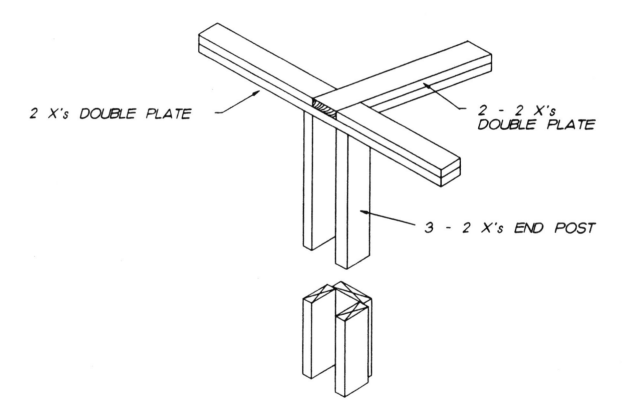

2 X's DOUBLE PLATE

2 - 2 X's
DOUBLE PLATE

3 - 2 X's END POST

STUD WALL INTERSECTION

Fig. 5.67

6

Construction Connections

The capacities of wood-framing connections are equally as important to the structure as the strength of the individual framing members. In fact, connection configurations may govern the size of the framing member. Edge distances and spacing dimensions of connection fasteners may necessitate that the size of a member be greater than the size designed to support structural loads. Accuracy in design, reliability of the strength of materials, and the quality of field workmanship are the determining factors in developing the strength of structural connections.

Products manufactured within a factory environment have the advantage of a high degree of control for both materials and workmanship; however, the same limits are not available for field construction. On-site inspections of completed construction work are effective in checking the major visible conditions. However, almost every practicing engineer can relate his or her own personal story about a field inspection in which a crucial connection was found to be deficient either in workmanship or materials. Recent records of structural failures indicate that in many instances the cause of a failure could be directly attributed to the inadequacy of a connection.

Standard types of connections for any structural material, whether wood, concrete, masonry, or steel, have their advantages as long as they are evaluated by calculations for each particular condition for which they are applied. Often the engineer will relegate the task of designing and drawing the connection details to the drafter. This is not realistic and represents a risk on the part of the engineer, since it is not the drafter's responsibility to perform engineering functions. The drafter may not have a sufficient knowledge of the forces involved, or of the structural calculation methods required to design connections. Design of structural connections often requires the drafter to produce an accurate scale drawing to determine the type, size, and spacing of the fasteners. The process of drawing a detail will reflect its actual fabrication. Explicit drawings of structural connections will verify the feasibility of the connection configuration. Verbal instruction of connection requirements may not disclose sufficient information; also, verbal instructions are open to multiple interpretations in the field. Communicating by rumor may leave a great deal of data to be desired. An engineer's lack of confidence in the capacity of structural connections can be a serious deterrent to a good night's sleep.

Each element of a structure must be capable of sustaining its own weight plus any externally applied live loads. The framing members of the structure must also be sequentially connected to transfer all design loads and forces. Detail drawings depicting frame connections serve to prescribe the total system as a unified structural entity. The design connections rely on the magnitude and direction of the forces to be resisted, the geometric pattern and spacing of the fastening hardware, the species and the specific gravity of the lumber, and the types of nails or bolts to be used.

The *National Design Specification for Wood Construction* (NDS), 1991 ed., Table 7.3.1, also requires that the connection be designed for certain modifying characteristics for each type of connection and hardware. Connections are classified according to their resistive direction either as a "shear," Z, connection or as a "withdrawal," W, connection. Shear connections resist forces that act laterally to the cross-sectional area of the fastener shank and the projected bearing area of the penetrated surface of the lumber. When a shear force passes through two cross-sectional areas of a single fastener, it is considered to be reacting in double shear. The resistive value of shear fasteners such as nails, bolts, or lag screws is calculated as the number of pounds of reactive resistance. Connections classified as withdrawal or pull-out joints operate by resisting forces acting parallel to the axis of a fastener shank. Also, withdrawal may react either in tension or in compression against the grain of the lumber. The withdrawal resistive value of a wood fastener is calculated as the number of pounds per inch of penetration of the fastener. High unit compressive stresses perpendicular to the surface of the lumber that result from withdrawal forces on the contact surface of the head of a bolt or lag bolt can be reduced by providing washers to spread the load over a larger area of the grain. When bolts or lag screws are installed, it is good practice to place a metal washer under the bolt head and the end nut. Design examples for connections reacting in shear and withdrawal are presented in this chapter. The example calculations are performed in accordance with the NDS and the third edition of the *American Institute of Timber Construction* (AITC) and the 1991 edition of the *Uniform Building Code*. It is recommended that the reader become familiar with the notation assignments presented in NDS 1.6. All chapter numbers, tables, and equation reference designations on the following pages are identified by the same numbers as those given in each of the above references.

Commercial lumber is divided into four separate groups depending on their average specific gravity designated as G. NDS Table 12A presents a tabulation of the value of G for a number of species of lumber. The species of lumber used in all of the design examples given in this chapter is Douglas fir–larch, which is classified in Group II with a specific gravity $G = 0.49$. As previously stated, NDS Section 1.6 denotes the nominal design shear value of a single fastener as Z and the nominal withdrawal design value as W. NDS gives the nominal value for each classification of connection for each of the different types of fasteners. The nominal values for Z and W need to be adjusted to determine their allowable working strength. They are adjusted by factors that are evaluated by such use conditions as moisture, duration of load, and temperature.

NDS Table 7.3.1 specifies the factors for each type of fastener and classification of connection. The adjusted nominal values of W and Z are converted to allowable working strength values designated as W' and Z'. Example 2, S-1 demonstrates that NDS provides for all contingencies of loading and method of fabrication. However, NDS Section 2.1.2 also recognizes that it is the responsibility of the designer to correlate the adjustment assumptions to the actual functioning conditions. An example of this type of design judgment can be found in the NDS,

Appendix B.2, which specifies adjustment factors for the duration of the load (C_d). The value of 0.90 for permanent duration of load may not be accurate. Wood, like other organic materials, becomes tired from hard work. UBC Tables 25-G and 25-H, respectively, specify allowable values for shear and withdrawal resistance for nails in Douglas fir–larch. Footnotes of these tables allow for some consideration for service modifiers; however, service adjustment factors are more individually analyzed in NDS Chapter 7.

Nails are the most frequently used type of wood-connection hardware because they are the least expensive and the easiest to install. Example 1, S-1, lines 1 to 35, presents the various shapes and sizes of the foremost types of nails and spikes. A nail specified as a 16d is spoken as a "sixteen-penny" nail. This type of designation started in England around the eighteenth century and is still being used in modern construction. The designation convention originated at a time when it was possible to purchase one hundred nails of a certain size or weight for a specific number of pennies or pence; consequently, the cost in the number of pennies per one hundred nails of a particular size becomes its numerical designation. Notice that although the designations and the shank length may be the same for two types of nails, the diameters increase for each succeeding type of nail or spike. For example, the shank diameter of a 16d box nail equals 0.135 in, while the shank diameter of a 16d common nail equals 0.162 in. Data from the *National Construction Estimator,* 1994 edition, stipulates the cost of materials and labor for 16d common nails to be approximately $0.065 per installed nail. It can be seen that it is relatively inexpensive to construct a nailed connection that may exceed the expected force requirements. It can be quite expensive in the long run to construct a nailed connection in which the number of nails is not commensurate to the forces involved.

Engineering design of nailed connections should be performed within the NDS parameters to determine that a connection has a sufficient quantity of nails. Very little is saved by an engineering design which attempts to cut construction costs by reducing the number of nails of a connection. Compared with the cost of nails, it is hardly worth the effort or the time.

UBC Table 25-Q, Nailing Schedule, is a tabulation of twenty-six of the most encountered wood-connection situations and their respective nailing requirements. A contractor or an engineer can use this table for most ordinary types of structures with a reasonable degree of assurance, but the user should also be aware that forces may occur in which design verification may be required. An example of this type of situation can be seen in developing a functional connection between a roof or floor diaphragm to a vertical shear wall. It is often necessary to calculate the size and spacing of the nails required to transfer the horizontal forces to the wall top double plates as shown in Figures 7.9, 7.10, and 7.11. Design of nailed connections relies on the magnitude and direction of the forces to be resisted, geometric patterns and spacing of the fastening hardware, species and specific gravity of the lumber, and the types of fasteners used. The examples in this chapter arrange the center of resistance pattern of the hardware to be mutually concentric with the connected members; otherwise an eccentric moment can occur and create combinations of secondary stresses.

Although item No. 7 of UBC Table 25-Q specifies two 16d end nails between the double plate and the top of the stud, end nailing is not recommended for designed nailed connections because the end grain of commercial lumber offers very low resistance to shear and withdrawal. Selection of the size and type of nail for a connection depends on the magnitude and direction of the forces to be resisted. Common nails have a larger shank diameter than box nails and therefore provide higher shear and withdrawal resistance. For this reason common nails are more often used for rough framing than box nails. Annular threaded nails have a high resistance to withdrawal due to the shape of the shank. Helically threaded nails are manufactured by a heat hardening process and have a greater capacity for shear and pull-out.

Nails classified as spikes have the same shear resistance as nails in either direction of the wood grain; however, spikes may be installed by using a predrilled hole equal to 75 percent of the shank diameter. Larger pilot holes are permitted for lumber having a higher specific gravity. The shank surface of a nail may be coated with cement or be galvanized to avoid corrosion; however, this does not substantially affect its structural value. NDS Section 12.3.4 requires the length of a nail or spike shank to extend 12 shank diameters into the connected lumber; however, the penetration shall not be less than 6 shank diameters. The penetration modifier for Z' is designated as C_d. Example 1, S-1, lines 25 to 35, presents the equation for the calculation of the modifier factor for nail penetration. AITC Table 6.36 presents a tabulation of required and minimum penetration values for nails and spikes for each group classification of commercial lumber. Example 1 shows four types of nails and nail heads.

Annularly and helically threaded nails offer the highest resistance to pull out. Flat-head nails are the most frequently used. The shape of a nail head is selected to fulfill a particular purpose. Sinker nail heads are used for the installation of gypsum board drywall. Roofing nail heads are flat with a large diameter to secure the material in place. Example 1 also shows diagrams for accepted nail spacing. Incorrect plywood edge nailing can substantially reduce the lateral force capacity of a diaphragm by splitting the supporting members. Example 1 shows the American Plywood Association recommended nail size and plywood thickness. Most building codes require that support members be at least a nominal 3 in wide for nails spaced at 2.5 in oc or less. Also, the nails are required to be staggered on both sides of the panel edge. It is good practice to inspect the installation of diaphragm nails from both sides of a floor or wall. Occasionally the edge member will be offset from the panel edge, and a carpenter may drive the nails at the panel edge but will miss the framing lumber. In this instance the nail penetration will equal zero, but they will be in a straight line.

Example 2, S-1, describes several design code methods of determining the shear and withdrawal resistance values of a nail in single shear. The example shows that there are slight differences in these values specified by each design code. It can be seen on line 3 that the UBC reduces the value of Z' by one-third for shear resistance parallel to the grain of the member, whereas other design codes assume the same value for any direction of the grain. Example 2, S-1, lines 16 to 38, lists the applicable adjustment factors for a number of conditions for values of Z and W. The factors are set equal to 1 in this case for the purpose of comparison. Also, NDS adjustment modifiers can make a significant difference in nail resistance; for instance, the toe-nail factor is equal to 0.67. The use of metal side plates can increase the use of the fastener by a factor of 25 percent. A table of NDS reference numbers is given for each particular factor. The nominal values for Z and W are factorially adjusted to calculate the working strength of the nail, which in this case is a 16d common nail.

Example 2, S-2, lines 1 to 21, demonstrates the equations used by the National Forest Products Association (NFPA) to calculate the nominal values of Z and W for each group of commercial lumber. It should be noted that these are only the nominal values and that the adjustment factors of the NDS are still applicable to calculate the working values. It can be seen that the values of Z and W derived by these equations are quite close to those specified by the NDS. Example 2, Case 1, demonstrates a lapped nailed splice in double shear. The total assembly is 3 in thick and the length of the 16d nail is 3.5 in. The nail's Z value may be increased by one-third if it passes through all three members and if the side members are at least one-third of the thickness of the center member. Example 2, Case 2, demonstrates a standard method of connecting a wall stud to the top of a floor double plate. UBC Table 25-Q, item number 8, calls for four 8d toe nails (two nails each side). NDS requires a one-third reduction for toe nails; however, since it is required to resist wind forces, the duration factor equals 1.6. Accurate workmanship and the quality of the lumber can be critical for installing toe nails to prevent lumber splitting and to ensure the required penetration.

Example 3, S-1, Case 1, is a calculation of a single-shear lapped splice. The factor of 0.67 is as per UBC Section 2510(c), which specifies a one-third reduction for nails parallel to the grain of the member. Note that NDS does have this requirement. Case 2 demonstrates the same type of lap connection, but since the nails are perpendicular to the grain, no reduction is taken. Example 3, S-1, Case 3, shows a double-member lap splice. This is not considered as a double-shear splice since the nails do not penetrate all three members. Example 3, S-2, Case 4, uses four 16d nails to react in withdrawal to a suspended wood stud partition. The horizontal load is designated as F_H and the vertical force as F_V. No grain direction is taken for the force vertical to the direction of the grain. Case 5 calculates the force capacity with a 25 percent increase allowed for the use of a metal side plate. Case 6 checks the sole plate nails for shear resistance. UBC allows a 33 percent increase for seismic forces.

Example 4, S-1, shows the nailing pattern on a horizontal plywood diaphragm. The boundary is defined as the panel edge adjacent to the vertical shear wall. Panel and boundary edge nail size and spacing are used to resist lateral wind or seismic forces. The intermediate field nails connect the plywood to the framing members. Plywood panels should be placed on horizontal diaphragms so that the exterior surface grain spans perpendicular to the framing members. Cases 1 and 2 show a nailed blocking method to resist shear forces at the double plate. Example 4, S-2, demonstrates the design calculation methods for shear and uplift on a plywood seismic wall. It is good practice to use nominal 4× members at the wall boundaries as opposed to using multiple studs. A problem arises when a number of 2× studs are substituted for a solid boundary member in that the nailing between the perimeter studs may not be sufficient to distribute the compression or uplift reactions, and the nailing may locate between stud surface joints, thus negating the required nail penetration. Also, when both sides of the wall require plywood, it is good practice to stagger the spacing of the nails on each side. Case 4 demonstrates a 4-ft-long lap splice of a wall top double plate. The designed number of nails exceed the required number by the UBC nailing table schedule.

Wire staples are used in wood construction generally as a substitute for nails for attaching surface materials to wood floors, ceilings, and stud walls. The use of mechanical devices to insert staples makes them relatively less expensive than hand-driven nails. Staples are shaped like an inverted U with two legs separated by a horizontal crown. Shear resistance of staple fasteners is calculated by the same method used for nails except that the value is doubled to account for the two legs of the configuration. Although NDS does not specify any strength values for staples for structural connections of commercial lumber, UBC Table 47-I does permit the use of 16-gage wire staples with $7/8$-in-long legs for attaching an expanded metal lath and a $7/8$-in-thick layer of cement stucco to exterior studs. The UBC allowed 180 lb/ft resistance to externally applied lateral forces for this cement stucco diaphragm assembly. However, since the Northridge earthquake, the allowable shear resistance value has been reduced by one-half. Many site inspections of wood-framed structures showed large areas of exterior cement plaster disengaged from the studs. The cause of this problem is still under investigation for the strength of materials and for the method of installation.

Wood screws are frequently used in manufacturing prefabricated wood connections in lieu of driven nails. Mass production techniques afford a higher degree of workmanship and output than regular on-site methods of construction. Use of shop-powered tools can make wood screws more economical than nails in wood manufacturing. Manual installation of screws requires more skill and accuracy for installation than driving nails. When screws are used for wood connections, their methods of installation should not be abused. NDS specifies that screws be installed by rotation and shall not be hammered in place, which is always a temptation at the job site. NDS permits screws to be installed by using predrilled holes or lead holes and light lubricants which can reduce surface resistance and prevent splitting of the wood. Among older carpenters, saliva seems to be the lubricant of choice. Wood screws are identified by two important dimensions. The first identifying designation is the gage number of the screw, which indicates the wire diameter of the shank portion of the screw. The second designation number is the length of the screw, which is used to calculate the penetration length of the threaded portion into the main connected member. Wood screw shear (Z) and withdrawal (W) values are modified by the same adjustment factors used for nails as specified in NDS Table 7.3.1.

NDS Part XI, Table 11.2A, presents a tabulation of withdrawal values per inch of penetration for each particular specific gravity of lumber and for each gage or shank diameter of a wood screw. The total withdrawal resistance of a screw is equal to W' multiplied by the penetrated threaded length. NDS Tables 11.3A and 11.3B present a tabulation of shear values for wood metal splices. The design examples of wood screw connections presented in this chapter use Douglas fir–larch lumber, Group II, $G = 0.49$, and 16-gage screws. NDS Table 11.2A specifies $W = 183$ lb/in of penetration. Table 3.A specifies $Z = 228$ lb for nominal 2× side members; and Table 11.3B, 16-gage side plates, 10-gage nail, $Z = 136$ lb. It should be noted that the working resistance values of wood screws may be increased 25 percent for the use of metal side plates, 33 percent for seismic or wind forces. The lateral value (Z) of wood screws placed to resist forces parallel to the grain shall be reduced by one-third.

Example 5, S-1, presents drawings of wood screws and their element designations. The countersink head screw is used for situations in which the head of the screw must be level with the wood surface. The root diameter is approximately 70 percent of the shank diameter. The screw penetration requirements and penetration adjustment factor are presented between lines 10 and 18. The length of penetration is defined as the length of thread that extends into the main member; it should not be considered as being the total thread length of the screw. Lines 19 to 36 present a table of screw sizes and their respective diameters. Also, the lead hole diameters are presented as a percentage of a diameter for withdrawal and shear for commercial lumber in Group I and Group II. No lead holes are required for lumber in Group III or Group IV.

Example 6, S-1, can be used to compare the strength of connections made with wood screws to the nailed connections presented in Example 3. The resultant values indicate that wood screws can offer higher shear and resistance strength. Example 6, S-2, Case 6, is a demonstration of wood screw resistance to forces acting in combination to shear and withdrawal. The length of penetration is a major factor in the calculation of withdrawal for wood screws and lag bolts.

Wood lag screws are often used as an alternate type of fastener in situations where it is either not possible to install a through bolt in the connection, or in instances when it is desired that the opposite side bolt head not be visible. Manual installation of lag screws is performed under the same general requirements for the smaller-sized wood screws, except that penetration, lead holes, and spacing vary due to the increased diameter of the lag screws and the hexagonal shape of the head. Example 7, S-1, presents a tabulation of dimensional data for lag screws. NDS Part XI permits screws to be installed by using predrilled holes or lead holes. Section 9.1.2.2 states that lead holes shall not be used for lag screws with a diameter of $\frac{3}{8}$ in or smaller. Wood lag screws are identified by the shank diameter and the total length. The penetration length of a lag screw should be eight times the shank diameter; however, this does not include the tip length. The minimum required penetration should not be less than four times the shank diameter. These values are used to calculate the penetration adjustment as per NDS Section 9.3.3.

Wood screw shear (Z) and withdrawal (W) values are modified by the same adjustment factors used for nails as specified in NDS Table 7.3.1. NDS Part IX presents a table of withdrawal values per inch of penetration for each particular specific gravity of lumber and for each size of lag screw. The withdrawal and shear values are calculated in the same manner as demonstrated for wood screws.

Installation of lag screws requires predrilled lead holes of a diameter equal to a percent of the shank diameter. The shear and pullout strength of lag screws relies on the grip of the thread surface of the penetrated member, plus the length of the threaded penetration. The strength of through bolts used for wood connections does not depend on the fastener thread grip on the material, but on the bearing area of the wood and the pattern of yield reaction of the bolt. It is good practice to predrill holes for through-bolt installation. These bolt holes should be approximately $\frac{1}{16}$ to $\frac{1}{32}$ in greater than the shank diameter. Driving bolts in a wood connection may split the surrounding lumber, thereby lessening their resistance value. Bolts should be placed with metal washers or side plates at the bolt head and at the nut to prevent high compression stress caused by tightening the nuts.

The NDS method of determining the lateral resistance of a dowel-shaped fastener for wood connections is based on the engineering mechanics of a yield limit model. NDS Appendix I diagrams assumed deformations of dowels for several cases of shear resistance. Calculating yield point shear resistance of bolts using the equations in NDS Section 8.2.1 may not be efficient. Tables 8.2A and 8.2C present a tabulation of bolt design single shear values of Z for each main member width, bolt size, width of side plates, and specific gravity of lumber. Table 8.2C is concerned only with single-shear bolts used in glued laminated wood. Double-shear bolt resistance values for commercial lumber and glued laminated lumbers are tabulated in Tables 8.3A and 8.3C, respectively. Single-shear or double-shear type connections are defined by the number of cross-sectional planes of the bolt through which the resisted load passes. The average bearing stress of a bolted shear connection can be calculated by dividing the resisted force by the projected area on the resisting members. The tables in NDS are for single-shear or double-shear arrangements. In cases in which the connection has more than two or multiple shear planes, NDS recommends evaluating each shear plane as a single shear plane and set the strength value of the connection as the product of the weakest plane times the number of planes. All adjustment factors specified in NDS Table 7.3.1 apply to the shear values specified for bolted connections. In view of the fact that holes for installation of bolts are drilled with a diameter greater than the bolt shank diameter, bolts offer no resistance to withdrawal. Tensing on a bolt can exert compression on the surface members sufficient to require extra size washers.

Example 8, S-1, presents drawings of two types of bolts used for wood connections. Bolts designated by ASTM Specification No. A307 are most commonly used for wood connections. This category of bolt has a square head and is not considered to be a high-strength fastener. The bolt designated as ASTM A325 is a high-strength bolt and is more commonly used for structural steel connections. High-strength bolts are tightened to much higher tension than wood bolts. Spacing of bolts can be quite complex depending on the direction of the grain of the lumber, the shank diameter, and the available space for edge distance and space between the bolts. It is good practice to sketch the proposed connection to ensure that bolts specified are feasible for the space available. The design methodology for wood-bolted connections is basically the same as presented in examples for lag screws. The bolt pattern of connections may require an adjustment factor to the allowable stress of the fasteners. When bolts are used with a metal side plate for tension splices, it is good practice to check unit tensile stress for the net cross section of the plates. The Hanison equation is used to calculate the connection just as is demonstrated in Example 6, Case 6.

The previous calculation examples and design code data were concerned with basic types of wood-fastening hardware such as nails, screws, and bolts. There are also available a number of manufactured light metal wood connectors designed to meet a broad variety of connection configurations and forces. The shapes of each part of metal connectors are designed to accommodate the actual dimensions of the wood members to be joined. These products have been certified by building departments and are presently used throughout the construction industry. Metal connectors that use nails and bolts have reduced construction labor costs. Extra metal hardware strategically added to a wood-framed structure can help to significantly add to its overall strength. This is particularly true for the use of metal straps and clips for seismic resistance. The ratio of cost to structural strength for manufactured hardware cannot be disputed. The hardware details presented on the following pages are manufactured by the Simpson Strong Tie Company. There are other qualified companies that manufacture these products throughout the United States. The designation number of each connection detail or part on the following pages matches the number in the Simpson Company catalog. Producers of metal connection products which are certified for use in a particular building code jurisdiction also publish design catalogs which give the approved load values for each condition of use.

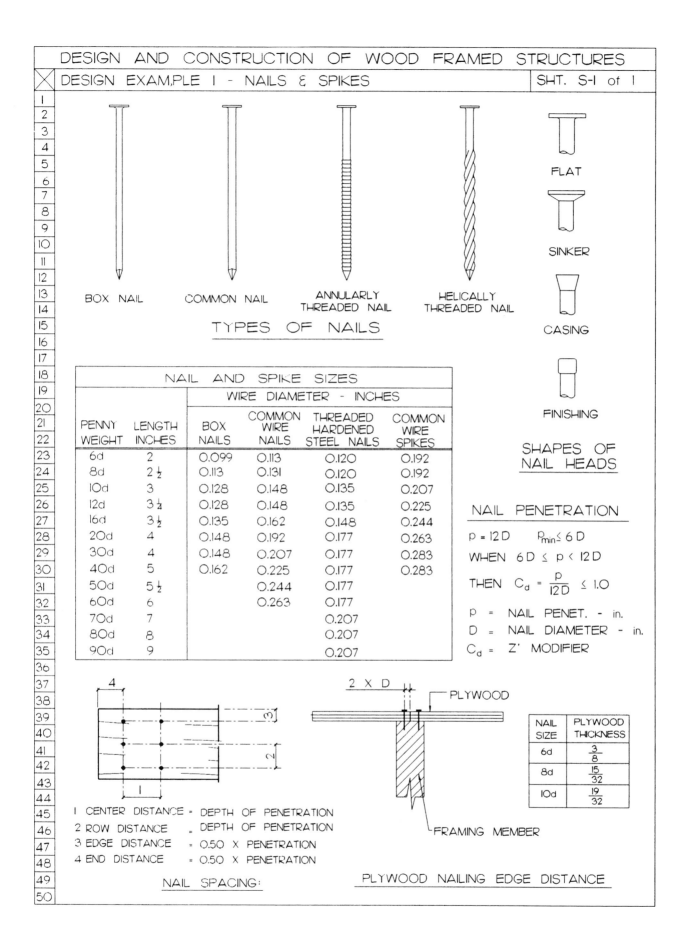

TYPES OF NAILS

FLAT

SINKER

CASING

FINISHING

SHAPES OF NAIL HEADS

BOX NAIL | COMMON NAIL | ANNULARLY THREADED NAIL | HELICALLY THREADED NAIL

NAIL AND SPIKE SIZES

		WIRE DIAMETER - INCHES			
PENNY WEIGHT	LENGTH INCHES	BOX NAILS	COMMON WIRE NAILS	THREADED HARDENED STEEL NAILS	COMMON WIRE SPIKES
6d	2	0.099	0.113	0.120	0.192
8d	2½	0.113	0.131	0.120	0.192
10d	3	0.128	0.148	0.135	0.207
12d	3¼	0.128	0.148	0.135	0.225
16d	3½	0.135	0.162	0.148	0.244
20d	4	0.148	0.192	0.177	0.263
30d	4	0.148	0.207	0.177	0.283
40d	5	0.162	0.225	0.177	0.283
50d	5½		0.244	0.177	
60d	6		0.263	0.177	
70d	7			0.207	
80d	8			0.207	
90d	9			0.207	

NAIL PENETRATION

$p = 12D$ $p_{min} \le 6D$

WHEN $6D \le p < 12D$

THEN $C_d = \dfrac{p}{12D} \le 1.0$

p = NAIL PENET. - in.

D = NAIL DIAMETER - in.

C_d = Z' MODIFIER

PLYWOOD

2 X D

FRAMING MEMBER

NAIL SIZE	PLYWOOD THICKNESS
6d	$\frac{3}{8}$
8d	$\frac{15}{32}$
10d	$\frac{19}{32}$

PLYWOOD NAILING EDGE DISTANCE

1 CENTER DISTANCE = DEPTH OF PENETRATION

2 ROW DISTANCE = DEPTH OF PENETRATION

3 EDGE DISTANCE = 0.50 X PENETRATION

4 END DISTANCE = 0.50 X PENETRATION

NAIL SPACING:

DESIGN AND CONSTRUCTION OF WOOD FRAMED STRUCTURES

DESIGN EXAMPLE 2 - NAILS & SPIKES — SHT. S-1 of 2

UBC - 16d COMMON NAIL FOR SHEAR AND WITHDRAWAL

REF. - UBC TABLE No. 25-G — Z'_q = 108#

REF. UBC SEC. 2510(c) $Z'_p = 0.67 \times Z'_q$ — Z'_p = 72#

REF. - UBC TABLE No. 25-H — W' = 42#

Note: tabulated values are for normal loading conditions

p = parallel to grain

q = perpendicular to grain

AITC - 16d COMMON NAIL FOR SHEAR AND WITHDRAWAL

REF. - AITC TABLE 6.36 $Z'_q = Z'_p$ = 108#

REF. - AITC TABLE 6.35

LUMBER: GROUP 2 G = 0.49 W' = 42#

NDS - 16d COMMON NAIL FOR SHEAR AND WITHDRAWAL

NDS TABLE 7.3.1 - NAILS AND SPIKES ADJUSTMENT FACTORS											
W'	C_D	C_M	C_t	o	o	o	o	o	o	o	C_{tn}
Z'	C_D	C_M	C_t	o	o	C_d	C_{eg}	o	o	C_{di}	C_{tn}

ADJUSTMENT FACTORS		NDS REF. No.
C_D = LOAD DURATION FACTOR	= 1.0	7.3.2
C_M = WET SERVICE FACTOR - DRY	= 1.0	7.3.3
C_t = TEMPERATURE FACTOR DRY	= 1.0	7.3.4
C_d = PENETRATION DEPTH FACTOR	= 1.0	12.3.4
C_{tn} = TOE NAIL FACTOR	= 1.0	12.2.3
C_{di} = DIAPHRAGM NAIL FACTOR	= 1.0	12.3.6
C_{eg} = END GRAIN FACTOR	= 1.0	12.3.5

NOTE THAT THE CODE ALSO ALLOWS THE FOLLOWING FACTORS

SEISMIC FORCES = 1.33

METAL SIDE PLATES = 1.25

LET C_F = FACTORIAL OF APPLICABLE ADJUSTMENT FACTORS

C_F = 1.0

REF. NDS TABLE 12.3B $Z'_q = Z'_p = C_F \times 138\# = 138\#$

REF. NDS TABLE 12.2A $W' = C_F \times 38\# = 38\#$

p = parallel to grain *q = perpendicular to grain*

REF. NDS 12.1.1 - MANUAL FOR WOOD FRAME CONSTRUCTION
NATIONAL FORREST PRODUCTS ASSOC. (NFPA) WASHINGTON, DC 1988

$$Z' = C_F \times K \times D^{1.5}$$

$$W' = C_F \times 1380 \times D \times G^{2.5}$$

GIVEN CONDITIONS:

LUMBER - DOUGLAS FIR LARCH
GROUP 2 - SPECIFIC GRAVITY = 0.49
16d COMMON NAILS   D = 0.162 in.
NORMAL DURATION LOAD
NORMAL TEMPERATURE
DRY CONDITIONS
*C_F = 1.0

$$Z' = 1680 \times 0.162^{1.5} = 109.5^{\#}$$

$$W' = 1380 \times 0.162 \times 0.49^{2.5} = 37.6^{\#}$$

* FACTORIAL OF ALL APPLICABLE ADJUSTMENT FACTORS

Z' = ALLOWABLE LATERAL LOAD ON
     A NAIL IN ANY DIRECTION - lbs.

W' = ALLOWABLE WITHDRAWAL LOAD

C_F = FACTORIAL OF APPLICABLE ADJUSTMENT

K = SPECIES FACTOR

LUMBER GROUP	K
I	2040
II	1650
III	1350
IV	1080

D = NAIL SHANK DIAMETETER - in⁊

G = SPECIFIC GRAVITY OF LUMBER

CASE 1 - DOUBLE SHEAR LAP SPLICE

PLAN

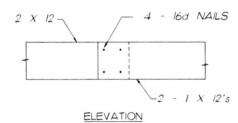

ELEVATION

GIVEN CONDITIONS:

LUMBER - DOUGLAS FIR LARCH
GROUP 2 - SPECIFIC GRAVITY = 0.49
16d COMMON NAILS   D = 0.162 in.
NORMAL DURATION LOAD
NORMAL TEMPERATURE
LENGTH OF NAIL = 3.5"
C_d = 1.33
DRY CONDITIONS

$$F = 1.33 \times 4 \times 109.5 = 582.4^{\#}$$

CASE 2 - STUD TOP & BOTTOM NAILS

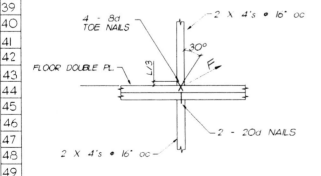

GIVEN CONDITIONS:

LUMBER - DOUGLAS FIR LARCH
GROUP 2 - SPECIFIC GRAVITY = 0.49
8d COMMON NAILS   D = 0.131 in.
WIND LOAD
NORMAL TEMPERATURE
LENGTH OF NAIL = 2.5"
C_{tn} = 0.67 C_D = 1.6
DRY CONDITIONS

$$F = 1.6 \times 0.67 \times 4 \times 1680 \times 0.131^{1.5} = 341.6^{\#}$$

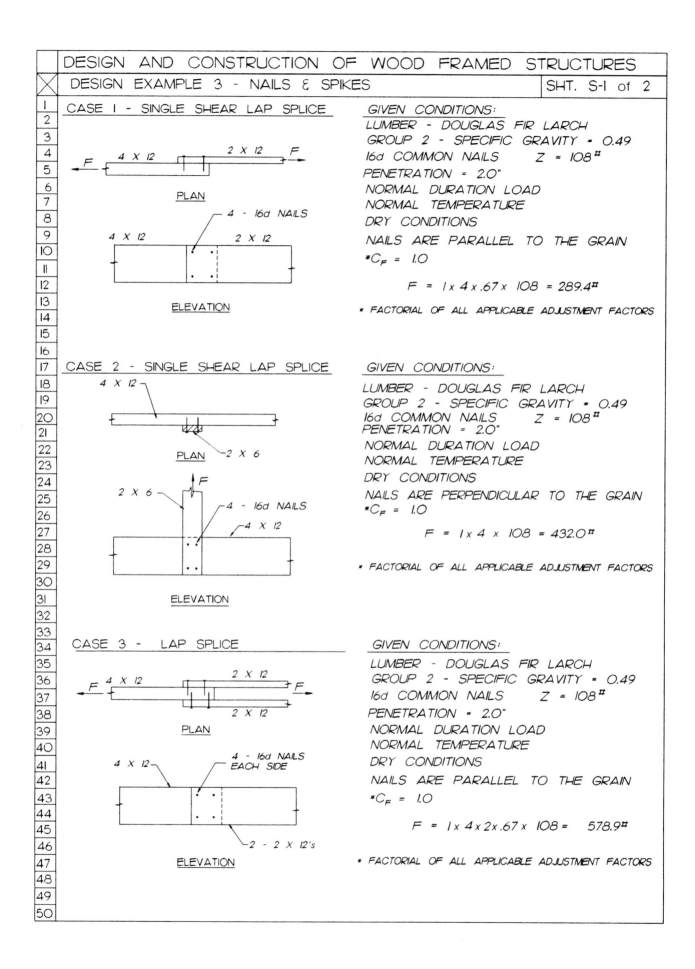

CASE I - SINGLE SHEAR LAP SPLICE

PLAN

4 X 12   2 X 12

ELEVATION

4 X 12   2 X 12

4 - 16d NAILS

GIVEN CONDITIONS:

LUMBER - DOUGLAS FIR LARCH
GROUP 2 - SPECIFIC GRAVITY = 0.49
16d COMMON NAILS $Z = 108^{\#}$
PENETRATION = 2.0"
NORMAL DURATION LOAD
NORMAL TEMPERATURE
DRY CONDITIONS
NAILS ARE PARALLEL TO THE GRAIN
$*C_F = 1.0$

$$F = 1 \times 4 \times .67 \times 108 = 289.4^{\#}$$

* FACTORIAL OF ALL APPLICABLE ADJUSTMENT FACTORS

CASE 2 - SINGLE SHEAR LAP SPLICE

PLAN

4 X 12

2 X 6

ELEVATION

2 X 6

4 - 16d NAILS

4 X 12

F

GIVEN CONDITIONS:

LUMBER - DOUGLAS FIR LARCH
GROUP 2 - SPECIFIC GRAVITY = 0.49
16d COMMON NAILS $Z = 108^{\#}$
PENETRATION = 2.0"
NORMAL DURATION LOAD
NORMAL TEMPERATURE
DRY CONDITIONS
NAILS ARE PERPENDICULAR TO THE GRAIN
$*C_F = 1.0$

$$F = 1 \times 4 \times 108 = 432.0^{\#}$$

* FACTORIAL OF ALL APPLICABLE ADJUSTMENT FACTORS

CASE 3 - LAP SPLICE

PLAN

4 X 12   2 X 12

2 X 12

ELEVATION

4 X 12

4 - 16d NAILS
EACH SIDE

2 - 2 X 12's

GIVEN CONDITIONS:

LUMBER - DOUGLAS FIR LARCH
GROUP 2 - SPECIFIC GRAVITY = 0.49
16d COMMON NAILS $Z = 108^{\#}$
PENETRATION = 2.0"
NORMAL DURATION LOAD
NORMAL TEMPERATURE
DRY CONDITIONS
NAILS ARE PARALLEL TO THE GRAIN
$*C_F = 1.0$

$$F = 1 \times 4 \times 2 \times .67 \times 108 = 578.9^{\#}$$

* FACTORIAL OF ALL APPLICABLE ADJUSTMENT FACTORS

CASE 4 - SINGLE SHEAR LAP SPLICE

SECTION

GIVEN CONDITIONS:

LUMBER - DOUGLAS FIR LARCH
GROUP 2 - SPECIFIC GRAVITY = 0.49
16d COMMON NAILS
$Z = 108$#
$W = 42$#
PENETRATION = 2.0"
NORMAL DURATION LOAD
NORMAL TEMPERATURE
DRY CONDITIONS
NAILS ARE PARALLEL TO THE GRAIN
*$C_F = 1.0$

$$F_H = 1 \times 2 \times .67 \times 108 = 144.7 \text{\#}$$
$$F_V = 1 \times 4 \times 42 \qquad = 168.0 \text{\#}$$

* FACTORIAL OF ALL APPLICABLE ADJUSTMENT FACTORS

CASE 5 - METAL SIDE PLATE CONNECTION

ELEVATION

GIVEN CONDITIONS:

LUMBER - DOUGLAS FIR LARCH
GROUP 2 - SPECIFIC GRAVITY = 0.49
16d COMMON NAILS $Z = 108$#
PENETRATION = 2.0"
NORMAL DURATION LOAD
NORMAL TEMPERATURE
DRY CONDITIONS
NAILS ARE PERPENDICULAR TO THE GRAIN
METAL SIDE PLATE FACTOR = 1.25
*$C_F = 1.25$

$$F = 1.25 \times 5 \times 108 = 675.0 \text{\#}$$

* FACTORIAL OF ALL APPLICABLE ADJUSTMENT FACTORS

CASE 6 - SEISMIC DIAPHRAGM CONNECTION

SECTION

GIVEN CONDITIONS:

LUMBER - DOUGLAS FIR LARCH
GROUP 2 - SPECIFIC GRAVITY = 0.49
16d COMMON NAILS $Z = 108$#
PENETRATION = 2.0"
SEISMIC DURATION LOAD = 1.33
NORMAL TEMPERATURE
DRY CONDITIONS
NAILS ARE PARALLEL TO THE GRAIN
*$C_F = 1.33$

SOLE PL. = $1.33 \times 2 \times 108 = 287.3$ #/FT.
DOUBLE PL. = $1.33 \times 2 \times 0.75 \times 108 = 210.6$ #/FT.

* FACTORIAL OF ALL APPLICABLE ADJUSTMENT FACTORS

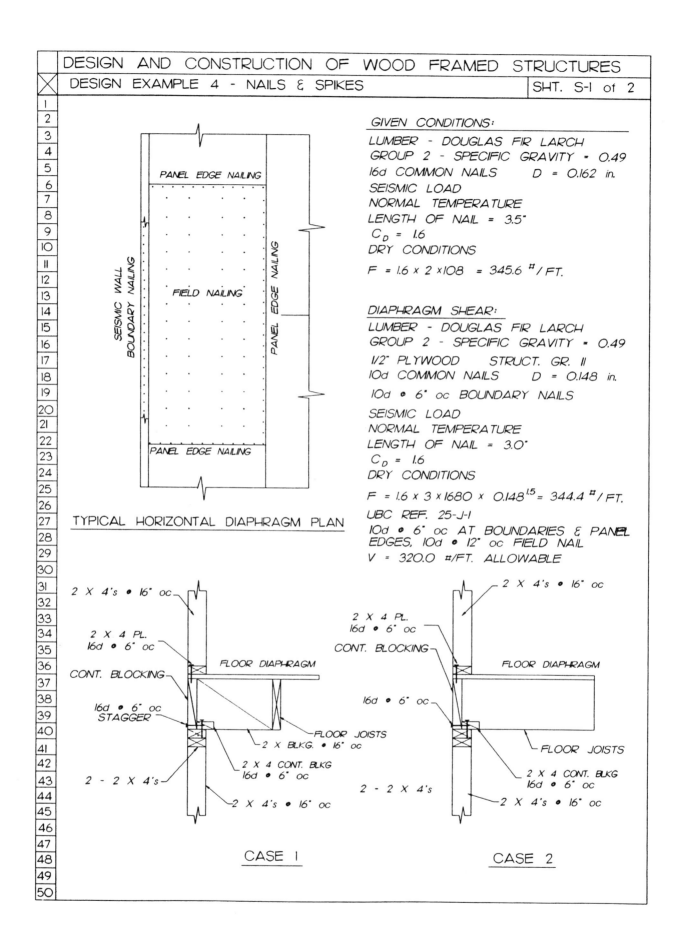

TYPICAL HORIZONTAL DIAPHRAGM PLAN

(plan labels: PANEL EDGE NAILING, SEISMIC WALL BOUNDARY NAILING, PANEL EDGE NAILING, FIELD NAILING, PANEL EDGE NAILING, PANEL EDGE NAILING)

GIVEN CONDITIONS:

LUMBER - DOUGLAS FIR LARCH
GROUP 2 - SPECIFIC GRAVITY = 0.49
16d COMMON NAILS   D = 0.162 in.
SEISMIC LOAD
NORMAL TEMPERATURE
LENGTH OF NAIL = 3.5"
C_D = 1.6
DRY CONDITIONS

$F = 1.6 \times 2 \times 108 = 345.6\ \#/FT.$

DIAPHRAGM SHEAR:

LUMBER - DOUGLAS FIR LARCH
GROUP 2 - SPECIFIC GRAVITY = 0.49
1/2" PLYWOOD   STRUCT. GR. II
10d COMMON NAILS   D = 0.148 in.
10d @ 6" oc BOUNDARY NAILS
SEISMIC LOAD
NORMAL TEMPERATURE
LENGTH OF NAIL = 3.0"
C_D = 1.6
DRY CONDITIONS

$F = 1.6 \times 3 \times 1680 \times 0.148^{1.5} = 344.4\ \#/FT.$

UBC REF. 25-J-I

10d @ 6" oc AT BOUNDARIES & PANEL EDGES, 10d @ 12" oc FIELD NAIL
V = 320.0 #/FT. ALLOWABLE

CASE I

(labels: 2 X 4's @ 16" oc; 2 X 4 PL. 16d @ 6" oc; CONT. BLOCKING; 16d @ 6" oc STAGGER; 2 - 2 X 4's; FLOOR DIAPHRAGM; FLOOR JOISTS; 2 X BLKG. @ 16" oc; 2 X 4 CONT. BLKG 16d @ 6" oc; 2 X 4's @ 16" oc)

CASE 2

(labels: 2 X 4's @ 16" oc; 2 X 4 PL. 16d @ 6" oc; CONT. BLOCKING; 16d @ 6" oc; 2 - 2 X 4's; FLOOR DIAPHRAGM; FLOOR JOISTS; 2 X 4 CONT. BLKG 16d @ 6" oc; 2 X 4's @ 16" oc)

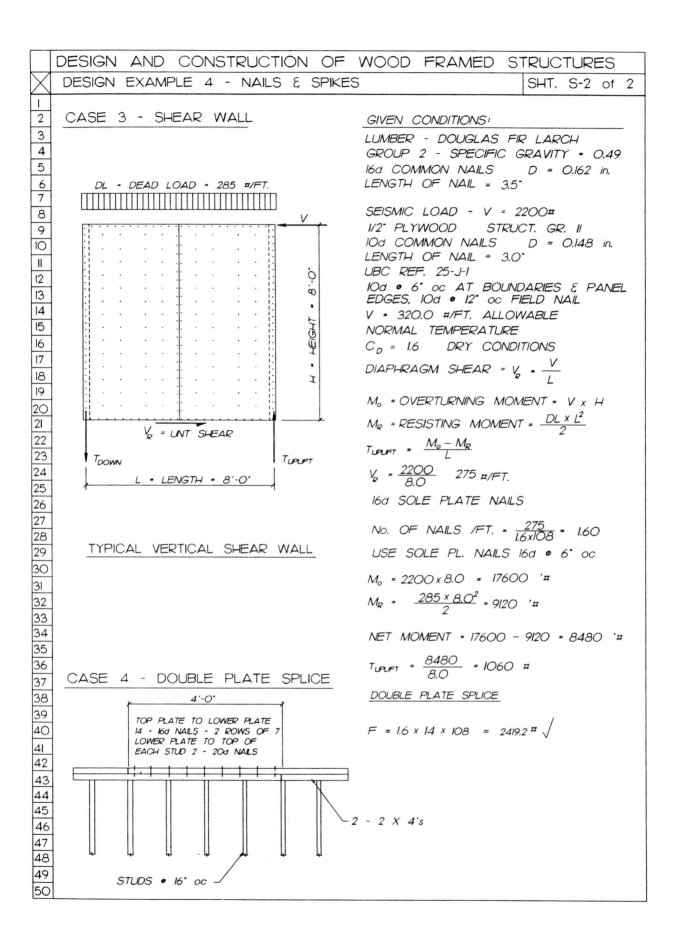

CASE 3 - SHEAR WALL

DL - DEAD LOAD = 285 #/FT.

H - HEIGHT = 8'-0"

V_R = UNT SHEAR

T_{DOWN} T_{UPLIFT}

L - LENGTH = 8'-0"

TYPICAL VERTICAL SHEAR WALL

CASE 4 - DOUBLE PLATE SPLICE

4'-0"

TOP PLATE TO LOWER PLATE
14 - 16d NAILS - 2 ROWS OF 7
LOWER PLATE TO TOP OF
EACH STUD 2 - 20d NAILS

2 - 2 X 4's

STUDS • 16" oc

GIVEN CONDITIONS:

LUMBER - DOUGLAS FIR LARCH
GROUP 2 - SPECIFIC GRAVITY = 0.49
16d COMMON NAILS   D = 0.162 in.
LENGTH OF NAIL = 3.5"

SEISMIC LOAD - V = 2200#
1/2" PLYWOOD   STRUCT. GR. II
10d COMMON NAILS   D = 0.148 in.
LENGTH OF NAIL = 3.0"
UBC REF. 25-J-1
10d • 6" oc AT BOUNDARIES & PANEL
EDGES, 10d • 12" oc FIELD NAIL
V = 320.0 #/FT. ALLOWABLE
NORMAL TEMPERATURE
$C_D = 1.6$ DRY CONDITIONS

$$\text{DIAPHRAGM SHEAR} = V_R = \frac{V}{L}$$

$$M_o = \text{OVERTURNING MOMENT} = V \times H$$

$$M_R = \text{RESISTING MOMENT} = \frac{DL \times L^2}{2}$$

$$T_{UPLIFT} = \frac{M_o - M_R}{L}$$

$$V_R = \frac{2200}{8.0}   275 \text{ #/FT.}$$

16d SOLE PLATE NAILS

$$\text{No. OF NAILS /FT.} = \frac{275}{1.6 \times 108} = 1.60$$

USE SOLE PL. NAILS 16d • 6" oc

$$M_o = 2200 \times 8.0 = 17600 \text{ '#}$$

$$M_R = \frac{285 \times 8.0^2}{2} = 9120 \text{ '#}$$

NET MOMENT = 17600 - 9120 = 8480 '#

$$T_{UPLIFT} = \frac{8480}{8.0} = 1060 \text{ #}$$

DOUBLE PLATE SPLICE

$$F = 1.6 \times 14 \times 108 = 2419.2 \text{ #} \checkmark$$

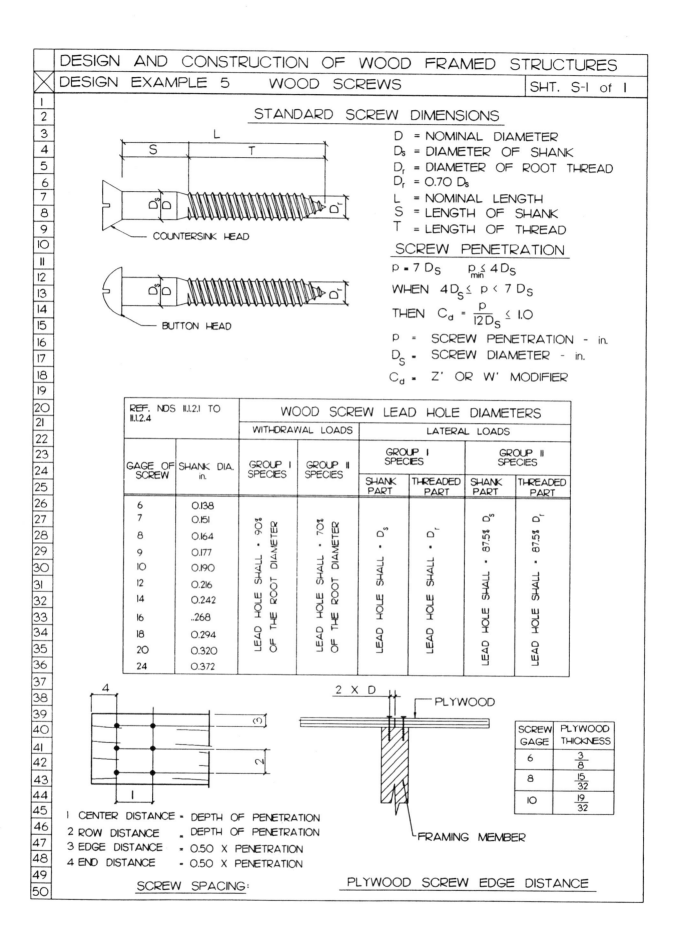

STANDARD SCREW DIMENSIONS

COUNTERSINK HEAD

BUTTON HEAD

D = NOMINAL DIAMETER
D_s = DIAMETER OF SHANK
D_r = DIAMETER OF ROOT THREAD
$D_r = 0.70\ D_s$
L = NOMINAL LENGTH
S = LENGTH OF SHANK
T = LENGTH OF THREAD

SCREW PENETRATION

$p = 7\ D_s \qquad p_{min} \le 4\ D_s$

WHEN $4\ D_s \le p < 7\ D_s$

THEN $C_d = \dfrac{p}{12\ D_s} \le 1.0$

p = SCREW PENETRATION - in.
D_s = SCREW DIAMETER - in.
C_d = Z' OR W' MODIFIER

REF. NDS 11.1.2.1 TO 11.1.2.4		WOOD SCREW LEAD HOLE DIAMETERS					
		WITHDRAWAL LOADS		LATERAL LOADS			
				GROUP I SPECIES		GROUP II SPECIES	
GAGE OF SCREW	SHANK DIA. in.	GROUP I SPECIES	GROUP II SPECIES	SHANK PART	THREADED PART	SHANK PART	THREADED PART
6	0.138	LEAD HOLE SHALL = 90% OF THE ROOT DIAMETER	LEAD HOLE SHALL = 70% OF THE ROOT DIAMETER	LEAD HOLE SHALL = D_s	LEAD HOLE SHALL = D_r	LEAD HOLE SHALL = 87.5% D_s	LEAD HOLE SHALL = 87.5% D_r
7	0.151						
8	0.164						
9	0.177						
10	0.190						
12	0.216						
14	0.242						
16	..268						
18	0.294						
20	0.320						
24	0.372						

1 CENTER DISTANCE = DEPTH OF PENETRATION
2 ROW DISTANCE = DEPTH OF PENETRATION
3 EDGE DISTANCE = 0.50 X PENETRATION
4 END DISTANCE = 0.50 X PENETRATION

SCREW SPACING:

SCREW GAGE	PLYWOOD THICKNESS
6	$\frac{3}{8}$
8	$\frac{15}{32}$
10	$\frac{19}{32}$

PLYWOOD SCREW EDGE DISTANCE

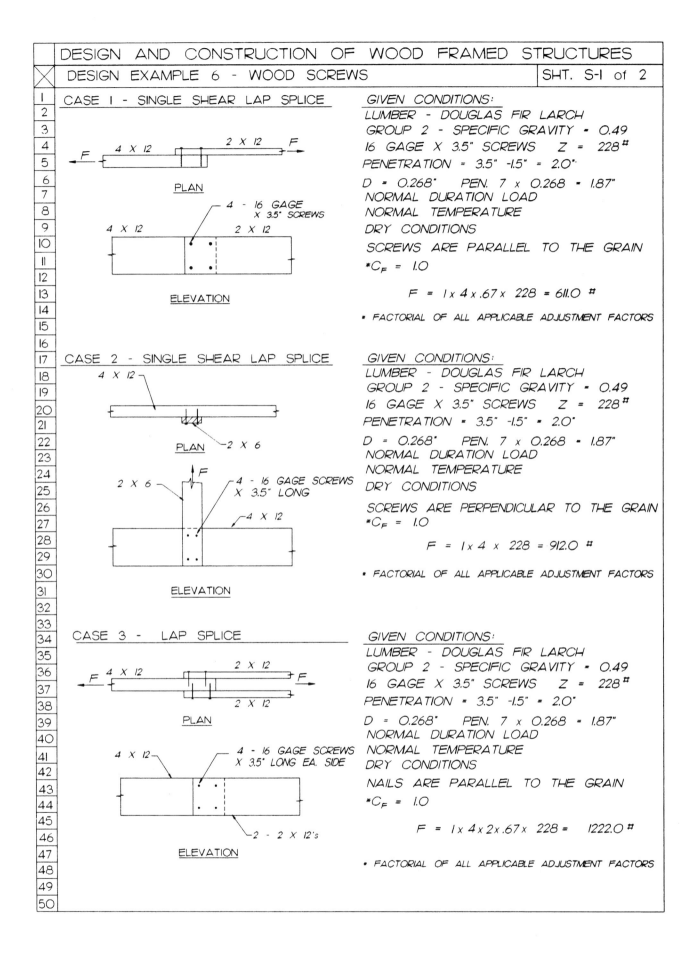

CASE 1 - SINGLE SHEAR LAP SPLICE

PLAN

ELEVATION

GIVEN CONDITIONS:

LUMBER - DOUGLAS FIR LARCH
GROUP 2 - SPECIFIC GRAVITY = 0.49
16 GAGE X 3.5" SCREWS   Z = 228#
PENETRATION = 3.5" -1.5" = 2.0"

$D = 0.268"$ PEN. 7 x 0.268 = 1.87"
NORMAL DURATION LOAD
NORMAL TEMPERATURE
DRY CONDITIONS
SCREWS ARE PARALLEL TO THE GRAIN
*$C_F = 1.0$

$$F = 1 \times 4 \times .67 \times 228 = 611.0 \#$$

* FACTORIAL OF ALL APPLICABLE ADJUSTMENT FACTORS

CASE 2 - SINGLE SHEAR LAP SPLICE

PLAN

ELEVATION

GIVEN CONDITIONS:

LUMBER - DOUGLAS FIR LARCH
GROUP 2 - SPECIFIC GRAVITY = 0.49
16 GAGE X 3.5" SCREWS   Z = 228#
PENETRATION = 3.5" -1.5" = 2.0"

$D = 0.268"$ PEN. 7 x 0.268 = 1.87"
NORMAL DURATION LOAD
NORMAL TEMPERATURE
DRY CONDITIONS
SCREWS ARE PERPENDICULAR TO THE GRAIN
*$C_F = 1.0$

$$F = 1 \times 4 \times 228 = 912.0 \#$$

* FACTORIAL OF ALL APPLICABLE ADJUSTMENT FACTORS

CASE 3 - LAP SPLICE

PLAN

ELEVATION

GIVEN CONDITIONS:

LUMBER - DOUGLAS FIR LARCH
GROUP 2 - SPECIFIC GRAVITY = 0.49
16 GAGE X 3.5" SCREWS   Z = 228#
PENETRATION = 3.5" -1.5" = 2.0"

$D = 0.268"$ PEN. 7 x 0.268 = 1.87"
NORMAL DURATION LOAD
NORMAL TEMPERATURE
DRY CONDITIONS
NAILS ARE PARALLEL TO THE GRAIN
*$C_F = 1.0$

$$F = 1 \times 4 \times 2 \times .67 \times 228 = 1222.0 \#$$

* FACTORIAL OF ALL APPLICABLE ADJUSTMENT FACTORS

CASE 4 - SINGLE SHEAR LAP SPLICE

4 X 12

F

4 X 12

2 X 8's • 16" oc

2 - 16 GAGE SCREWS
X 3.5 " LONG EA. END

SECTION

GIVEN CONDITIONS:

LUMBER - DOUGLAS FIR LARCH
GROUP 2 - SPECIFIC GRAVITY = 0.49
16 GAGE WOOD SCREWS X 3.5" LONG
W = 183#
PENETRATION = 1.87"
NORMAL DURATION LOAD
NORMAL TEMPERATURE
DRY CONDITIONS
SCREWS ARE PERPENDICULAR TO THE GRAIN
*C_F = 1.0

$$F_V = 1 \times 4 \times 183 \times 1.87 = 1368.8\#$$

* FACTORIAL OF ALL APPLICABLE ADJUSTMENT FACTORS

CASE 5 - METAL SIDE PLATE CONNECTION

F

4 - 16 GAGE SCREWS
3.5" LONG - EA. END

METAL SIDE PLATE
ONE SIDE

2 X 6

4 X 12

ELEVATION

GIVEN CONDITIONS:

LUMBER - DOUGLAS FIR LARCH
GROUP 2 - SPECIFIC GRAVITY = 0.49
16 GAGE WOOD SCREWS X 3.5# LONG
Z = 228#
PENETRATION = 1.87"
NORMAL DURATION LOAD
NORMAL TEMPERATURE
DRY CONDITIONS
NAILS ARE PARALLEL TO THE GRAIN
METAL SIDE PLATE FACTOR = 1.25
*C_F = 1.25 x 0.67 = 0.8375

$$F = 0.8375 \times 4 \times 228 = 763.8\#$$

* FACTORIAL OF ALL APPLICABLE ADJUSTMENT FACTORS

CASE 6 - COMBINED SHEAR & WITHDRAWAL

4 X 12

30°

2 - 10 GAGE SCREWS
X 4" LONG

L 4 X 4 X 3/8

F

GIVEN CONDITIONS:

LUMBER - DOUGLAS FIR LARCH
GROUP 2 - SPECIFIC GRAVITY = 0.49
10 GAGE WOOD SCREWS X 4.0" LONG
Z = 136#   W = 130#
PENETRATION = 4-.375 = 3.625"
NORMAL DURATION LOAD
NORMAL TEMPERATURE
DRY CONDITIONS
NAILS ARE PARALLEL TO THE GRAIN
METAL SIDE PLATE FACTOR = 1.25
*C_F = 1.25 x 0.67 = 0.8375
NDS 11.3.5   a = ANGLE TO GRAIN

$$Z'_a = \frac{(W'p)Z'}{(W'p)\sin^2 a + Z'\cos^2 a}$$

$Z' = 0.8375 \times 136 = 114$
$W' = 0.8375 \times 130 = 108.9$

$$Z'_a = \frac{108.9 \times 3.625 \times 114}{108.9 \times 3.625 \times .25 + 114 \times .75} = 244.3\#$$

$$F = 2 \times 244.3 = 488.6\#$$

DESIGN AND CONSTRUCTION OF WOOD FRAMED STRUCTURES

DESIGN EXAMPLE 7 - LAG SCREWS — SHT. S-I of I

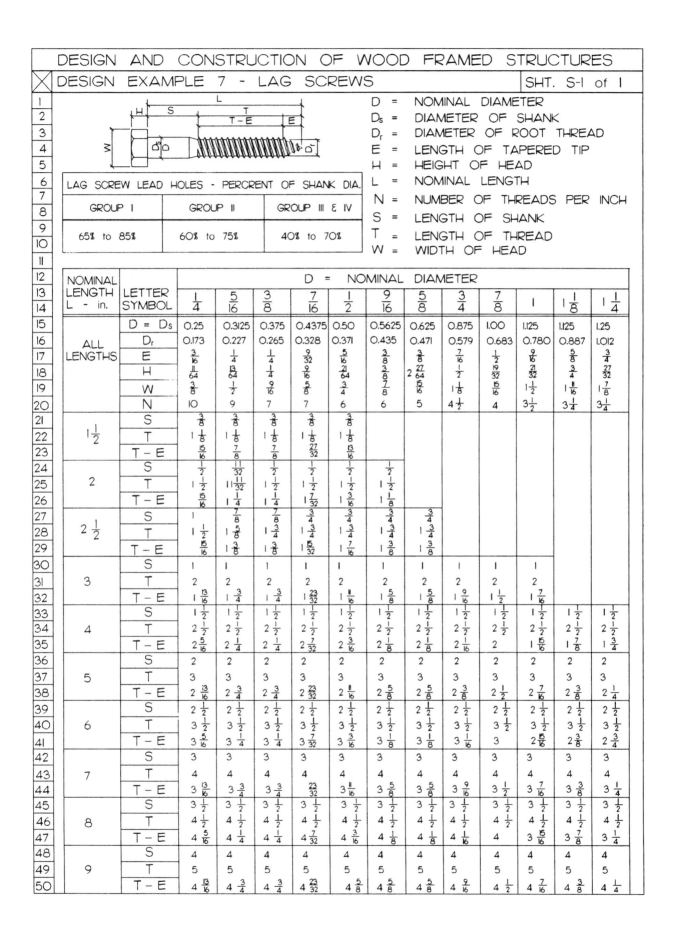

Legend:

- D = NOMINAL DIAMETER
- D_s = DIAMETER OF SHANK
- D_r = DIAMETER OF ROOT THREAD
- E = LENGTH OF TAPERED TIP
- H = HEIGHT OF HEAD
- L = NOMINAL LENGTH
- N = NUMBER OF THREADS PER INCH
- S = LENGTH OF SHANK
- T = LENGTH OF THREAD
- W = WIDTH OF HEAD

LAG SCREW LEAD HOLES - PERCRENT OF SHANK DIA.

GROUP I	GROUP II	GROUP III & IV
65% to 85%	60% to 75%	40% to 70%

Nominal Length L - in.	Letter Symbol	$\frac{1}{4}$	$\frac{5}{16}$	$\frac{3}{8}$	$\frac{7}{16}$	$\frac{1}{2}$	$\frac{9}{16}$	$\frac{5}{8}$	$\frac{3}{4}$	$\frac{7}{8}$	1	$1\frac{1}{8}$	$1\frac{1}{4}$
ALL LENGTHS	$D = D_s$	0.25	0.3125	0.375	0.4375	0.50	0.5625	0.625	0.875	1.00	1.125	1.125	1.25
	D_r	0.173	0.227	0.265	0.328	0.371	0.435	0.471	0.579	0.683	0.780	0.887	1.012
	E	$\frac{3}{16}$	$\frac{1}{4}$	$\frac{1}{4}$	$\frac{9}{32}$	$\frac{5}{16}$	$\frac{3}{8}$	$\frac{3}{8}$	$\frac{7}{16}$	$\frac{1}{2}$	$\frac{9}{16}$	$\frac{5}{8}$	$\frac{3}{4}$
	H	$\frac{11}{64}$	$\frac{13}{64}$	$\frac{1}{4}$	$\frac{9}{32}$	$\frac{21}{64}$	$\frac{3}{8}$	$\frac{27}{64}$	$\frac{1}{2}$	$\frac{19}{32}$	$\frac{21}{32}$	$\frac{3}{4}$	$\frac{27}{32}$
	W	$\frac{3}{8}$	$\frac{1}{2}$	$\frac{9}{16}$	$\frac{5}{8}$	$\frac{3}{4}$	$\frac{7}{8}$	$\frac{15}{16}$	$1\frac{1}{8}$	$1\frac{5}{16}$	$1\frac{1}{2}$	$1\frac{11}{16}$	$1\frac{7}{8}$
	N	10	9	7	7	6	6	5	$4\frac{1}{2}$	4	$3\frac{1}{2}$	$3\frac{1}{4}$	$3\frac{1}{4}$
$1\frac{1}{2}$	S	$\frac{3}{8}$	$\frac{3}{8}$	$\frac{3}{8}$	$\frac{3}{8}$	$\frac{3}{8}$							
	T	$1\frac{1}{8}$	$1\frac{1}{8}$	$1\frac{1}{8}$	$1\frac{1}{8}$	$1\frac{1}{8}$							
	T − E	$\frac{15}{16}$	$\frac{7}{8}$	$\frac{7}{8}$	$\frac{27}{32}$	$\frac{13}{16}$							
2	S	$\frac{1}{2}$	$\frac{1}{2}$	$\frac{1}{2}$	$\frac{1}{2}$	$\frac{1}{2}$	$\frac{1}{2}$						
	T	$1\frac{1}{2}$	$1\frac{1}{2}$	$1\frac{1}{2}$	$1\frac{1}{2}$	$1\frac{1}{2}$	$1\frac{1}{2}$						
	T − E	$1\frac{5}{16}$	$1\frac{1}{4}$	$1\frac{1}{4}$	$1\frac{7}{32}$	$1\frac{3}{16}$	$1\frac{1}{8}$						
$2\frac{1}{2}$	S	1	$\frac{7}{8}$	$\frac{7}{8}$	$\frac{3}{4}$	$\frac{3}{4}$	$\frac{3}{4}$	$\frac{3}{4}$					
	T	$1\frac{1}{2}$	$1\frac{5}{8}$	$1\frac{5}{8}$	$1\frac{3}{4}$	$1\frac{3}{4}$	$1\frac{3}{4}$	$1\frac{3}{4}$					
	T − E	$1\frac{5}{16}$	$1\frac{3}{8}$	$1\frac{3}{8}$	$1\frac{15}{32}$	$1\frac{7}{16}$	$1\frac{3}{8}$	$1\frac{3}{8}$					
3	S	1	1	1	1	1	1	1	1	1			
	T	2	2	2	2	2	2	2	2	2			
	T − E	$1\frac{13}{16}$	$1\frac{3}{4}$	$1\frac{3}{4}$	$1\frac{23}{32}$	$1\frac{11}{16}$	$1\frac{5}{8}$	$1\frac{5}{8}$	$1\frac{9}{16}$	$1\frac{1}{2}$	$1\frac{7}{16}$		
4	S	$1\frac{1}{2}$	$1\frac{1}{2}$	$1\frac{1}{2}$	$1\frac{1}{2}$	$1\frac{1}{2}$	$1\frac{1}{2}$	$1\frac{1}{2}$	$1\frac{1}{2}$	$1\frac{1}{2}$	$1\frac{1}{2}$	$1\frac{1}{2}$	$1\frac{1}{2}$
	T	$2\frac{1}{2}$	$2\frac{1}{2}$	$2\frac{1}{2}$	$2\frac{1}{2}$	$2\frac{1}{2}$	$2\frac{1}{2}$	$2\frac{1}{2}$	$2\frac{1}{2}$	$2\frac{1}{2}$	$2\frac{1}{2}$	$2\frac{1}{2}$	$2\frac{1}{2}$
	T − E	$2\frac{5}{16}$	$2\frac{1}{4}$	$2\frac{1}{4}$	$2\frac{7}{32}$	$2\frac{3}{16}$	$2\frac{1}{8}$	$2\frac{1}{8}$	$2\frac{1}{16}$	2	$1\frac{15}{16}$	$1\frac{7}{8}$	$1\frac{3}{4}$
5	S	2	2	2	2	2	2	2	2	2	2	2	2
	T	3	3	3	3	3	3	3	3	3	3	3	3
	T − E	$2\frac{13}{16}$	$2\frac{3}{4}$	$2\frac{3}{4}$	$2\frac{23}{32}$	$2\frac{11}{16}$	$2\frac{5}{8}$	$2\frac{5}{8}$	$2\frac{9}{16}$	$2\frac{1}{2}$	$2\frac{7}{16}$	$2\frac{3}{8}$	$2\frac{1}{4}$
6	S	$2\frac{1}{2}$	$2\frac{1}{2}$	$2\frac{1}{2}$	$2\frac{1}{2}$	$2\frac{1}{2}$	$2\frac{1}{2}$	$2\frac{1}{2}$	$2\frac{1}{2}$	$2\frac{1}{2}$	$2\frac{1}{2}$	$2\frac{1}{2}$	$2\frac{1}{2}$
	T	$3\frac{1}{2}$	$3\frac{1}{2}$	$3\frac{1}{2}$	$3\frac{1}{2}$	$3\frac{1}{2}$	$3\frac{1}{2}$	$3\frac{1}{2}$	$3\frac{1}{2}$	$3\frac{1}{2}$	$3\frac{1}{2}$	$3\frac{1}{2}$	$3\frac{1}{2}$
	T − E	$3\frac{5}{16}$	$3\frac{1}{4}$	$3\frac{1}{4}$	$3\frac{7}{32}$	$3\frac{3}{16}$	$3\frac{1}{8}$	$3\frac{1}{8}$	$3\frac{1}{16}$	3	$2\frac{15}{16}$	$2\frac{7}{8}$	$2\frac{3}{4}$
7	S	3	3	3	3	3	3	3	3	3	3	3	3
	T	4	4	4	4	4	4	4	4	4	4	4	4
	T − E	$3\frac{13}{16}$	$3\frac{3}{4}$	$3\frac{3}{4}$	$3\frac{23}{32}$	$3\frac{11}{16}$	$3\frac{5}{8}$	$3\frac{5}{8}$	$3\frac{9}{16}$	$3\frac{1}{2}$	$3\frac{7}{16}$	$3\frac{3}{8}$	$3\frac{1}{4}$
8	S	$3\frac{1}{2}$	$3\frac{1}{2}$	$3\frac{1}{2}$	$3\frac{1}{2}$	$3\frac{1}{2}$	$3\frac{1}{2}$	$3\frac{1}{2}$	$3\frac{1}{2}$	$3\frac{1}{2}$	$3\frac{1}{2}$	$3\frac{1}{2}$	$3\frac{1}{2}$
	T	$4\frac{1}{2}$	$4\frac{1}{2}$	$4\frac{1}{2}$	$4\frac{1}{2}$	$4\frac{1}{2}$	$4\frac{1}{2}$	$4\frac{1}{2}$	$4\frac{1}{2}$	$4\frac{1}{2}$	$4\frac{1}{2}$	$4\frac{1}{2}$	$4\frac{1}{2}$
	T − E	$4\frac{5}{16}$	$4\frac{1}{4}$	$4\frac{1}{4}$	$4\frac{7}{32}$	$4\frac{3}{16}$	$4\frac{1}{8}$	$4\frac{1}{8}$	$4\frac{1}{16}$	4	$3\frac{15}{16}$	$3\frac{7}{8}$	$3\frac{3}{4}$
9	S	4	4	4	4	4	4	4	4	4	4	4	4
	T	5	5	5	5	5	5	5	5	5	5	5	5
	T − E	$4\frac{13}{16}$	$4\frac{3}{4}$	$4\frac{3}{4}$	$4\frac{23}{32}$	$4\frac{11}{16}$	$4\frac{5}{8}$	$4\frac{5}{8}$	$4\frac{9}{16}$	$4\frac{1}{2}$	$4\frac{7}{16}$	$4\frac{3}{8}$	$4\frac{1}{4}$

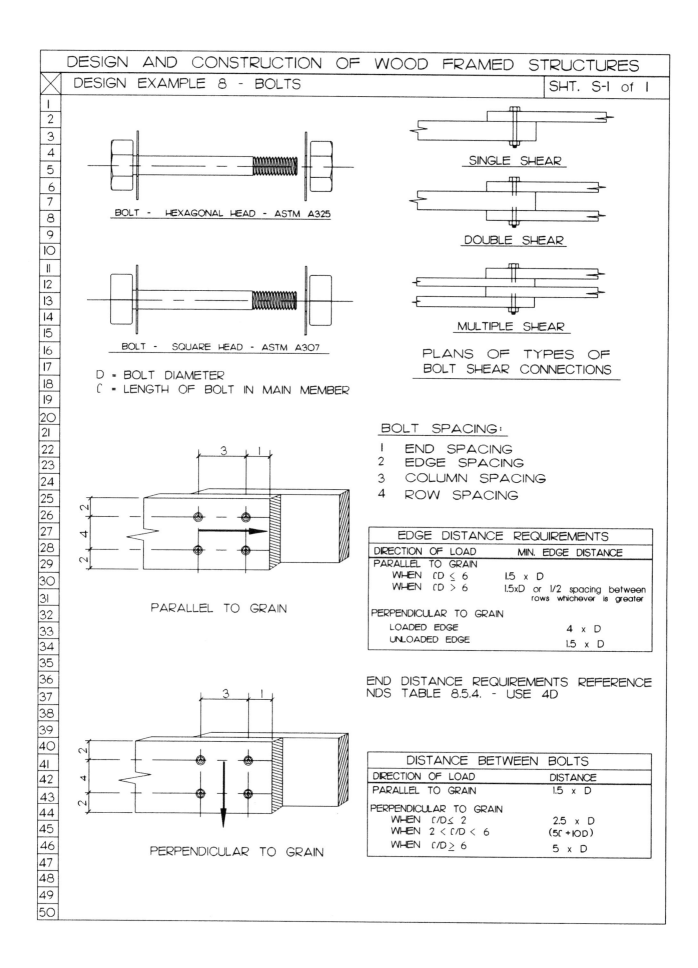

BOLT - HEXAGONAL HEAD - ASTM A325

BOLT - SQUARE HEAD - ASTM A307

D = BOLT DIAMETER
ℓ = LENGTH OF BOLT IN MAIN MEMBER

SINGLE SHEAR

DOUBLE SHEAR

MULTIPLE SHEAR

PLANS OF TYPES OF
BOLT SHEAR CONNECTIONS

PARALLEL TO GRAIN

PERPENDICULAR TO GRAIN

BOLT SPACING:

1 END SPACING
2 EDGE SPACING
3 COLUMN SPACING
4 ROW SPACING

EDGE DISTANCE REQUIREMENTS	
DIRECTION OF LOAD	MIN. EDGE DISTANCE
PARALLEL TO GRAIN	
WHEN $\ell D \leq 6$	1.5 x D
WHEN $\ell D > 6$	1.5xD or 1/2 spacing between rows whichever is greater
PERPENDICULAR TO GRAIN	
LOADED EDGE	4 x D
UNLOADED EDGE	1.5 x D

END DISTANCE REQUIREMENTS REFERENCE
NDS TABLE 8.5.4. - USE 4D

DISTANCE BETWEEN BOLTS	
DIRECTION OF LOAD	DISTANCE
PARALLEL TO GRAIN	1.5 x D
PERPENDICULAR TO GRAIN	
WHEN $\ell/D \leq 2$	2.5 x D
WHEN $2 < \ell/D < 6$	$(5\ell + 10D)$
WHEN $\ell/D \geq 6$	5 x D

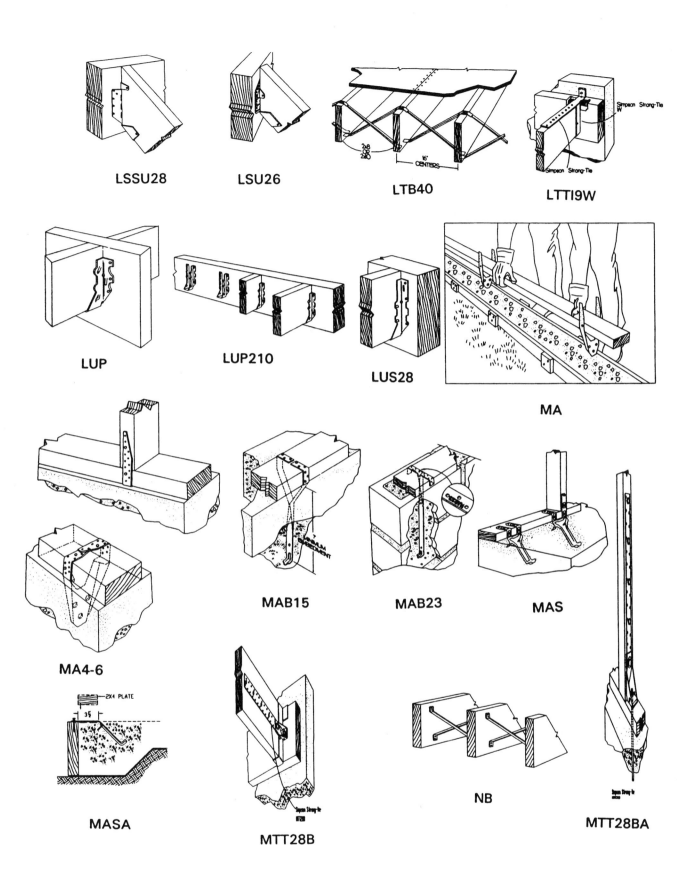

LSSU28

LSU26

LTB40

LTTI9W

LUP

LUP210

LUS28

MA

MA4-6

MAB15

MAB23

MAS

MASA

MTT28B

NB

MTT28BA

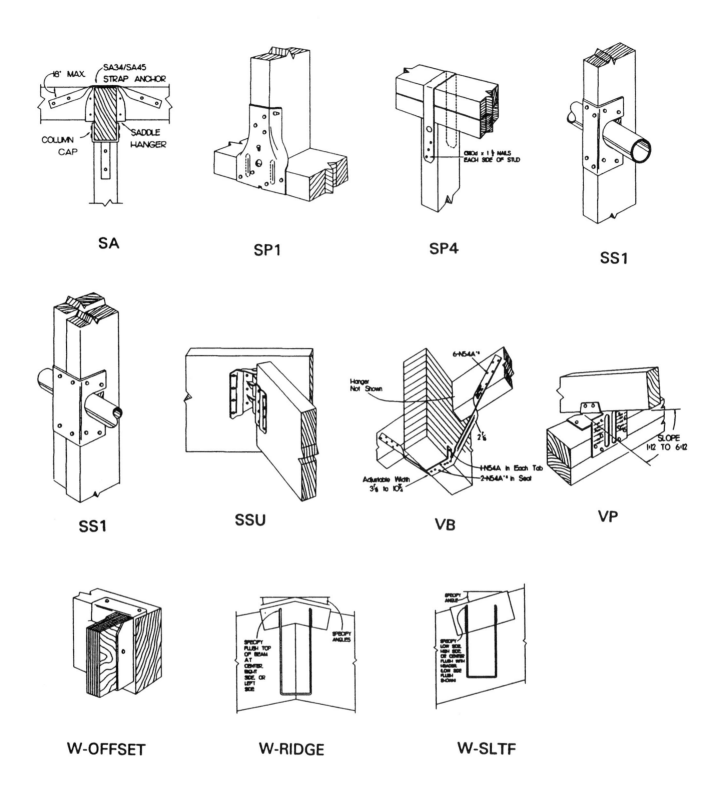

SA

SP1

SP4

SS1

SS1

SSU

VB

VP

W-OFFSET

W-RIDGE

W-SLTF

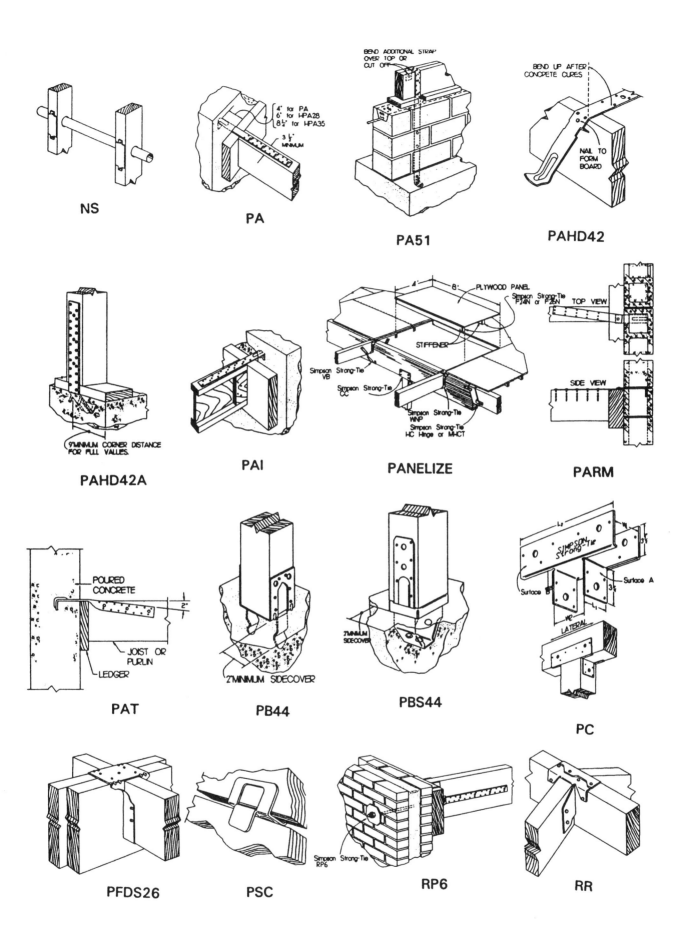

NS

PA

BEND ADDITIONAL STRAP OVER TOP OR CUT OFF

4" for PA
6" for HPA28
8½" for HPA35

3½" MINIMUM

PA51

BEND UP AFTER CONCRETE CURES

NAIL TO FORM BOARD

PAHD42

9"MINIMUM CORNER DISTANCE FOR FULL VALUES.

PAHD42A

PAI

PLYWOOD PANEL

Simpson Strong-Tie F24N or F26N

STIFFENER

Simpson Strong-Tie VB

Simpson Strong-Tie CC

Simpson Strong-Tie WNP

Simpson Strong-Tie HC Hinge or MHCT

PANELIZE

TOP VIEW

SIDE VIEW

PARM

POURED CONCRETE

2"

JOIST OR PURLIN

LEDGER

PAT

2"MINIMUM SIDECOVER

PB44

7"MINIMUM SIDECOVER

PBS44

SIMPSON Strong Tie

Surface

Surface A

LATERAL

PC

PFDS26

PSC

Simpson Strong-Tie RP6

RP6

RR

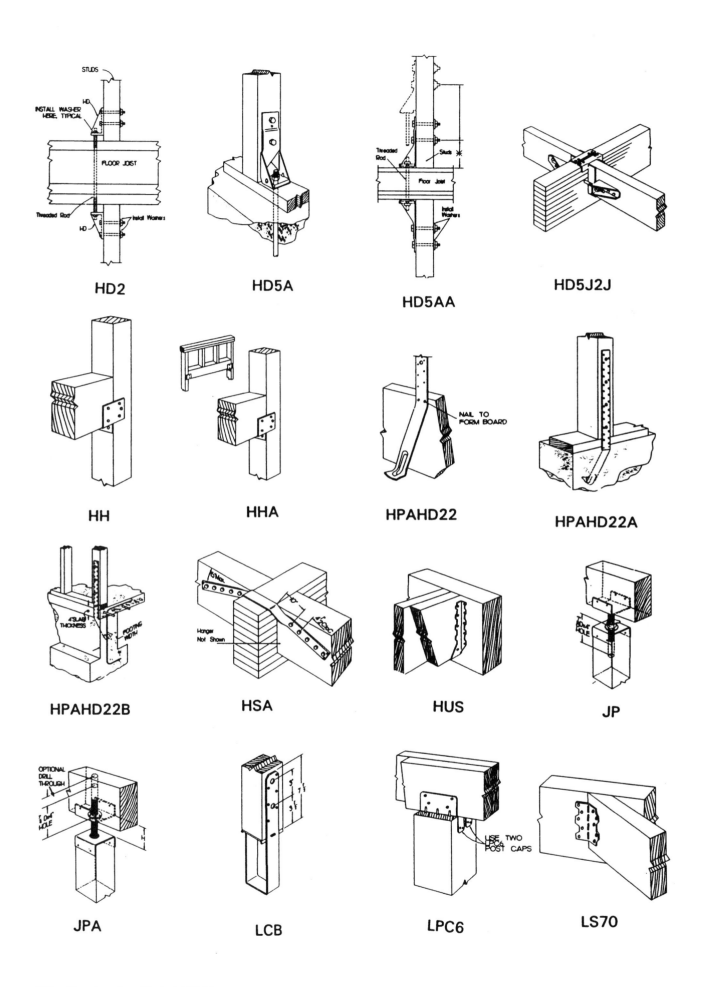

HD2

HD5A

HD5AA

HD5J2J

HH

HHA

HPAHD22

HPAHD22A

HPAHD22B

HSA

HUS

JP

JPA

LCB

LPC6

LS70

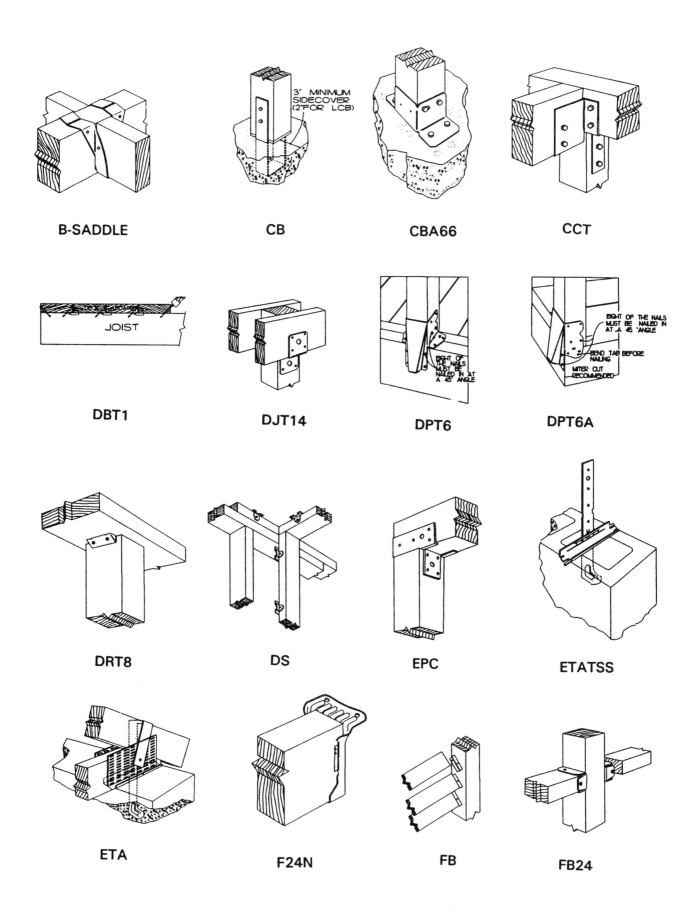

B-SADDLE

CB

3" MINIMUM SIDECOVER (2"FOR LCB)

CBA66

CCT

JOIST

DBT1

DJT14

EIGHT OF THE NAILS MUST BE NAILED IN AT A 45° ANGLE

DPT6

EIGHT OF THE NAILS MUST BE NAILED IN AT A 45° ANGLE

BEND TAB BEFORE NAILING

MITER CUT RECOMMENDED

DPT6A

DRT8

DS

EPC

ETATSS

ETA

F24N

FB

FB24

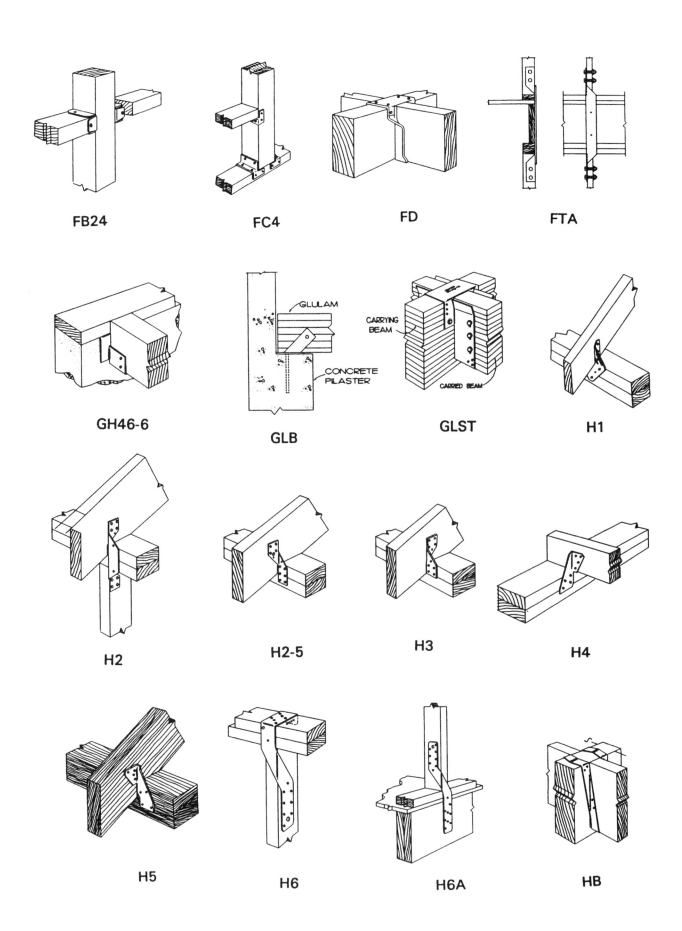

FB24

FC4

FD

FTA

GH46-6

GLB

GLULAM

CONCRETE PILASTER

GLST

CARRYING BEAM

CARRIED BEAM

H1

H2

H2-5

H3

H4

H5

H6

H6A

HB

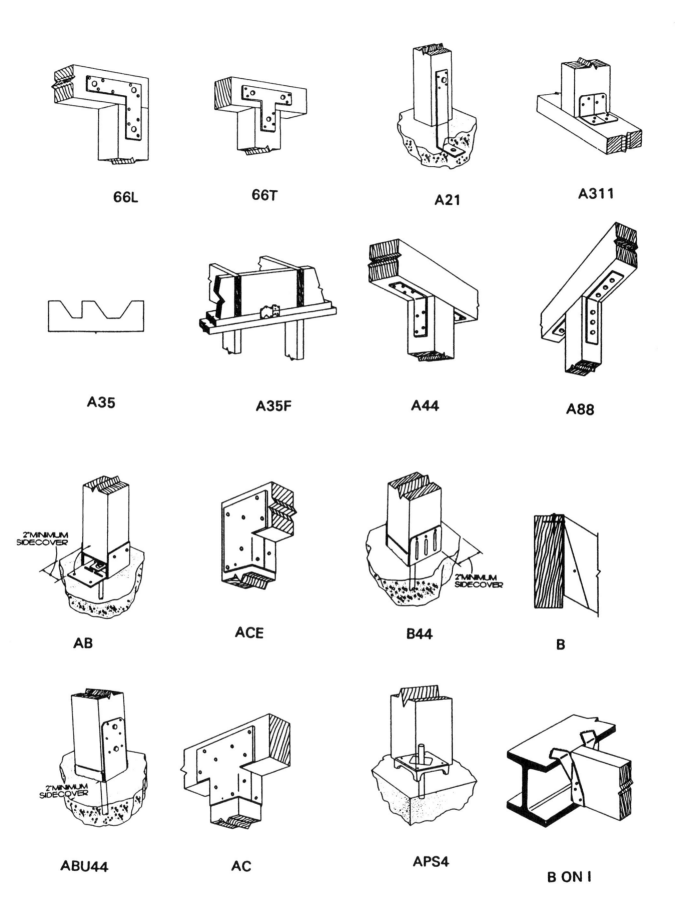

66L

66T

A21

A311

A35

A35F

A44

A88

2" MINIMUM SIDECOVER

AB

ACE

2" MINIMUM SIDECOVER

B44

B

2" MINIMUM SIDECOVER

ABU44

AC

APS4

B ON I

7

Wind and Seismic Design

Wind and seismic forces originate from two unpredictable natural occurrences. In general, earthquake forces result from irregular ground motion acceleration and are usually greater in magnitude than wind forces. Seismic forces are less predictable and less commonplace than forces generated by high-velocity wind motion. On the other hand, although wind forces may have less magnitude than seismic forces (Hurricane Andrew not included), they are more prevalent and also more predictable. Since these forces hypothetically act in any direction on a horizontal plane, they are referred to as shear forces. The source of a lateral force may depend on the local geology, the area's climate, or the history of seismic or wind activity within the particular locale. Until the last fifteen years, the general opinion has been that earthquakes occurred almost exclusively in certain parts of the world. The State of California especially has a large number of seismic faults with a history of activity within relatively short time cycles (ten to fifteen years); however, recent investigations made by the Building Seismic Safety Council (BSSC) indicate that there are also several major faults located around the Missouri area, the Midwest, and along the eastern seaboard of the United States. Historical records disclose the following seismic events: 1775—Cape Ann, MA, VII (Modified Mercalli intensity); 1884—New York City; 1868—Charleston, SC, 7.7 Richter scale; 1812—New Madrid, MO, 8.4 Richter scale; 1968—Southern, IL, 5.7 Modified Mercalli intensity. Measured movement of the earth's geology adjacent to these midwest and eastern faults alerts us that they may eventually become active, but within a longer time cycle than those faults located in the western states.

Although seismic forces appear to present a major threat to structures, there are regions in which forces derived from high wind velocity may likewise be equally as damaging. Typhoons, hurricanes, and tornados often occur on a seasonal basis in many parts of the world, and the populations in these locations often draw on their past experiences to construct reliable buildings to withstand these dynamic wind forces. On August 24, 1992, Hurricane Andrew reached Dade County, Florida. The wind velocity was measured to be between 140 and 160 miles per hour (mph), and extended over an area defined by 20 miles (north-south) by 12 miles (east-west) and to a lesser degree north to Broward County. The hurricane passed over the Gulf of Mexico and regained intensity and struck the Louisiana coast, west of New Orleans. The UBC wind map Table 23-1 specifies a maximum basic wind speed of 110 mph for this area. The wind speed of Hurricane Andrew exceeded the building code value by almost 50 percent, with an incremental increase in the magnitude of wind force of more than 100 percent. This is based on calculating the force of wind (lb/sq ft) equal to $0.00275 \times$ wind velocity (mph). Hurricane Andrew was the most destructive hurricane to ever hit a United States coast. The financial damage resulting from this ordeal was estimated to be $20 to $30 billion in Florida and $1 billion in Louisiana.

Wind and seismic forces may be regarded as an act of God; however, the responsibility for the resultant damage to structures to a certain degree may be placed on the citizens of the community. In contrast to this statement, it may be stated that rain is also an act of God, but modern technology has taught us how not to get wet. Information compiled by the BSSC discloses that between the years 1900 and 1986 that approximately 3500 lives were lost in the lower forty-eight United States due to earthquake damage. Using dollars as a measuring gauge, the value of property damage (based on 1979 dollars) experienced between 1900 and 1986 has been thus far exceeded since 1987. The vital concern of the engineer is that regardless of the source of the force, and at any random point in time, every structure should be designed and constructed with a reasonable expectation to resist a certain exceptional magnitude of externally applied lateral force.

For an applied technology to accomplish its intended purpose, pure science must take precedence in developing its methodology; therefore, resistance calculations to natural forces generated by wind or seismic activity should not be compromised by inaccurate assumptions. The procedure used to calculate seismic lateral forces is based on two related assumptions which are within the logic of scientific principles. The first assumption is that seismic forces are generated by dynamic lateral motion of the ground, and thus yield a Force $= M \times A$; M is the mass of the ground, and A is the vibration acceleration of the motion in a particular direction. The second assumption views the complete building entity as a body at rest or in a static state of equilibrium. The seismic force imparted to a wood-framed structure is calculated as a static inertial response to the force of the ground motion at the instant of impact. An analogy to this action would be a person standing in an elevator that suddenly starts to move upward.

A wood structure's capacity to resist externally applied lateral forces originating from either wind force or seismic shock depends on the strength of its opposing horizontal and vertical diaphragm plane surfaces. The distribution of lateral forces throughout the internal structure of a wood building is calculated on the principle of the tributary area to horizontal or vertical diaphragms. The relatively low modulus of elasticity of structural lumber as compared with concrete or steel, and the correlated degree of resistance to distortion of wood connection joints between diaphragms, tends to produce a proportionally resilient structure. The limit of the amount of horizontal deflection of the building may also regulate the dimensional ratios of interacting diaphragms. Structures consisting of steel or concrete columns, beams, and floors are considered as being more inelastic than wood structures; therefore the lateral forces are apportioned to the structural frame based on the relative rigidity of the component parts. Also, the material's higher modulus of elasticity produces joint connections with a more reliable degree of rigidity than those fabricated with structural lumber.

In either case, the connections between the structural parts and diaphragms are essential to transfer or distribute the forces within the structural frame. The endurance of the structure as a complete entity requires that its fundamental connections be capable of transferring lateral forces to the subsequent resisting walls and floors without independent movement of the parts. The horizontal and vertical structural diaphragms of a wood structure are usually the roof or the floors and the walls. The limits of the structural capacity of diaphragms are specified within the constraints of a governing code criteria; in this book the allowable values used are specified in UBC Table 47-G. UBC Tables 25-J-1 and 25-K-1 present a tabulation of the allowable shear resistance for horizontal and vertical diaphragms, respectively, for various combinations of plywood thickness, nail sizes, and spacing. UBC Table 25-I presents the ratio limits of width to length of horizontal and vertical diaphragms for each type of material. These tables can be found in Appendix A of this book. Horizontal diaphragms are designed to operate as flat beams which are supported by shear walls to resist uniform loads of distributed wind or seismic forces. The vertical shear wall panels react as a vertical cantilever from floor to floor and must be capable of resisting sliding and overturning. A demonstration of these two important requirements is presented in the design example of this chapter.

The Northridge earthquake of January 1994 has given the construction industry an opportunity to verify the strength of the materials and the methods of design used to resist lateral forces on wood structures. After an intense period of inspection, it was determined that several of the Los Angeles City Building Code specifications did not yield sufficient strength against the lateral forces. Also, it was found that the shear wall dimension ratios had to be substantially increased. Several of the shear resistance values specified in Table 47-G were revised; for example, the allowable resistance value of exterior stucco was reduced from 180 lb/ft to 90 lb/ft; interior gypsum $\frac{5}{8}$-in-thick board allowable resistance value was reduced from 175 lb/ft to 75 lb/ft. The tabulated resistance values of plywood shear walls were also reduced by 25 percent. All of the studies and inspections of seismic damage led to a consensus by the engineers that wood-framed structures required materials with a higher shear value than was previously used. The proposed revisions to the building code were not arbitrary; the earthquake supplied more than sufficient visual data for their justification. As a result of these elevated standards, future wood structures will require more plywood for shear walls, longer shear panels, additional anchor bolts, and holddown connections and the use of common nails in lieu of box nails for panels and connections.

The stress grade, thickness, nailing, and the direction of the placement of plywood are the major factors in determining the amount of shear resistance of horizontal and vertical diaphragms. Plywood panels are usually produced in standard size sheets of 4 ft wide by 8 ft long. Larger-size sheets are available for special configurations; however, in most cases 4 ft × 8 ft sheets can be adapted to meet the majority of requirements. A plywood panel consists of an odd number of laminated layers or plies of lumber. The thickness of a ply can vary from $\frac{1}{8}$ to $\frac{5}{16}$ in. The surface grain of each ply is alternately placed perpendicular to the previous layer. A plywood panel is fabricated by coating the surfaces of each ply with an adhesive and bonding them together under high pressure. The types of adhesives used for bonding the layers are based on interior or exterior exposure of the panel. Although the surface grains of the layers are alternated, the exterior surface grain on each side of the finished panel runs in the same direction. The cross-grain assembly of sheet plies provides the panel strength required to span horizontally between supports or to resist transverse shear from seismic or wind forces. Since plywood can support loads in bending, horizontal diaphragms are constructed with plywood placed with the surface grain perpendicular to the span of the joists or rafters. Construction of shear walls requires that plywood surface grain be parallel to the vertical studs to resist the cross-grain shear resulting from lateral forces. In either case the surface grain is normal to the direction of the applied load. Plywood is manufactured with a moisture content of less than 5 percent, therefore, no substantial shrinkage should be anticipated. However, it is good practice to place the panels with approximately $\frac{1}{16}$-in space between panel edges to allow for any movement of supporting members.

The American Plywood Association (APA) has created standards to establish a performance rating for the structural capacity of plywood (APA publication "Performance Rated Panels"). Each plywood panel is stamped with a mark which consists of specification data such as grade of lumber, allowable exposure of the adhesives, manufacturer's mill number, and the APA index number. The thickness and stress grade of a particular type of plywood used for the support of vertical load is usually identified by its thickness and stress grade or by its index number as tabulated in UBC Table S-1. The selection of a plywood panel used for lateral load resistance must also specify the size and spacing of the edge shear panel boundary nailing, the panel edge nailing, and the intermediate field nailing.

The *Uniform Building Code* (1991 ed.) is quite specific concerning the parameters for seismic resistance calculations and construction requirements. Judgment gained through experience can also be a major factor in determining structural resistance to lateral forces. It is the engineer's responsibility to make knowledgeable alternative decisions for size and location of shear walls within the building plan configuration. A lateral force design example is presented in this chapter to demonstrate the calculation methods for wind and seismic forces on a three-story office building. Also, a commentary is given in the following paragraphs to explain the UBC requirements and the design procedures. It is suggested that the reader refer to UBC Chapter 23—Parts II and III to become familiar with the design definitions, notations, and equations. The demonstration example will refer to the UBC notations, equations, and table numbers in the discourse of the calculations. The reference numbers given in the example are for the code tables, equations, and sections of the new UBC 1994 edition. Either edition of the code may be used for this example.

Sheet S-1 presents the cross section of a three-story medical office building plus the roof and floor loads for each area of the building. The building is completely constructed with wood members except for the first floor slab and footings. The walls are constructed with 2 × 6 wood studs spaced at 16 in o.c. from the second floor to the roof. The studs used from the first floor are 3 × 6's at 16 in o.c. The ceilings in the offices and corridor are suspended and covered with $\frac{5}{8}$-in-thick gypsum board. The second and third floors are constructed with wood joists. Notice that there is a 2500-lb (operating weight) mechanical heating and ventilating unit placed at the center of the roof.

Sheets S-2 and S-3 present seismic design key plans for each floor of the building. The wall panels to be designed for lateral resistance are dimensioned and shown in heavy lines. The walls at grid lines 1 and 6 were selected for calculation demonstration since there is a positive connection of the wall to the floor. The walls adjacent to the stairs are not connected to the floor diaphragm; however, they are connected at the roof level. The example is performed so that all perimeter vertical panel edges stack up vertically. This allows for an easy transfer of tension or compression uplift loads from floor to floor. In instances where the shear walls are not vertically contiguous, that is they do not stack up, the lateral and vertical shear wall reactions are required to be transferred horizontally to the next set of wall panels at the level below. It is good practice to use shear panels that coincide vertically at each floor.

The lateral force vectors are labeled either as V for vertical direction or H for horizontal direction and subscripted according to the grid line number. The reader should not construe this to mean the earthquake forces will coincide with a building's x and y coordinate axes. UBC Sections 2311 and 2334(a) state that wind and seismic forces can impact a structure from any direction; however, it may be assumed that lateral forces act nonconcurrently in the direction of the principal axis of the building. The values for the forces designated as *W1* and *W2* are calculated to act as a uniformly distributed force normal to the horizontal diaphragm, which acts as a flat beam. The values specified as T on the plan are calculated as the chord load of the horizontal beam.

Sheet S-4 presents the UBC equations and notations for the seismic base shear for the entire building. The values are calculated and substituted into the equations to determine a factor of the dead load to calculate the value of V. The values of the variables listed between lines 12 and 25 are specified in tables in the code for their respective conditions. Although the value of $C = 2.91$ on line 27, the code allows a maximum value of $C = 2.75$. The value of W is determined by the dead load on each level of the building. UBC Section 2334(a)2 specifies a partition dead load of 10 lb/sq ft. In the case of live loads greater than 100 lb/sq ft, such as in storage and warehouses, the code requires that the dead load must also include 25 percent of the live load.

The variable I, the importance designation in Equation 34-1, requires some practical judgment by the design engineer. Importance values greater than 1.0 as specified by the UBC are based on related considerations such as occupancies of hospitals or convalescent homes, the ambulatory state of tenants, and the essential importance of the building at the time of a disaster. UBC Section 2336(a) requires that the value of I for the seismic force on an individual component be equal to 1.5. It is assumed that the code specifies general minimum requirements for human safety against wind or seismic forces; however, since the code cannot address every particular situation, two added factors should also be considered. First, all buildings are not created equal, either because of architectural requirements, construction materials, workmanship, or structural design. The second factor to be considered is the actual magnitude of the lateral force. The Richter scale rating of a seismic event may yield only a recorded value; however, it could be somewhat greater than that value depending on the distance from the epicenter at the instant of shock.

Sheet S-4, L40 presents the mathematical method used for the vertical distribution of the base shear on the building. The value F_T is included in the dead load of the roof to the second floor since it is relatively less than the total dead load and it occupies a small surface plan area.

Sheet S-5, L16 to L34, gives the conditions set forth in the UBC used to determine a wind load of 22.0 lb/sq ft. Note that L37 to L48 calculate that Hurricane Andrew generated a wind force equal to approximately 98 lb/sq ft, which produced wind forces on the surface of the example structure that are significantly greater than the seismic base shear.

Sheet S-6 shows a tabulated calculation of the dead loads at each level of the building. Line 36 gives the cumulative value of the total dead load, and L38 uses that value for the calculation of the seismic base shear. Sheet S-4, line 31 calculates a factor of 0.183 × Dead Load equals the total lateral force or the base shear for the conditions given for this example building. Equation 28-8 on L40 of Sheet S-4 is used to determine the vertical distribution of the base shear at the roof, and at each floor level. The total dead load of the superstructure equals 728,812 lb; the seismic factor calculated on Sheet S-4, L31 equals 0.183; L38 calculates the base shear by multiplying the seismic design factor by the total dead load of the superstructure which equals to 133,372 lb. L36 to L49 demonstrates the calculation for the proportional vertical distribution of the base shear to each level of the structure. The horizontal force at each floor is used to determine the design of the horizontal diaphragm at that particular level. The force used to design the vertical resisting diaphragms or shear walls is cumulative from the top of the structure down; for example, shear walls between the second and third floors must be designed to resist a total force of F_R plus F_3. Also, L49 checks to see that the total base shear is totally distributed.

Sheet S-7 calculates the resistance of the building to overturning from either seismic or wind forces. Note that the code allows 85 percent of the dead load to be used for uplift resistance and that the resistance is required to be greater than a ratio $M_R / M_o = 1.5$. L27 to L43 calculate the shear per foot of the roof diaphragm.

Sheets S-8 to S-11 show the calculations for the seismic north-south walls on plan grid lines 1, 2, 5, and 6 and for the east-west walls on plan grid lines A and B. One shear wall panel on each of these walls is calculated from the floor to the foundation. A full seismic design requires that each shear panel of each wall, and at each level be calculated for unit shear stress, resistance to sliding, resistance to uplift and the continuity tie to the structure.

In Sheet S-8, L11 to L23, the unit shear transverse to the building = 367.7 lb/ft. The tributary width to the seismic walls on L12 = 18 ft. The seismic force is calculated by multiplying the tributary width times the unit shear. Note that the resistance to uplift is calculated on the assumption that the shear panel cantilevers about a point located at a lower corner point on the sole plate below. M_O = overturning moment; M_R = resisting moment; the net moment = $M_O - M_R$. When the M_R is greater than M_O, there is no uplift on the wall panel; however, when a converse condition exists, the uplift resistance is required and is calculated as the net moment divided by the panel length. The tie strap load of the panel is calculated as the cumulative lateral load between shear panels. The resistance to panel sliding is calculated as the resistance of the sole plate nailing. The value of 108 on L20 represents the allowable lateral resistance of a 16d common nail. The code allows that this value be increased by one-third for lateral forces. On Sheet S-11, L29, the mudsill anchor bolt spacing is calculated based on the resistance value of a $\frac{5}{8}$-in-diameter bolt acting in single shear parallel to the grain of the mudsill. The size and spacing of anchor bolts are critical to the resistance capacity of a shear panel at the foundation wall. The bolts are usually installed at the early stage of the construction. By the time the wood stud wall is to be covered, the mudsill compresses from creep caused by the progressive addition of vertical load, and some shrinkage can occur due to exposure. This reduction of the size of the wood mudsill can leave the anchor bolt nuts in a loose position. It is good practice to tighten the foundation nuts of the anchor just prior to closing the wall. This is especially true in the case of holddown hardware.

Sheet S-12 presents a calculation of an exterior bearing wall stud for a combination of vertical and horizontal wind load. The stud is blocked at midheight to reduce the slenderness ratio. The combined stress results are presented as a summation of the ratios of the calculated stress to the allowable stress. The code requires that this ratio not be greater than 1.33. Plywood shear panels required to resist high shear stress often use 3-in-wide studs to permit the nail spacing at 2-in o.c. When plywood is placed on both sides of a stud wall to gain the necessary shear resistance, it is good practice to stagger the surface nail spacing on each side. The high compression or tension load on a shear panel resulting from severe uplift can distort the panel edge member to the point that the plywood nailing will pop out. It is good practice to oversize panel edge members to maintain the strength of the panel and to provide for an effective connection for the holddowns.

Figures 7.1 to 7.4 show several possible types of holddown conditions that may be encountered in seismic design and construction. There are many types of wood-framing metal hardware available. Each brand has its own advantages and disadvantages. Substitution of materials should be done on an equal basis. Figures 7.5 to 7.8 show several standard hardware connections of mudsills to foundation walls. Figures 7.9 to 7.11 demonstrate several methods of connecting shear walls to horizontal diaphragms. Although the use of toe nails may appear to be the least costly method of construction, it should be noted that it is also the least resistive. The use of metal hardware can significantly increase the strength of the wall and diaphragm connection with only a small incremental cost of labor and materials. Figures 7.13 to 7.16 present methods of connecting shear panels at wall openings. The shear panels must be horizontally and vertically tied together for the structure to react as an assembly. Figures 7.17 to 7.19 are used in places where the first-floor framing is supported by high cripple stud walls or posts. The ground motion of an earthquake can move the stud off of the foundation wall, and thus break the exterior wall cover material at the mudsills. The blocking and cross-bracing of the underfloor posts and beams will serve to maintain the first-floor level and reduce possible partition damage. A great deal depends on the quality of workmanship, additional nailing and the strategic use of metal hardware, none of which is expensive compared to the safety of the structure.

The previous discussions and calculation examples present ideal situations and conditions to attain structural resistance to seismic and wind forces. There are, however, important essentials that are not completely represented in the design equations or within the UBC requirements. The Northridge earthquake of January 17, 1994, in Los Angeles has manifested several other factors necessary for seismic safety. The visible severe damage to many of the wood structures was not a great surprise to the independent engineers who inspected them after the shock; in point of fact, some of the damage could have even been predicted. Inspections disclosed such deficiencies as inaccurate design, the lack of required shear walls, inadequate or wrong size nails and bolts, lack of sufficient connections between shear walls and floor diaphragms, lack of necessary anchor bolts or seismic hold-down hardware, careless plan checking, no evidence of field inspection by either the engineer of record or by the city inspector, poor workmanship, and unapproved substitutions of inexpensive materials. Inspection of seismic damage following the Northridge earthquake verified that application of experience and judgment in structural design, quality of field workmanship, and responsible inspection are the best sources of earthquake insurance.

The American Plywood Association (APA) damage reports (APA Report T92-21) of Hurricane Andrew found that more than 60,000 wood-framed residential structures were either severely damaged or destroyed due to the lack of, or because of, inadequate structural connections between the lateral load–resisting walls. APA inspectors also found remarkably poor workmanship, weak diaphragms, the absence of shear walls and nailed joints, and in many cases the top plates of walls were not lapped at the corners. After the wood roof diaphragms were blown away, the rain saturated the gypsum wallboard ceilings, which resulted in their collapse. APA inspectors found shear walls on which gypsum wallboard was installed over resilient metal channels, significantly limiting their lateral resistance value.

Structural damage to a building is not exclusively an attribute of field workmanship or the strength of materials. There are architects who design buildings with little or no regard for structural stability. They proceed with the attitude that no matter what they conceive, the engineer will make it work. Basic structural requirements or experienced judgment may limit the scope of the design; however, architecture cannot exist without a structure.

It would seem that in the course of construction, any one of the above-cited deficiencies would have become self-evident; but when the cost of construction becomes the primary consideration, it can also be said that, "A closed mouth will gather no foot." The objectives of structural design and construction are bound together by a process of sharing of expertise and designating responsibility and individual accountability. The hierarchy of the persons involved to accomplish these objectives interreact as the links of a chain; however, the strength of the chain is determined only by its weakest link. One person within the system who does not effectively perform his or her function diminishes the capability of the total system. Ideally speaking, failure of the structural design should not happen, unless you, as the engineer, stop thinking and stop trying.

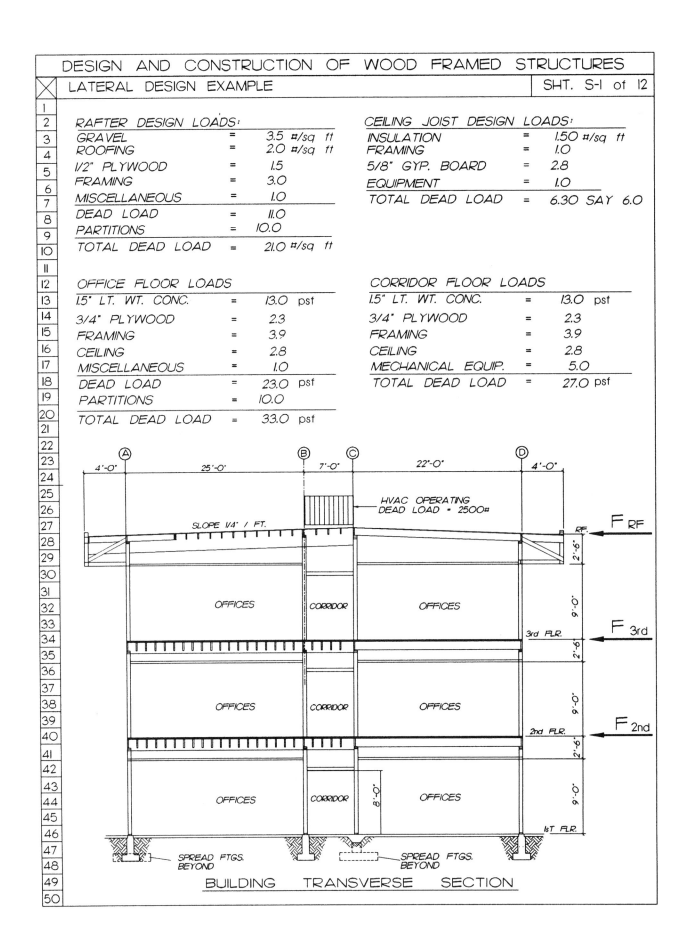

RAFTER DESIGN LOADS:

GRAVEL	=	3.5 #/sq ft
ROOFING	=	2.0 #/sq ft
1/2" PLYWOOD	=	1.5
FRAMING	=	3.0
MISCELLANEOUS	=	1.0
DEAD LOAD	=	11.0
PARTITIONS	=	10.0
TOTAL DEAD LOAD	=	21.0 #/sq ft

CEILING JOIST DESIGN LOADS:

INSULATION	=	1.50 #/sq ft
FRAMING	=	1.0
5/8" GYP. BOARD	=	2.8
EQUIPMENT	=	1.0
TOTAL DEAD LOAD	=	6.30 SAY 6.0

OFFICE FLOOR LOADS

1.5" LT. WT. CONC.	=	13.0 psf
3/4" PLYWOOD	=	2.3
FRAMING	=	3.9
CEILING	=	2.8
MISCELLANEOUS	=	1.0
DEAD LOAD	=	23.0 psf
PARTITIONS	=	10.0
TOTAL DEAD LOAD	=	33.0 psf

CORRIDOR FLOOR LOADS

1.5" LT. WT. CONC.	=	13.0 psf
3/4" PLYWOOD	=	2.3
FRAMING	=	3.9
CEILING	=	2.8
MECHANICAL EQUIP.	=	5.0
TOTAL DEAD LOAD	=	27.0 psf

BUILDING TRANSVERSE SECTION

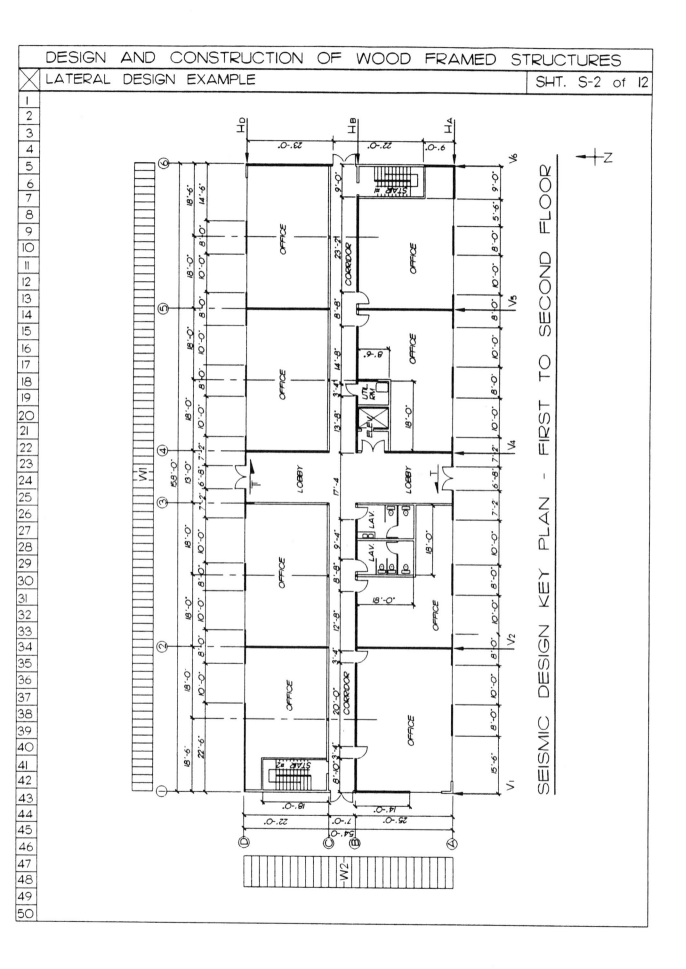

SEISMIC DESIGN KEY PLAN - FIRST TO SECOND FLOOR

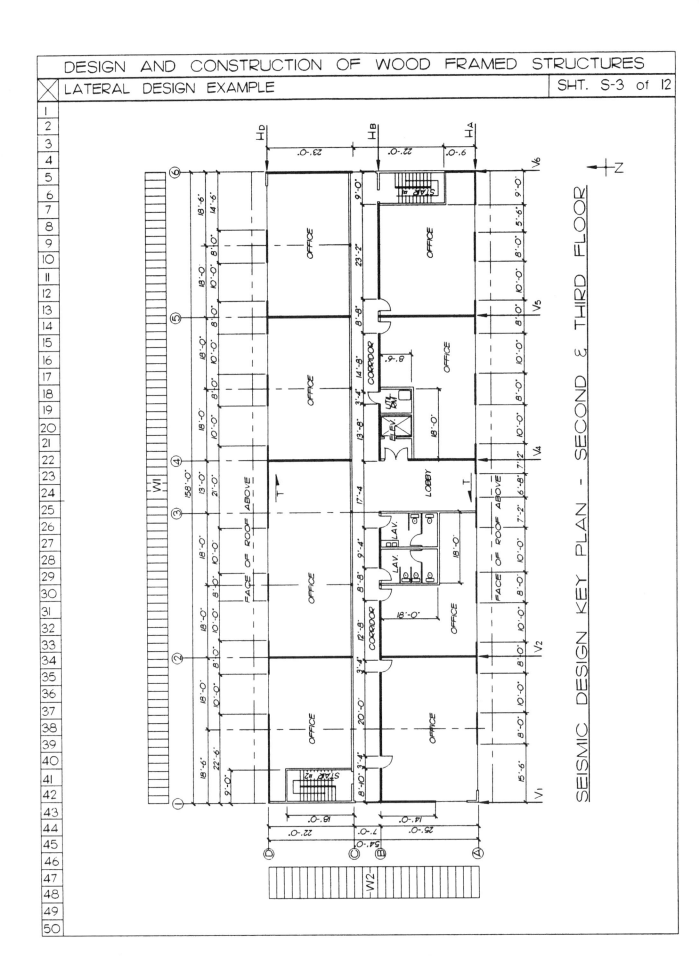

SEISMIC DESIGN KEY PLAN - SECOND & THIRD FLOOR

CALCULATION - BASE SHEAR V - STATIC FORCE PROCEDURE - REF. UBC 1628.2

$$Eq. (28\text{-}1) \qquad V = \left(\frac{Z \times I \times C}{R_w}\right) W$$

$$Eq. (28\text{-}2) \qquad C = \frac{1.25 \times S}{T^{2/3}}$$

V = THE TOTAL LATERAL DESIGN FORCE OR SHEAR AT THE BASE OF THE BUILDING

C = NUMERICAL COEFFICIENT SPECIFIED IN SECTION 1628.2.1

I = IMPORTANCE FACTOR GIVEN IN TABLE No. 16-K

R_w = NUMERICAL COEFFICIENT GIVEN IN TABLES No. 16-N AND 16-P

S = SITE COEFFICIENTS FOR SOIL CHARACTERISTICS GIVEN IN TABLE No. 23-J

T = THE FUNDAMENTAL PERIOD OF VIBRATION, IN SECONDS, OF THE STRUCTURE IN THE DIRECTION UNDER CONSIDERATION

W = THE TOTAL SEISMIC DEAD LOAD DEFINED IN SECTION 1628.1

Z = THE SEISMIC ZONE FACTOR GIVEN IN TABLE No. 16 - 1

$C_t = .02 \qquad S = 1 \qquad T = .02 \, (3 \times 11.5)^{3/4} = 0.284 \qquad C = \frac{1.25 \times 1}{(0.284)^{2/3}} = 2.91$

CODE MAX. REQ'D = 2.75 $I = 1.0$ SEISMIC ZONE 4, $Z = 0.4$ $R_w = 6.0$

$$Eq. (34\text{-}1) \quad V = \left(\frac{Z \times I \times C}{R_w}\right) W = \left(\frac{0.4 \times 1 \times 2.75}{6}\right) W = 0.183 \times W$$

VERTICAL DISTRIBUTION OF SEISMIC FORCES:

$$EQ\ (28\text{-}6) \qquad V = F_t + \sum_{i=1}^{n} F_i$$

$$EQ\ (28\text{-}7) \qquad F_t = 0.07 \times T \times V$$

$$EQ\ (28\text{-}8) \qquad F_x = \frac{(V - F_t)\, w_x\, h_x}{\sum\limits_{i=1}^{n} w_i\, h_i}$$

F_t = THAT PORTION OF THE BASE SHEAR, V, CONSIDERED AND CONCENTRATED AT THE TOP OF THE STRUCTURE IN ADDITION TO F_n

F_i = LATERAL FORCE APPLIED TO LEVEL i, n OR x RESPECTIVELY

n = THAT LEVEL WHICH IS UPPERMOST IN THE MAIN PORTION OF THE STRUCTURE

h_i, h_n, h_x = HEIGHT IN FEET ABOVE THE BASE TO LEVEL i, n, OR x RESPECTIVELY

$w_i\ OR\ w_x$ = THAT PORTION OF , W, WHICH IS LOCATED OR ASSIGNED TO LEVEL i OR x RESPECTIVELY

LATERAL FORCE ON ELEMENTS OF STRUCTURES AND NONSTRUCTURAL COMPONENTS SUPPORTED BY STRUCTURES – REF. UBC 1630.2

$$Eq.\ (30\text{-}1) \qquad F_p = Z \times I_p \times C_p \times W_p$$

F_p = LATERAL FORCE ON PART OF THE STRUCTURE

C_p = NUMERICAL COEFFICIENT SPECIFIED IN TABLE 16-O

W_p = WEIGHT OF AN ELEMENT OR COMPONENT

WIND DESIGN UBC SECTION 1614

$$EQ.\ (18\text{-}1) \qquad P = C_e \times C_q \times q_s \times I_w$$

P = DESIGN WIND PRESSURE

C_e = COMBINE HEIGHT, EXPOSURE AND GUST FACTOR COEFFICIENTS AS GIVEN IN TABLE No. 16-G $C_e = 1.31$ EXPOSURE C

C_q = PRESSURE COEFFICIENT FOR THE STRUCTURE OR PORTION OF THE STRUCTURE UNDER CONSIDERATION AS GIVEN IN TABLE No. 16-H METHOD 2, $C_q = 1.30$

q_s = WIND STAGNATION PRESSURE AT THE STANDARD HEIGHT OF 33 FT. AS SET FORTH IN TABLE No. 16-F   WIND AT 70 mph $q_s = 12.6$

I_w = IMPORTANCE FACTOR AS SET FORTH IN TABLE No. 16-K , $I = 1$

$$P = 1.31 \times 1.30 \times q_s \times 12.6 \times 1 = 21.5\ psf \qquad USE\ 22.0\ psf$$

NOTE THAT THE WIND VELOCITY OF HURRICANE ANDREW WAS RECORDED AT APPROXIMATELY 160 mph. EXTENDING THE VALUE IN TABLE 16-F GIVES $q_s = 58.$ (approx.)

THEN: $P = 1.31 \times 1.30 \times q_s \times 58 \times 1 = 98\ psf$ (ALL OTHER CONDITIONS BEING EQUAL)

WIND SURFACE AREA: N-S ELEVATION = $(11.5/2 + 2 \times 11.5)158 = 4542.5$ sq ft

E-W ELEVATION = $(11.5/2 + 2 \times 11.5)54 = 1552.5$ sq ft

WIND FORCE $_{N-S}$ = $98 \times 4542.5 = 445,156$ #

WIND FORCE $_{E-W}$ = $98 \times 1552.5 = 147,487$ #

SUPERSTRUCTURE DEAD LOADS

DEAD LOAD - ROOF TO 3rd FLOOR

ROOF	$= 54 \times 158 \times (11 + 10) =$	179172 #
CORRIDOR CEIL.	$= 7 \times 158 \times 6 =$	6636
HVAC	$=$	2500
MANSARD	$= 4 \times 2 \times 158 \times 11 =$	13904
	DEAD LOAD $=$	202212 #

FLOOR SPACE AREAS

LOBBY	$= 13 \times 25 =$	325 sq. ft.
CORRIDOR	$= 158 \times 7 =$	1106
STAIR No. 1	$= 9 \times 22 =$	198
STAIR No. 2	$= 9 \times 18 =$	162
LAVATORIES	$= 18 \times 18 =$	324
ELEV. & UTILITY RM.	$= 18 \times 8.5 =$	153
		2268 sq. ft.

TOTAL FLOOR AREA $= 54 \times 158 = 8532$ sq. ft.

OFFICE SPACE AREA $= 8532 - 2268 = 6264$ sq. ft.

DEAD LOAD - 3rd TO 2nd FLOOR

LOBBY	$= 325 \times 23 =$	7475 #
CORRIDOR	$= 1106 \times 27 =$	29862
STAIR No. 1	$= 198 \times 23 =$	4554
STAIR No. 2	$= 162 \times 23 =$	3726
LAVATORIES	$= 324 \times 23 =$	7452
ELEV. & UTILITY RM.	$= 153 \times 23 =$	3519
OFFICE AREA	$= 6264 \times 33 =$	206712
	DEAD LOAD $=$	263300 #

SUPERSTRUCTURE DEAD LOAD

ROOF TO 3rd FLOOR	$=$	202212 #
3rd FLOOR TO 2nd FLOOR	$=$	263300
2nd FLOOR TO 1sT FLOOR	$=$	263300
TOTAL DEAD LOAD	$=$	728812 #

BUILDING SEISMIC BASE SHEAR $= 0.183 \times 728812 = 133372$ #

$$F_R = \frac{133372 \times (202212 \times 3 \times 11.5)}{(202212 \times 3 \times 11.5 + 2 \times 11.5 \times 263300 + 11.5 \times 263300)} = 57935 \text{ #}$$

$$F_3 = \frac{133372 \times (263300 \times 2 \times 11.5)}{(202212 \times 3 \times 11.5 + 2 \times 11.5 \times 263300 + 11.5 \times 263300)} = 50292 \text{ #}$$

$$F_2 = \frac{133372 \times (263300 \times 11.5)}{(202212 \times 3 \times 11.5 + 2 \times 11.5 \times 263300 + 11.5 \times 263300)} = 25145 \text{ #}$$

$V = F_R + F_3 + F_2 \qquad V = 57935 + 50292 + 25145 = 133372$ # ✓

Wind and Seismic Design **181**

BUILDING OVERTURNING - NORTH SOUTH DIRECTION

ROOF TO 3rd FLR.

$\text{SEISMIC } W1 = \dfrac{57935}{158} = 367.7 \, ^\#/ft.$ $\qquad$ $\text{WIND} = 11.5 \times .5 \times 22 = 126.5 \, ^\#/ft.$

3rd FLR. TO 2nd FLR.

$\text{SEISMIC } W1 = \dfrac{50292}{158} = 318.3 \, ^\#/ft.$ $\qquad$ $\text{WIND} = 11.5 \times 22 = 253.0 \, ^\#/ft.$

2nd FLR. 1st FLR

$\text{SEISMIC } W1 = \dfrac{25145}{158} = 159.1 \, ^\#/ft.$ $\qquad$ $\text{WIND} = 11.5 \times 22 = 253.0 \, ^\#/ft.$

NOTE SEISMIC LOADS GOVERN

$\text{OVERTURN. } M = 367.7 \times 3 \times 11.5 + 318.3 \times 2 \times 11.5 + 159.1 \times 11.5 = 21,836.2 \, ft.$

$\text{UPLIFT} = \dfrac{21,836.2 \, ft.}{54} = 404.4 \, ^\#/ft.$

$\text{DEAD LOAD RESISTANCE TO UPLIFT} = 0.85(3 \times 11.5 \times 20 + 8 \times 11 + 2 \times .67 \times 33) = 698.6 \, ^\#/ft.$

ROOF MANSARD

UBC SEC. 2337

EXTERIOR WALL

FLOORS

$$\text{OVERTURNING RESISTANCE RATIO} = \dfrac{698.6}{404.4} = 1.72 < 1.50 \checkmark$$

CHECK ROOF DIAPHRAGM SHEAR

$W1 = \dfrac{57935}{158} = 367.7 \, ^\#/ft.$ $\qquad$ $W2 = \dfrac{57935}{54} = 1072.9 \, ^\#/ft.$

$T = \dfrac{367.7 \times 36^2}{8 \times 54} = 1103 \, ^\#$ $\qquad$ $H_B = 1072.9 \times 54 \times .5 = 28968.3 \, ^\#$

$\text{DIAPHRAGM SHEAR} = \dfrac{28968.3}{158} = 183.3 \, ^\#/ft.$ $\quad$ 1/2" PLYWOOD OK

$V_4 = 367.7 \times 36 = 13237.2 \, ^\#$

$\text{DIAPHRAGM SHEAR} = \dfrac{13237.2}{54} = 245.1 \, ^\#/ft.$ $\quad$ 1/2" PLYWOOD OK

CHECK FLOOR DIAPHRAGM SHEAR

$$W1 = \frac{50292}{158} = 318.3 \,^\#/ft. \qquad W2 = \frac{50292}{54} = 931.3 \,^\#/ft. \qquad T = \frac{318.3 \times 36}{8 \times 54^2} = 955.0 \,^\#$$

$$H_B = 931.3 \times 54 \times .5 = 2524.1 \,^\# \qquad DIAPHRAGM \ SHEAR = \frac{2524.1}{158} = 159.1 \,^\#/ft.$$

$$V_4 = 318.3 \times 36 = 11458.8 \,^\# \qquad DIAPHRAGM \ SHEAR = \frac{11458.8}{54} = 212.2 \,^\#/ft.$$

1/2" THICK ROOF PLYWOOD   -OK - UBC TABLE No. 23-1-J-1

CASE 1 - ROOF TO 3rd FLOOR - SHEAR WALL - GRID LINE 1

$$W1 = 367.7 \,^\# \qquad V1 = V6 = 9 \times 367.7 = 3309.3^\# \qquad V2 = V4 = V5 = 18 \times 367.7 = 6618.6^\#$$

$$V1 = \frac{3309.3}{54} = 61.3 \,^\#/ft. \quad PANEL \ LENGTH = 14' \quad PANEL \ SHEAR = \frac{3309.3}{14} = 236.4 \,^\#/ft.$$

DEAD LOAD / TIE STRAP

OVERTURN. M. $= 3309.3 \times 11.5 = 38057 \,^\#$

DEAD LOAD $= 0.85 (11.5 \times 20 + 9.25 \times 33) = 455 \,^\#/ft.$

RESISTING. M. $= \frac{455 \times 14^2}{2} = 44586.3 \,'^\# \ M_R > M_O \ \therefore \ NO \ UPLIFT$

TIE STRAP LOAD $= 61.3 \times 29 = 1777.7 \,^\# \ USE \ SIMPSON \ ST6224$

SOLE PLATE NAILS $= \frac{108 \times 1.33 \times 12}{236.4} = 7.3 \ SAY \ 16d \ COMMON \ NAILS \bullet 6" \ oc$

14' | 11.5'

R | R

GRID LINE 1

USE 1/2" THICK PLYWOOD, GRADE CD, NAIL WITH 10d NAILS, 6" oc AT PANEL EDGES 4" oc AT BOUNDARIES AND 12" oc FIELD NAIL. UBC TABLE 25-K-1

CASE 2 - ROOF TO 3rd FLOOR - SHEAR WALL - GRID LINES 2 & 5

$$W1 = 367.7 \,^\# \qquad V2 = V5 = 18 \times 367.7 = 6619 \,^\# \qquad V2 = V4 = V5 = 18 \times 367.7 = 6618.6 \,^\#$$

$$V = \frac{6618.6}{54} = 122.6 \,^\#/ft. \quad PANEL \ LENGTH = 25 + 22 = 47' \quad PANEL \ SHEAR = \frac{6618.6}{47} = 140.8 \,^\#/ft.$$

SOLE PLATE NAILS $= \frac{108 \times 1.33 \times 12}{140.8} = 12.4 \quad SAY \ 16d \ COMMON \ NAILS \bullet 12" \ oc$

USE 5/8" THICK GYPSUM WALL BOARD ON ONE SIDE, ALL PANEL EDGES SHALL BE BLOCKED, 6d COOLER NAILS AT 7" oc   UBC TABLE 25-1

CASE 3 - ROOF TO 3rd FLOOR - SHEAR WALL - GRID LINE A

$$W2 = 931.3 \,^\# \quad H_A = 16.5 \times 931.3 = 15366.5 \,^\# \quad TOTAL \ LENGTH \ OF \ SHEAR \ PANEL = 71.34 \ ft$$

$$V_A = \frac{15366.5}{158} = 97.3 \,^\#/ft. \quad PANEL \ LENGTH = 8' \quad PANEL \ SHEAR = \frac{15366.5}{71.34} = 215.4 \,^\#/ft.$$

DEAD LOAD / TIE STRAP

OVERTURN. M. $= 8 \times 215.4 \times 11.5 = 19816.8 \,'^\#$

DEAD LOAD $= 0.85 (11.5 \times 20 + 4 \times 11) = 224.4 \,^\#/ft.$

RESISTING. M. $= \frac{224.4 \times 8^2}{2} = 7180.8 \,'^\# \quad M_O > M_R$

NET OTM $= 19816.8 - 7180.8 = 12636 \,'^\# \quad USE \ SIMPSON \ ST6236$

UPLIFT $= \frac{12636}{8} = 1579.5 \,^\#$

8' | 11.5'

R | R

GRID LINE A

TIE STRAP LOAD $= 61.3 \times 29 = 1777.7 \,^\# \ USE \ SIMPSON \ ST6224$

SOLE PLATE NAILS $= \frac{108 \times 1.33 \times 12}{215.4} = 8 \ USE \ 18d \ COMMON \ NAILS \bullet 8" \ oc$

CASE 4 - ROOF TO 3rd FLOOR - SHEAR WALL - GRID LINE B

$W2 = 931.3$ # $H_B = 27 \times 931.3 = 25145$ #   TOTAL LENGTH OF SHEAR PANEL = 102.33 ft

$V_B = \dfrac{25145}{158} = 159.1$ #/ft.   PANEL LENGTH = 8.83' PANEL SHEAR $= \dfrac{25145}{102.33} = 245.7$ #/ft.

DEAD LOAD — TIE STRAP

OVERTURN. M. = $8.83 \times 245.7 \times 11.5 = 24949.6$ '#

DEAD LOAD = $0.85 (11.5 \times 20 + 4 \times 11) = 233$ #/ft.

11.5'

RESISTING. M. = $\dfrac{233 \times 8.83^2}{2} = 9083$ '# $M_O > M_R$

8.83'

NET OTM = $24949.6 - 9083 = 15866.6$ '#

R   R

UPLIFT = $\dfrac{15866.6}{8.83} = 1796.9$ #   USE SIMPSON ST6236

GRID LINE B

SOLE PLATE NAILS = $\dfrac{108 \times 1.33 \times 12}{245.7} = 7$ USE 16d COMMON NAILS ● 6" oc

CASE 5 - 3rd FLOOR TO 2nd FLOOR - SHEAR WALL - GRID LINE 1

$\Sigma V = 57935 + 50292 = 108227$ # $W1 = \dfrac{108227}{158} = 685$ #/ft.

V1 PANEL LENGTH = 14' $V1 = 685 \times 9 = 6165$ #   PANEL SHEAR $= \dfrac{6165}{14} = 440.3$ #/ft.

DEAD LOAD — TIE STRAP

OVERTURN. M. = $6165 \times 11.5 = 70897.5$ '#

DEAD LOAD = $0.85 (2 \times 11.5 \times 20 + 9.25 \times (33 + 11)) = 737$ #/ft.

11.5'

RESISTING. M. = $\dfrac{737 \times 14^2}{2} = 72226$ '# $M_R > M_O$ ∴ NO UPLIFT

14'

SOLE PLATE NAILS = $\dfrac{108 \times 1.33 \times 12}{440.3} = 3.9$

R   R

SAY 16d COMMON NAILS ● 4" oc

GRID LINE 1

USE 1/2" THICK PLYWOOD, GRADE CD, NAIL WITH 10d NAILS, 4" oc AT PANEL EDGES
3" oc AT BOUNDARIES AND 12" oc FIELD NAIL.   UBC TABLE 25-K-1

CASE 6 - 3rd FLOOR TO 2nd FLOOR - SHEAR WALL - GRID LINES 2 & 5

$\Sigma V = 57935 + 50292 = 108227$ # $W1 = \dfrac{108227}{158} = 685$ #/ft. $V4 = V5 = 18 \times 685 = 12330$ #

PANEL LENGTH = 25 + 22 = 47'   PANEL SHEAR $= \dfrac{12330}{47} = 262.3$ #/ft.

SOLE PLATE NAILS = $\dfrac{108 \times 1.33 \times 12}{262.3} = 6.57$ SAY 16d COMMON NAILS ● 6" oc

USE 5/8" GYPSUM WALL BOARD ON EACH SIDE, BLOCK PANEL EDGES
NAIL WITH 6d COOLER NAILS AT ALL EDGES AND FIELD NAIL   UBC TABLE 25-1

CASE 7 - 3rd FLOOR TO 2nd FLOOR - SHEAR WALL - GRID LINE A

$\Sigma V = 57935 + 50292 = 108227$ # $W1 = \dfrac{108227}{54} = 2004.2$ #/ft. $V_A = 18 \times 2004.2 = 36075.7$ #

$V_A = \dfrac{36075.7}{158} = 228.3$ #/ft.   PANEL LENGTH = 71.34' PANEL SHEAR $= \dfrac{36075.7}{71.34} = 505.7$ #/ft.

DEAD LOAD — TIE STRAP

OVERTURN. M. = $8 \times 505.7 \times 11.5 = 46524.4$ '#

DEAD LOAD = $0.85 (2 \times 9.5 \times 20 + 4 \times 11) = 428.4$ #/ft.

11.5'

RESISTING. M. = $\dfrac{424.4 \times 8^2}{2} = 13708.8$ '# $M_O > M_R$

8'

NET OTM = $46524.4 - 13708.8 = 32815.6$ '#

R   R

UPLIFT = $\dfrac{32815.6}{8} = 4102$ #   USE SIMPSON MST48

GRID LINE A

TIE STRAP LOAD = $228.3 \times 10 = 2283$ #   USE SIMPSON ST6236

SOLE PLATE NAILS = $\dfrac{108 \times 1.33 \times 12}{505.7} = 3.4$ USE 16d COMMON NAILS ● 3" oc

CASE 8 - 3rd FLOOR TO 2nd FLOOR - SHEAR WALL - GRID LINE B

$\Sigma = 57935 + 50292 = 108227^{\#}$ $W2 = \dfrac{108227}{54} = 2004.2^{\#}/ft.$

$H_B = 27 \times 2004.2 = 54113.5^{\#}$ TOTAL LENGTH OF SHEAR PANEL = 102.33 ft

$V = \dfrac{54113.5}{158} = 342.5^{\#}/ft.$ PANEL LENGTH = 8.83'   PANEL SHEAR = $\dfrac{54113.5}{102.33} = 528.8^{\#}/ft.$

OVERTURN. M. = $8.83 \times 528.8 \times 11.5 = 53697'^{\#}$

DEAD LOAD = $0.85(11.5 \times 2 \times 20 + 4 \times 11) = 428.4^{\#}/ft.$

RESISTING. M. = $\dfrac{428.4 \times 8.83^2}{2} = 16701'^{\#}$ $M_O > M_R$

NET OTM = $53697 - 16701 = 36996'^{\#}$

UPLIFT = $\dfrac{36996}{8.83} = 4189.8^{\#}$ USE SIMPSON MST48

TIE STRAP LOAD = $342.5 \times 10 = 342.5^{\#}$

SOLE PLATE NAILS = $\dfrac{108 \times 1.33 \times 12}{528.8} = 3.25$

USE 16d COMMON NAILS @ 3" oc

GRID LINE B

CASE 9 - 2nd FLOOR TO 1st FLOOR - SHEAR WALL - GRID LINE 1

$\Sigma V = 57935 + 50292 + 25145 = 133372^{\#}$ $W1 = \dfrac{133372}{158} = 844.1^{\#}/ft.$

V1 PANEL LENGTH = 14' $V1 = 844.1 \times 9.25 = 7808^{\#}$ PANEL SHEAR = $\dfrac{7808}{14} = 557.7^{\#}/ft.$

OVERTURN. M. = $7808 \times 11.5 = 89792'^{\#}$

DEAD LOAD = $0.85(3 \times 11.5 \times 20 + 9.25 \times (2 \times 33 + 11)) = 1192^{\#}/ft.$

RESISTING. M. = $\dfrac{1192 \times 14^2}{2} = 116816'^{\#}$ $M_R > M_O$ ∴ NO UPLIFT

MUDSILL ANCHOR BOLTS = $\dfrac{590 \times 1.33 \times 12}{557.7} = 16.9$

GRID LINE 1   USE 5/8" DIA. BOLTS AT 16" oc

USE 1/2" THICK PLYWOOD, GRADE CD, NAIL WITH 10d NAILS, 4" oc AT PANEL EDGES
3" oc AT BOUNDARIES AND 12" oc FIELD NAIL.   UBC TABLE 25-K-1

CASE 10 - 2nd FLOOR TO 1st FLOOR - SHEAR WALL - GRID LINES 2 & 5

$\Sigma V = 57935 + 50292 + 25145 = 133372^{\#}$ $W1 = \dfrac{133372}{158} = 844.1^{\#}/ft.$

$V4 = V5 = 18 \times 844.1 = 15194^{\#}$ PANEL LENGTH = $25 + 22 = 47'$

PANEL SHEAR = $\dfrac{15194}{47} = 323.3^{\#}/ft.$ TRY 5/8" DIA. ANCHOR BOLTS

MUDSILL ANCHOR BOLT SPACING = $\dfrac{1.33 \times 590 \times 12}{323.3} = 29.1"$ USE SPACING = 24" oc

USE 5/8" GYPSUM WALL BOARD ON EACH SIDE, BLOCK PANEL EDGES
NAIL WITH 6d COOLER NAILS AT ALL EDGES AND FIELD NAIL   UBC TABLE 47-1

CASE 11 - 1st FLOOR TO - 2nd FLOOR SHEAR WALL GRID LINE A

$\Sigma = 57935 + 50292 + 25145 = 133372^{\#}$ $W2 = \dfrac{133372}{54} = 2469.9^{\#}/ft.$

$H_A = 12.5 \times 2469.9 = 30873^{\#}$ TOTAL LENGTH OF SHEAR PANEL $= 71.34$ ft

$V = \dfrac{133372}{158} = 844^{\#}/ft.$ PANEL LENGTH $= 8.0'$ PANEL SHEAR $= \dfrac{30873}{71.34} = 432.8^{\#}/ft.$

OVERTURN. M. $= 8.0' \times 432.8 \times 11.5 = 39819'^{\#}$

DEAD LOAD $= 0.85 (11.5 \times 3 \times 20 + 4 \times 11) = 624^{\#}/ft.$

RESISTING. M. $= \dfrac{624 \times 8.0^2}{2} = 19964.8'^{\#}$ $M_o > M_R$

NET OTM $= 39819 - 19964.8 = 19854.2'^{\#}$

UPLIFT $= \dfrac{19854.2}{8.0} = 2481.9^{\#}$ USE SIMPSON HD2A

TIE STRAP LOAD $= 844 \times 10 = 8440^{\#}$

TIE STRAPS - 2 SIMPSON ST6236 EACH SIDE AT EACH END OF EACH PANEL

ANCHOR BOLT SPACING $= \dfrac{1.33 \times 710 \times 12}{432.8} = 26.2"$ USE 3/4" DIA. ANCHOR BOLTS @ 24" oc

(figure, left: DEAD LOAD, TIE STRAP, 11.5', 8.0', R, R — GRID LINE A)

CASE 12 - 2nd FLOOR TO 1st FLOOR - SHEAR WALL - GRID LINE B

$\Sigma V = 57935 + 50292 + 25145 = 133372^{\#}$ $W2 = \dfrac{133372}{54} = 2469.9^{\#}/ft.$

TOTAL LENGTH OF SHEAR WALL $= 102.34'$ $V_B = 2469.9 \times 27 = 66687.3^{\#}$

PANEL SHEAR $= \dfrac{66687.3}{102.34} = 651.6^{\#}/ft.$ DIAPH. V $= \dfrac{66687.3}{158} = 422.^{\#}/ft.$

V_B PANEL LENGTH $= 8.83'$

OVERTURN. M. $= 651.6 \times 8.83' \times 11.5 = 66166.7'^{\#}$

DEAD LOAD $= 0.85 (3 \times 11.5 \times 20 + 3 \times 3.5 \times 27) = 827.5^{\#}/ft.$

RESISTING. M. $= \dfrac{827.5 \times 8.83^2}{2} = 32258.7'^{\#}$ $M_o > M_R$ ∴ UPLIFT

NET OTM $= 66166.7 - 32258.7 = 33908'^{\#}$

UPLIFT $= \dfrac{33908}{8.83} = 4070.6^{\#}$ USE SIMPSON HD2A

TIE STRAP LOAD $= 422. \times 17.33 = 7300^{\#}$

TIE STRAPS - 2 SIMPSON MST48 EACH SIDE AT EACH END OF EACH PANEL AT LOBBY

ANCHOR BOLT SPACING $= \dfrac{1.33 \times 710 \times 12}{651.6} = 17.4"$ USE 3/4" DIA. ANCHOR BOLTS @ 16" oc

(figure, left: DEAD LOAD, TIE STRAP, 11.5', 8.83', R, R — GRID LINE B)

USE 1/2" THICK PLYWOOD EA. SIDE, GRADE CD, NAIL WITH 10d NAILS; 4" oc AT PANEL EDGES
3" oc AT BOUNDARIES AND 12" oc FIELD NAIL.   UBC TABLE 25-K-1

CHECK EXTERIOR WALL STUDS AT FIRST FLOOR FOR VERTICAL LOAD AND WIND LOAD

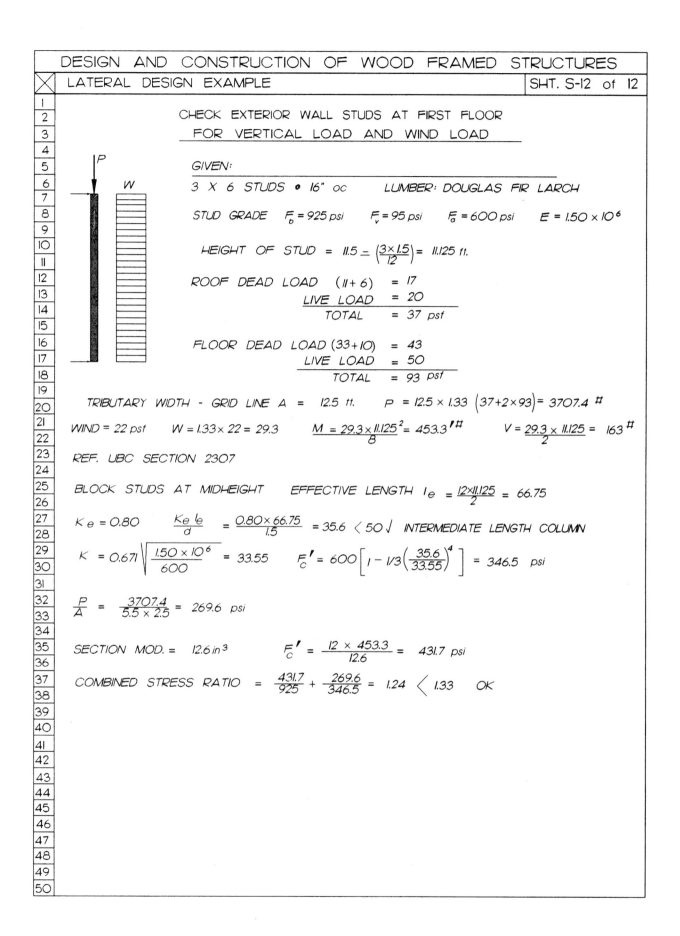

GIVEN:

3 X 6 STUDS @ 16" oc   LUMBER: DOUGLAS FIR LARCH

STUD GRADE $F_b = 925\,psi$ $F_v = 95\,psi$ $F_a = 600\,psi$ $E = 1.50 \times 10^6$

HEIGHT OF STUD = $11.5 - \left(\dfrac{3 \times 1.5}{12}\right) = 11.125\ ft.$

$$
\begin{array}{lrl}
\text{ROOF DEAD LOAD} & (11+6) & = 17 \\
\text{LIVE LOAD} & & = 20 \\
\hline
\text{TOTAL} & & = 37\ psf
\end{array}
$$

$$
\begin{array}{lrl}
\text{FLOOR DEAD LOAD} & (33+10) & = 43 \\
\text{LIVE LOAD} & & = 50 \\
\hline
\text{TOTAL} & & = 93\ psf
\end{array}
$$

TRIBUTARY WIDTH – GRID LINE A = 12.5 ft. $P = 12.5 \times 1.33\,(37 + 2 \times 93) = 3707.4^{\#}$

WIND = 22 psf $W = 1.33 \times 22 = 29.3$ $M = \dfrac{29.3 \times 11.125^2}{8} = 453.3^{'\#}$ $V = \dfrac{29.3 \times 11.125}{2} = 163^{\#}$

REF. UBC SECTION 2307

BLOCK STUDS AT MIDHEIGHT   EFFECTIVE LENGTH $l_e = \dfrac{12 \times 11.125}{2} = 66.75$

$K_e = 0.80$ $\dfrac{K_e\,l_e}{d} = \dfrac{0.80 \times 66.75}{1.5} = 35.6 < 50\ \checkmark$ INTERMEDIATE LENGTH COLUMN

$K = 0.671\sqrt{\dfrac{1.50 \times 10^6}{600}} = 33.55$ $F_c' = 600\left[1 - 1/3\left(\dfrac{35.6}{33.55}\right)^4\right] = 346.5\ psi$

$\dfrac{P}{A} = \dfrac{3707.4}{5.5 \times 2.5} = 269.6\ psi$

SECTION MOD. = $12.6\ in^3$ $F_c' = \dfrac{12 \times 453.3}{12.6} = 431.7\ psi$

COMBINED STRESS RATIO = $\dfrac{431.7}{925} + \dfrac{269.6}{346.5} = 1.24 < 1.33$ OK

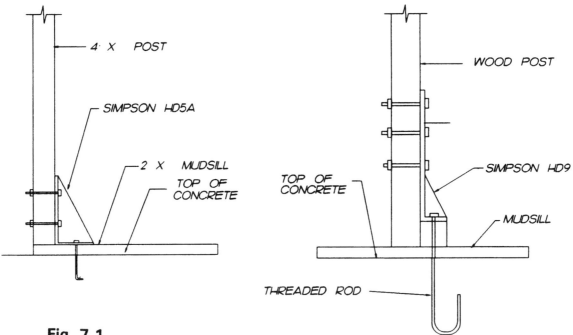

4· X   POST

SIMPSON HD5A

2 X   MUDSILL
TOP OF
CONCRETE

Fig. 7.1

WOOD POST

TOP OF
CONCRETE

SIMPSON HD9

MUDSILL

THREADED ROD

Fig. 7.2

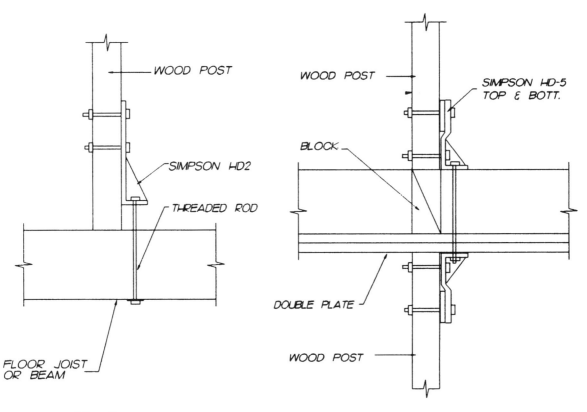

WOOD POST

SIMPSON HD2

THREADED ROD

FLOOR JOIST
OR BEAM

Fig. 7.3

WOOD POST

SIMPSON HD-5
TOP & BOTT.

BLOCK

DOUBLE PLATE

WOOD POST

Fig. 7.4

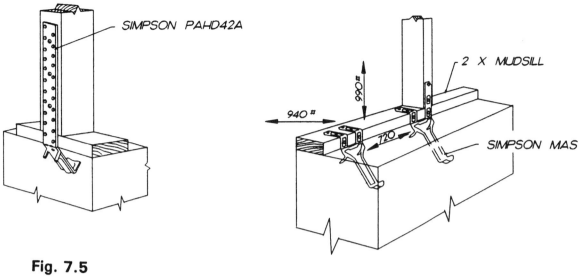

Fig. 7.5

Fig. 7.6

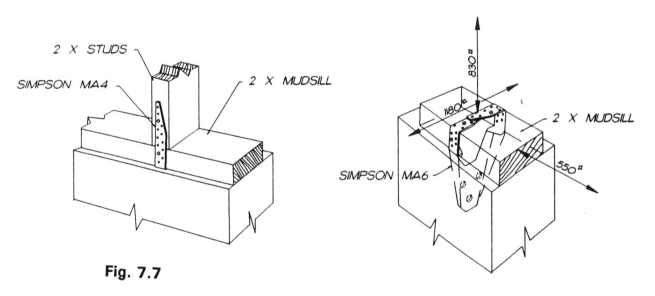

Fig. 7.7

Fig. 7.8

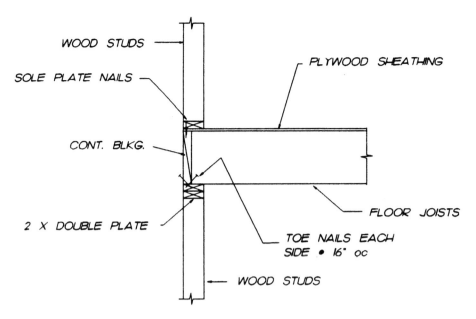

FLOOR & WALL CONNECTION

TOE NAIL 16d's ● 6" oc STAGGER EACH SIDE

SHEAR RESISTANCE $= 108 \times 1.33 \times 2 \times .67 = 192.5$ #/ft

Fig. 7.9

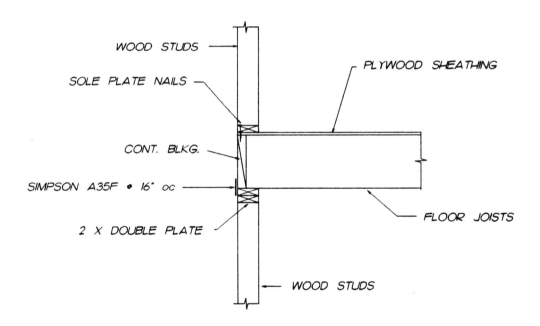

FLOOR & WALL CONNECTION

SHEAR RESISTANCE $= 500 \times \left(\dfrac{12}{16} \right) = 375.0$ #/ft

Fig. 7.10

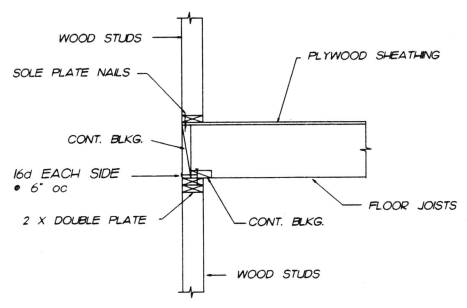

FLOOR & WALL CONNECTION

TOE NAIL 16d's • 6" oc STAGGER EACH SIDE

SHEAR RESISTANCE $= 108 \times 1.33 \times \left(\dfrac{12}{6}\right) = 287.3$ #/ft

Fig. 7.11

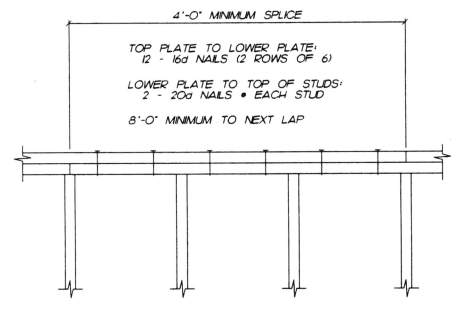

STUDS • 16" oc UNLESS OTHERWISE NOTED

TYPICAL STUD WALL DOUBLE PLATE SPLICE

$12 - 16d$ NAILS $= \dfrac{12 \times 108 \times 1.33}{4'} = 431$ #/ft

Fig. 7.12

WOOD POST
EDGE OF SHEAR PANEL
NAILED METAL STRAP
FIN. FLR.
DOUBLE PL.
WOOD POST
WOOD STUD WALL

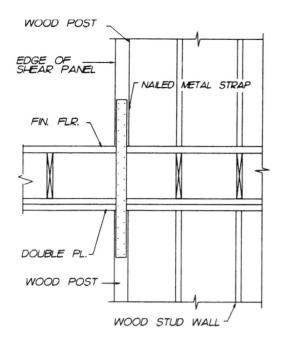

Fig. 7.13

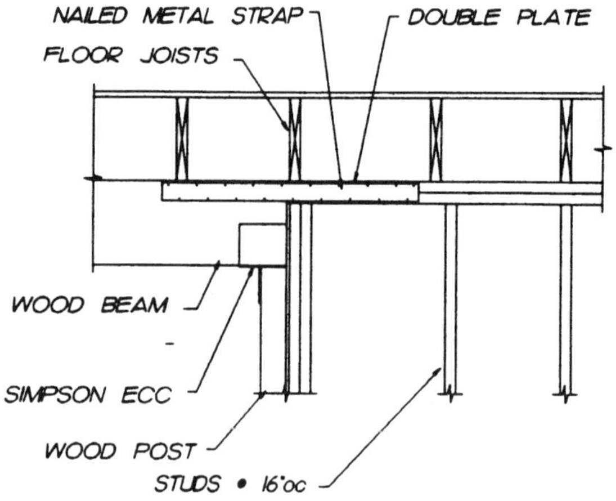

NAILED METAL STRAP
DOUBLE PLATE
FLOOR JOISTS
WOOD BEAM
SIMPSON ECC
WOOD POST
STUDS • 16"oc

Fig. 7.14

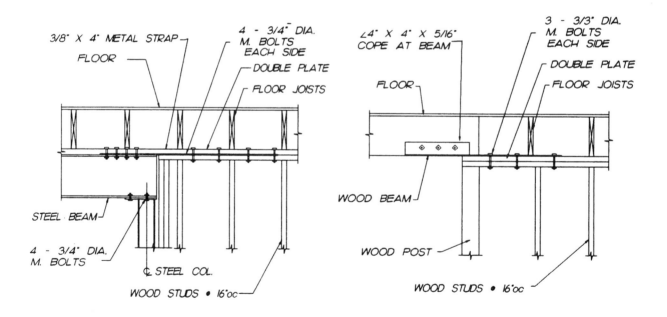

3/8" X 4" METAL STRAP
4 - 3/4" DIA. M. BOLTS EACH SIDE
FLOOR
DOUBLE PLATE
FLOOR JOISTS
STEEL BEAM
4 - 3/4" DIA. M. BOLTS
℄ STEEL COL.
WOOD STUDS • 16"oc

Fig. 7.15

∠4" X 4" X 5/16" COPE AT BEAM
3 - 3/3" DIA. M. BOLTS EACH SIDE
DOUBLE PLATE
FLOOR
FLOOR JOISTS
WOOD BEAM
WOOD POST
WOOD STUDS • 16"oc

Fig. 7.16

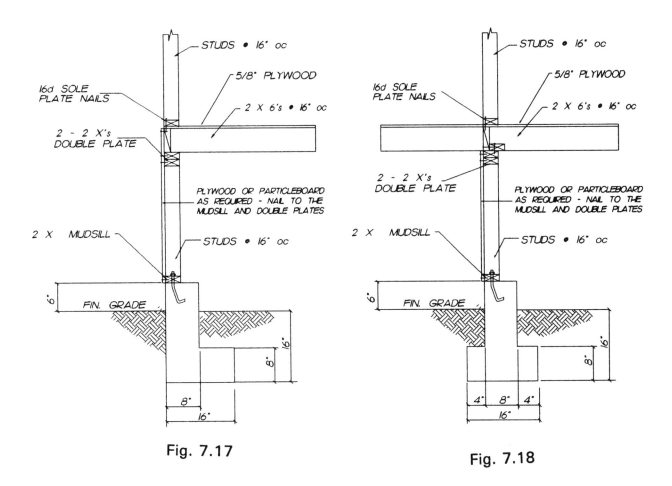

STUDS • 16" oc

5/8" PLYWOOD

16d SOLE
PLATE NAILS

2 X 6's • 16" oc

2 - 2 X's
DOUBLE PLATE

PLYWOOD OR PARTICLEBOARD
AS REQUIRED - NAIL TO THE
MUDSILL AND DOUBLE PLATES

2 X   MUDSILL

STUDS • 16" oc

6"

FIN. GRADE

16"

8"

8"

16"

Fig. 7.17

STUDS • 16" oc

5/8" PLYWOOD

16d SOLE
PLATE NAILS

2 X 6's • 16" oc

2 - 2 X's
DOUBLE PLATE

PLYWOOD OR PARTICLEBOARD
AS REQUIRED - NAIL TO THE
MUDSILL AND DOUBLE PLATES

2 X   MUDSILL

STUDS • 16" oc

6"

FIN. GRADE

16"

8"

4"   8"   4"

16"

Fig. 7.18

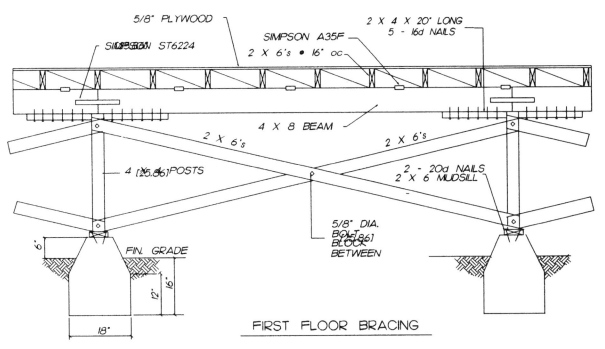

5/8" PLYWOOD

2 X 4 X 20" LONG
5 - 16d NAILS

SIMPSON ST6224

SIMPSON A35F

2 X 6's • 16" oc

4 X 8 BEAM

2 X 6's

2 X 6's

4 [25.86] POSTS

2 - 20d NAILS
2 X 6 MUDSILL

5/8" DIA.
BOLT [25.86]
BLOCK
BETWEEN

6"

FIN. GRADE

16"

12"

18"

FIRST FLOOR BRACING

Fig. 7.19

Appendix A

Uniform Building Code Requirements and Tables

TABLE NO. 23-A—UNIFORM AND CONCENTRATED LOADS

USE OR OCCUPANCY		UNIFORM LOAD[1]	CONCEN-TRATED LOAD
Category	Description		
1. Access floor systems	Office use	50	2,000[2]
	Computer use	100	2,000[2]
2. Armories		150	0
3. Assembly areas[3] and auditoriums and balconies therewith	Fixed seating areas	50	0
	Movable seating and other areas	100	0
	Stage areas and enclosed platforms	125	0
4. Cornices, marquees and residential balconies		60	0
5. Exit facilities[4]		100	0[5]
6. Garages	General storage and/or repair	100	6
	Private or pleasure-type motor vehicle storage	50	6
7. Hospitals	Wards and rooms	40	1,000[2]
8. Libraries	Reading rooms	60	1,000[2]
	Stack rooms	125	1,500[2]
9. Manufacturing	Light	75	2,000[2]
	Heavy	125	3,000[2]
10. Offices		50	2,000[2]
11. Printing plants	Press rooms	150	2,500[2]
	Composing and linotype rooms	100	2,000[2]
12. Residential[7]		40	0[5]
13. Restrooms[8]			
14. Reviewing stands, grandstands, bleachers, and folding and telescoping seating		100	0
15. Roof decks	Same as area served or for the type of occupancy accommodated		
16. Schools	Classrooms	40	1,000[2]
17. Sidewalks and driveways	Public access	250	6
18. Storage	Light	125	
	Heavy	250	
19. Stores	Retail	75	2,000[2]
	Wholesale	100	3,000[2]

[1]See Section 2306 for live load reductions.

[2]See Section 2304 (c), first paragraph, for area of load application.

[3]Assembly areas include such occupancies as dance halls, drill rooms, gymnasiums, playgrounds, plazas, terraces and similar occupancies which are generally accessible to the public.

[4]Exit facilities shall include such uses as corridors serving an occupant load of 10 or more persons, exterior exit balconies, stairways, fire escapes and similar uses.

[5]Individual stair treads shall be designed to support a 300-pound concentrated load placed in a position which would cause maximum stress. Stair stringers may be designed for the uniform load set forth in the table.

[6]See Section 2304 (c), second paragraph, for concentrated loads.

[7]Residential occupancies include private dwellings, apartments and hotel guest rooms.

[8]Restroom loads shall not be less than the load for the occupancy with which they are associated, but need not exceed 50 pounds per square foot.

TABLE NO. 23-B—SPECIAL LOADS[1]

USE		VERTICAL LOAD	LATERAL LOAD
Category	Description	(Pounds per Square Foot unless Otherwise Noted)	
1. Construction, public access at site (live load)	Walkway, see Sec. 4406	150	
	Canopy, see Sec. 4407	150	
2. Grandstands, reviewing stands, bleachers, and folding and telescoping seating (live load)	Seats and footboards	120[2]	See Footnote No. 3
3. Stage accessories (live load)	Gridirons and fly galleries	75	
	Loft block wells[4]	250	250
	Head block wells and sheave beams[4]	250	250
4. Ceiling framing (live load)	Over stages	20	
	All uses except over stages	10[5]	
5. Partitions and interior walls, see Sec. 2309 (live load)			5
6. Elevators and dumbwaiters (dead and live load)		2 x Total loads[6]	
7. Mechanical and electrical equipment (dead load)		Total loads	
8. Cranes (dead and live load)	Total load including impact increase	1.25 x Total load[7]	0.10 x Total load[8]
9. Balcony railings and guardrails	Exit facilities serving an occupant load greater than 50		50[9]
	Other		20[9]
10. Handrails		See Footnote No. 10	See Footnote No. 10
11. Storage racks	Over 8 feet high	Total loads[11]	See Table No. 23-P
12. Fire sprinkler structural support		250 pounds plus weight of water-filled pipe[12]	See Table No. 23-P
13. Explosion exposure	Hazardous occupancies, see Sec. 910		

[1]The tabulated loads are minimum loads. Where other vertical loads required by this code or required by the design would cause greater stresses, they shall be used.

[2]Pounds per lineal foot.

[3]Lateral sway bracing loads of 24 pounds per foot parallel and 10 pounds per foot perpendicular to seat and footboards.

[4]All loads are in pounds per lineal foot. Head block wells and sheave beams shall be designed for all loft block well loads tributary thereto. Sheave blocks shall be designed with a factor of safety of five.

[5]Does not apply to ceilings which have sufficient total access from below, such that access is not required within the space above the ceiling. Does not apply to ceilings if the attic areas above the ceiling are not provided with access. This live load need not be considered as acting simultaneously with other live loads imposed upon the ceiling framing or its supporting structure.

[6]Where Appendix Chapter 51 has been adopted, see reference standard cited therein for additional design requirements.

[7]The impact factors included are for cranes with steel wheels riding on steel rails. They may be modified if substantiating technical data acceptable to the building official is submitted. Live loads on crane support girders and their connections shall be taken as the maximum crane wheel loads. For pendant-operated traveling crane support girders and their connections, the impact factors shall be 1.10.

[8]This applies in the direction parallel to the runway rails (longitudinal). The factor for forces perpendicular to the rail is 0.20 x the transverse traveling loads (trolley, cab, hooks and lifted loads). Forces shall be applied at top of rail and may be distributed among rails of multiple rail cranes and shall be distributed with due regard for lateral stiffness of the structures supporting these rails.

[9]A load per lineal foot to be applied horizontally at right angles to the top rail.

[10]The mounting of handrails shall be such that the completed handrail and supporting structure are capable of withstanding a load of at least 200 pounds applied in any direction at any point on the rail. These loads shall not be assumed to act cumulatively with Item 9.

[11]Vertical members of storage racks shall be protected from impact forces of operating equipment, or racks shall be designed so that failure of one vertical member will not cause collapse of more than the bay or bays directly supported by that member.

[12]The 250-pound load is to be applied to any single fire sprinkler support point but not simultaneously to all support joints.

TABLE NO. 23-C—MINIMUM ROOF LIVE LOADS[1]

	METHOD 1			METHOD 2		
	TRIBUTARY LOADED AREA IN SQUARE FEET FOR ANY STRUCTURAL MEMBER			UNIFORM LOAD[2]	RATE OF REDUCTION r (Percent)	MAXIMUM REDUCTION R (Percent)
ROOF SLOPE	0 to 200	201 to 600	Over 600			
1. Flat or rise less than 4 inches per foot. Arch or dome with rise less than one eighth of span	20	16	12	20	.08	40
2. Rise 4 inches per foot to less than 12 inches per foot. Arch or dome with rise one eighth of span to less than three eighths of span	16	14	12	16	.06	25
3. Rise 12 inches per foot and greater. Arch or dome with rise three eighths of span or greater	12	12	12	12	No Reductions Permitted	
4. Awnings except cloth covered[3]	5	5	5	5		
5. Greenhouses, lath houses and agricultural buildings[4]	10	10	10	10		

[1]Where snow loads occur, the roof structure shall be designed for such loads as determined by the building official. See Section 2305 (d). For special-purpose roofs, see Section 2305 (e).

[2]See Section 2306 for live load reductions. The rate of reduction r in Section 2306 Formula (6-1) shall be as indicated in the table. The maximum reduction R shall not exceed the value indicated in the table.

[3]As defined in Section 4506.

[4]See Section 2305 (e) for concentrated load requirements for greenhouse roof members.

TABLE 23-D—MAXIMUM ALLOWABLE DEFLECTION FOR STRUCTURAL MEMBERS[1]

TYPE OF MEMBER	MEMBER LOADED WITH LIVE LOAD ONLY (L.L.)	MEMBER LOADED WITH LIVE LOAD PLUS DEAD LOAD (L.L. + K.D.L.)
Roof member supporting plaster or floor member	L/360	L/240

[1]Sufficient slope or camber shall be provided for flat roofs in accordance with Section 2305 (f).

L.L. = live load.
D.L. = dead load.
K = factor as determined by Table No. 23-E.
L = length of member in same units as deflection.

TABLE 23-E—VALUE OF "K"

WOOD		REINFORCED CONCRETE[2]	STEEL
Unseasoned	Seasoned[1]		
1.0	0.5	$[2 - 1.2\,(A'_s/A_s)] \geq 0.6$	0

[1]Seasoned lumber is lumber having a moisture content of less than 16 percent at time of installation and used under dry conditions of use such as in covered structures.

[2]See also Section 2609.

A'_s = area of compression reinforcement.
A_s = area of nonprestressed tension reinforcement.

Basic wind speed (mph)[1]	70	80	90	100	110	120	130
Pressure q_s (psf)	12.6	16.4	20.8	25.6	31.0	36.9	43.3

[1]Wind speed from Section 2314.

**TABLE NO. 23-G—COMBINED HEIGHT, EXPOSURE AND
GUST FACTOR COEFFICIENT (C_e)[1]**

HEIGHT ABOVE AVERAGE LEVEL OF ADJOINING GROUND (feet)	EXPOSURE D	EXPOSURE C	EXPOSURE B
0-15	1.39	1.06	0.62
20	1.45	1.13	0.67
25	1.50	1.19	0.72
30	1.54	1.23	0.76
40	1.62	1.31	0.84
60	1.73	1.43	0.95
80	1.81	1.53	1.04
100	1.88	1.61	1.13
120	1.93	1.67	1.20
160	2.02	1.79	1.31
200	2.10	1.87	1.42
300	2.23	2.05	1.63
400	2.34	2.19	1.80

[1]Values for intermediate heights above 15 feet may be interpolated.

TABLE NO. 23-H—PRESSURE COEFFICIENTS (C_q)

STRUCTURE OR PART THEREOF	DESCRIPTION	C_q FACTOR

1. Primary frames and systems	**Method 1 (Normal force method)**
	Walls:
	  Windward wall
	  Leeward wall
	Roofs[1]:
	  Wind perpendicular to ridge
	  Leeward roof or flat roof
	  Windward roof
	    less than 2:12
	    Slope 2:12 to less than 9:12
	
	    Slope 9:12 to 12:12
	    Slope > 12:12
	  Wind parallel to ridge and flat roofs
		
		0.8 inward
		0.5 outward
		
		0.7 outward
		
		0.7 outward
		0.9 outward or
		  0.3 inward
		0.4 inward
		0.7 inward
		0.7 outward

	Method 2 (Projected area method)
	On vertical projected area
	  Structures 40 feet or less in height
	  Structures over 40 feet in height
	On horizontal projected area[1]
		
		1.3 horizontal any direction
		1.4 horizontal any direction
		0.7 upward

2. Elements and components not in areas of discontinuity[2]	Wall elements
	  All structures
	  Enclosed and unenclosed structures
	  Open structures
	  Parapets walls
		
		1.2 inward
		1.2 outward
		1.6 outward
		1.3 inward or outward

	Roof elements[3]
	  Enclosed and unenclosed structures
	    Slope < 7:12
	    Slope 7:12 to 12:12
	
	  Open structures
	    Slope < 2:12
	    Slope 2:12 to 7:12
	
	    Slope > 7:12 to 12:12
		
		1.3 outward
		1.3 outward or inward
		
		1.7 outward
		1.6 outward or 0.8 inward
		1.7 outward or inward

3. Elements and components in areas of discontinuities[2,4,6]	Wall corners[7]
	
	Roof eaves, rakes or ridges without overhangs[7]
	  Slope < 2:12
	  Slope 2:12 to 7:12
	  Slope > 7:12 to 12:12
	For slopes less than 2:12
	  Overhangs at roof eaves, rakes or ridges, and canopies
		1.5 outward or 1.2 inward
		
		2.3 upward
		2.6 outward
		1.6 outward
		
		0.5 added to values above

STRUCTURE OR PART THEREOF	DESCRIPTION	C_q FACTOR
4. Chimneys, tanks and solid towers	Square or rectangular Hexagonal or octagonal Round or elliptical	1.4 any direction 1.1 any direction 0.8 any direction

5. Open-frame towers[5,8]	Square and rectangular
	   Diagonal
	   Normal
	Triangular
		
		4.0
		3.6
		3.2

6. Tower accessories (such as ladders, conduit, lights and elevators)	Cylindrical members
	   2 inches or less in diameter
	   Over 2 inches in diameter
	Flat or angular members
		
		1.0
		0.8
		1.3

7. Signs, flagpoles, lightpoles, minor structures[8]		1.4 any direction

[1]For one story or the top story of multistory open structures, an additional value of 0.5 shall be added to the outward C_q. The most critical combination shall be used for design. For definition of open structures, see Section 2312.

[2]C_q values listed are for 10-square-foot tributary areas. For tributary areas of 100 square feet, the value of 0.3 may be subtracted from C_q, except for areas at discontinuities with slopes less than 7:12 where the value of 0.8 may be subtracted from C_q. Interpolation may be used for tributary areas between 10 and 100 square feet. For tributary areas greater than 1,000 square feet, use primary frame values.

[3]For slopes greater than 12:12, use wall element values.

[4]Local pressures shall apply over a distance from the discontinuity of 10 feet or 0.1 times the least width of the structure, whichever is smaller.

[5]Wind pressures shall be applied to the total normal projected area of all elements on one face. The forces shall be assumed to act parallel to the wind direction.

[6]Discontinuities at wall corners or roof ridges are defined as discontinuous breaks in the surface where the included interior angle measures 170 degrees or less.

[7]Load is to be applied on either side of discontinuity but not simultaneously on both sides.

[8]Factors for cylindrical elements are two thirds of those for flat or angular elements.

TABLE NO. 23-I
SEISMIC ZONE FACTOR Z

ZONE	1	2A	2B	3	4
Z	0.075	0.15	0.20	0.30	0.40

The zone shall be determined from the seismic zone map in Figure No. 23-2.

TABLE NO. 23-J
SITE COEFFICIENTS[1]

TYPE	DESCRIPTION	S FACTOR
S_1	A soil profile with either: (a) A rock-like material characterized by a shear-wave velocity greater than 2,500 feet per second or by other suitable means of classification, or (b) Stiff or dense soil condition where the soil depth is less than 200 feet.	1.0
S_2	A soil profile with dense or stiff soil conditions, where the soil depth exceeds 200 feet.	1.2
S_3	A soil profile 70 feet or more in depth and containing more than 20 feet of soft to medium stiff clay but not more than 40 feet of soft clay.	1.5
S_4	A soil profile containing more than 40 feet of soft clay characterized by a shear wave velocity less than 500 feet per second.	2.0

[1]The site factor shall be established from properly substantiated geotechnical data. In locations where the soil properties are not known in sufficient detail to determine the soil profile type, soil profile S_3 shall be used. Soil profile S_4 need not be assumed unless the building official determines that soil profile S_4 may be present at the site, or in the event that soil profile S_4 is established by geotechnical data.

TABLE NO. 23-K
OCCUPANCY CATEGORIES

OCCUPANCY CATEGORIES	OCCUPANCY TYPE OR FUNCTIONS OF STRUCTURE
I. Essential Facilities[1]	Hospitals and other medical facilities having surgery and emergency treatment areas.
	Fire and police stations.
	Tanks or other structures containing, housing or supporting water or other fire-suppression materials or equipment required for the protection of essential or hazardous facilities, or special occupancy structures.
	Emergency vehicle shelters and garages.
	Structures and equipment in emergency-preparedness centers.
	Standby power-generating equipment for essential facilities.
	Structures and equipment in government communication centers and other facilities required for emergency response.
II. Hazardous Facilities	Structures housing, supporting or containing sufficient quantities of toxic or explosive substances to be dangerous to the safety of the general public if released.
III. Special Occupancy Structure	Covered structures whose primary occupancy is public assembly–capacity > 300 persons.
	Buildings for schools through secondary or day-care centers–capacity > 250 students.
	Buildings for colleges or adult education schools–capacity > 500 students.
	Medical facilities with 50 or more resident incapacitated patients, but not included above.
	Jails and detention facilities.
	All structures with occupancy > 5,000 persons.
	Structures and equipment in power-generating stations and other public utility facilities not included above, and required for continued operation.
IV. Standard Occupancy Structure	All structures having occupancies or functions not listed above.

[1]Essential facilities are those structures which are necessary for emergency operations subsequent to a natural disaster.

TABLE NO. 23-L—OCCUPANCY REQUIREMENTS

OCCUPANCY CATEGORY[1]	IMPORTANCE FACTOR I	
	Earthquake[2]	Wind
I. Essential facilities	1.25	1.15
II. Hazardous facilities	1.25	1.15
III. Special occupancy structures	1.00	1.00
IV. Standard occupancy structures	1.00	1.00

[1]Occupancy types or functions of structures within each category are listed in Table No. 23-K and structural observation requirements are given in Sections 305, 306 and 307.
[2]For life-safety-related equipment, see Section 2336 (a).

TABLE NO. 23-O—STRUCTURAL SYSTEMS

BASIC STRUCTURAL SYSTEM[1]	LATERAL LOAD-RESISTING SYSTEM—DESCRIPTION	R_w[2]	H[3]
A. Bearing Wall System	1. Light-framed walls with shear panels		
	a. Plywood walls for structures three stories or less	8	65
	b. All other light-framed walls	6	65
	2. Shear walls		
	a. Concrete	6	160
	b. Masonry	6	160
	3. Light steel-framed bearing walls with tension-only bracing	4	65
	4. Braced frames where bracing carries gravity loads		
	a. Steel	6	160
	b. Concrete[4]	4	—
	c. Heavy timber	4	65
B. Building Frame System	1. Steel eccentrically braced frame (EBF)	10	240
	2. Light-framed walls with shear panels		
	a. Plywood walls for structures three stories or less	9	65
	b. All other light-framed walls	7	65
	3. Shear walls		
	a. Concrete	8	240
	b. Masonry	8	160
	4. Concentrically braced frames		
	a. Steel	8	160
	b. Concrete[4]	8	—
	c. Heavy timber	8	65
C. Moment-resisting Frame System	1. Special moment-resisting frames (SMRF)		
	a. Steel	12	N.L.
	b. Concrete	12	N.L.
	2. Concrete intermediate moment-resisting frames (IMRF)[6]	8	—
	3. Ordinary moment-resisting frames (OMRF)		
	a. Steel	6	160
	b. Concrete[7]	5	—
D. Dual Systems	1. Shear walls		
	a. Concrete with SMRF	12	N.L.
	b. Concrete with steel OMRF	6	160
	c. Concrete with concrete IMRF[6]	9	160
	d. Masonry with SMRF	8	160
	e. Masonry with steel OMRF	6	160
	f. Masonry with concrete IMRF[4]	7	—
	2. Steel EBF		
	a. With steel SMRF	12	N.L.
	b. With steel OMRF	6	160
	3. Concentrically braced frames		
	a. Steel with steel SMRF	10	N.L.
	b. Steel with steel OMRF	6	160
	c. Concrete with concrete SMRF[4]	9	—
	d. Concrete with concrete IMRF[4]	6	—
E. Undefined Systems	See Sections 2333 (h) 3 and 2333 (i) 2	—	—

[1]Basic structural systems are defined in Section 2333 (f).
[2]See Section 2334 (c) for combination of structural system.
[3]*H*—Height limit applicable to Seismic Zones Nos. 3 and 4. See Section 2333 (g).
[4]Prohibited in Seismic Zones Nos. 3 and 4.
[5]N.L.—No limit.
[6]Prohibited in Seismic Zones Nos. 3 and 4, except as permitted in Section 2338 (b).
[7]Prohibited in Seismic Zones Nos. 2, 3 and 4.

TABLE NO. 23-P—HORIZONTAL FORCE FACTOR, C_p

ELEMENTS OF STRUCTURES AND NONSTRUCTURAL COMPONENTS AND EQUIPMENT[1]	VALUE OF C_p	FOOTNOTE
I. Part or Portion of Structure		
1. Walls including the following:		
a. Unbraced (cantilevered) parapets	2.00	
b. Other exterior walls above the ground floor	0.75	2,3
c. All interior bearing and nonbearing walls and partitions	0.75	3
d. Masonry or concrete fences over 6 feet high	0.75	
2. Penthouse (except when framed by an extension of the structural frame)	0.75	
3. Connections for prefabricated structural elements other than walls, with force applied at center of gravity	0.75	4
4. Diaphragms	—	5
II. Nonstructural Components		
1. Exterior and interior ornamentations and appendages	2.00	
2. Chimneys, stacks, trussed towers and tanks on legs:		
a. Supported on or projecting as an unbraced cantilever above the roof more than one half their total height	2.00	
b. All others, including those supported below the roof with unbraced projection above the roof less than one half its height, or braced or guyed to the structural frame at or above their centers of mass	0.75	
3. Signs and billboards	2.00	
4. Storage racks (include contents)	0.75	10
5. Anchorage for permanent floor-supported cabinets and book stacks more than 5 feet in height (include contents)	0.75	
6. Anchorage for suspended ceilings and light fixtures	0.75	4,6,7
7. Access floor systems	0.75	4,9
III. Equipment		
1. Tanks and vessels (include contents), including support systems and anchorage	0.75	
2. Electrical, mechanical and plumbing equipment and associated conduit, ductwork and piping, and machinery	0.75	8

[1]See Section 2336 (b) for items supported at or below grade.

[2]See Section 2337 (b) 4 and Section 2336 (b).

[3]Where flexible diaphragms, as defined in Section 2334 (f), provide lateral support for walls and partitions, the value of C_p for anchorage shall be increased 50 percent for the center one half of the diaphragm span.

[4]Applies to Seismic Zones Nos. 2, 3 and 4 only.

[5]See Section 2337 (b) 9.

[6]Ceiling weight shall include all light fixtures and other equipment or partitions which are laterally supported by the ceiling. For purposes of determining the seismic force, a ceiling weight of not less than four pounds per square foot shall be used.

[7]Ceilings constructed of lath and plaster or gypsum board screw or nail attached to suspended members that support a ceiling at one level extending from wall to wall need not be analyzed provided the walls are not over 50 feet apart.

[8]Machinery and equipment include, but are not limited to, boilers, chillers, heat exchangers, pumps, air-handling units, cooling towers, control panels, motors, switch gear, transformers and life-safety equipment. It shall include major conduit, ducting and piping serving such machinery and equipment and fire sprinkler systems. See Section 2336 (b) for additional requirements for determining C_p for nonrigid or flexibly mounted equipment.

[9]W_p for access floor systems shall be the dead load of the access floor system plus 25 percent of the floor live load plus a 10 psf partition load allowance.

[10]In lieu of the tabulated values, steel storage racks may be designed in accordance with U.B.C. Standard No. 27-11.

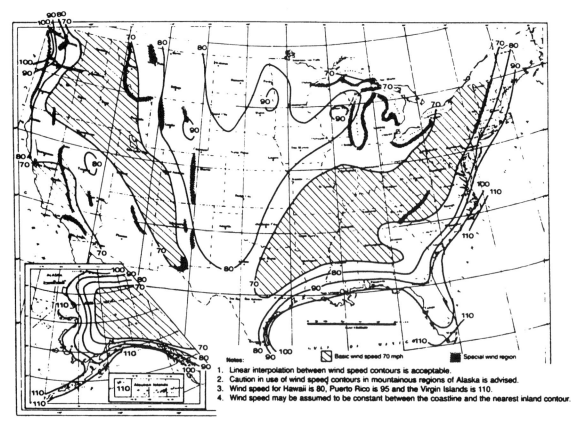

Notes:
1. Linear interpolation between wind speed contours is acceptable.
2. Caution in use of wind speed contours in mountainous regions of Alaska is advised.
3. Wind speed for Hawaii is 80, Puerto Rico is 95 and the Virgin Islands is 110.
4. Wind speed may be assumed to be constant between the coastline and the nearest inland contour.

FIGURE NO. 23-1—MINIMUM BASIC WIND SPEEDS IN MILES PER HOUR

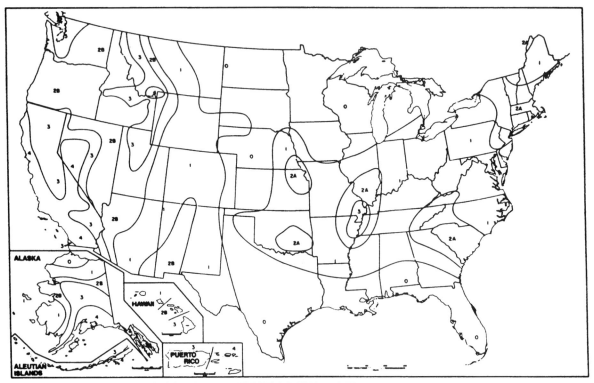

FIGURE NO. 23-2—SEISMIC ZONE MAP OF THE UNITED STATES

For areas outside of the United States, see Appendix Chapter 23.

SPECIES AND COMMERCIAL GRADE	SIZE CLASSIFI- CATION	ALLOWABLE UNIT STRESSES IN POUNDS PER SQUARE INCH								GRADING RULES UNDER WHICH GRADED
		EXTREME FIBER IN BENDING F_b		Tension Parallel to Grain F_t	Horizontal Shear F_v	Compres- sion per- pendicular to Grain $F_c\perp$ [21]	Compres- sion Parallel to Grain F_c	MODULUS OF ELASTICITY E [21]		
		Single- member Uses	Repetitive- member Uses							
DOUGLAS FIR – LARCH (Surfaced dry or surfaced green. Used at 19% max. m.c.)										
DOUGLAS FIR – LARCH (North)										
Dense Select Structural		2450	2800	1400	95	730	1850	1,900,000		
Select Structural		2100	2400	1200	95	625	1600	1,800,000		
Dense No. 1		2050	2400	1200	95	730	1450	1,900,000		
No. 1	2" to 4"	1750	2050	1050	95	625	1250	1,800,000		
Dense No. 2	thick	1700	1950	1000	95	730	1150	1,700,000		
No. 2	2" to 4"	1450	1650	850	95	625	1000	1,700,000		NLGA,
No. 3	wide	800	925	475	95	625	600	1,500,000		WCLIB,
Appearance		1750	2050	1050	95	625	1500	1,800,000		and
Stud		800	925	475	95	625	600	1,500,000		WWPA
Construction	2" to 4"	1050	1200	625	95	625	1150	1,500,000		(See footnotes
Standard	thick	600	675	350	95	625	925	1,500,000		2 through 9,
Utility	4" wide	275	325	175	95	625	600	1,500,000		11, 13, 15
Dense Select Structural		2100	2400	1400	95	730	1650	1,900,000		and 16)
Select Structural		1800	2050	1200	95	625	1400	1,800,000		
Dense No. 1		1800	2050	1200	95	730	1450	1,900,000		
No. 1	2" to 4"	1500	1750	1000	95	625	1250	1,800,000		
Dense No. 2	thick	1450	1700	775	95	730	1250	1,700,000		
No. 2	5" and	1250	1450	650	95	625	1050	1,700,000		
No. 3 and Stud	wider	725	850	375	95	625	675	1,500,000		
Appearance		1500	1750	1000	95	625	1500	1,800,000		

[1]Where eastern spruce and balsam fir are shipped in a combination, the tabulated values for balsam fir shall apply.

[2]The design values shown in Table No. 25-A-1 are applicable to lumber that will be used under dry conditions such as in most covered structures. For 2-inch- to 4-inch-thick lumber the DRY surfaced size shall be used. In calculating design values, the natural gain in strength and stiffness that occurs as lumber dries has been taken into consideration as well as the reduction in size that occurs when unseasoned lumber shrinks. The gain in load-carrying capacity due to increased strength and stiffness resulting from drying more than offsets the design effect of size reductions due to shrinkage. For 5-inch and thicker lumber, the surfaced sizes also may be used because design values have been adjusted to compensate for any loss in size by shrinkage which may occur.

[3]Values for F_b, F_t and F_c for the grades of Construction, Standard and Utility apply only to 4-inch widths.

[4]The values in Table No. 25-A-1 for dimension 2 inches to 4 inches are based on edgewise use. Where such lumber is used flatwise, the recommended design values for extreme fiber stress in bending may be multiplied by the following factors:

WIDTH	THICKNESS		
	2"	3"	4"
2 inches to 4 inches	1.10	1.04	1.00
5 inches and wider	1.22	1.16	1.11

Values for decking may be increased by 10 percent for 2-inch decking and 4 percent for 3-inch decking.

[5]When 2-inch- to 4-inch-thick lumber is manufactured at a maximum moisture content of 15 percent and used in a condition where the moisture content does not exceed 15 percent, the design values shown in Table No. 25-A-1 for surfaced dry and surfaced green may be multiplied by the following factors:

EXTREME FIBER IN BENDING F_b	TENSION PARALLEL TO GRAIN F_t	HORIZONTAL SHEAR F_v	COMPRESSION PERPENDICULAR TO GRAIN $F_c\perp$	COMPRESSION PARALLEL TO GRAIN F_c	MODULUS OF ELASTICITY E
1.08	1.08	1.05	1.00	1.17*	1.05*

*For redwood use 1.15 for F_c and 1.04 for E.

[6]When 2-inch- to 4-inch-thick lumber is designed for use where the moisture content will exceed 19 percent for an extended period of time, the values shown in Table No. 25-A-1 shall be multiplied by the following factors:

EXTREME FIBER IN BENDING F_b	TENSION PARALLEL TO GRAIN F_t	HORIZONTAL SHEAR F_v	COMPRESSION PERPENDICULAR TO GRAIN $F_c\perp$	COMPRESSION PARALLEL TO GRAIN F_c	MODULUS OF ELASTICITY E
0.86	0.84	0.97	0.67	0.70	0.97

[7]When lumber 5 inches thick and thicker is designed for use where the moisture content will exceed 19 percent for an extended period of time, the values shown in Table No. 25-A-1 shall be multiplied by the following factors:

EXTREME FIBER IN BENDING F_b	TENSION PARALLEL TO GRAIN F_t	HORIZONTAL SHEAR F_v	COMPRESSION PERPENDICULAR TO GRAIN $F_{c\perp}$	COMPRESSION PARALLEL TO GRAIN F_c	MODULUS OF ELASTICITY E
1.00	1.00	1.00	0.67	0.91	1.00

[8]Specific horizontal shear values may be established by use of the following tabulation when length of split or size of check or shake is known and no increase in them is anticipated. For California redwood, southern pine, Virginia pine-pond pine, or yellow poplar, the provisions in this footnote apply only to the following F_v values: 80 psi, California redwood; 95 psi, southern pine (KD-15); 90 psi, southern pine (S-dry); 85 psi, southern pine (S-green); 95 psi, Virginia pine-pond pine (KD-15); 90 psi, Virginia pine-pond pine (S-dry); 85 psi, Virginia pine-pond pine (KD-15); 90 psi, Virginia pine-pond pine (S-dry); 85 psi, Virginia pine-pond pine (S-green); and 75 psi, yellow poplar.

SHEAR STRESS MODIFICATION FACTOR					
Length of Split on Wide Face of 2" Lumber (nominal):	Multiply Tabulated F_v Value by:	Length of Split on Wide Face of 3" and Thicker Lumber (nominal):	Multiply Tabulated F_v Value by:	Size of Shake* in 3" and Thicker Lumber (nominal):	Multiply Tabulated F_v Value by:
No split	2.00	No split	2.00	No shake	2.00
$1/2$ by wide face	1.67	$1/2$ by narrow face	1.67	$1/6$ by narrow face	1.67
$3/4$ by wide face	1.50	1 by narrow face	1.33	$1/3$ by narrow face	1.33
1 by wide face	1.33	$1^1/2$ by narrow face or more .	1.00	$1/2$ by narrow face or more ...	1.00
$1^1/2$ by wide face or more ..	1.00				

*Shake is measured at the end between lines enclosing the shake and parallel to the wide face.

[9]Stress-rated boards of nominal 1-inch, $1^1/4$-inch and $1^1/2$-inch thickness, 2 inches and wider, are permitted the recommended design values shown for Select Structural, No. 1, No. 2, No. 3, Construction, Standard, Utility, Appearance, Clear Heart Structural and Clear Structural grades as shown in the 2-inch- to 4-inch-thick categories herein, where graded in accordance with the stress-rated board provisions in the applicable grading rules.

[10]When decking is used where the moisture content will exceed 15 percent for an extended period of time, the tabulated design values shall be multiplied by the following factors: extreme fiber in bending F_b – 0.79; modulus of elasticity E – 0.92.

[11]Where lumber is graded under the NLGA values shown for Select Structural, No. 1, No. 2, No. 3, and Stud grades are not applicable to 3-inch x 4-inch and 4-inch x 4-inch sizes.

[12]Lumber in the beam and stringer or post and timber size classification may be assigned different working stresses for the same grade name and species based on the grading rules of the specific agency involved. It is therefore necessary that the grading rule agency be identified to properly correlate permitted design stresses with the grademark.

[13]Utility grades of all species may be used only under conditions specifically approved by the building official.

[14]A horizontal shear F_v of 70 may be used for eastern white pine graded under the NHPMA and NELMA grading rules.

[15]Tabulated tension parallel to grain values for species 5 inches and wider, 2 inches to 4 inches thick (and $2^1/2$ inches to 4 inches thick) size classifications apply to 5-inch and 6-inch widths only, for grades of Select Structural, No. 1, No. 2, No. 3, Appearance and Stud (including dense grades). For lumber wider than 6 inches in these grades, the tabulated F_t values shall be multiplied by the following factors:

GRADE (2 inches to 4 inches thick, 5 inches and wider) ($2^1/2$ inches to 4 inches thick, 5 inches and wider) (Includes "Dense" grades)	Multiply tabulated F_t values by		
	5 inches and 6 inches wide	8 inches wide	10 inches and wider
Select Structural	1.00	0.90	0.80
No. 1, No. 2, No. 3 and Appearance	1.00	0.80	0.60
Stud	1.00		

[16]Design values for all species of Stud grade in 5-inch and wider size classifications apply to 5-inch and 6-inch widths only.

[17]Repetitive member design values for extreme fiber in bending for southern pine grades of Dense Structural 86, 72 and 65 apply to 2-inch to 4-inch thicknesses only.

[18]When 2-inch-to 4-inch-thick southern pine lumber is surfaced dry or at 15 percent maximum moisture content (KD) and is designed for use where the moisture content will exceed 19 percent for an extended period of time, the design values in Table No. 25-A-1 for the corresponding grades of $2^1/2$-inch- to 4-inch-thick surfaced green southern pine lumber shall be used. The net green size may be used in such designs.

[19]When 2-inch-to 4-inch-thick southern pine lumber is surfaced dry or at 15 percent maximum moisture content (KD) and is designed for use under dry conditions, such as in most covered structures, the net dry size shall be used in design. For other sizes and conditions of use, the net green size may be used in design.

[20]Values apply only to ponderosa pine graded under the NLGA grading rules.

[21]The duration of load modification factors given in Section 2504 (c) 4 shall not apply.

Members stressed principally in bending with load applied perpendicular to the wide faces of the laminations

Combination Symbol [10]	Species Outer Laminations/ Core Laminations [4]	Bending About X-X Axis — Extreme Fiber in Bending F_{bxx} — Tension Zone Stressed in Tension [22] psi	Compression Zone Stressed in Tension psi	Compression Perpendicular to Grain $F_{c\perp xx}$ [21] — Tension Face psi	Compression Face psi	Horizontal Shear F_{vxx} psi	Modulus of Elasticity E_{xx} [21] x 10⁶ psi	Bending About Y-Y Axis — Extreme Fiber in Bending [5,17] F_{byy} psi	Compression Perpendicular to Grain $F_{c\perp yy}$ [21] psi	Horizontal Shear F_{vyy} psi	Horizontal Shear F_{vyy} psi (For members with multiple-piece laminations which are not edge glued) [20]	Modulus of Elasticity E_{yy} [21] x 10⁶ psi	Axially Loaded — Tension Parallel to Grain F_t psi	Compression Parallel to Grain F_c psi	Modulus of Elasticity E [21] x 10⁶ psi
1	2	3	4	5	6	7	8	9	10	11	12	13	14	15	16
Visually Graded Western Species—(Continued)															
The following three combinations are balanced and are intended for members continuous or cantilevered over supports and provide equal capacity in both positive and negative bending.															
22F-V7	DF/DF			650	650	165	1.8	1450	560	145	75	1.6	1100	1650	1.6
22F-V8	DF/DF	2200	2200	590[8]	590[7,8]	165	1.7	1450	560	145	75	1.6	1050	1650	1.6
22F-V9	HF/HF			500[9]	500[9]	155	1.5	1250	375	135	70	1.4	975	1400	1.4
24F-V1	DF/WW			650	650	140[2,3]	1.7[3,4]	1250	255	130	70	1.4[3,4]	1000	1300	1.4
24F-V2	HF/HF			500[9]	500[9]	155	1.5	1250	375	135	70	1.4	950	1300	1.4
24F-V3	DF/DF	2400	1200	650	560[7]	165	1.8	1500	560	145	75	1.6	1100	1600	1.6
24F-V4	DF/DF			650	650	165	1.8	1500	560	145	75	1.6	1150	1650	1.6
24F-V5	DF/HF			650	650	155	1.7	1350	375	140	70	1.5	1100	1450	1.5
24F-V11	DF/DFS			650	560[7]	165	1.7	1600	500	145	75	1.4	1150	1700	1.4

[1]The combinations in this table are applicable to members consisting of four or more laminations and are intended primarily for members stressed in bending due to loads applied perpendicular to the wide faces of the laminations. Design values are tabulated, however, for loading both perpendicular and parallel to the wide faces of the laminations. For combinations and design values applicable to members loaded primarily axially or parallel to the wide faces of the laminations, see Table No. 25-C-1, Part B. For members of two or three laminations, see Table No. 25-C-1, Part B.

[2]The tabulated design values are for dry conditions of use. To obtain wet-use design values, multiply the tabulated values by the factors shown at the end of the table.

[3]The tabulated design values are for normal duration of loading. For other durations of loading, see Section 2504 (c) 4.

[4]The symbols used for species are AC = Alaska cedar, DF = Douglas fir-larch, DFS = Douglas fir south, HF = hem-fir, WW = softwood species. SP = southern pine and ES = eastern spruce. (N3 refers to No. 3 structural joists and planks or structural light framing grade.) Softwood species (WW) and eastern spruce are included in the general category of western species although eastern spruce and some softwood species are produced in other areas.

[5]The tabulated design values in bending are applicable to members 12 inches or less in depth. For members greater than 12 inches in depth, the requirements of Section 2511 (d) 5 apply.

[6]Design values in this column are for extreme fiber stress in bending when the member is loaded such that the compression zone laminations are subjected to tensile stresses. The values in this column may be increased 200 psi where end joint spacing restrictions are applied to the compression zone when stressed in tension.

[7]Where specified, this value may be increased to 650 psi by providing in the bearing area at least one dense 2-inch nominal thickness lamination of Douglas fir-larch for western species combinations, or southern pine for southern pine combinations. These dense laminations must be backed by a medium-grain lamination of the same species.

[8]For bending members greater than 15 inches in depth, the design value for compression stress perpendicular to grain is 650 psi on the tension face.

[9]Where specified, this value may be increased by providing at least two 2-inch nominal thickness Douglas fir-larch laminations in the bearing area. The compression-perpendicular-to-grain design values for Douglas fir-larch are 560 psi for medium grain and 650 psi for dense.

[10]These combinations are for dry conditions of use only because they may contain wane. They are recommended for industrial appearance grade and for straight or slightly cambered members only. If wane is omitted these restrictions do not apply.

[11]This value may be increased to 140 psi for softwood species (WW) and to 155 psi for hem-fir when the member does not contain wane on both sides; to 115 psi for softwood species (WW) and to 130 psi for hem-fir when the member does not contain wane on one side.

[12]This value may be increased to 110 psi when the member does not contain coarse-grain material; to 140 psi when the member does not contain wane on both sides or the member does not contain coarse-grain material and wane on one side; to 165 psi when the member does not contain coarse-grain material and wane on both sides.

[13]The compression-perpendicular-to-grain design value of 255 psi is based on the lowest strength species of the western woods group. If at least one 2-inch nominal thickness lamination of E-rated hem-fir with the same E value, or E-rated Douglas fir-larch 200,000 psi higher in modulus of elasticity (E) than that specified is used in the bearing area on the face of the member subjected to the compression-perpendicular-to-grain stress, $F_c\perp$ may be increased to 375 psi. If at least two 2-inch nominal thickness laminations of E-rated hem-fir with the same E value, or E-rated Douglas fir-larch 200,000 psi higher in modulus of elasticity than that specified are used in the bearing area on the face of the member subjected to the compression-perpendicular-to-grain stress, $F_c\perp$ may be increased to 500 psi.

[14]Where specified, this value may be increased to 650 psi by providing in the bearing area at least one 2-inch nominal thickness lamination of Douglas fir-larch for western species combinations, or one 2-inch nominal thickness lamination of southern pine for southern pine combinations having a modulus of elasticity (E) value 200,000 psi higher than the E value specified.

[15]E-rated Douglas fir-larch 200,000 psi higher in modulus of elasticity may be substituted for the specified E-rated hem-fir.

[16]This value may be increased to 140 psi when the member does not contain coarse-grain material or when the member does not contain wane on both sides; to 165 psi when members do not contain coarse-grain material or wane on one side; or to 200 psi when the member does not contain both coarse-grain material and wane on both sides of the member.

[17]Footnote 5 to Table No. 25-C-1, Part B, also applies.

[18]When Douglas fir south is used in place of all of the western wood laminations required in western species combinations 16F-V1, 16F-V4, 20F-V1, 20F-V5, 22F-V1, 22F-V5, 24F-V1, 24F-V6, 16F-E1, 16F-E4, 20F-E1, 20F-E4, 22F-E3, 24F-E6 and 24F-E7, the design value for horizontal shear is the same as for combinations using all Douglas fir-larch (F_{vu} = 165 psi and F_{vm} = 145 psi for L3; and F_{vx} = 90 psi and F_{vm} = 135 psi for N3).

[19]The combination symbols relate to a specific combination of grades and species in U.B.C. Standard No. 25-11 that will provide the design values shown for the combinations. The first two numbers in the combination symbol correspond to the design value in bending shown in column 3. The letter in the combination symbol (either a "V" or an "E") indicates whether the combination is made from visually graded (V) or E-rated (E) lumber in the outer zones.

[20]These values for horizontal shear, F_{vm} apply to members manufactured using multiple-piece laminations with unbonded edge joints. For members manufactured using single-piece laminations or using multiple-piece laminations with bonded edge joints, the horizontal shear values in column 11 apply.

[21]The duration of load modification factors given in Section 2504 (c) 4 shall not apply.

[22]The design values in bending about the x-x axis (F_{bx}) in this column for bending members shall be multiplied by 0.75 when the member is manufactured without the required special tension laminations.

[23]The following species may be used for softwood species (WW), provided the design values in horizontal shear in column 7 (F_{vx}) and in Column 11 (F_{vm}) are reduced by 10 psi and the design values in horizontal shear in Column 12 (F_{vy}) are reduced by 5 psi: Coast sitka spruce, coast species, eastern white pine (north) and western white pine.

[24]The following species may be used for softwood species (WW), provided the design values in modulus of elasticity (E_x and E_y) in Columns 8 and 13 are reduced by 100,000 psi: Western cedars, western cedars (north), white woods (western woods) and California redwood—open grain.

TABLE NO. 25-D—PART B—VALUES FOR USE IN COMPUTING WORKING STRESSES WITH FACTORS OF PART A TOGETHER WITH LIMITATIONS REQUIRED TO PERMIT THE USE OF SUCH STRESSES [3]

COMBINATION SYMBOL	RATIO OF SIZE OF MAXIMUM PERMITTED KNOT TO FINISHED WIDTH OF LAMINATION[4]	NUMBER OF LAMINATIONS[5]	EXTREME FIBER IN BENDING		TENSION PARALLEL TO GRAIN		COMPRESSION PARALLEL TO GRAIN		MODULUS OF ELASTICITY (E)[6]
			Stress Module	Steepest Grain Slope	Stress Module	Steepest Grain Slope	Stress Module	Steepest Grain Slope	Stress Module
A	0.1	4 to 14	800	1:16	500	1:16	970	1:15	1,000,000
		15 or more	800	1:16	500	1:16	970	1:15	
B	.2	4 to 14	770	1:16	500	1:16	920	1:15	1,000,000
		15 or more	800	1:16	500	1:16	930	1:15	
C	.3	4 to 14	600	1:12	450	1:15	860	1:14	900,000
		15 or more	660	1:12	450	1:16	870	1:14	
D	.4	4 to 14	450	1:8	350	1:10	780	1:12	800,000
		15 or more	520	1:8	350	1:12	810	1:12	
E	.5	4 to 14	300	1:8	300	1:8	690	1:10	800,000
		15 or more	380	1:8	300	1:8	730	1:10	

[1]The allowable unit stresses in bending obtained from Table No. 25-D apply when the wide faces of the laminations are normal to the direction of the load.

[2]Allowable stresses for dry conditions of use shall be applicable when the moisture content in service is 16 percent or less as in most covered structures. For wet conditions of use the following maximum percentage of the dry-use stresses shall be permitted:

F_b (bending) and F_t (tension) 80 percent F_v (horizontal shear 88 percent)

F_c (compression parallel to grain) 70 percent $F_c\perp$ (compression perpendicular to grain) 67 percent

E (modulus of elasticity) 83 percent

[3]For modification of allowable unit stresses for structural glued-laminated lumber, see Section 2504.

[4]Factors for knot sizes of 0.1 and 0.2 are identical in case of extreme fiber in bending and in tension parallel to grain because slope of grain of 1:16 is a greater limitation than knot size. The smaller knot size may be specified for reasons other than strength.

[5]When laminations of different thicknesses are used, divide the depth of the member by the thickest lamination used and then assume the quotient to be the number of laminations in the member for use in determining the allowable stress.

[6]The duration of load modification factors given in Section 2504 (c) 4 shall not apply.

(See U.B.C. Standard No. 25-17 where members are not of equal size and for values in other species.)

p = Safe loads parallel to grain in pounds
q = Safe loads perpendicular to grain in pounds

Length of Bolt in Main Wood Member[3] (in inches)		DIAMETER OF BOLT (IN INCHES)								
		⅜	½	⅝	¾	⅞	1	1⅛	1¼	1½
1½	Single p	325	470	590	710	830	945			
	Shear q	185	215	245	270	300	325			
	Double p	650	940	1180	1420	1660	1890			
	Shear q	370	430	490	540	600	650			
2½	Single p		630	910	1155	1370	1575			
	Shear q		360	405	450	495	540			
	Double p	710	1260	1820	2310	2740	3150			
	Shear q	620	720	810	900	990	1080			
3½	Single p			990	1400	1790	2135	2455	2740	3305
	Shear q			565	630	695	760	825	895	1020
	Double p	710	1270	1980	2800	3580	4270	4910	5480	6610
	Shear q	640	980	1130	1260	1390	1520	1650	1780	2040
5½	Single p					1950	2535	3190	3820	4975
	Shear q					1090	1190	1300	1395	1605
	Double p		1270	1990	2860	3900	5070	6380	7640	9950
	Shear q		930	1410	1880	2180	2380	2600	2790	3210
7½	Single p								3975	5680
	Shear q								1900	2185
	Double p			1990	2860	3890	5080	6440	7950	11,360
	Shear q			1260	1820	2430	3030	3500	3800	4370
9½	Single p									5730
	Shear q									2765
	Double p				2860	3900	5080	6440	7950	11,460
	Shear q				1640	2270	2960	3710	4450	5530
11½	Single p									
	Shear q									
	Double p					3900	5080	6440	7950	11,450
	Shear q					2050	2770	3540	4360	6150
13½	Single p									
	Shear q									
	Double p						5100	6440	7960	11,450
	Shear q						2530	3310	4160	6040

[1]Tabulated values are on a normal load-duration basis and apply to joints made of seasoned lumber used in dry locations. See U.B.C. Standard No. 25-17 for other service conditions.

[2]Double shear values are for joints consisting of three wood members in which the side members are one half the thickness of the main member. Single shear values are for joints consisting of two wood members having a minimum thickness not less than that specified.

[3]The length specified is the length of the bolt in the main member of double shear joints or the length of the bolt in the thinner member of single shear joints.

[4]See U.B.C. Standard No. 25-17 for wood-to-metal bolted joints.

TABLE NO. 25-G—SAFE LATERAL STRENGTH AND REQUIRED PENETRATION OF BOX AND COMMON WIRE NAILS DRIVEN PERPENDICULAR TO GRAIN OF WOOD

SIZE OF NAIL	STANDARD LENGTH (Inches)	WIRE GAUGE	PENETRATION REQUIRED (Inches)	LOADS (Pounds)[1][2][3]	
				Douglas Fir Larch or Southern Pine	Other Species
BOX NAILS					
6d	2	12½	1⅛	51	See U.B.C. Standard No. 25-17
8d	2½	11½	1¼	63	
10d	3	10½	1½	76	
12d	3¼	10½	1½	76	
16d	3½	10	1½	82	
20d	4	9	1⅝	94	
30d	4½	9	1⅝	94	
40d	5	8	1¾	108	
COMMON NAILS					
6d	2	11½	1¼	63	See U.B.C. Standard No. 25-17
8d	2½	10¼	1½	78	
10d	3	9	1⅝	94	
12d	3¼	9	1⅝	94	
16d	3½	8	1¾	·108	
20d	4	6	2⅛	139	
30d	4½	5	2¼	155	
40d	5	4	2½	176	
50d	5½	3	2¾	199	
60d	6	2	2⅞	223	

[1]The safe lateral strength values may be increased 25 percent where metal side plates are used.

[2]For wood diaphragm calculations these values may be increased 30 percent. (See U.B.C. Standard No. 25-17.)

[3]Tabulated values are on a normal load-duration basis and apply to joints made of seasoned lumber used in dry locations. See U.B.C. Standard No. 25-17 for other service conditions.

TABLE NO. 25-H—SAFE RESISTANCE TO WITHDRAWAL OF COMMON WIRE NAILS

Inserted Perpendicular to Grain of the Wood, in Pounds per Linear Inch of Penetration into the Main Member

KIND OF WOOD	SIZE OF NAIL									
	6d	8d	10d	12d	16d	20d	30d	40d	50d	60d
1. Douglas Fir, Larch	29	34	38	38	42	49	53	58	63	67
2. Southern Pine	35	41	46	46	50	59	64	70	76	81
3. Other Species	See U.B.C. Standard No. 25-17									

TABLE NO. 25-I—MAXIMUM DIAPHRAGM DIMENSION RATIOS

MATERIAL	HORIZONTAL DIAPHRAGMS	VERTICAL DIAPHRAGMS
	Maximum Span-Width Ratios	Maximum Height-Width Ratios
1. Diagonal sheathing, conventional	3:1	2:1
2. Diagonal sheathing, special	4:1	3½:1
3. Plywood and particleboard, nailed all edges	4:1	3½:1
4. Plywood and particleboard, blocking omitted at intermediate joints	4:1	2:1

TABLE NO. 25-J-1—ALLOWABLE SHEAR IN POUNDS PER FOOT FOR HORIZONTAL PLYWOOD DIAPHRAGMS WITH FRAMING OF DOUGLAS FIR-LARCH OR SOUTHERN PINE[1]

PLYWOOD GRADE	Common Nail Size	Minimum Nominal Penetration in Framing (in inches)	Minimum Nominal Plywood Thickness (in inches)	Minimum Nominal Width of Framing Member (in inches)	BLOCKED DIAPHRAGMS — Nail spacing at diaphragm boundaries (all cases), at continuous panel edges parallel to load (Cases 3 and 4) and at all panel edges (Cases 5 and 6)				UNBLOCKED DIAPHRAGM — Nails spaced 6" max. at supported end	
					6	4	2½/2	2	Load perpendicular to unblocked edges and continuous panel joints (Case 1)	Other configurations (Cases 2, 3, 4, 5 and 6)
					\[Nail spacing at other plywood panel edges\] 6	6	4	3		
STRUCTURAL I	6d	1¼	5/16	2	185	250	375	420	165	125
				3	210	280	420	475	185	140
	8d	1½	3/8	2	270	360	530	600	240	180
				3	300	400	600	675	265	200
	10d[3]	1⅝	15/32	2	320	425	640	730	285	215
				3	360	480	720	820	320	240
C-D, C-C, STRUCTURAL II and other grades covered in U.B.C. Standard No. 25-9	6d	1¼	5/16	2	170	225	335	380	150	110
				3	190	250	380	430	170	125
			3/8	2	185	250	375	420	165	125
				3	210	280	420	475	185	140
	8d	1½	3/8	2	240	320	480	545	215	160
				3	270	360	540	610	240	180
			15/32	2	270	360	530	600	240	180
				3	300	400	600	675	265	200
	10d[3]	1⅝	15/32	2	290	385	575	655	255	190
				3	325	430	650	735	290	215
			19/32	2	320	425	640	730	285	215
				3	360	480	720	820	320	240

[1]These values are for short-time loads due to wind or earthquake and must be reduced 25 percent for normal loading. Space nails 12 inches on center along intermediate framing members.

Allowable shear values for nails in framing members of other species set forth in Table No. 25-17-J of the U.B.C. Standards shall be calculated for all grades by multiplying the values for nails in Structural I by the following factors: Group III, 0.82 and Group IV, 0.65.

[2]Framing at adjoining panel edges shall be 3-inch nominal or wider and nails shall be staggered where nails are spaced 2 inches or 2½ inches on center.

[3]Framing at adjoining panel edges shall be 3-inch nominal or wider and nails shall be staggered where 10d nails having penetration into framing of more than 1⅝ inches are spaced 3 inches or less on center.

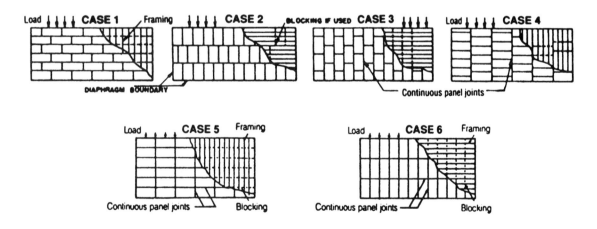

Note: Framing may be oriented in either direction for diaphragms, provided sheathing is properly designed for vertical loading.

TABLE NO. 25-J-2—ALLOWABLE SHEAR IN POUNDS PER FOOT FOR HORIZONTAL PARTICLEBOARD DIAPHRAGMS WITH FRAMING OF DOUGLAS FIR-LARCH OR SOUTHERN PINE[1]

PANEL GRADE	COMMON NAIL SIZE	MINIMUM NAIL PENETRATION IN FRAMING (Inches)	MINIMUM NOMINAL PANEL THICKNESS (Inch)	MINIMUM NOMINAL WIDTH OF FRAMING MEMBER (Inches)	BLOCKED DIAPHRAGMS Nail Spacing (In.) at diaphragm boundaries (all cases), at continuous panel edges parallel to load (Cases 3 & 4), and at all panel edges (Cases 5 & 6) 6	4	2½[2]	2[2]	UNBLOCKED DIAPHRAGMS Nails Spaced 6" max. at Supported Edges Case 1 (No unblocked edges or continuous joints parallel to load)	All other configurations (Cases 2, 3 4, 5 & 6)
					Nail Spacing (In.) at other panel edges (Cases 1, 2, 3 & 4) 6	6	4	3		
2-M-W	6d	1¼	5/16	2	170	225	335	380	150	110
				3	190	250	380	430	170	125
			⅜	2	185	250	375	420	165	125
				3	210	280	420	475	185	140
	8d	1½	⅜	2	240	320	480	545	215	160
				3	270	360	540	610	240	180
			7/16	2	255	340	505	575	230	170
				3	285	380	570	645	255	190
			½	2	270	360	530	600	240	180
				3	300	400	600	675	265	200
	10d[3]	1⅝	½	2	290	385	575	655	255	190
				3	325	430	650	735	290	215
			⅝	2	320	425	640	730	285	215
				3	360	480	720	820	320	240
2-M-3	10d[3]	1⅝	¾	2	320	425	640	730	285	215
				3	360	480	720	820	320	240

[1]These values are for short-time loads due to wind or earthquake and must be reduced 25 percent for normal loading. Space nails 12 inches on center along intermediate framing members.

Allowable shear values for nails in framing members of other species set forth in Table No. 25-17-J of the U.B.C. Standards shall be calculated for all grades by multiplying the values for nails by the following factors: Group III, 0.82 and Group IV, 0.65.

[2]Framing at adjoining panel edges shall be 3-inch nominal or wider and nails shall be staggered where nails are spaced 2 inches or $2^{1}/_{2}$ inches on center.

[3]Framing at adjoining panel edges shall be 3-inch nominal or wider and nails shall be staggered where 10d nails having penetration into framing of more than $1^{5}/_{8}$ inches are spaced 3 inches or less on center.

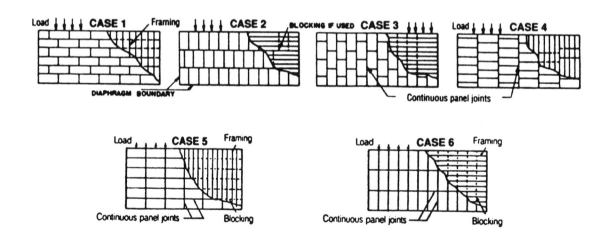

Note: Framing may be oriented in either direction for diaphragms, provided sheathing is properly designed for vertical loading.

TABLE NO. 25-K-1—ALLOWABLE SHEAR FOR WIND OR SEISMIC FORCES IN POUNDS PER FOOT FOR PLYWOOD SHEAR WALLS WITH FRAMING OF DOUGLAS FIR-LARCH OR SOUTHERN PINE[1][4]

PLYWOOD GRADE	MINIMUM NOMINAL PLYWOOD THICKNESS (Inches)	MINIMUM NAIL PENETRATION IN FRAMING (Inches)	NAIL SIZE (Common or Galvanized Box)	PLYWOOD APPLIED DIRECT TO FRAMING — Nail Spacing at Plywood Panel Edges				NAIL SIZE (Common or Galvanized Box)	PLYWOOD APPLIED OVER ½-INCH OR ⅝-INCH GYPSUM SHEATHING — Nail Spacing at Plywood Panel Edges			
				6	4	3	2[2]		6	4	3	2[2]
STRUCTURAL I	5/16	1¼	6d	200	300	390	510	8d	200	300	390	510
	3/8	1½	8d	230[3]	360[3]	460[3]	610[3]	10d[5]	280	430	550	730[2]
	15/32	1½	8d	280	430	550	730	10d[5]	280	430	550	730
	15/32	1⅝	10d[5]	340	510	665	870	—	—	—	—	—
C-D, C-C STRUCTURAL II, plywood panel siding and other grades covered in U.B.C. Standard No. 25-9.	5/16	1¼	6d	180	270	350	450	8d	180	270	350	450
	3/8	1¼	6d	200	300	390	510	8d	200	300	390	510
	3/8	1½	8d	220[3]	320[3]	410[3]	530[3]	10d[5]	260	380	490	640
	15/32	1½	8d	260	380	490	640	10d[5]	260	380	490	640
	15/32	1⅝	10d[5]	310	460	600	770	—	—	—	—	—
	19/32	1⅝	10d[5]	340	510	665	870	—	—	—	—	—
			NAIL SIZE (Galvanized Casing)					**NAIL SIZE (Galvanized Casing)**				
Plywood panel siding in grades covered in U.B.C. Standard No. 25-9	5/16	1¼	6d	140	210	275	360	8d	140	210	275	360
	3/8	1½	8d	130[3]	200[3]	260[3]	340[3]	10d[5]	160	240	310	410

[1]All panel edges backed with 2-inch nominal or wider framing. Plywood installed either horizontally or vertically. Space nails at 6 inches on center along intermediate framing members for 3/8-inch plywood installed with face grain parallel to studs spaced 24 inches on center and 12 inches on center for other conditions and plywood thicknesses. These values are for short-time loads due to wind or earthquake and must be reduced 25 percent for normal loading.

Allowable shear values for nails in framing members of other species set forth in Table No. 25-17-J of U.B.C. Standards shall be calculated for all grades by multiplying the values for common and galvanized box nails in STRUCTURAL I and galvanized casing nails in other grades by the following factors: Group III, 0.82 and Group IV, 0.65.

[2]Framing at adjoining panel edges shall be 3-inch nominal or wider and nails shall be staggered where nails are spaced 2 inches on center.

[3]The values for 3/8-inch-thick plywood applied direct to framing may be increased 20 percent, provided studs are spaced a maximum of 16 inches on center or plywood is applied with face grain across studs.

[4]Where plywood is applied on both faces of a wall and nail spacing is less than 6 inches on center on either side, panel joints shall be offset to fall on different framing members or framing shall be 3-inch nominal or thicker and nails on each side shall be staggered.

[5]Framing at adjoining panel edges shall be 3-inch nominal or wider and nails shall be staggered where 10d nails having penetration into framing of more than 1⅝ inches are spaced 3 inches or less on center.

TABLE NO. 25-K-2—ALLOWABLE SHEAR FOR WIND OR SEISMIC FORCES IN POUNDS PER FOOT FOR PARTICLEBOARD SHEAR WALLS WITH FRAMING OF DOUGLAS FIR-LARCH OR SOUTHERN PINE[1] [4]

PANEL GRADE	MINIMUM NOMINAL PANEL THICKNESS (In.)	MINIMUM NAIL PENETRATION IN FRAMING (In.)	PANELS APPLIED DIRECT TO FRAMING					PANELS APPLIED OVER 1/2" GYPSUM SHEATHING				
			Nail Size (Common or galvanized box)	Nail Spacing at Panel Edges (In.)				Nail Size (Common or galvanized box)	Nail Spacing at Panel Edges (In.)			
				6	4	3	2[2]		6	4	3	2[2]
2-M-W	5/16	1 1/4	6d	180	270	350	450	8d	180	270	350	450
	3/8			200	300	390	510		200	300	390	510
	3/8	1 1/2	8d	220[3]	320[3]	410[3]	530[3]	10d[5]	260	380	490	640
	7/16			240[3]	350[3]	450[3]	585[3]					
	1/2			260	380	490	640					
	1/2	1 5/8	10d[5]	310	460	600	770	—	—	—	—	—
	5/8			340	510	665	870	—	—	—	—	—

[1]All panel edges backed with 2-inch nominal or wider framing. Panels installed either horizontally or vertically. Space nails at 6 inches on center along intermediate framing members for 3/8-inch panel installed with the long dimension parallel to studs spaced 24 inches on center and 12 inches on center for other conditions and panel thicknesses. These values are for short-time loads due to wind or earthquake and must be reduced 25 percent for normal loading.

Allowable shear values for nails in framing members of other species set forth in Table No. 25-17-J of U.B.C. Standards shall be calculated for all grades by multiplying the values for common and galvanized box nails by the following factors: Group III, 0.82 and Group IV, 0.65.

[2]Framing at adjoining panel edges shall be 3-inch nominal or wider and nails shall be staggered where nails are spaced 2 inches on center.

[3]The allowable shear values may be increased to the values shown for 1/2-inch-thick sheathing with the same nailing, provided:
    (a) The studs are spaced a maximum of 16 inches on center, or
    (b) The panels are applied with the long dimension perpendicular to studs.

[4]Where particleboard is applied on both faces of a wall and nail spacing is less than 6 inches on center on either side, panel joints shall be offset to fall on different framing members, or framing shall be 3-inch nominal or thicker and nails on each side shall be staggered.

[5]Framing at adjoining panel edges shall be 3-inch nominal or wider and nails shall be staggered where 10d nails having penetration into framing of more than 1 5/8 inches are spaced 3 inches or less on center.

TABLE NO. 25-P—ALLOWABLE SHEARS FOR WIND OR SEISMIC LOADING ON VERTICAL DIAPHRAGMS OF FIBERBOARD SHEATHING BOARD CONSTRUCTION FOR TYPE V CONSTRUCTION ONLY[1]

SIZE AND APPLICATION	NAIL SIZE	SHEAR VALUE 3-INCH NAIL SPACING AROUND PERIMETER AND 6-INCH AT INTERMEDIATE POINTS
1. 1/2" x 4' x 8'	No. 11 gauge galvanized roofing nail 1 1/2" long, 7/16" head	125[2]
2. 25/32" x 4' x 8'.	No. 11 gauge galvanized roofing nail 1 3/4" long, 7/16" head	175

[1]Fiberboard sheathing diaphragms shall not be used to brace concrete or masonry walls.
[2]The shear value may be 175 for 1/2-inch x 4-foot x 8-foot fiberboard nail-base sheathing.

CONNECTION	NAILING[1]
1. Joist to sill or girder, toenail	3-8d
2. Bridging to joist, toenail each end	2-8d
3. 1" x 6" subfloor or less to each joist, face nail	2-8d
4. Wider than 1" x 6" subfloor to each joist, face nail	3-8d
5. 2" subfloor to joist or girder, blind and face nail	2-16d
6. Sole plate to joist or blocking, face nail	16d at 16" o.c.
7. Top plate to stud, end nail	2-16d
8. Stud to sole plate	4-8d, toenail or 2-16d, end nail
9. Double studs, face nail	16d at 24" o.c.
10. Doubled top plates, face nail	16d at 16" o.c.
11. Top plates, laps and intersections, face nail	2-16d
12. Continuous header, two pieces	16d at 16" o.c. along each edge
13. Ceiling joists to plate, toenail	3-8d
14. Continuous header to stud, toenail	4-8d
15. Ceiling joists, laps over partitions, face nail	3-16d
16. Ceiling joists to parallel rafters, face nail	3-16d
17. Rafter to plate, toenail	3-8d
18. 1" brace to each stud and plate, face nail	2-8d
19. 1" x 8" sheathing or less to each bearing, face nail	2-8d
20. Wider than 1" x 8" sheathing to each bearing, face nail	3-8d
21. Built-up corner studs	16d at 24" o.c.
22. Built-up girder and beams	20d at 32" o.c. at top and bottom and staggered 2-20d at ends and at each splice
23. 2" planks	2-16d at each bearing
24. Plywood and particleboard:[5] Subfloor, roof and wall sheathing (to framing): 1/2" and less	6d[2]
19/32"-3/4"	8d[3] or 6d[4]
7/8"-1"	8d[2]
1 1/8"-1 1/4"	10d[3] or 8d[4]
Combination Subfloor-underlayment (to framing): 3/4" and less	6d[4]
7/8"-1"	8d[4]
1 1/8"-1 1/4"	10d[3] or 8d[4]
25. Panel Siding (to framing): 1/2" or less	6d[6]
5/8"	8d[6]
26. Fiberboard Sheathing:[7] 1/2"	No. 11 ga.[8] 6d[3] No. 16 ga.[9]
25/32"	No. 11 ga.[8] 8d[3] No. 16 ga.[9]

[1]Common or box nails may be used except where otherwise stated.
[2]Common or deformed shank.
[3]Common.
[4]Deformed shank.
[5]Nails spaced at 6 inches on center at edges, 12 inches at intermediate supports except 6 inches at all supports where spans are 48 inches or more. For nailing of plywood and particleboard diaphragms and shear walls, refer to Section 2513 (c). Nails for wall sheathing may be common, box or casing.
[6]Corrosion-resistant siding or casing nails conforming to the requirements of Section 2516 (j) 1.
[7]Fasteners spaced 3 inches on center at exterior edges and 6 inches on center at intermediate supports.
[8]Corrosion-resistant roofing nails with $7/16$-inch-diameter head and $1 1/2$-inch length for $1/2$-inch sheathing and $1 3/4$-inch length for $25/32$-inch sheathing conforming to the requirements of Section 2516 (j) 1.
[9]Corrosion-resistant staples with nominal $7/16$-inch crown and $1 1/8$-inch length for $1/2$-inch sheathing and $1 1/2$-inch length for $25/32$-inch sheathing conforming to the requirements of Section 2516 (j) 1.

TABLE NO. 25-R-1—ALLOWABLE SPANS FOR LUMBER FLOOR AND ROOF SHEATHING[1] [3]

SPAN (Inches)	MINIMUM NET THICKNESS (Inches) OF LUMBER PLACED			
	PERPENDICULAR TO SUPPORTS		DIAGONALLY TO SUPPORTS	
	Surfaced Dry[2]	Surfaced Unseasoned	Surfaced Dry[2]	Surfaced Unseasoned
FLOORS				
1. 24	3/4	25/32	3/4	25/32
2. 16	5/8	11/16	5/8	11/16
ROOFS				
3. 24	5/8	11/16	3/4	25/32

[1]Installation details shall conform to Sections 2517 (e) 1 and 2517 (h) 7 for floor and roof sheathing, respectively.

[2]Maximum 19 percent moisture content.

[3]Floor or roof sheathing conforming with this table shall be deemed to meet the design criteria of Section 2516.

TABLE NO. 25-R-2—SHEATHING LUMBER SHALL MEET THE FOLLOWING MINIMUM GRADE REQUIREMENTS: BOARD GRADE

SOLID FLOOR OR ROOF SHEATHING	SPACED ROOF SHEATHING	GRADING RULES
1. Utility	Standard	NLGA, WCLIB, WWPA
2. 4 Common or Utility	3 Common or Standard	NLGA, WCLIB, WWPA, NHPMA or NELMA
3. No. 3	No. 2	SPIB
4. Merchantable	Construction Common	RIS

TABLE NO. 25-R-3—SIZE, HEIGHT AND SPACING OF WOOD STUDS[1]

STUD SIZE (Inches)	BEARING WALLS				NONBEARING WALLS	
	LATERALLY UNSUPPORTED STUD HEIGHT[3] (Feet)	SUPPORTING ROOF AND CEILING ONLY	SUPPORTING ONE FLOOR, ROOF AND CEILING	SUPPORTING TWO FLOORS, ROOF AND CEILING	LATERALLY UNSUPPORTED STUD HEIGHT[3] (Feet)	SPACING (Inches)
		SPACING (Inches)				
1. 2 x 3[2]	—	—	—	—	10	16
2. 2 x 4	10	24	16	—	14	24
3. 3 x 4	10	24	24	16	14	24
4. 2 x 5	10	24	24	—	16	24
5. 2 x 6	10	24	24	16	20	24

TABLE NO. 25-S-1—ALLOWABLE SPANS FOR PLYWOOD SUBFLOOR AND ROOF SHEATHING CONTINUOUS OVER TWO OR MORE SPANS AND FACE GRAIN PERPENDICULAR TO SUPPORTS[1][8]

PANEL SPAN RATING[3]	PLYWOOD THICKNESS (Inch)	ROOF[2] Maximum Span (In Inches)		Load (In Pounds per Square Foot)		FLOOR MAXIMUM SPAN[4] (In Inches)
		Edges Blocked	Edges Unblocked	Total Load	Live Load	
1. 12/0	5/16	12		135	130	0
2. 16/0	5/16, 3/8	16		80	65	0
3. 20/0	5/16, 3/8	20		70	55	0
4. 24/0	3/8	24	16	60	45	0
5. 24/0	15/32, 1/2	24	24	60	45	0
6. 32/16	15/32, 1/2, 19/32, 5/8	32	28	55	35[5]	16[6]
7. 40/20	19/32, 5/8, 23/32, 3/4, 7/8	40	32	40[5]	35[5]	20[6][7]
8. 48/24	23/32, 3/4, 7/8	48	36	40[5]	35[5]	24

[1]These values apply for C-C, C-D, Structural I and II grades only. Spans shall be limited to values shown because of possible effect of concentrated loads.

[2]Uniform load deflection limitations $^1/_{180}$ of the span under live load plus dead load, $^1/_{240}$ under live load only. Edges may be blocked with lumber or other approved type of edge support.

[3]Span rating appears on all panels in the construction grades listed in Footnote No. 1.

[4]Plywood edges shall have approved tongue-and-groove joints or shall be supported with blocking unless $^1/_4$-inch minimum thickness underlayment, or $1^1/_2$ inches of approved cellular or lightweight concrete is placed over the subfloor, or finish floor is $^3/_4$-inch wood strip. Allowable uniform load based on deflection of $^1/_{360}$ of span is 165 pounds per square foot (psf).

[5]For roof live load of 40 psf or total load of 55 psf, decrease spans by 13 percent or use panel with next greater span rating.

[6]May be 24 inches if $^3/_4$-inch wood strip flooring is installed at right angles to joists.

[7]May be 24 inches where a minimum of $1^1/_2$ inches of approved cellular or lightweight concrete is placed over the subfloor and the plywood sheathing is manufactured with exterior glue.

[8]Floor or roof sheathing conforming with this table shall be deemed to meet the design criteria of Section 2516.

TABLE NO. 25-S-2—ALLOWABLE LOADS FOR PLYWOOD ROOF SHEATHING CONTINUOUS OVER TWO OR MORE SPANS AND FACE GRAIN PARALLEL TO SUPPORTS[1][2]

	THICKNESS	NO. OF PLIES	SPAN	TOTAL LOAD	LIVE LOAD
STRUCTURAL I	15/32	4	24	30	20
		5	24	45	35
	1/2	4	24	35	25
		5	24	55	40
Other grades covered in U.B.C. Standard No. 25-9	15/32	5	24	25	20
	1/2	5	24	30	25
	19/32	4	24	35	25
		5	24	50	40
	5/8	4	24	40	30
		5	24	55	45

[1]Uniform load deflection limitations: $^1/_{180}$ of span under live load plus dead load, $^1/_{240}$ under live load only. Edges shall be blocked with lumber or other approved type of edge supports.

[2]Roof sheathing conforming with this table shall be deemed to meet the design criteria of Section 2516.

TABLE NO. 25-S-3—ALLOWABLE LOADS FOR PARTICLEBOARD ROOF SHEATHING[1][2][4]

GRADE	THICKNESS (Inches)	MAXIMUM ON-CENTER SPACING OF SUPPORTS (Inches)	LIVE LOAD (Pounds Per Square Foot)	TOTAL LOAD (Pounds Per Square Foot)
2-M-W	3/8[3]	16	45	65
	7/16	16	105	105
	7/16[3]	24	30	40
	1/2	16	110	150
	1/2	24	40	55

[1]Panels are continuous over two or more spans.

[2]Uniform load deflection limitation: $^1/_{180}$ of the span under live load plus dead load and $^1/_{240}$ of the span under live load only.

[3]Edges shall be tongue-and-groove or supported with blocking or edge clips.

[4]Roof sheathing conforming with this table shall be deemed to meet the design criteria of Section 2516.

Appendix B

Size and Properties of Structural Members

PROPERTIES OF GEOMETRIC SECTIONS

SQUARE:

THE AXIS OF MOMENTS IS LOCATED THROUGH CENTER OF THE SQUARE

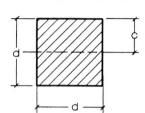

$$A = d^2$$

$$C = \frac{d}{2}$$

$$I = \frac{d^4}{12}$$

$$S = \frac{d^3}{6}$$

$$r = \frac{d}{\sqrt{12}} = 0.288d$$

RECTANGLE:

THE AXIS OF MOMENTS IS LOCATED THROUGH BASE OF THE RECTANGLE

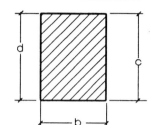

$$A = b\,d$$

$$C = d$$

$$I = \frac{b\,d^3}{3}$$

$$S = \frac{b\,d^2}{3}$$

$$r = \frac{d}{\sqrt{3}} = 0.577d$$

SQUARE:

THE AXIS OF MOMENTS IS LOCATED AT THE BASE OF THE SQUARE

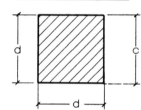

$$A = d^2$$

$$C = d$$

$$I = \frac{d^4}{3}$$

$$S = \frac{d^3}{3}$$

$$r = \frac{d}{\sqrt{3}} = 0.577d$$

CIRCLE:

THE AXIS OF MOMENTS IS LOCATED THROUGH CENTER OF THE CIRCLE

$$A = \frac{\pi d^2}{4}$$

$$C = \frac{d}{2} = \text{RADIUS} = R$$

$$I = \frac{\pi d^4}{64} = 0.785R^4$$

$$S = \frac{d^3}{32} = 0.785R^3$$

$$r = \frac{d}{4} = \frac{R}{2}$$

SQUARE:

THE AXIS OF MOMENTS IS LOCATED AT THE DIAGONAL OF THE SQUARE

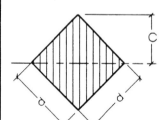

$$A = d^2$$

$$C = \frac{d}{\sqrt{2}}$$

$$I = \frac{d^4}{12}$$

$$S = \frac{d^3}{6\sqrt{2}} = 0.1178d^3$$

$$r = \frac{d}{\sqrt{12}} = 0.288d$$

A = AREA
I = MOMENT OF INERTIA
S = SECTION MODULUS
r = RADIUS OF GYRATION

EXAMPLE No. 1

GIVEN - 4 X 12 BEAM
DIMENSIONS = 3 1/2" X 11 1/4"
AREA = 3.5 x 11.25 = 39.375 sq. in.

$$I = \frac{3.5 \times 11.25^3}{12} = 415.25 \text{ in}^4$$

$$S = \frac{3.5 \times 11.25^2}{6} = 73.83 \text{ in}^3$$

$$r = \frac{415.25}{39.375} = 10.56 \text{ in.}$$

EXAMPLE No. 2

GIVEN - 12" DIAMETER COLUMN
DIMENSIONS = DIA = 11 1/4" RADIUS = 5.625"
AREA = 0.785 x 11.25² = 99.35 sq. in.²

$$I = 0.785 \times 5.625 = 785.88 \text{ in.}^4$$

$$S = 0.785 \times 5.625 = 134.37 \text{ in.}^3$$

$$r = \frac{785.88}{99.35} = 7.91 \text{ in.}$$

RECTANGLE:

THE AXIS OF MOMENTS IS LOCATED THROUGH CENTER OF THE RECTANGLE

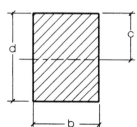

$$A = b\,d$$

$$C = \frac{d}{2}$$

$$I = \frac{b\,d^3}{12}$$

$$S = \frac{b\,d^2}{6}$$

$$r = \frac{d}{\sqrt{12}} = 0.288d$$

NOMINAL SIZE in. b x d	STANDARD DRESSED SIZE (in.) (S4S) b x d	AREA of SECTION (in.²)	MOMENT of INERTIA I (in.⁴)	SECTION MODULUS S (in.³)
2 X 4	$1\frac{1}{2}$ X $3\frac{1}{2}$	5.25	5.36	3.063
2 X 6	$1\frac{1}{2}$ X $5\frac{1}{2}$	8.25	20.80	7.563
2 X 8	$1\frac{1}{2}$ X $7\frac{1}{2}$	10.88	47.64	13.14
2 X 10	$1\frac{1}{2}$ X $9\frac{1}{2}$	13.88	98.93	21.39
2 X 12	$1\frac{1}{2}$ X $11\frac{1}{2}$	16.88	178.0	31.64
2 X 14	$1\frac{1}{2}$ X $13\frac{1}{2}$	19.88	290.0	43.89
3 X 4	$2\frac{1}{2}$ X $3\frac{1}{2}$	8.75	8.93	5.104
3 X 6	$2\frac{1}{2}$ X $5\frac{1}{2}$	13.75	34.66	12.60
3 X 8	$2\frac{1}{2}$ X $7\frac{1}{2}$	18.12	70.39	21.90
3 X 10	$2\frac{1}{2}$ X $9\frac{1}{4}$	23.12	164.9	35.65
3 X 12	$2\frac{1}{2}$ X $11\frac{1}{4}$	28.12	296.6	52.73
3 X 14	$2\frac{1}{2}$ X $13\frac{1}{4}$	33.12	484.6	73.15
3 X 16	$2\frac{1}{2}$ X $15\frac{1}{4}$	38.12	738.9	96.90
4 X 4	$3\frac{1}{2}$ X $3\frac{1}{2}$	12.25	12.50	7.146
4 X 6	$3\frac{1}{2}$ X $5\frac{1}{2}$	19.25	48.53	17.65
4 X 8	$3\frac{1}{2}$ X $7\frac{1}{2}$	25.38	111.10	30.66
4 X 10	$3\frac{1}{2}$ X $9\frac{1}{4}$	32.38	230.8	49.91
4 X 12	$3\frac{1}{2}$ X $11\frac{1}{4}$	39.38	415.3	73.83
4 X 14	$3\frac{1}{2}$ X $13\frac{1}{4}$	46.38	678.5	102.4
4 X 16	$3\frac{1}{2}$ X $15\frac{1}{4}$	53.38	1034	135.7
6 X 6	$5\frac{1}{2}$ X $5\frac{1}{2}$	30.25	76.26	27.73
6 X 8	$5\frac{1}{2}$ X $7\frac{1}{2}$	41.25	193.4	51.56
6 X 10	$5\frac{1}{2}$ X $9\frac{1}{4}$	52.25	393.0	82.73
6 X 12	$5\frac{1}{2}$ X $11\frac{1}{4}$	63.25	697.1	121.10
6 X 14	$5\frac{1}{2}$ X $13\frac{1}{4}$	74.25	1128.0	167.10
6 X 16	$5\frac{1}{2}$ X $15\frac{1}{4}$	83.25	1707.0	220.2

NOMINAL SIZE in. b x d	STANDARD DRESSED SIZE (in.) (S4S) b x d	AREA of SECTION (in.²)	MOMENT of INERTIA I (in.⁴)	SECTION MODULUS S (in.³)
8 X 6	7½ X 5½	41.25	104.0	37.81
8 X 8	7½ X 7½	56.25	263.7	70.31
8 X 10	7½ X 9½	71.25	535.9	112.8
8 X 12	7½ X 11½	86.25	950.5	165.3
8 X 14	7½ X 13½	101.2	1538	227.8
8 X 16	7½ X 15½	116.2	2327	300.3
8 X 18	7½ X 17½	131.2	3350	382.8
10 X 6	9½ X 5½	52.25	131.7	47.9
10 X 8	9½ X 7½	71.25	334.0	89.06
10 X 10	9½ X 9½	90.25	678.8	142.9
10 X 12	9½ X 11½	109.2	1204	209.4
10 X 14	9½ X 13½	128.2	1948	288.6
10 X 16	9½ X 15½	147.2	2948	380.4
10 X 18	9½ X 17½	166.2	4243	484.9
12 X 6	11½ X 5½	63.25	159.4	57.98
12 X 8	11½ X 7½	86.25	404.3	107.8
12 X 10	11½ X 9½	109.2	821.7	173.0
12 X 12	11½ X 11½	132.2	1458	253.5
12 X 14	11½ X 13½	155.2	2358	349.3
12 X 16	11½ X 15½	178.2	3569	460.5
12 X 18	11½ X 17½	201.2	5136	587.0

DESIGN AND CONSTRUCTION OF WOOD FRAMED STRUCTURES

SIZES AND PROPERTIES OF GLUED LAMINATED TIMBER

WIDTH	NUMBER OF LAMINATIONS	DEPTH d (in.)	AREA of SECTION (in.²)	SIZE FACTOR $C_F = (12/d)^{1/9}$	SECTION MODULUS S (in.³)	SECTION MODULUS $S_n = C_F \times S$ (in.³)	MOMENT of INERTIA I (in.⁴)	WEIGHT PER FT. (35 pcf)
2⅛ in.	2	3	6.375	1.00	3.188	3.188	4.781	1.50
	3	4½	9.562	1.00	7.172	7.172	16.137	2.30
	4	6	12.75	1.00	12.75	12.75	38.25	3.10
	5	7½	15.94	1.00	19.92	19.92	74.71	3.90
	6	9	19.12	1.00	28.69	28.69	129.1	4.60
	7	10½	22.31	1.00	39.05	39.05	205.0	5.40
	8	12	25.50	1.00	51.00	51.00	306.0	6.20
	9	13½	28.69	0.99	64.50	63.71	435.7	7.70
	10	15	79.69	0.98	79.69	77.74	597.7	7.70
3⅛ in.	2	3	9.375	1.00	4.688	4.688	7.031	2.30
	3	4½	14.06	1.00	10.55	10.55	23.73	3.40
	4	6	18.75	1.00	18.75	18.75	56.25	4.60
	5	7½	23.44	1.00	29.30	29.30	109.9	5.70
	6	9	28.12	1.00	42.19	42.19	189.8	6.80
	7	10½	32.81	1.00	57.42	57.42	301.5	8.00
	8	12	37.50	1.00	75.00	75.00	450.0	9.10
	9	13½	42.19	0.99	94.92	94.92	640.7	10.3
	10	15	46.88	0.98	117.2	117.2	878.9	11.4
	11	16½	51.56	0.97	141.8	141.8	1170.0	12.5
	12	18	56.25	0.96	168.8	168.8	1519.0	13.7
	13	19½	60.94	0.95	198.0	198.0	1931.0	14.8
	14	21	65.62	0.94	229.7	229.7	2412.0	16.0
	15	22½	70.31	0.93	263.7	263.7	2966.0	17.1
	16	24	75.00	0.93	300.0	300.0	3600.0	18.2
	17	25½	79.69	0.92	338.7	338.7	4318.0	19.4
	18	27	84.38	0.91	379.7	379.7	6126.0	20.5
	19	28½	89.06	0.91	423.0	423.0	6028.0	21.6
	20	30	93.75	0.90	468.8	468.8	7031.0	22.8

WIDTH	NUMBER OF LAMINATIONS	DEPTH d (in.)	AREA of SECTION (in.²)	SIZE FACTOR $C_F=(12/d)^{1/9}$	SECTION MODULUS S (in.³)	SECTION MODULUS $S_n = C_F \times S$ (in.³)	MOMENT of INERTIA I (in.⁴)	WEIGHT PER FT. (35 pcf)
5 1/8 in.	2	3	15.38	1.00	7.688	7.688	11.53	3.7
	3	4½	23.06	1.00	17.30	17.30	38.92	5.6
	4	6	30.75	1.00	30.75	30.75	92.25	7.5
	5	7½	38.44	1.00	48.05	48.05	180.2	9.3
	6	9	46.12	1.00	69.19	69.19	311.3	11.2
	7	10½	53.81	1.00	94.17	94.17	494.4	13.1
	8	12	61.50	1.00	123.0	123.0	738.0	14.9
	9	13½	69.19	0.99	155.7	153.6	1051	16.8
	10	15	76.88	0.98	192.2	187.5	1441	18.7
	11	16½	84.56	0.97	232.5	224.5	1919	20.6
	12	18	92.25	0.96	276.8	264.6	2491	22.4
	13	19½	99.98	0.95	324.8	307.7	3167	24.3
	14	21	107.6	0.94	376.7	354.0	3955	26.2
	15	22½	115.3	0.93	432.4	403.2	4865	28.0
	16	24	123.0	0.93	492.0	455.5	5904	29.9
	17	25½	130.7	0.92	555.4	510.8	7082	31.8
	18	27	138.4	0.91	622.7	569.0	8406	33.6
	19	28½	146.1	0.91	693.8	630.2	9887	35.5
	20	30	153.8	0.90	768.8	694.3	11,530	37.4
	21	31½	161.4	0.90	847.5	761.4	13,350	39.2
	22	33	169.1	0.89	930.2	831.3	15,350	41.1
	23	34½	176.8	0.89	1017	904.1	17,540	43.0
	24	36	184.5	0.89	1107	979.8	19,930	44.8
6 3/4 in.	2	3	20.25	1.00	10.12	10.12	15.19	4.9
	3	4½	30.38	1.00	22.78	22.78	51.26	7.4
	4	6	40.50	1.00	40.50	40.50	121.5	9.8
	5	7½	50.62	1.00	63.28	63.28	237.3	12.3
	6	9	60.75	1.00	91.12	91.12	410.1	14.8
	7	10½	70.88	1.00	124.0	124.0	651.2	17.2
	8	12	81.00	1.00	162.0	162.0	972.0	19.7
	9	13½	91.12	0.99	205.0	202.4	1384	22.1
	10	15	101.3	0.98	253.1	246.9	1898	24.6
	11	16½	111.4	0.97	306.3	295.6	2527	27.1
	12	18	121.5	0.96	364.5	348.4	3280	29.5
	13	19½	131.6	0.95	427.8	405.3	4171	32.0
	14	21	141.8	0.94	496.1	466.2	5209	34.5
	15	22½	151.9	0.93	569.5	531.1	6407	36.9
	16	24	162.0	0.93	648.0	600.0	7776	39.4
	17	25½	172.1	0.92	731.5	672.8	9327	41.8
	18	27	182.3	0.91	820.1	749.5	11,070	44.3
	19	28½	192.4	0.91	913.8	830.0	13,020	46.8
	20	30	202.5	0.90	202.5	914.5	11,190	49.2
	21	31½	212.6	0.90	212.6	1003	17,580	51.7
	22	33	222.8	0.89	222.8	1095	20,220	54.1
	23	34½	232.9	0.89	232.9	1190	23,100	56.6
	24	36	243.0	0.89	243.0	1290	26,240	59.1
	25	37½	253.1	0.88	253.1	1394	29,660	61.5
	26	39	263.3	0.88	263.3	1501	33,270	64.0
	27	40½	273.4	0.87	273.4	1612	37,370	66.4
	28	42	283.5	0.87	283.5	1727	41,670	68.9
	29	43½	293.6	0.87	293.6	1845	46,300	71.4
	30	45	303.8	0.86	303.8	1967	51,260	73.8
	31	46½	313.9	0.86	313.9	2093	56,560	76.3
	32	48	324.0	0.86	324.0	2222	62,210	78.8

WIDTH	NUMBER OF LAMINATIONS	DEPTH d (in.)	AREA of SECTION (in.^{2})	SIZE FACTOR $C_F = (12/d)^{1/9}$	SECTION MODULUS S (in.^{3})	SECTION MODULUS $S_n = C_F \times S$ (in.^{3})	MOMENT of INERTIA I (in.^{4})	WEIGHT PER FT. (35 pcf)
	2	3	26.25	1.00	13.12	13.12	19.69	6.4
	3	4 ½	39.38	1.00	29.53	29.53	66.45	9.6
	4	6	52.50	1.00	52.50	52.50	157.5	12.8
	5	7 ½	65.62	1.00	82.03	82.03	307.6	16.0
	6	9	78.75	1.00	118.1	118.1	531.6	19.1
	7	10 ½	91.88	1.00	160.8	160.8	844.1	22.3
	8	12	105.0	1.00	210.0	210.0	1200	25.5
	9	13 ½	118.1	0.99	265.8	262.3	1794	28.7
	10	15	131.3	0.98	328.1	320.1	2461	31.9
	11	16 ½	144.4	0.97	397.0	383.2	3276	35.1
	12	18	157.5	0.96	472.5	451.7	4252	39.3
	13	19 ½	170.6	0.95	554.5	525.4	5407	41.5
	14	21	183.8	0.94	643.1	604.4	6753	44.7
	15	22 ½	196.9	0.93	738.3	688.5	8306	47.9
	16	24	210.0	0.93	840.0	777.7	10,080	51.0
	17	25 ½	223.1	0.92	948.3	872.1	12,090	54.2
8 ¾ in.	18	27	236.3	0.91	1063	971.5	14,350	57.4
	19	28 ½	249.4	0.91	1184	1076	16,880	60.6
	20	30	262.5	0.90	1312	1186	19,690	63.8
	21	31 ½	275.6	0.90	1447	1230	22,790	67.0
	22	33	288.8	0.89	1588	1419	26,200	70.2
	23	34 ½	301.9	0.89	1736	1544	29,940	73.4
	24	36	315.0	0.89	1890	1673	34,020	76.6
	25	37 ½	328.1	0.88	2051	1807	38,450	79.8
	26	39	341.3	0.88	2218	1946	43,250	82.9
	27	40 ½	354.4	0.87	2392	2090	48,440	86.1
	28	42	367.5	0.87	2572	2238	54,020	89.3
	29	43 ½	380.6	0.87	2760	2392	60,020	92.5
	30	45	393.8	0.86	2953	2550	66,440	95.7
	31	46 ½	406.9	0.86	3154	2713	73,310	98.9
	32	48	420.0	0.86	3360	2880	80,640	102.1
	33	49 ½	433.1	0.85	3573	3053	88,440	105.3
	34	51	446.3	0.85	3793	3230	96,720	108.5
	35	52 ½	459.4	0.85	4020	3412	105,500	111.7
	36	54	472.5	0.85	4252	3598	114,800	114.8
	37	55 ½	485.6	0.84	4492	3789	124,700	118.0
	38	57	498.8	0.84	4738	3985	135,000	121.2
	39	58 ½	511.9	0.84	4991	4185	146,000	124.4
	40	60	525.0	0.84	5250	4390	157,500	127.6
	41	61 ½	538.1	0.83	5516	4600	169,600	130.8
	42	63	551.3	0.83	5788	4814	182,300	134.0

WIDTH	NUMBER OF LAMINATIONS	DEPTH d (in.)	AREA of SECTION (in.²)	SIZE FACTOR $C_F = (12/d)^{1/9}$	SECTION MODULUS S (in.³)	SECTION MODULUS $S_n = C_F \times S$ (in.³)	MOMENT of INERTIA I (in.⁴)	WEIGHT PER FT. (35 pcf)
	2	3	32.25	1.00	16.12	16.12	24.19	7.8
	3	4½	48.38	1.00	36.28	36.28	81.63	11.8
	4	6	64.50	1.00	64.50	64.50	193.5	15.7
	5	7½	80.62	1.00	100.8	100.8	377.9	19.6
	6	9	96.75	1.00	145.1	145.1	653.1	23.5
	7	10½	112.9	1.00	197.3	197.3	1037	27.4
	8	12	129.0	1.00	258.0	258.0	1548	31.4
	9	13½	145.1	0.99	326.5	322.3	2204	35.3
	10	15	161.3	0.98	403.1	393.3	3023	39.2
	11	16½	177.4	0.97	487.8	470.8	4024	43.1
	12	18	193.5	0.96	580.5	554.9	4224	47.0
	13	19½	209.6	0.95	681.3	645.5	6642	51.0
	14	21	225.8	0.94	790.1	742.5	8296	54.9
	15	22½	241.9	0.93	907.0	845.8	10,200	58.8
	16	24	258.0	0.93	1032	955.5	12,380	62.7
	17	25½	274.1	0.92	1165	1072	14,850	66.6
	18	27	290.3	0.91	1306	1194	17,630	70.5
	19	28½	306.4	0.91	1455	1322	20,740	74.5
	20	30	322.5	0.90	1612	1456	24,190	78.4
10¾ in.	21	31½	338.6	0.90	1778	1597	28,000	82.3
	22	33	354.8	0.89	1951	1744	32,190	86.2
	23	34½	370.9	0.89	2132	1896	36,790	90.1
	24	36	387.0	0.89	2322	2055	41,800	94.1
	25	37½	403.1	0.88	2520	2220	47,240	98.0
	26	39	419.3	0.88	2725	2391	53,140	101.9
	27	40½	435.4	0.87	2939	2567	59,510	105.8
	28	42	451.5	0.87	3160	2750	66,370	109.7
	29	43½	467.6	0.87	3390	2938	73,740	113.7
	30	45	483.8	0.86	3628	3133	81,630	117.6
	31	46½	499.9	0.86	3874	3333	90,070	121.5
	32	48	516.0	0.86	4128	3539	99,070	125.4
	33	49½	532.1	0.85	4390	3750	108,700	129.3
	34	51	548.3	0.85	4660	3968	118,900	133.3
	35	52½	564.4	0.85	4938	4191	129,600	137.2
	36	54	580.5	0.85	5224	4420	141,100	141.1
	37	55½	596.6	0.84	5519	4655	153,100	145.0
	38	57	612.8	0.84	5821	4896	165,900	148.9
	39	58½	628.9	0.84	6132	5142	179,300	152.9
	40	60	645.0	0.84	6450	5394	193,500	156.8
	41	61½	661.1	0.83	6776	5651	208,400	160.7
	42	63	677.3	0.83	7111	5915	224,000	164.6
	43	64½	693.4	0.83	7454	6183	240,400	168.5
	44	66	709.5	0.83	7804	6458	257,500	172.4
	45	67½	725.6	0.83	8163	6738	275,500	176.4
	46	69	741.8	0.82	8530	7023	294,300	180.3
	47	70½	757.9	0.82	8905	7315	313,900	184.2
	48	72	774.0	0.82	9288	7611	334,400	188.1
	49	73½	790.1	0.82	9679	7914	355,700	192.0
	50	75	806.3	0.82	10080	8222	377,900	196.0

WIDTH	NUMBER OF LAMINATIONS	DEPTH d (in.)	AREA of SECTION (in.²)	SIZE FACTOR $C_F=(12/d)^{1/9}$	SECTION MODULUS S (in.³)	SECTION MODULUS $S_n = C_F \times S$ (in.³)	MOMENT of INERTIA I (in.⁴)	WEIGHT PER FT. (35 pcf)
$12\frac{1}{4}$ in.	2	3	36.75	1.00	18.38	18.38	27.56	8.9
	3	$4\frac{1}{2}$	55.12	1.00	41.34	41.34	93.02	13.4
	4	6	73.50	1.00	73.50	73.50	220.5	17.9
	5	$7\frac{1}{2}$	91.88	1.00	114.8	114.8	430.7	22.3
	6	9	110.3	1.00	165.4	165.4	744.2	26.8
	7	$10\frac{1}{2}$	128.6	1.00	225.1	225.1	1182	31.3
	8	12	147.0	1.00	294.0	294.0	1764	35.7
	9	$13\frac{1}{2}$	165.4	0.99	372.1	367.3	2512	40.2
	10	15	183.8	0.98	459.4	448.1	3445	44.7
	11	$16\frac{1}{2}$	202.1	0.97	555.8	536.5	4586	49.1
	12	18	220.5	0.96	661.5	632.4	5953	53.6
	13	$19\frac{1}{2}$	238.9	0.95	776.3	735.6	7569	58.1
	14	21	257.3	0.94	900.4	846.1	9454	62.5
	15	$22\frac{1}{2}$	275.6	0.93	1034	963.9	11,630	67.0
	16	24	294.0	0.93	1176	1089	14,110	71.5
	17	$25\frac{1}{2}$	312.4	0.92	1328	1221	16,930	75.9
	18	27	330.8	0.91	1488	1360	20,090	80.4
	19	$28\frac{1}{2}$	349.1	0.91	1658	1506	23,630	84.9
	20	30	367.5	0.90	1838	1660	27,560	89.3
	21	$31\frac{1}{2}$	385.9	0.90	2926	1820	31,910	93.8
	22	33	404.3	0.89	2223	1987	36,690	98.3
	23	$34\frac{1}{2}$	422.6	0.89	2430	2161	41,920	102.7
	24	36	441.0	0.89	2646	2342	47,630	107.2
	25	$37\frac{1}{2}$	459.4	0.88	2871	2530	53,830	111.7
	26	39	477.8	0.88	3105	2724	60,560	116.1
	27	$40\frac{1}{2}$	496.1	0.87	3349	2926	67,810	120.6
	28	42	514.5	0.87	3602	3134	75,630	125.1
	29	$43\frac{1}{2}$	532.9	0.87	3863	3348	84,030	129.5
	30	45	551.3	0.86	4134	3570	93,020	134.0
	31	$46\frac{1}{2}$	569.6	0.86	4415	3798	102,600	138.5
	32	48	588.0	0.86	4704	4032	112,900	142.9
	33	$49\frac{1}{2}$	606.4	0.85	5003	4274	123,800	147.4
	34	51	624.8	0.85	5310	4522	135,400	151.8
	35	$52\frac{1}{2}$	641.3	0.85	5627	4776	147,700	156.3
	36	54	661.5	0.85	5954	5037	160,700	160.8
	37	$55\frac{1}{2}$	679.9	0.84	6289	5305	174,500	165.2
	38	57	698.3	0.84	6633	5579	189,100	169.7
	39	$58\frac{1}{2}$	716.6	0.84	6987	5859	204,400	174.2
	40	60	735.0	0.84	7350	6146	220,500	178.6
	41	$61\frac{1}{2}$	753.4	0.83	7720	6440	237,500	183.1
	42	63	771.8	0.83	8103	6740	255,300	187.6
	43	$64\frac{1}{2}$	790.1	0.83	8494	7046	274,000	192.0
	44	66	808.5	0.83	8894	7359	293,500	196.6
	45	$67\frac{1}{2}$	826.9	0.83	9302	7678	314,000	201.0
	46	69	845.3	0.82	9720	8003	335,400	205.4
	47	$70\frac{1}{2}$	863.6	0.82	10150	8335	357,700	209.9
	48	72	882.0	0.82	10580	8673	381,000	214.4
	49	$73\frac{1}{2}$	900.4	0.82	11030	9018	404,300	218.8
	50	75	918.8	0.82	11480	9369	430,700	223.3

WIDTH	NUMBER OF LAMINATIONS	DEPTH d (in.)	AREA of SECTION (in.^{2})	SIZE FACTOR $C_F=(12/d)^{1/9}$	SECTION MODULUS S (in.^{3})	SECTION MODULUS $S_n = C_F \times S$ (in.^{3})	MOMENT of INERTIA I (in.^{4})	WEIGHT PER FT. (35 pcf)
$14\frac{1}{4}$ in.	2	3	42.75	1.00	21.38	21.38	32.06	10.4
	3	$4\frac{1}{2}$	64.12	1.00	48.09	48.09	108.2	15.6
	4	6	85.5	1.00	85.50	85.50	256.5	20.8
	5	$7\frac{1}{2}$	106.9	1.00	133.6	133.6	501.0	26.0
	6	9	128.3	1.00	192.4	192.4	865.7	31.2
	7	$10\frac{1}{2}$	149.6	1.00	261.8	261.8	1375	36.4
	8	12	171.0	1.00	342.0	342.0	2052	41.6
	9	$13\frac{1}{2}$	192.4	0.99	432.8	427.2	2922	46.8
	10	15	213.8	0.98	534.4	521.3	4008	52.0
	11	$16\frac{1}{2}$	235.1	0.97	646.6	624.1	5334	57.1
	12	18	256.5	0.96	769.5	735.6	6925	62.3
	13	$19\frac{1}{2}$	277.9	0.95	903.1	855.7	8805	67.5
	14	21	299.3	0.94	1047	984.2	11,000	72.7
	15	$22\frac{1}{2}$	320.6	0.93	1202	1121	13,530	77.9
	16	24	342.0	0.93	1368	1267	16,420	83.1
	17	$25\frac{1}{2}$	363.4	0.92	1544	1420	19,690	88.3
	18	27	384.8	0.91	1731	1582	23,370	93.5
	19	$28\frac{1}{2}$	406.1	0.91	1929	1752	27,490	98.7
	20	30	427.5	0.90	2138	1930	32,060	103.9
	21	$31\frac{1}{2}$	448.9	0.90	2357	2117	37,120	109.1
	22	33	470.3	0.89	2586	2311	42,680	114.3
	23	$34\frac{1}{2}$	491.6	0.89	2827	2514	48,760	119.5
	24	36	513.0	0.89	3078	2724	55,400	124.7
	25	$37\frac{1}{2}$	534.4	0.88	3340	2943	62,620	129.9
	26	39	555.8	0.88	3612	3169	70,440	135.1
	27	$40\frac{1}{2}$	577.1	0.87	3896	3403	78,890	140.3
	28	42	598.5	0.87	4190	3645	87,980	145.5
	29	$43\frac{1}{2}$	619.9	0.87	4494	3895	97,750	150.7
	30	45	641.3	0.86	4809	4153	108,200	155.9
	31	$46\frac{1}{2}$	662.6	0.86	5135	4418	119,400	161.1
	32	48	684.0	0.86	5472	4690	1,31,300	166.3
	33	$49\frac{1}{2}$	705.4	0.85	5819	4972	144,000	171.4
	34	51	726.8	0.85	6177	5260	157,500	176.6
	35	$52\frac{1}{2}$	748.1	0.85	6546	5556	171,800	181.8
	36	54	769.5	0.85	6926	5860	187,000	187.0
	37	$55\frac{1}{2}$	790.9	0.84	7316	6171	203,000	192.2
	38	57	812.3	0.84	7716	6490	219,900	197.4
	39	$58\frac{1}{2}$	833.6	0.84	8128	6816	237,700	202.6
	40	60	855.0	0.84	8550	7150	256,500	207.8
	41	$61\frac{1}{2}$	876.4	0.83	8983	7491	276,200	213.0
	42	63	897.8	0.83	9426	7840	296,900	218.2
	43	$64\frac{1}{2}$	919.1	0.83	9881	8196	318,600	223.4
	44	66	940.5	0.83	10350	8560	341,400	228.6
	45	$67\frac{1}{2}$	961.9	0.83	10820	8932	365,200	233.8
	46	69	983.3	0.82	11310	9310	390,100	239.0
	47	$70\frac{1}{2}$	1005	0.82	11800	9696	416,100	244.2
	48	72	1026	0.82	12310	10090	443,200	249.4
	49	$73\frac{1}{2}$	1047	0.82	12830	10490	471,500	254.6
	50	75	1069	0.82	13360	10900	501,000	259.8

Index

About the Author

Morton Newman heads his own engineering company in Los Angeles, California, and has worked in the field of structural engineering since 1958. He previously held positions with US Steel, Welton Becket and Associates/Architects, and Perriera & Luckman/Architects. Mr. Newman is also the author of the *Standard Handbook of Structural Details for Building Construction*, Second Edition, available from McGraw-Hill.

NOTES

NOTES

NOTES

NOTES

NOTES

NOTES